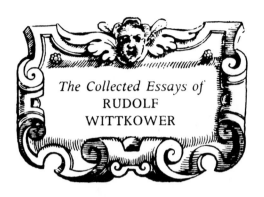

The Collected Essays of
RUDOLF
WITTKOWER

STUDIES IN
THE ITALIAN BAROQUE

Frontispiece: PIRANESI. Pl. III from *Prima parte di Architetture e Prospettive,* 1743, showing an imaginary mausoleum for a Roman emperor

RUDOLF WITTKOWER

STUDIES
IN
THE ITALIAN
BAROQUE

with 357 illustrations

WESTVIEW PRESS · BOULDER, COLORADO

Published 1975 in London, England, by Thames and Hudson, Ltd.

Published 1975 in the United States of America
by Westview Press, Inc.
1898 Flatiron Court
Boulder, Colorado 80301
Frederick A. Praeger, Publisher and Editorial Director

Filmset and printed by BAS Printers Limited, Wallop, Hampshire, England

Library of Congress Cataloging in Publication Data

Wittkower, Rudolf.
  Studies in the Italian Baroque.

  (The Collected essays of Rudolf Wittkower)
  Includes bibliographical references and index.
  1. Architecture—Baroque—Italy.   2. Architecture
—Italy. I. Title.
NA1116.5.B3W57   720'.945   75-22083
ISBN 0-89158-506-0

CONTENTS

FOREWORD

WHEN Rudolf Wittkower, aged twenty-one, went to Rome in 1922, Baroque studies were still in their infancy. Despite the ground-breaking works of scholars such as Cornelius Gurlitt, Wölfflin and Alois Riegl (to name only the three earliest pioneers in the re-evaluation of Baroque art), the conviction that the pinnacle of human achievement had been reached in the Renaissance and everything that followed 'was but an after-bloom, rapidly tending to decadence' (Symonds) was still shared by the majority of art-historians. Travellers, reading the introductory chapter on the arts in Rome in the latest available edition of Baedeker – that most widely used guide book – were informed that 'the degenerate Renaissance [is] known as Baroque'. Should they harbour a sneaking admiration for the works of Bernini, they were warned 'to . . . beware of being led captive by art essentially flimsy and meretricious'; and Maderno, Borromini and Carlo Fontana were presented to them as 'the leaders of that band of artists who conspired to rob architecture of its fitting repose'. This distaste for Baroque art in general and for Roman Baroque in particular did not essentially change until after the First World War when travelling and publishing were possible again and a new generation of art-historians could carry on what their teachers had begun.

The 1920s were exhilarating years for a young scholar living in Rome: a whole phase of history to be re-interpreted; a wealth of documents to be found in as yet unexplored archives; new insights to be gained into the works of the great masters and due recognition to be restored to a host of artists whose very names had been forgotten. They were years of intense work, but also of great fun. The commission, for instance, to revise the old Baedeker (new edition published 1927) required a re-appraisal of not only all the Baroque art and architecture but also of delicious *trattorie* and *osterie* in and near Rome.

Much of the groundwork for Rudolf Wittkower's later writings on Roman subjects was laid in those early years. In the 1930s he began to extend his interest to northern Italy, first to Vicenza and Venice, and after the Second World War to Piedmont. It is from these three focal areas that the subjects for this, the second volume of *Collected Essays*, have been chosen. The papers were written over a period of more than thirty years. They vary in length from a few pages to almost book size, but quantitative conformity was not, and I believe should not have been, a guide for their choice. Texts and illustrations have been reprinted virtually unchanged with the following exceptions: the drawings from Filippo Juvarra's sketchbook at Chatsworth, originally illustrated with eleven examples, are here reproduced in full; certain overlappings in the three Piranesi essays have been eliminated, and the style of the Rainaldi article has been extensively revised. My husband had often been asked to have this paper reprinted, because the old number of the *Art Bulletin* in which it appeared is not always readily available. But he grudged the time it would have taken him to correct the English translation of the original German text — a necessity which in no way casts any blame upon the translator whose task was indeed formidable on account of those intractable German compound nouns and the many technical terms for which there was as yet no English equivalent because they were newly coined even in German. I have now tried to simplify too-involved sentences, rectified some shifts of meaning and corrected actual mistranslations — without, however, re-writing an article which, in its way, is still considered a milestone in the history of architecture and as such has become in itself a historical document.

It remains to thank those friends from the Department of Art and Archaeology, Columbia University, who never failed to give encouragement and advice. I am grateful to Adolf K. Placzek, Avery Librarian, Columbia University, and to Thomas Wragg, Librarian and Keeper of the Chatsworth Collections, for their generous help with photographic material, as well as to all those who kindly gave their permission to reprint the original essays. I deeply regret that 'house rules' prevent me from publicly acknowledging my greatest indebtedness. I hope my mute but sincere thanks will be accepted.

New York, July 1974   MARGOT WITTKOWER

1 CARLO RAINALDI. S. Maria in Campitelli, Rome

I CARLO RAINALDI AND THE ARCHITECTURE OF THE HIGH BAROQUE IN ROME

Carlo Rainaldi and the Architecture of the High Baroque in Rome

2 Foundation medal of the two churches in the Piazza del Popolo, Rome
Carlo Rainaldi's project, 1662

THERE are three reasons why Carlo Rainaldi's architecture ought to command a more lasting interest than his actual talent might seem to justify: 1 his works and projects are connected with the most important architectural enterprises in Rome during the seventeenth century; 2 in his process of working we can observe the modification of his own principles of design through the influence of his greater contemporaries; 3 those principles of design which are distinctly his own can be defined as a carrying over of 'Mannerist' architecture into the High Baroque.

The last point is my chief topic in this paper, which is to be taken as a continuation of my essay on Michelangelo's Biblioteca Laurenziana,[1] the most outstanding and epoch-making example of Mannerist architecture.

It is evident that the historical significance of Rainaldi (1611–91) can be understood only in the light of an exhaustive study of his principal works. As my purpose, however, is not to write a monograph but to trace the evolution of a particular architectural conception, it is not necessary to deal with all his works, nor to take them in strict chronological order.[2]

My method of procedure will be this: I shall first demonstrate the interaction between Rainaldi's principles and those of the 'true' Baroque in the history of the following three buildings: 1 the two parallel churches in the Piazza del Popolo; 2 S. Agnese in Piazza Navona; 3 S.

Andrea della Valle. I shall, secondly, discuss Rainaldi's contribution to the problem of centrally planned churches. This will offer an opportunity for discussing the evolution of this type in the works of Bernini, Cortona and Borromini and for defining Rainaldi's own position in the development of the Baroque style as a whole. Thirdly I shall give a detailed analysis of his most important work: S. Maria in Campitelli; and finally I shall present some material for adjudging Rainaldi's artistic development.

S. Maria di Monte Santo and S. Maria de' Miracoli in the Piazza del Popolo

The history of the building of the two churches in the Piazza del Popolo as given by Hempel[3] and other writers,[4] must be corrected and amplified in some points. On 15 March 1662, the foundation stones of the churches were laid and building continued until the death of Alexander VII (22 May 1667). Then came a pause for four years. From 1671 onwards the future Cardinal Giovanni Gastaldi had the work carried on at his own expense. S. Maria di Monte 4, 6 Santo, the building to the left, was practically completed by the Holy Year 1675,[5] but was

3 Engraving by Falda of the Piazza del Popolo,
1665

consecrated only in 1678; S. Maria de' Miracoli
11 was consecrated in 1679.[6]

The architect of the first period (1662–67)
was Rainaldi, but after 1671 the work was
carried on by Bernini. Since the researches of
Hempel it has been taken as proved that when
Bernini took over he modified the original plan
in two respects: first, as regards S. Maria di
Monte Santo, by substituting an elongated oval
for the circular ground-plan of the original
design; and secondly, by altering the exterior
of both buildings, especially through the
enlargement of the domes and the rejection of
the high attic between the lower structure and
the drum. Hempel seeks to prove the first point
by referring to the *Guida* of the Abbate Titi
from 1686,[7] which on the whole may be
regarded as a reliable authority, and the second
by comparing the completed buildings with the
3 Falda engraving, made in 1665[8] and therefore
during the time when Rainaldi was still in
charge of the work.

Hempel does not raise the question of what
may have caused Bernini to alter the ground-
plan of S. Maria di Monte Santo, nor whether
the church had not been already begun during
the long five-year period under Rainaldi, so
that any important alterations in the ground-

4 S. Maria di Monte Santo, Rome

11

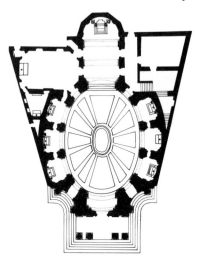

5 CARLO FONTANA. Project for the alteration of the dome of S. Maria di Monte Santo. Engraving of 1674

6 S. Maria di Monte Santo, Rome. Ground-plan

plan would have been impossible. Misgivings are indeed aroused by the fact that the first edition of Titi's work, published in 1674,[9] contains a statement which directly contradicts that made in the second edition, to which Hempel refers. This can be shown by a comparison between the two texts:

> Titi, 1st ed., 1674, p. 427: . . . 'fù Architetto il Cav. Rainaldi, e ne diede il disegno bellissimo, che và in stampa. Hora si finisce quella di Monte Santo mediante la generosità dell'Eminentissimo Castaldi della quale con la direttione del Bernino, e assistenza del Cav. Fontana si è mutato il disegno *fuori che del Cupolino*, e Altar maggiore, che è del medemo Rainaldi.'

> Titi, 2nd ed., 1686, p. 355: . . .'col pensiero del Bernino e assistenza del Cav. Fontana si mutò il Cuppolino, e ridusse in ovato la Chiesa che prima era rotonda seguitando il disegno del Rainaldi.'

In the first edition Titi attributes the '*Cupolino*' (by which he can only mean the relatively small dome) and therefore the corresponding ground-plan of the building to Rainaldi himself. That this is the correct view (which Titi, twelve years later, erroneously changed) is confirmed

by an independent authority, the editor of *Roma sacra antica e moderna* in the edition of 1687;[10] he states, apparently in refutation of the statement in Titi's second edition, that on 15 March 1662, the monks began to build a '*riguardevole Chiesa in forma ovata*'. And the text of the first edition of Titi is obviously followed by the critical editor of *Descrizione di Roma moderna* of 1697,[11] who makes the characteristic change of term from '*Cupolino*' into '*Cupola*'.[12]

That there can be finally no doubt that the ground-plan of S. Maria di Monte Santo derives from Rainaldi himself is proved by an engraving by Carlo Fontana dedicated to Cardinal Matteo Orlandi in 1674.[13] For here Fontana actually proposed to counteract the irregular aspect of the dodecagonal dome, a form of dome which was necessitated by the oval ground-plan, by thickening the walls of the drum latitudinally so that outwardly an appearance of regular quasi-circular form would be produced. By this means he was therefore proposing to correct the disparate dodecagonal design by Rainaldi, which from his classical standpoint he would feel compelled to condemn.

12

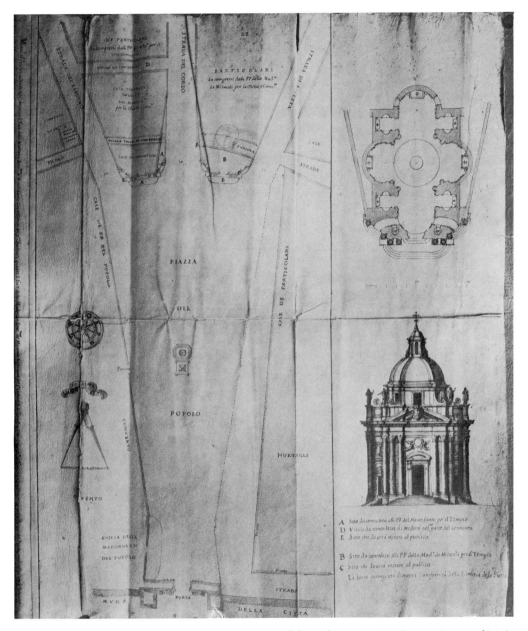

7 CARLO RAINALDI. Project for the churches in the Piazza del Popolo, Rome, 1661 (Roman State Archives)

8 The Piazza del Popolo before Rainaldi. Detail of the Pianta di Roma of Maggi-Maudin-Losi, 1616–21

9 CARLO RAINALDI. Drawing of the Piazza del Popolo

It may be asked, however, whether Rainaldi's own plans are not at variance with the literary authorities and with Fontana's engraving. Up to the present Rainaldi's design has been known only from the foundation medal of 1662,[14] the design which was used by Falda in the above-mentioned engraving in the *Teatro Nuovo* of 1665. Here certainly both churches are represented as completely symmetrical, and this has so far been regarded as Rainaldi's last word. But though we have no later plan of his hand it can be proved that building was never begun on the lines of the official plan.

What was actually the ground-plan of the project shown on the medal? The answer is to be found in a large design which was made a short time before the foundation medal and which is now in the Roman State Archives.[15] On the left-hand side of the sheet is a papal *chirografo* – an official command in the margin, handwritten or at least signed by whoever gave it – dated 16 November 1661 (the text of which is not shown in the illustration) whereby the execution of the design was officially sanctioned. By comparing this drawing with the design on the medal, one can see that although Rainaldi seems to have intended this to be the final and definitive design, and although as such it received the papal confirmation, by the time the medal was cast some important modifications had been made in the elevation of both buildings, notably by replacing the attached columns by a portico with free-standing columns and by substituting the concave outer bay for convex ones. But as in both churches

the proportions between the dome and the lower structure remained unchanged, it is evident that in neither case could the general lines of the ground-plan have been altered. Consequently both churches as shown on the medal would have had to be based on a Greek cross plan.

For what reason then did Rainaldi, even after the foundation stone was laid, make extensive changes in the ground-plans? One must seek for the explanation in the nature of Rainaldi's task. In this case the architect had to be first and foremost a town-planner. It was a question of creating a worthy forecourt to receive the traveller entering Rome by the Porta del Popolo. From here, three main streets radiate through the city between the Pincio and Tiber. The decisive point in the planning of the square would be the front elevation of the two blocks of houses between the radiating streets. The idea was to organize the wide thoroughfare in such a way that the line of vision from the Porta del Popolo met an important focus. Its effectiveness would depend on two things, first on absolute symmetry, and secondly on making the chief features in the line of vision, i.e. the two domes, as large as possible. But these essential conditions were not easily attained, and it was a slow process to find the correct solution. Rainaldi had first to tackle the problem of symmetry. Before he began his work, the two blocks of houses reached out into the square in varying length and width. To bring the façades into line on the square was not a matter of great difficulty, but the different

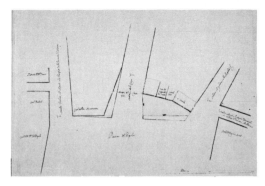

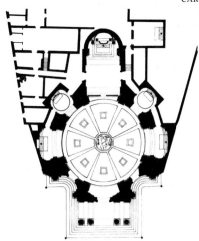

10 CARLO RAINALDI. Drawing of the south side of
the Piazza del Popolo
11 S. Maria de' Miracoli, Rome. Ground-plan

width of the blocks could not be altogether
eliminated. The design in the State Archives
shows very clearly not only the situation as it
was, but also by what means Rainaldi sought
to equalize the irregularities of the site. It shows
further that the alterations to the square could
not be confined to the south side alone, but
that, as was inevitable in the Rome of the
Seicento, the design of the whole square would
have to be changed. The idea of correcting the
irregular aspect of this important Piazza was
not new and dates doubtless from the time of
the erection of the obelisk under Sixtus V.[16]

The plan by Rainaldi in the State Archives
makes it clear that in two other sheets we have
his preliminary drafts for the regulation of the
church sites and the square. The first of these
9 is a large plan[17] which, to judge by the character
of the work (pencil and heavy sepia lines), is by
Rainaldi himself. It shows the existing situation
in ink, with pencil additions indicating the
10 proposed alterations. The second sheet, depicting the south side of the square only, is drawn
to scale and has detailed inscriptions.[18] It is an
elaboration of the first sheet by Rainaldi's own
hand. From this sketch one can see very clearly
how greatly the two blocks vary in width and
that the farther they recede from the front the
greater this difference becomes. These facts are
only shown correctly in the new material.[19]

So much for the question of symmetry which,
as one can see, was essential and had to be
solved before the planning of the churches
could be started. Once the two sites had been
equalized as far as possible, it was not difficult

to build two symmetrical churches. A plan in
the form of a Greek cross was the simplest
solution. The difference in the diameters of the
two buildings could be minimized by transepts
and chapels of slightly differing depths, while
the domes of both churches would be equal in
size, which was essential for a symmetrical
impression. This was still the position when the
foundation medal was struck.

It was the desire to enlarge the domes to the
greatest possible extent which made the subsequent alterations necessary. That enlargement could only be accomplished by abandoning the Greek cross in favour of a circular plan,
where the dome could extend over the full
width of the available space. But such a solution
would have meant that the diameter of the dome
of S. Maria di Monte Santo, the church on the
narrower site, would be considerably smaller
than that of S. Maria de' Miracoli. As this would
have been inconsistent with the idea of complete exterior symmetry, there was no other
solution but to make the plan of S. Maria di
Monte Santo an elongated oval. Only by thus 6
placing the diameter of the dome farther back,
at a wider point in the wedge-shaped site, could
the domes, seen from the square, give the
impression of identity of size and form. It is
clear therefore that the circular ground-plan
which was finally adopted for S. Maria de' 11
Miracoli – the plan for which alone Rainaldi is
usually held to be responsible – inevitably
necessitated the adoption of an oval ground-
plan for S. Maria di Monte Santo: they are the
complementary halves of one idea.

Although it must be assumed that both ground-plans belong to the first building period under Rainaldi (an assumption which is confirmed by the written documents), yet we have to admit that the basic idea behind this solution is very much indebted to Bernini. The visitor who approaches the churches from the square (from where alone he can see both domes simultaneously)[20] is under the optical illusion that the round and the oval dome are equal – an illusion which is based on the law of subjective perception. One accepts as 'real' what one sees, not what exists in fact.[21] This law is of great importance in Bernini's psychological approach to architecture. He took it into account in a manner unknown before and had it in mind even in the very preliminary planning stages of his work.[22]

Rainaldi did not, however, adopt this attitude of Bernini's spontaneously, but he was influenced here by his assistant, Carlo Fontana. Up to the present the position of the young Fontana in Rainaldi's studio has attracted little attention.[23] But many facts illustrate it, and it may even be shown that Rainaldi was, though to varying degrees, constantly dependent on his young assistant. This was due not so much to Fontana's artistic capacity as to his intimate knowledge of Bernini's principles and working method.

The collaboration between Rainaldi and Fontana during these years will be proved later from documents. Meanwhile I shall discuss a plan which is even earlier than that in the State Archives and which could never have been conceived without Fontana's influence. This careful and detailed drawing of the two churches,[24] rendered almost like a picture, was undoubtedly meant to give Alexander VII a clear idea of the projected buildings. It certainly concludes a long series of preliminary drafts and sketches. The serene semicircular domes rise above a flatly modelled drum with a strongly emphasized unbroken cornice dividing drum and dome. Behind this rather unimaginative design lies a feeling for stability and harmonious proportion quite foreign to Rainaldi but typical of Fontana.[25]

The design of the façades in the sketch is certainly more authentically Rainaldi's than that of the domes, for the inner coupled pilasters fulfil a dual function:[26] the triangular pediment links them together as the frame of the central unit, and the eye therefore demands that the outer units be similarly framed, which is not the case; they have only an outer and no inner boundary. If one could disregard the pediment, the inner pilasters would fall into line with the outer pilasters, and the façade would become a simple alternation of order and wall. But the pediment at once reasserts itself and this produces a constantly shifting emphasis. By this simple device an impression of fluctuation and of flowing unstable movement is produced, very characteristic of Rainaldi's individual architectural conceptions, but fundamentally different from Fontana's principles.

In the second stage, the plan in the State Archives, the Fontana element in the design of the dome has largely disappeared. Instead of the serene circular form one finds an octagonal dome with massive ribs. Large decorative scrolls unite the base of the dome with the attic below, with the result that the functional significance of the drum is diminished and the weight of the dome seems to bear directly on the lower structure – another example of the functional ambiguity characteristic of Rainaldi's style. The alterations in the lower zone – the replacement of the pilasters by columns and the fact that the outer bays are convex and slope back – serve to emphasize the town-planning intention of the first project. This intention is made clear by the fact that in the drawing of that project the perspective of the streets extends to the horizon. The first idea of the artist was to preserve the impression of cubic mass in the two blocks of buildings, a tendency which in the second project becomes even more emphasized by the greater plasticity and the shield-like bending of the outer units of the two façades. By this means the wedges of buildings seem to push into the square with compelling force. On the traveller entering through the Porta del Popolo they would have made almost an aggressive impression.

The façades of the design on the medals, with which the final construction in the main corresponds, reflect a different idea of town planning. Here the concave outer bays and the tetra-prostyle express welcome and invitation. While in the two earlier plans the rows of houses were terminated by the two massive structures, in the final plan everything is conceived from

12 CARLO RAINALDI. Project for the churches in the Piazza del Popolo, 1661 (Chigiana)

13 The Piazza del Popolo, Rome. Left: S. Maria di Monte Santo. Right: S. Maria de' Miracoli

the point of view of the spectator, and all is designed to draw him into the spell of the long receding streets. From what has been said before one can easily guess to whose influence this new orientation is due. As to the tetra-prostyle, its model can of course be found in the portico of the Pantheon and in the prostyle which Michelangelo planned for St Peter's. But (and this is of decisive importance) there is a plan of Bernini's of 1659, to erect a portico with *four* columns in front of Maderno's façade of St Peter's.[27] Carlo Fontana was for many years Bernini's assistant in the planning of the Piazza S. Pietro, and it must be due to him that the type of classical temple façade, never executed at St Peter's, was realized in the churches of the Piazza del Popolo. The pure lines of this classical portico are as far removed as possible from Rainaldi's architectural conceptions. It is this motif which gives to the two façades a Berninesque character.[28]

When Bernini actually took over the construction of the churches in 1671 the only thing that remained to be done was to abolish the high attic of Rainaldi's design so that the pediment regained its full classical value.[29]

The various stages in the development of the plans can be summarized as follows: **1** the plan 12 in the Chigiana with a dome on classical lines, characteristic of Fontana; **2** the plan in the State 7 Archives. Here Rainaldi's conception of functional ambiguity which was expressed previously only in the façade, was applied to the zone of the dome. At both stages the approach to town planning is essentially the same: it is objective, i.e. it is concentrated on the rows of houses and the street perspective; **3** the project 2 of the medals. Here a new conception appears in town planning. It is subjective, i.e. it takes account of the spectator. The tetra-prostyle is in the style of Bernini but the drum and dome express Rainaldi's architectural principles of the second stage; **4** a further alteration in the design, between the laying of the foundation stone and the beginning of the work. In order to enhance their effect on the townscape, the volume of the two domes is increased, which entails a re-forming of the ground-plans on a pseudo-symmetrical basis, a second concession to the subjectivism of Bernini; **5** the abolition of the attic behind the pediment during the completion of the work by Bernini in accord-

ance with his three-dimensional planning. This defines approximately the main lines in the history of the building of the churches and their significance in the *oeuvre* of Rainaldi. In order to follow the above analysis one must have an eye open for the conflict between two different architectural conceptions and their extraordinary intermingling, crossing and overlapping. Before, however, turning to the interiors of both churches, it is advisable to approach the problems before us from another side.

S. Agnese in Piazza Navona

A large plan for the building of S. Agnese was 14 first by Egger,[30] and later by Hempel,[31] attributed to Girolamo, the father of Carlo Rainaldi, but it reveals without any doubt the authorship of Carlo Rainaldi himself. It can be dated 1652 and is closely related to the design made ten years later for the churches on the Piazza del Popolo. The treatment of the large order corresponds exactly with the design in 12 the Chigiana: division by double columns or double pilasters projecting entablature, and a pediment over the central orders. In the design for S. Agnese the sequence pilasters-columns naturally produces a concentration towards the centre, but this quantitative increase in volume

14 CARLO RAINALDI. Project for S. Agnese in
Piazza Navona, Rome, 1652

15 BORROMINI. Project for S. Agnese in Piazza
Navona

16 Façade of S. Agnese in Piazza Navona

unfolds before a neutral, non-projecting wall,
so that one is forced to regard these disparate
members of the order as qualitatively equal.[32]
Because of this arrangement the impression of
ambiguity is even stronger in the design for S.
Agnese than in the two later churches.

It has been observed that Rainaldi was
69 influenced here by the design of St Peter's,[33]
but in every respect his plan shows alterations
pointing in a new direction. In St Peter's the
graduation of the orders is accompanied by
corresponding projections of the wall behind,[34]
while in S. Agnese the wall remains flat. The
attic, which in St Peter's is already too high for
harmonious classical proportions, is in Rainaldi's design carried to a still more disproportionate height. Rainaldi also entirely omits the
drum; it is true that in St Peter's, after the later
addition of the nave, the drum became practically invisible at a short distance from the
church, but the structural incongruity which
in the case of St Peter's is merely apparent,
would have been a fact in that of S. Agnese.

Rainaldi's plan was never carried out.[35] A
year after the building was begun he was superseded by Borromini (7 August 1653), who
completely revised the designs. When Rainaldi
ten years later had to erect S. Maria in Campitelli, he reasserted the principles of his plan for

S. Agnese, although the foundation medal of 46
S. Maria in Campitelli shows several modifications inspired by contemporary ideas. In the
actually built façade of S. Maria we can still see 1
the original combination of small and colossal
orders. The circumstances in which Rainaldi in
the year 1657 in turn succeeded Borromini have
been fully described by Hempel. The façade 16
had by then reached the crowning cornice and
it was from this point upwards that Rainaldi set
out to 'rectify' Borromini's design. In a project
of Borromini's[36] which can be only slightly
earlier than his final design, the attic and
pediment are represented other than they
actually are in the existing building. In this
sketch a low balustrade runs along the top
cornice, and over the centre appear *pentimenti*
which show that Borromini's intentions were
still fluctuating. But their realization would
obviously have implied a considerable heightening of the centre, such as indeed he had
already planned in his first design.[37] The high 15
attic of the present building which, because of
the interrupting horizontal panels, continues
the vertical lines of the façade rather weakly, is
as little expressive of Borromini's architectural
style as is its unsubstantial, cardboardlike
appearance and its disproportional relation to
the main storey of the façade. These are features

19

17 GIOVANNI MARIA BARATTA (?). Project for
S. Agnese in Piazza Navona, Rome. A clumsy
attempt to combine Rainaldi and Borromini

essentially typical of Rainaldi. Also the unbroken classical triangular pediment would
have been an unparalleled and anomalous
feature in Borromini's work. To be sure, this
classical formula does not correspond to Rainaldi's treatment of detail either. But considering
that the work on the campanili of the building
did not begin until about 1666 and that the
attic and pediment were therefore probably
erected not earlier than the sixties, the classicism of the pediment may well be derived from
the same source as the idea of the tetra-prostyle
of the churches on the Piazza del Popolo.

Thus, three quite distinct artistic tendencies
can be traced in the façade of S. Agnese. The
imaginative and dynamic centre of Borromini's
modulated façade is transformed by Rainaldi
into a classicist, pedimented front of Berninesque derivation. Standing relief-like against
the attic wall it has, however, lost the richly
sculptural, three-dimensional quality of Bernini's own creations.[38]

In view of this situation one cannot simply
speak of the influence of 'Borromini's' façade of
S. Agnese on the design for the churches on the
Piazza del Popolo – such a statement would
ignore the complications of the S. Agnese
design. But one can certainly say that the
change of the outer sections of these churches
into concave bays was directly inspired by the
design which Borromini contributed to S.
Agnese.

S. Andrea della Valle

In our first example, the churches on the Piazza
del Popolo, we found Rainaldi profoundly
affected by Bernini's architectural ideas; in our
second example, S. Agnese, we saw a façade by
Borromini transformed by Rainaldi during his
Berninesque period. We now come to a still
more complicated case, the façade of S. Andrea,
the history of which clarifies also Fontana's
position in Rainaldi's studio.

Carlo Maderno, the first architect to S.
Andrea, published an engraving of his design 20
for the façade in 1624.[39] The logical gradation
of the orders and the projecting wall, which
distinguishes his façade for S. Susanna, do not
recur in the works that followed. Already, a
few years later, in the façade of St Peter's, the 69
projection of the entablature above the pilasters
which enclose the outer compartments with the
niches is an inconsistency. The design for S.
Andrea, which followed that for S. Susanna by
almost a generation, represents another important step in the same direction. In the ground
storey the artist has, it is true, made the wall
units project clearly on three planes, though he
has abandoned the finely differentiated gradation of the orders and decoration of S. Susanna;
but the arrangement of the upper storey follows
quite a different system. The four coupled
columns with their respective projecting entablatures are attached to a neutral straight wall
and are equal in value; Maderno's principle
here is one of simple serial sequence. The two
storeys are therefore not based on a homogeneous conception. Instead of the unity of S.
Susanna, we have in this late work a problem-
atic hybrid composition.[40]

When Carlo Rainaldi took over the construction of the building he had no longer a free
hand. The socle of the ground floor had already
been erected according to Maderno's design.
Rainaldi's intentions can be inferred from a
design by his hand.[41] His alterations to Maderno 18
were twofold. He had first of all to satisfy an
imperative demand of contemporary taste. In
the second half of the seventeenth century a
vertical unification of the two storeys was
always aimed at and to this end the entablature
above each order is broken, thus forcing the eye
to connect the pedestals of the upper order with
the cornices of the order below. As a result, the

top pediment, together with the outer columns which carry it, is to be seen as a frame to the centre motif, graded and verticalized in its turn. The vertical movement of the two motifs one within the other, is further accentuated by the projecting outer pilasters with their crowning figures. But within this High Baroque system of unity and verticality Rainaldi was able to develop his own idiosyncrasies. The sequence of bays can, of course, also be seen as a horizontal succession. But if we do this, we find that the outer pilasters with their projecting entablature have no counterpart in inner half-pilasters as they do in Maderno's design, but compete with the next following column. This qualitative equation of pilaster and column we found to be typical for the principle of ambiguity.[42] In the upper storey, the entablature over the inner columns of the side bays is an extension of the entablature of the segmental pediment; it differs greatly from the entablature over the corresponding outer columns and thereby obscures the framing function of the columns.

Rainaldi's suggested alterations of Maderno's design were not carried out. In the executed building he eliminated the ambiguous elements. Here the entablature over the outer pilasters of the lower storey does not project, and in the upper storey the entablature above the inner columns of the side bays is no longer developed from the segmental pediment over the centre.

18 CARLO RAINALDI. Project for the façade of S. Andrea della Valle, Rome, 1662

19 Façade of S. Andrea della Valle

20 MADERNO. Project for the façade of S. Andrea della Valle, 1624

21

21 CARLO FONTANA. Project for S. Andrea della Valle

22 Foundation medal of S. Andrea della Valle. Carlo Rainaldi's project, 1662–63

Other modifications point in the same direction and affect every part of the building:

1 Greater severity in the treatment of details: The illusionistic effect of the central window in the upper storey and the ornate, broken segmental pediments over the niches in the side bays have been eliminated; so has the broken pediment over the entrance door. The massive scrolls have disappeared, and the half-pilasters of the lower storey are now logically carried on in the upper storey.

2 Simplification of framework and profile: Instead of the conical connection of the lower with the upper part, which softened the transition from storey to storey, the attic is now placed squarely over the main storey and the plinths below.

3 Separation of architectural and ornamental elements: Incongruous combinations such as those in the niches of pediments and Chigi arms (outer bays, lower part) are discarded, and the pediments are restored to their pure, architectonic function. Likewise, the jejune, broken segmental pediments (intertwined with the framed cartouche) over the central door, is replaced by a simple, large segmental pediment.

4 Detachment of sculptural decoration from architectural ornamentation: The *putti* bearing palm branches and arms now hover freely over the tabernacles.

5 Balanced proportions and alternating rhythms: The upper and lower part are made almost equivalent by increasing the height of the upper columns and by relating the attic more closely to the upper storey. This is achieved by placing the balustrade beneath the central window not above but within the attic.[43]

In the design Rainaldi had crowned the tabernacles in the inner bays of both storeys with segmental pediments; only the lower outer bays have triangular pediments – a clear indication of how he wanted the façade to be interpreted. In the actual building, however, he reverted to the classical rhythm of alternating segments and triangles, so that every tabernacle has its place in an easily readable network of logical correspondences. A diagram will show clearly how the design and the completed façade differ:

(a: segmental gable; b: triangular gable)

Design	Façade
b	b
a	a
a a a	a b a
a	a b a b a
b a a a b	

From our previous experience, we may guess that this purposeful alteration of Rainaldi's design was the work of Carlo Fontana. The conjecture here becomes a certainty because a pen and wash drawing signed Carlo Fontana exists[44] which shows the alterations of Rainaldi's design almost exactly as we have described them and which therefore must have served as model for the design of the foundation medal of 1662[45] and for the actual construction.

Here we have documentary proof that Fontana, although only an assistant, actually corrected a design by his master. Fontana had Rainaldi's design before him, but in some respects turned its substance into the opposite sense. The tendency of these changes is away from Rainaldi's ambiguous forms towards Fontana's own Berninesque classicism, which – in the final construction of the building – was almost entirely accepted by Rainaldi. The present façade of S. Andrea therefore is based on a design by Maderno which was modified by Carlo Rainaldi and finally 'purified' by Carlo Fontana.

If the historical significance of Fontana as Rainaldi's assistant during the years 1661–62 has thus now been established, we may ask whether his classicist intrusion into Rainaldi's work is more than a sporadic episode or whether Rainaldi's principles of design are as clearly maintained over long stretches of time as we have suggested. The answer to this question will be given in the chapter on the development of Rainaldi's style. But first I wish to turn to the problems presented by the interior of the churches on the Piazza del Popolo, though this will lead us rather far afield.

The problem of direction in centrally planned buildings

The main problem in all Christian church architecture is the shape of the interior. Christianity inherited from antiquity two fundamentally different types: the basilica and the centralized building crowned by a dome. Both forms were adopted but employed for separate ends: the hall as the assembling place for the congregation, therefore as the actual church, the domed form as baptistry and burial chapel.

It is well known that the architects of the Renaissance set out systematically to adapt the circular structure to the purposes of an assembling place. Brunelleschi was the initiator with S. Maria degli Angeli (begun in 1434 and never completed). From that time onwards the problem was tackled ever anew, but the connection of form and purpose contained from the outset many elements of conflict.

In the centrally planned buildings of the Renaissance[46] all parts are equally grouped around one point. The essential character of such a building consists therefore in a perfect balance between all parts; in other words, it is a building without particular orientation. This is true without exception of all central structures. Up to the second half of the sixteenth century the apparent multiplicity of forms can be resolved into two fundamental types: the simple circular form (or a form developed from the polygonal shape) and the Greek cross, which is a centralized building with four equal arms.[47]

The lack of orientation in both these shapes conflicts irreconcilably with the liturgical requirements of the church.[48] The altar is the spiritual centre of the church and must therefore stand in the most prominent place; in a central structure this is naturally the centre, but to place the altar in the centre is unusual because of liturgical reasons. For, to take only the most obvious objections, how, with this arrangement is it possible to separate clergy from laity and to secure enough space in front of the altar in which to assemble a large congregation?[49] An accentuated wall altar is the only solution, but such an altar gives an axial direction to the interior which does not accord with the aesthetic laws of a circle. The architects of the Renaissance attempted to solve the problem by not accentuating the wall altars, thus giving full value to the circular form. And we may here mention that although this form of building was not dictated by liturgical purposes, it was nevertheless an outcome of religious considerations, for the circle was felt to be in itself the most perfect form and therefore the most suitable for the worship of God.

These essential difficulties explain the failure of the centralized type of building during the Renaissance. Not only were the most important plans never executed and most of the designs remain fantasies on paper, but nearly all the buildings that were constructed in this form were later felt to be inadequate.[50]

23, 24 VIGNOLA. S. Anna dei Palafrenieri, Rome.
Plan and interior

From the Counter-Reformation onwards liturgical considerations came again to the fore. But that did not mean a general return to the nave structure. Instead one finds new architectural attempts to adapt the central form to liturgical requirements. Before, however, going further into the matter, we must review briefly the history of *oval* buildings. For it is significant that about the middle of the sixteenth century a third type was added to the two fundamental types of centralized buildings. The oval is a pseudo-circular shape which offers to a certain extent a sense of direction, but makes it possible to combine a circular and a directional conception without conflict. In the oval structure the directional intention is merely implied, and the domed interior preserves its centralized character. It is possible for the architect, through the articulation of the walls and the structure of dome and chapels, to emphasize either one or the other of these two tendencies; he has to decide which he will develop and which he will suppress.

The evolution of the oval ground-plan. The first tentative introduction of the oval form was that by Vignola in S. Andrea in Via Flaminia in about 1552, where an oval dome is erected over an oblong ground-plan.[51] The decisive step, however, towards an oval structure was not taken till twenty years later in S. Anna dei Palafrenieri, the last work of Vignola, who died (1573) a year after the completion of the plans.[52] Up to the level of the cornice over the columns the structure is based on his design, but the attic, vaulting, choir and façade were completed only much later and with considerable alterations. In the original parts, however, Vignola's intentions are clearly to be seen. The recessed columns articulate the wall surface in an alternating rhythm of a, b, a, b, a, b, a, b, while the large bays at each end of the two principal axes are made to correspond to each other by four identical arches over the columns. One is here aware of the intersection of two directions embedded as it were in the oval form; but that these intersecting lines are subordinated to the conception of centralization is made abundantly clear by the top cornice, which is carried unbroken all round the oval interior.

The next important step in the same direction was the construction of S. Giacomo degli Incurabili by the now almost forgotten Francesco Volterrano from 1592 onwards.[53] The latent tendencies in S. Anna dei Palafrenieri are here clearly developed, but by a completely new variation in the design predominance is given to the cross-lines. The cornice round the interior breaks through the oval at each end of the long axis and is carried round the walls of the choir and entrance bay respectively,[54] thereby uniting heterogeneous parts of the building, so that the whole church must now be seen as one structure with a very definite directive tendency. But the transverse axis is also accentuated, though in a completely different way from the longitudinal axis by emphasizing the centre of each half of the oval, because each half now forms a unit of five bays, articulated in the rhythm usual in façade designs: a, b, c, b, a. The zone of the dome too makes it especially clear that the members articulating the walls must be seen as symmetrical responses and not as rhythmical divisions of the oval, for above each of the two bays on the transverse axis is an important lunette with a window, correspond-

23,
24

25–
27

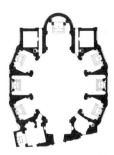

ing in size to the wall unit and flanked on each side by a smaller lunette. On the longitudinal axis, on the other hand, there are no lunettes; instead, the entrance and choir vaults cut into the vaulted ceiling. The longitudinal division of the structure into two independent concave parts, is thereby made absolutely clear.

Francesco Volterrano accentuated therefore in the oval structure the direction from entrance to altar, but he did not carry the movement through without a break, for half-way down it is interrupted by the equally accentuated transverse axis. So here the conflict arising from the crossing of axial lines in a centralized oval is very evident, with the result that the tension between purpose and form (liturgical requirements and spatial law) finds for the first time conscious and visible expression.[55]

The three solutions. In the course of these analyses we have indicated the possible solutions of the conflict latent in centralized churches. To summarize before passing on to further investigation: there are two ways of evading the conflict. One is to retain the completely pure centralized form, the other, to subordinate this form so much to axial directions that the interior gives the impression of an inflated nave. But it is also possible to tackle the problem from the opposite side; instead of suppressing the conflict, to intensity it and make us conscious of it. This can be achieved by counteracting one axial line by the other, so that the centralized form which is disintegrated by the accentuation of the longitudinal axis is reconstituted by emphasizing the transverse one. In the construction of a centrally planned building every architect must, in principle, adopt one of these three solutions.

The churches on the Piazza del Popolo. If after these observations we turn again to these churches we can see at the first glance – even from the illustrations – that we are dealing with two fundamentally different attempts to solve
6 the problem. In S. Maria di Monte Santo we see the predominance of the longitudinal axis. The design is influenced by that of S. Giacomo in so far as the cornice is likewise carried round the whole building, but there is no marked transverse axis. S. Maria de' Miracoli, on the other hand, closely follows the design of S. Giacomo

25, 26, 27 FRANCESCO VOLTERRANO. S. Giacomo degli Incurabili, 1592. Plan and interior looking north and east

25

28, 29, 30 CARLO RAINALDI. Interior of S. Maria de' Miracoli

with its complications. We need not here say much about S. Maria di Monte Santo. From the elevation, which does not represent Rainaldi's architectural conceptions, we can infer that when Bernini took over the construction the building was not so far advanced that every feature had been determined. But although the completion of the building is credited to Bernini, he cannot be held responsible for all the details. It seems probable that these were worked out by Mattia de Rossi, Bernini's trusted though not very gifted pupil.[56]

The design of S. Maria de' Miracoli is much more complicated than that of S. Maria di Monte Santo.[57] We find here, it is true, the same break
28 in the cornice of the longitudinal axis and the same emphasis on the centre of the walls
29 surrounding the chapels on the transverse axis, but all contrasts are much more intensified than in S. Giacomo. The very form of the ground-
11 plan – circle and a very long choir instead of the oval and short choir in S. Giacomo – implies conflicting elements. The two chapels on the transverse axis are also made still more prom-

inent by their increased size. The sharp accentuation of the transverse axis is, however, mainly achieved by the device of carrying the projection of the pilasters into the entablature of the projecting aedicule. Rainaldi was not content to preserve the idea of centralization by merely accentuating the transverse axis. He wished to make the circular form clearly perceptible. The projecting pilasters of the transverse axis are repeated on the longitudinal axis, where they carry the entrance arch and the arch of the choir respectively. By this arrangement the sequence of the orders represents a regular rhythm, a, b, a, b, a, b, a, b. But this intention is again opposed by another tendency, for the pilasters of the choir in contradistinction to 30 those of the main structure are fluted, and correspond in this particular to those attached to the walls of the choir. Through the colour scheme too they are sharply differentiated from the main structure and related, with their respective entablature and arch, to the choir; so that these pilasters appear as two arms, which, reaching from the choir into the central

26

building, break the continuity of the circular articulation and accentuate the long axis.

Obviously, Rainaldi is here not satisfied with a simple conflict of axial lines. Despite the interrupting projections in the entablature on the longitudinal axis, he tries to preserve the impression of a complete circle by his treatment of the walls, but counteracts this intention again by the dual function of the pilasters before the choir, so that there is not only a discord due to the intersecting of axial lines but also an inextricable fusion of circular hall and rectangular choir at the points where their walls meet.

A more detailed analysis would elucidate the problem still further, but the present investigations suffice to show the genesis of Rainaldi's design for the plan and elevation of S. Maria de' Miracoli. Undoubtedly the interior of the building is determined by the same ambiguous principles which inform the façade, where they are more obvious and can be more easily analysed.

At this point it may be asked whether so much importance should be assigned to a structure so insignificant in size, especially since its external aspect was the primary consideration. Two

things may be said in reply: first that Rainaldi used the same principles in the interior of his other buildings, although it may be only in S. Maria in Campitelli that they are carried through with the same precision; and secondly, that it is an error to think that in Baroque architecture the largest buildings are the most important. On the contrary, all the Italian buildings of the seventeenth century which are most decisive not only in the history of architectural development but also as expressions of individual styles, are of medium size or even quite small, and they are centrally planned. The rich possibilities of centralized structures stimulated new and individual inventions in a way that the nave type of church could never do. One can even say that it was the experience gathered from building centralized structures which stimulated new ventures in the design of longitudinal buildings.

But before further discussion of Rainaldi's work we must compare his particular interpretation of the centralized buildings with other important contemporary churches in Rome of the same type. Only thus can Rainaldi's originality and his place in the history of architecture be understood.

Centrally planned buildings by Bernini, Cortona and Borromini

Bernini: S. Andrea al Quirinale. Bernini constructed three centrally planned churches, all three extremely small in size but of immense effect. In each case he used one of the three possible shapes in its purest form: the pure circle for the Chiesa della Assunta in Ariccia near Rome, the pure Greek cross for S. Tomaso in Castel Gandolfo, the pure oval for S. Andrea al Quirinale in Rome.[58] The most important and most ornate of the three churches is the last, and it is here therefore that Bernini's conception of a central structure can best be studied.

It has often been said that in S. Andrea Bernini was the first to make the transverse oval the basis of a church plan. He was forced to do so by lack of space, for the site at his disposal was wide but shallow. But he knew how to turn disadvantages such as these to good account. This is indeed one of the most striking characteristics of his work: material difficulties spur him to new artistic solutions. The important

32, 33

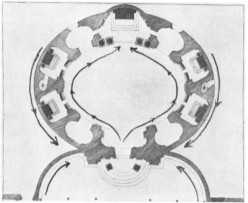

31, 32, 33 BERNINI. S. Andrea al Quirinale, Rome.
Project for the façade, plan and section

point in this design is that the transverse axis
(which is longer than the main axis), instead of
opening, as usual, at each end into a chapel, is
here blocked by pilasters. The long axis of the
oval, therefore, which determines our sense of
direction, is closed at the decisive spots, so that
the unified space of the oval is immediately
evident even in the ground-plan. This unity is
further emphasized in the elevation. The
cornice, supported by pilasters, forms a smooth
ring (no projecting entablature); the chapels are
dark, and thus completely isolated from the
brightly lit central space; the choir too forms
an independent entity not only because of the
columns which divide it from the rest of the
building, but also because it is bathed in
brilliant light. But although the centralized
shape is most strongly emphasized, the effect is
not centripetal in accordance with the static
principles of the Renaissance – that is, there is
no suggested movement towards an ideal
centre. We find, on the contrary, a very marked
concentration upon the aedicule in front of the
choir so that the altar, though part of another
world and strictly isolated, is at once felt to be
the spiritual centre. The eye sweeps round the
ring of the cornice to the columned aedicule and 34
on to the apotheosis of the saint to which every
worshipper becomes a witness: here, in a
concave break in the pediment, he beholds St
Andrew soaring to heaven.

Corresponding to the centrifugal pressure of
the interior, the powerful ring of the exterior
is held together by the aedicule of the façade. 31
Just as in the interior the semicircular choir lies
outside of the closed ring of the oval, so in the
exterior, the loggia, borne by columns, stands
outside the encircling ring. Exterior and
interior are two parts of one whole, but the
emphasis on the direction is reversed: outside,
the structure is bound together by the convex
aedicule of the façade, inside by the concave
aedicule of the altar; overflowing vitality
creates the loggia outside, the choir inside. The
exterior concave walls which form, as it were,
an inviting forecourt, seem to grip the building
like pincers at the crucial joints and to rivet the
structure together against the explosive force
of the inner space. Bernini's structure is a completely organic unit, a dynamic creation, the
result of a masterful handling and total control
over form and mass.

By distinguishing between the component parts of the building and by defining clearly and unequivocally the form and function of every architectural member, Bernini belongs distinctly to the classical school. But he interprets those two fundamental elements – the shape of the ground-plan and the articulation of the structure – in a way unknown to the Renaissance. His conceptions are based on a dynamic principle of controlled and directed forces instead of on a succession of independent units.

This was of great significance inasmuch as it paved the way for the real solution of centralized structures, which the architects of the fifteenth and sixteenth centuries had been unable to find. Only by shifting the centrifugal tension on to the outer ring, was it possible, without provoking a conflict of axial directions, to retain the effect of a closed centralized interior, and at the same time to accentuate the altar (which stands outside the dynamic ring) in accordance with liturgical demands.

At this point one must consider the part which sculpture plays in S. Andrea. We have seen how all the visual directives given in the interior lead up to the sculptured figure that is borne to heaven on clouds.[59] Whoever enters this church participates in a particular event, fixed in time and space. He sees the glorification of the saint who is flying upwards in the golden dome towards the Holy Dove surrounded by *putti*. But it is at the altar that the mystery itself is consummated; here angels bear aloft the image of the martyred saint and human suffering is transfigured by divine reward. Thereafter, the deliverance is complete and if our eyes turn back to the church they rest again upon the soaring figure of the saint.

Formerly, churches had been neutral spaces, as it were, vast shrines, where the mediation between man and the Divine was accomplished. In Bernini's S. Andrea the entire space is dominated by one particular event and because the whole interior is dedicated to the ascension of the saint, the architectural setting is eclipsed by the soul-moving story itself. In this space the sculpture serves to evoke conscious, subjective reactions in the contemplating mind, and so to 'psychologize' or dramatize the objective purport of the architecture.[60]

From what has been said, it must be clear

34 BERNINI. S. Andrea al Quirinale. Interior looking east

that in S. Andrea architecture and sculpture never conflict, but the architecture prepares for the sculpture and all its specific meaning, as is shown by the way in which the lines of the architecture converge upon the figure of the ascending saint, and also by the colour scheme of the interior: dark marble below, gold and white above. Architecture and sculpture are here the two sides of one grand conception, unmistakably expressing, and unmistakably conveying one single, clearly defined experience.

Pietro da Cortona: SS. Luca e Martina. Cortona set out to solve the problem of centralized buildings by means completely different from those used by Rainaldi and Bernini. SS. Luca e Martina is designed in the form of a Greek cross with a slight accentuation of the longitudinal axis.[61] Entrance and choir have at each side, between the arches of the crossing and the termination of the apse, a wide bay with a door surmounted by a balcony, while on the transverse axis, at the corresponding places, are only

35, 36

29

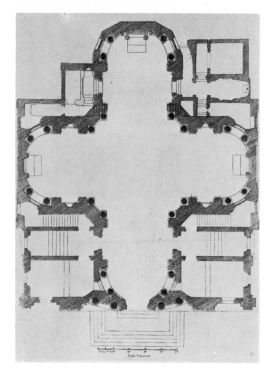

35, 36 PIETRO DA CORTONA. SS. Luca e Martina,
Rome. Plan and section

small niches for statues. But this unimportant accentuation of the direction is almost entirely neutralized by those other features which give the building its specific character. Here again it is on the surrounding wall that interest is concentrated, but the means employed are very different from those used by Bernini. Even in the ground-plan one is struck by the complication and breaking up of the wall surface, in contrast to the clarity and severity of Bernini. This activation of the wall structure in depth is based on a systematic pattern, the principle of which at least can here be outlined. The boundaries of the interior are conceived on three planes one behind the other, which are visible in each arm at alternating but always corresponding points. The innermost layer can be seen at the end of the four apses; the outermost lies behind the columns in the rounded bays of the apses; while the middle layer is the one in the bays between the crossing and the apses. To the eye accustomed to Renaissance buildings this three-plane boundary may appear violently agitated and indiscriminately broken up, but in fact it represents a regular rhythm of undulating movement. Once this is realized one will easily recognize the different planes and the corresponding articulations as a unity.

To activate a wall by splitting it into different layers seems the basic principle of Cortona's architecture. This principle of differentiation implies again a dynamic, centrifugal movement and it is therefore another means of solving the old problem of direction in centralized structures.[62]

Borromini: S. Ivo della Sapienza. To become acquainted with Borromini's final conception of centralized buildings one must turn to the church of S. Ivo, the construction of which was 37, 38 begun about ten years after that of S. Carlo alle Quattro Fontane. Those tendencies which in S. Carlo were only indicated are here fully developed.[63] From the geometrical point of view the plan of the building has always and correctly been described as an intersection of two equilateral triangles. The angles of one triangle are turned into concave semicircles, while the points of the other are 'cut off' by convex walls. Concave and convex boundaries therefore alternate. On entering the church it is not possible to perceive the geometric pattern of the ground-plan; as one's eye wanders along the walls one has instead the impression of a single star shape. This primary impression is due to, and indeed only made possible by, the design of the elevation and the articulation of the walls. In order to emphasize the unity and indivisibility of the wall articulation, the mouldings, colour scheme and ornamentation are identical throughout, the pilasters are made to articulate the wall surface in a simple rhythmical sequence along which the eye moves smoothly; finally, the clear-cut crowning cornice runs around the whole interior in one unbroken, precisely defined line.

The structure of the dome, although clearly differentiated from the body of the church by the wide, unbroken entablature and the lighter colour scheme, nevertheless continues the articulation of the walls, for the vertical thrust of the pilasters is carried on in the system of the dome panels. But these panels, alternately convex and concave at their base, lose their contrasting movement as they approach the apex. They are finally united under the lantern by a homogeneous ring of twelve stars. In this transformation of multiplicity into unity, of differentiation and complication into the pure form of the circle consists the fascinating richness of the interior. If one traces the movement into the opposite direction, one can follow the lines downward from the simplicity of the apex in the heavenly sphere to the increasing complexity in the earthly.

In this star-shaped church it is again the activation of the walls which compel the visitor to see them as encompassing a centrifugally conceived space – an impression which is in no way disturbed by the accentuation of the main altar, because no axial relations can be established in a room in which the confronting units are of different shapes.[64]

The significance of Rainaldi's centralized buildings

The centralized buildings of Bernini, Cortona and Borromini are all highly individual solutions of the problems discussed, widely apart in conception and attained by completely different means. Yet the three architects had the same object in view – the complete reconciliation of liturgical purpose with spatial

37, 38 BORROMINI. S. Ivo della Sapienza, Rome. Dome and interior

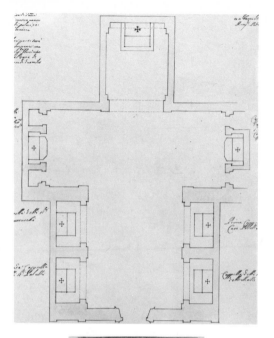

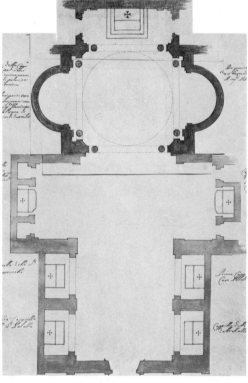

39, 40 S. Maria in Campitelli, Rome. Ground-plans, showing (top) choir of 1619 and nave of 1642–48 and (bottom) Rainaldi's project for the enlargement of the choir, 1658

demands. They all three pursue the only way by which this can be obtained, namely, by activating our conscious perception of space. In all three cases their buildings give the clearest directives of how they should be seen and one is made to follow these spatial indications in what we may term a time sequence – the only possible solution of the old problem. The spectator is made aware of the unity of the centralized form, yet his eyes are led to the predominant position of the high altar. Bernini attained this end by the dynamic articulation of the whole structure; Cortona by the effect of walls broken up by the active intrusion of space; Borromini by space-shaping wall formations.

Rainaldi's solution too is a centrifugal one. But, as we have seen, it is obscured by the simultaneous accentuation of the two axes. This inconsistency, and wavering between two possibilities, is entirely different from the conceptions of the great masters of the Roman High Baroque. Rainaldi is the only one who, by applying his principles of ambiguity to the construction of centralized buildings, carried over into High Baroque ideas inherited from the late sixteenth century. Compared with the three buildings we have analysed Rainaldi's work is conventional. If Rainaldi may thus be regarded as an heir to the Roman Mannerist tradition, further analysis will show how strongly his work was also influenced by the north Italian school of architecture. In his most important building, S. Maria in Campitelli, he grappled with the problem of direction in the nave type of church, a problem which arose not on Roman but on north Italian soil.

S. Maria in Campitelli: history of the building

In the light of new material and new arguments an attempt will here be made to establish the different stages by which Rainaldi's most important building and one of the most significant examples of Roman Baroque architecture took shape.[65]

The original building. In 1619 Paul V had ordered a church to be erected on the site of the present building; enlarged and richly adorned during 1642 and the following years, it was

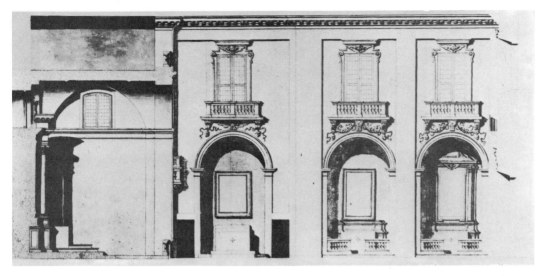

41 S. Maria in Campitelli, Rome. Section corresponding to the plan in pl. 39, showing the church before Rainaldi

consecrated by Cardinal Marc Antonio Franci-otti on 3 May 1648. According to Marracci's description,[66] this church consisted of a nave with two chapels at each side and a transept in front of the old choir of 1619. Two sheets in the codex Chigianus P VII 10 have preserved the plan[67] and elevation of this church which correspond exactly with Marracci's description. The conjunction of the older choir of 1619 with the wider, higher and much more ornate nave of 1642–48 is clearly visible.

The proposed enlargement of the original building. As a protection against the plague which had been raging in Rome since 1656, the Roman senate decided to erect a new church in honour of the miracle-working picture of the Madonna which was then in S. Maria in Portico. On 29 November 1656, the papal consent was obtained,[68] but on 21 January 1657, the pope paid a personal visit to S. Maria in Portico and declared that such a site, in the dirty and crowded Ripa district was unsuitable for a new building.

In the course of the year 1657 it was decided to erect the new church for the holy picture on the site of S. Maria in Campitelli on Piazza Campizucchi, and on 13 March 1658, the conservators and priors laid before Alexander VII plans for a building on this site.[69] These plans probably included the scheme for en-

larging the existing building which is preserved in the codex Chigianus. By this scheme the 'modern' nave of 1642–48 was to be kept intact, but the small old-fashioned choir of 1619 was to be replaced.

A flap which is pasted on to the ground-plan so as to cover the old rectangular choir depicts an imposing domed interior, with isolated columns supporting the crossing, lateral apses, and an extended rectangular altar space. The section of the proposed alterations on sheet 107v/8r shows a feature which is not yet indicated in the ground-plan. The third large bay forming the transept is here covered by a flap on which the whole width of the transept is divided into two parts, one of which consists of a chapel corresponding in size to the other two chapels, and the other of a small compartment (with an entrance door) which fills the remaining width. By this elimination of the transept and the introduction of a domed zone, the plan now follows the classical example of the Gesù in Rome.

In other respects the design of the section agrees with the ground-plan on fol. 104r. The proposed domed zone is not only distinctly separated from the nave by the triumphal arch supported by isolated and projecting columns, but stylistically too it differs markedly from the nave. The new design entailed quite new proportions. Mighty columns over twenty *palmi*

33

42 S. Maria in Campitelli, Rome. Section corresponding to the plan in pl. 40, showing Rainaldi's project for the enlargement of the choir

high (as stated in the inscription on the plan) give a monumental character to the domed area; the serried, sculptural group of free-standing columns, the ornate high crowning cornice, the richly articulated mouldings of the arches of the crossing – all these features contrast sharply with the flat pilaster strips along the walls and the studied simplicity of the entablature of the nave.

The proportions of the domed sanctuary itself are unusual. The arches of the crossing are extremely elongated and have especially wide mouldings so that the zone of the arches is exceptionally high; the drum, on the other hand, is so compressed that it is reduced to a rudimentary strip with four small oblong windows on the two main axes of the building.

A number of small flaps attached to the elevation over the side apse and the choir depict an alternative treatment of various details. At the altar of the side apse the undermost flap shows 43 the sculptural figure of a cardinal turning in an attitude of prayer towards the high altar; over 42 that is pasted a small flap with four noblemen in the same praying attitude, and finally on top

there is a larger flap which depicts the altar without any sculptural decoration, obviously left empty for a picture.[70] On the side wall near the high altar are three superimposed designs, the lowest showing the group of four praying 43 noblemen, the next the same figure of the 42 cardinal, and the topmost only a simple door.

Another sheet in the same volume of the Chigiana (fol. 109r) makes the intentions of the artist quite clear.[71] Here in the transverse sec- 44 tion of the domed sanctuary we have the same groups of figures in the side apses which we saw depicted on the flaps: on one side the cardinal, and on the other side the group of four figures turned in prayer towards the picture of the Madonna borne aloft by angels and adored by two other praying figures. Beneath the design for the group of figures on the high altar is a second design which shows the altar unadorned by any figures.

The artist thus proposes three alternative solutions: 1 to place figures in the side apses and on the high altar; 2 to place the same figures against the walls left and right of the high altar; 3 to leave the architecture bare of sculptural

43 S. Maria in Campitelli, Rome. Section showing Rainaldi's project for dividing the transept into two parts

decoration. The praying figures in the side apses are intimately related to the high altar so that there is a spiritual connection across the intervening space, the same space in which the spectator moves.[72] This fusion of art and reality, this transcending of the boundaries of art was foreshadowed already in the late Cinquecento and – a typical feature of Italian High Baroque – was first given 'classical' expression in Bernini's Cappella Cornaro in S. Maria della Vittoria. It is here extended to include the whole of the sanctuary.

Who then is the author of this plan? Two of the sheets mentioned bear the signature of the architect Gregorio Tomassini.[73] We know practically nothing about this artist. An example of his style can be seen in a plan in the same codex of the Chigiana, P VII 10. It represents a design 45 by Tomassini for S. Salvatore at the end of the Via Giulia, suggesting a spacious central building to replace an older church.[74] This design is decidedly more conventional than the plan for the enlargement of S. Maria in Campitelli, and prototypes can easily be found. The façade is composed under the influence of Rainaldi's S.

Maria in Campitelli and S. Andrea della Valle, while the dome depends on the church of S. Agnese in Piazza Navona. Even in his draughtsmanship and type of details used Tomassini follows Rainaldi closely.

This example of Tomassini's mediocre talent entitles us to attribute those remarkable features in the plan for S. Maria in Campitelli to a more distinguished mind, namely to Carlo Rainaldi. Tomassini must have been working during these years in Rainaldi's studio, and some details of the plan suggest that in minor matters he was allowed a free hand. His position was probably that of a fairly independent pupil, similar to that of the incomparably more important Carlo Fontana. The design for S. Salvatore in Via Giulia, although made during the pontificate of Alexander VII, may be therefore regarded as an independent work by Tomassini after he had left Rainaldi's studio.

To return to S. Maria in Campitelli: the fact that the existing domed sanctuary of today was 60, constructed essentially in accordance with the 61 plan for the enlargement, points most clearly to Rainaldi's authorship of the project. The com-

44 S. Maria in Campitelli. Rainaldi's project for the new choir, looking east, 1658

plete identification – through the specific disposition of the sculpture – of the ritual and functional purpose of the interior is also characteristic of Rainaldi. The life-size praying figures, kneeling and looking towards the altar across wide intervening spaces – an adoption of Bernini's idea – are used here in the same way as later in his church of Gesù e Maria.

The plan with the large dome. Apparently the Pope was not satisfied with the plan for the enlargement. But it was not till the beginning of 1660[75] that the decision was reached to erect a completely new building and a large sum of money was allocated to that purpose. On 9 March 1662, a start was made in pulling down the neighbouring houses and laying the foundations of the new church, but the ceremonial laying of the foundation stone took place only six months later, on 29 September 1662.[76] On this occasion the Pope himself buried medals in the foundation depicting Rainaldi's project.[77] What then exactly was this project, in accordance with which work had most probably been going on since March 1662?

The reverse of the foundation medal has nothing in common with the present building. Behind a one-storey concave façade, articulated by colossal orders, rises an imposing dome. The similarity of this design to that in the State 7 Archives for the churches on the Piazza del Popolo, of November 1661, is so obvious that it need not be elaborated. It should be noted, however, that the design of S. Maria in Campitelli is enriched by a new and important feature; following Pietro da Cortona's front of SS. Luca e Martina, the concave middle part of the façade is here framed by two strongly projecting piers. Though the connection with the design in the State Archives is clear it does not throw any light on the form of the ground-plan of the medal design for S. Maria in Campitelli. An exact reconstruction of the ground-plan is impossible and even the general features of the design can only be inferred. But if we assume that we have in the medal a reliable representation also of the lesser details – and the quality of the medal entitles us to do so – we may reconstruct a dome with sixteen ribs and panels of varying width.[78] This means in all likelihood that the dome was to have been erected over an oval ground-plan. From the great circumference

45 GREGORIO TOMASSINI. Project for S. Salvatore, Rome

46 Foundation medal of S. Maria in Campitelli. Carlo Rainaldi's project, 1662

of the dome we may conclude that the intended oval interior was to be wider than the present nave. After the laying of the foundation stone, Alexander VII gave orders that the construction of the apse and of the façade should both be begun, so that the imposing dimensions of the building would be established once for all.[79] From the start therefore the overall size of the church was planned to be that of the present building. As this measurement exceeds by far even that of the proposed great oval dome, we must infer that the domed sanctuary, such as we found it on the plan for the enlargement and as it actually exists, was also projected at this phase. We can therefore reconstruct the design

47, 48 CARLO RAINALDI. Drawings for façade and section of S. Maria in Campitelli, Rome (Archivio di S. Maria in Campitelli)

49 Second foundation medal of S. Maria in Campitelli. Carlo Rainaldi's project of 1662–63

as a sequence of two domed parts, one of superior and dominating dimensions and one decidedly smaller which would be the actual shrine of the holy picture.[80]

This reconstruction is confirmed in two original drawings by Rainaldi from the Archivio di S. Maria in Campitelli.[81] The façade is here still curved, but has already two storeys. The section shows a sequence of a very large domed oblong central room, and a small domed circular one; but the dome of the main room, formed by alternating large and small lunettes, has no drum and is very low. This decrease in the size of the dome as compared with the design on the medal proves that a reduction of the ambitious medal design was discussed – still without the intention of giving up the dome completely. The second storey of the façade now became a necessity, because this low type of dome had to be hidden. It is not without interest to note that the important influence of Pietro da Cortona is even more evident in this façade. It is a combination of the curved façade of SS. Martina e Luca with loggias in two storeys supported by double columns, and that of S. Maria in Via Lata. 47, 48

The plan as executed. A few months after the foundation medal had been buried, a new medal was struck which represents a fundamental change of design.[82] The large dome has been given up. The façade has two storeys and the fact that it is no longer curved points to the abandoning of an oval interior. The actual construction of the building was carried out in accordance with this plan and the completed façade agrees largely with the design on this medal. A representation of the entire wall facing the square can be seen in a drawing by Rainaldi himself, preserved in the codex Chigianus P VII 10. The design on the medal and later the engraving by Falda of 1665 must have been based on this or a similar drawing.[83] 49, 1, 53, 52

This change of plan, which took place shortly after the laying of the foundation stone, meant a substantial reduction of the original project. We do not know why the idea of a large dome was given up, but most probably it was for fear of the immense cost. It seems that the new façade on the second medal was projected at the same time as the present ground-plan; there is rather curious documentary evidence for this assumption in a drawing[84] which may reason- 50, 51 ably be presumed to date from the period between the laying of the foundation stone and the issuing of the second medal. This drawing shows only the barest outlines of the architectural block, but from these outlines one can see that the final decision on the ground-plan had already been taken.

The main body of the church, though designed early in 1663, was not constructed till much later. Work first proceeded on the façade and on the sanctuary for the picture of the Madonna while the old church in between remained intact for a long time. Shortly after the death of Alexander VII the work on the façade and sanctuary was completed.[85] On 24 October 1667, i.e. about five years after the beginning of building, the wall between the old church and the sanctuary was pulled down, and the picture of the Madonna was transferred to the new apse.[86] Then followed a complete pause. It was not until 1673 that work was taken up again with feverish intensity because of the hoped-for consecration of the finished building in the Holy Year of 1675. This actually took place on 8 December 1675, although the church was still largely lacking in decoration. The subsequent work of completion lasted till 1728.

The façade of S. Maria in Campitelli

It is with reason that the façade of this church has time and again been described as reminiscent of late classical antiquity and of craggy classical ruins.[87] Undoubtedly this work shows a profound empathy with Late Roman architecture. The façade strikes one as an artistic recreation of the wall in a Roman bath. This impression is due to a profusion of columns arranged on different planes and in different groupings.

In Rome from the beginning of the seventeenth century onwards the column was an element of ever-increasing importance, till in edifices of the High Baroque such as Longhi's façade of SS. Vincenzo ed Anastasio, Cortona's S. Maria in Via Lata and Bernini's colonnade on Piazza S. Pietro, it reached its full sculptural climax. In this respect S. Maria in Campitelli is only a link in the general line of development. But each artist had his own special way of employing columns in his structural scheme. To anyone who has followed the analysis of S.

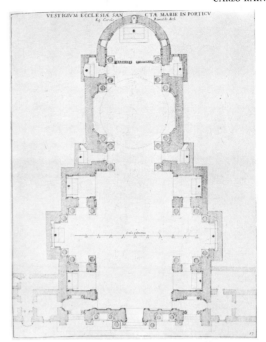

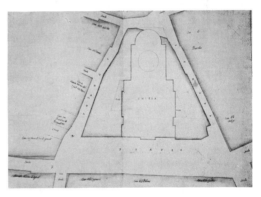

50, 51, 52 CARLO RAINALDI. S. Maria in Campitelli. Ground-plan, plan showing the site (Codex Chigianus P VII 10), and engraving by Falda, 1665

53 CARLO RAINALDI. Project for S. Maria in Campitelli (Codex Chigianus P VII 10)

Andrea della Valle it will be at once evident that the structural frame of S. Maria in Campitelli is identical with that of S. Andrea. Here again an aedicule extending through the two storeys is enclosed in a still larger aedicule and the two outer bays of the lower storey are, as it were, added to this closed system.

On the other hand, just as in S. Andrea, the outermost bays must also be regarded as an integral part of the whole façade, especially as they are organically related by the small orders and window pediments to the central bay.[88] Seen this way, they are bounded on one side by a pilaster and on the other by a half-column. Although these two orders lack equivalence in quality, the fact that they are placed on the same level gives them equivalence of function. This equation is however immediately contradicted by the dual role of the pilasters crowned by the Chigi *monti*. They are not only tied to the half-columns of the aedicule, but they also function as the inner boundaries of the palace

53 façades to the right and left, because they are exact repetitions of the pilasters which frame the palaces at the outer ends.

The half-columns in the lower as well as the upper storey correspond to the full columns forming the inner boundary of the bays, so that we have here – much as in S. Susanna – a gradation from pilaster to half-column to full column. But instead of enhancing the clarity of the system as this gradation does in S. Susanna, the dual function of Rainaldi's orders is even strengthened by their progressively increased volume. This façade clearly shows the survival of the Early Baroque striving for gradated, crescendo movement coupled with that intentionally fluctuating, boundary-blurring movement characteristic of the Mannerist period. It is this fusion of two totally different principles which gives the façade of S. Maria in Campitelli its unique character – the peculiar attraction as well as the aversion it sometimes provokes.[89]

Rainaldi's method was only possible if applied to an aediculated structure. In order, therefore, to place this work into its proper historical setting, we have to turn to the genesis of the aedicule façade.

Girolamo Rainaldi and the aedicule façade

The type of façade with two aedicules enclosed one in the other, is definitely not Roman, as will be confirmed by anyone acquainted with the development of church façades in Rome. A long and logical process of evolution, a progressive plasticity of wall, order and decoration, reaches a conclusion in S. Susanna.[90] Subsequently, as could be seen even in the later works of

Maderno himself, a disintegration of that fully developed concept set in. But at no time during this development, any more than in the works of the great masters of the High Baroque, was the aedicule articulation used. If in some cases there is an approximation to it, as in the façade of S. Ignazio, it was always considered an unusual phenomenon on Roman soil. In S. Ignazio the north Italian derivation has been proved.[91] It is in north Italy too that one finds the first fully developed aedicule façade.

Aedicule façades, as against those based on the grouping of compact masses, express an entirely different approach to the basic elements of architecture – wall and order. Façades built on the aedicule principle have a forceful vertical thrust and are strongly accentuated, but they allow the artist a much greater freedom than block compositions which affect and determine every detail of the architecture. This freedom from the compelling laws of mass grouping is as characteristic of north Italian buildings as is the high regard for columns which remained a vital, north Italian feature throughout the Cinquecento.

It is not possible to trace here the evolution of the aedicule principle step by step. We can only note that in the first half of the seventeenth century characteristic examples of the fully developed type are to be found in Milan, for instance in Francesco Maria Ricchini's entrance to the Ospedale Maggiore (after 1625) or in his façade of S. Giuseppe.[92] Meanwhile this type of structure had also begun to extend southwards. The most important document in our context is Girolamo Rainaldi's project for the façade of S. Lucia in Bologna, the construction of which never advanced beyond the first stages.[93]

Girolamo's design represents an early elaboration of the simple aedicule motif which was not actually executed till thirty years later, when S. Maria in Campitelli was constructed by his son Carlo. Its arrangement of the orders represents a graduated increase in volume from simple to projecting pilasters and from half-columns to three-quarter-columns. Girolamo was a Roman; but as a result of years of activity at Parma and Piacenza, he took over not only many architectural details, but also the north Italian canon of façade composition and united it with the Roman principle of mass grouping.

54 GIROLAMO RAINALDI. Project for S. Lucia, Bologna, 1623

Clearly Carlo Rainaldi remained faithful to the paternal tradition, even though he far exceeded his father's ideas in his own severe, truly Roman systematization of High Baroque grandeur and plasticity.

The combination in S. Maria in Campitelli of the north Italian aedicule with the Roman conception of mass concentration bore unexpected fruit. The very individual and unique façades of the great architects of the High Baroque period could not be easily popularized. S. Maria in Campitelli provided a more adaptable type of façade, with the aedicule in Roman guise, the vertical impulse and rich articulation reflecting the tendencies of the mid-century. After the construction of this church, the same type of façade, but with individual simplifications, appeared repeatedly in Rome,[94] and from there spread throughout Italy[95] and Europe. In a building such as the church of Johann Nepomuk by the brothers Asam in Munich (1733–46) we see its final and Late Baroque development.

The interior of S. Maria in Campitelli

The enlargement scheme of the first church stands in a clearly defined line of development. From the fifteenth century onwards the old problem of combining a central domed zone

55 PAOLO MAGGI. SS. Trinità de' Pellegrini, Rome, 1614

56 MARTINO LONGHI THE YOUNGER. S. Adriano, Rome, c. 1656

with a nave had been solved in two fundamentally different ways. According to one conception the two different spatial units were fused into an organic entity, that is, the units were subordinated to one principle – be it the principle of sequence, or of mass combination, or the dynamic principle – while according to the other conception their divergent character was preserved by keeping their contiguity undisguised.

The organic principle can be traced from Brunelleschi's S. Spirito to Scamozzi's plan for the cathedral of Salzburg, and from S. Andrea in Mantua to the Gesù and the numerous buildings which derive from it. The second principle, by which the two fundamental structural forms remain isolated, was perhaps developed for the first time by Michelozzi in the Annunziata in Florence, and was later often employed in cases where a domed part had to be added to an existing nave. This solution, however, was no mere makeshift; it represents, on the contrary, definite intentions manifested, for instance, in such a homogeneous church as S. Maria della Pace in Rome or in Antonio da Sangallo's designs for S. Tolomeo di Nepi.[96]

If the organic unification of complex spaces may be regarded as an inheritance from the Gothic, one may justly see the separable

juxtaposition of individual units as a survival of classical principles.[97] This is quite evident in the ground-plan. But if we consider the elevation – that is, the optical impression – we are faced with a different situation. It is the 'Gothic' conception which can be clearly and immediately apprehended on entering, while the 'classical' conception is in comparison complicated and full of unexpected surprises. For in this type of church the nave opens into a domed space, of whose form the planning of the nave has given us no indication. It is to this type of design that Rainaldi's proposed enlargement of S. Maria in Campitelli obviously belongs. Characteristically, he unites two incongruous spatial shapes and thereby creates a structure rich in optical effects.

In the ground-plan of the enlargement scheme the eight isolated columns have a very special function: together they carry the arches of the crossing, but at the same time the four columns, which stand on the longitudinal axis, serve as guide posts to the visitor's sense of orientation. Particularly if seen from the entrance, they would have directed his eye along the nave and would have appeared like a rich orchestration of the choir part. But this dynamic Baroque idea is only one component of the total conception. As one approaches the domed space one faces not only a complete re-orientation, but one also realizes that, despite their functional equality as supports of the arches, the second group of four columns has a totally different relation to the adjacent walls. The columns in the transverse axis stand at an angle of 90 degrees to the piers of the crossing and are placed in rectangular wall niches; the columns on the longitudinal axis stand free and isolated in front of the wall.

Here we must turn for a moment to the general question of the position of columns in domed interiors. During the second half of the Quattrocento the idea of the early Renaissance was, in accordance with classical prototypes, to support the arches of the crossing on four columns placed in the four corners of the room. A significant example of this arrangement can be found in S. Bernardino in Urbino.[98] The other possible arrangement – placing free-standing columns in front of the piers of the crossing – can already be seen in Bramante's early designs for St Peter's. A great many subsequent buildings were erected in accordance with one or the other of these two principles. In Rome itself it was not till the end of the sixteenth and the beginning of the seventeenth century that, as a result of north Italian influence, churches were erected in which the crossing was supported by columns, as for instance Mascherino's S. Salvatore in 55 Lauro[99] or Paolo Maggi's SS. Trinità de' Pellegrini.[100]

But besides these simple and unambiguous arrangements, there exists a third possibility, namely to combine the two principles – attached and free-standing columns – in one and the same crossing. One of the earliest examples of this is in Genga's S. Giovanni Battista in Pesaro, and it is significant that the construction of this church was begun in 1543.[101] Thereafter a small number of buildings were erected which incorporate the same idea, and where again columns with the same structural function are related in different ways 57 to the wall. These were followed by still more complicated designs, e.g. that for the church of 56 S. Adriano in Rome by Martino Longhi the Younger,[102] where the arches of the crossing under the oval dome are supported by columns on the side of the nave and by pilasters on the side of the apse.

57 S. Pietro, Bologna

The Cathedral at Monte Compatri. The same problems which were presented by the proposed enlargement of S. Maria in Campitelli, had had to be dealt with by Rainaldi in his earliest building, the Cathedral at Monte Compatri.[103] Here it was a question of enlarging a small country church and Rainaldi solved it in the same way as he did thirty years later in the enlargement plan for S. Maria in Campitelli. The domed extension is simply attached to the older nave by means of a narrow bay which, by casting a deep shadow between the two parts, serves to accentuate the complete independence of the two spatial units.

In this church the disposition of the isolated columns in the domed interior is especially informative. The eight functionally identical columns which support the arches of the crossing correspond more or less to the design of SS. Trinità de' Pellegrini. But Rainaldi was not satisfied here with the columns merely placed at angles before the piers of the crossing but has in each case combined one pair of columns with another pair in the form of a cross, in which each of the two columns on the same axis has a different function: the free-standing, arch-supporting column corresponds to one which has no similar structural function and which is half recessed in the wall.[104]

58, 59

43

58, 59 Cathedral of Monte Compatri. *Far left:* south transept by Rainaldi, nave by G. B. Soria. *Left:* bay between nave and Rainaldi's domed extension

The rich complexity of this domed interior is not due merely to the large number of columns but also to the conflicting way in which they are related. For here equal elements are united in a compact group and are yet made to fulfil divergent functions.

The elements of the present ground-plan of S. Maria in Campitelli. It has always been 50 recognized that the ground-plan of the building as finally built may be analysed as consisting of two different but connected units. The anterior and larger structure consists of the oblong main building with three chapels on each side. Both in size and significance the chapels differ completely; the middle chapels are richly adorned with columns and are so large that they give the impression of a transept flanked on each side by a small chapel. This impression is most 60, strongly confirmed by the elevation of the 61 interior, for the vaulting of the 'transept' is almost as high as the barrel roof of the nave, while the dark flanking chapels are so low that between them and the main cornice there is still room for *choretti.*

The next smaller unit consists of a domed central part preceded and followed each side by bays with doors which open into four small chapels. Fundamentally then the ground-plans of the two structures are similar in design, although it must be emphasized at once that the actual visual impression of the building would never lead one to surmise it. Nevertheless, the fact remains that in both cases Rainaldi used the same basic elements and that it is only because of his particular treatment of the wall that this is not obvious. The common denominator in the ground-plans of both parts of S. Maria in Campitelli can be seen in the State Archive project of 1661 for the churches on the Piazza del Popolo.

The project in the State Archives. The ground- 7 plan of this project can be read in two ways. On the one hand it can be seen as a Greek cross of the type of St Peter's, but with the important difference that the side chapels do not open into the transept. It is this very alteration which makes possible the alternative way of reading the plan: as the two small chapels on each side are open only on the longitudinal axis one has the impression of a row of three chapels on each side, with a transeptlike dominating central feature. The idea of a nave crossed by a predominant transverse axis and flanked by side chapels is, as it were, superimposed on the centralized conception of a Greek cross.

But it does not follow that the design of S. Maria in Campitelli is a direct transcription of the project in the State Archives for the churches on the Piazza del Popolo. There was another more immediate source of inspiration.

S. Salvatore in Bologna. Nave-type churches with accentuated transverse axes had been built from the second half of the sixteenth 62, century onwards.[105] Magenta's S. Salvatore in 63

FACIES INTERIOR ECCLESIAE SANTAE MARIAE IN PORTICV IN REGIONE CAMPITELLI
Eq. Carolo Rainaldo Archit.

60, 61 CARLO RAINALDI. S. Maria in Campitelli. Section and interior looking towards the choir

45

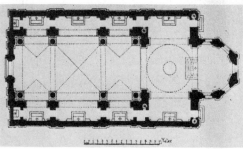

62, 63 MAGENTA. S. Salvatore, Bologna. View towards dome, and plan

Bologna is an example in which this tendency is definitely evolved.[106] In this case the derivation from the halls of classical baths is quite obvious. The evolution of the conception can be traced from Michelangelo's S. Maria degli Angeli to Pellegrino Tibaldi's S. Fedele in Milan, and finally to S. Salvatore.

The main hall of a classical bath (*tepidarium*) was used for passage both in the longitudinal and the transverse directions. But because the three arches were always identical in size the crossing of axial lines is not perceptible in the ground-plan, but only in the elevation of the building, where the high vaulting of the central bays contrasts with the low doorways of the 64 rooms left and right. Magenta was the first to reinforce these differences in the elevation by corresponding variations in the ground-plan.

The similarity between S. Salvatore and S. Maria in Campitelli is not confined to a fundamentally identical treatment of the transverse axis. In S. Salvatore too a domed interior is attached to the nave. But Magenta's domed zone is an integral part of the articulation of the whole building, and does not form a new and independent unit, as it does with Rainaldi.[107]

The significance of the transverse axis. The crossing of the nave midway by an accentuated transept must be interpreted in the same way as the 'cross of directions' in centralized buildings. The sense of orientation in the nave is disturbed: on entering the church the eye is immediately drawn to the transept and the crossing of axial lines confronts one with a perplexing situation. This contradiction in the longitudinal and transverse directives is the most effective means for creating an impression of unrest in the structural form itself. It is yet another manifestation of that conception which we have already defined as the 'principle of ambiguity'.

It is hardly necessary to point out that this complicated system of directions is far removed from 'classical' ideas. But it depends on the scheme of wall decoration whether and to what extent perplexity is turned into open conflict.[108]

The system of wall articulation in S. Maria in 60, *Campitelli* fulfils two completely different 61 functions: it represents at once a dynamic concentration upon the choir and an accentuation of the conflict inherent in the shape of the building. In contrast to the designs inspired by classical baths, such as S. Salvatore in Bologna, there are no columns in Rainaldi's nave but only flat wall pilasters; free-standing columns are only found in the 'transept' and in the rear part of the church. If instead of the large central chapel on each side of the nave we could imagine the walls to be evenly articulated, e.g., in a succession of four small chapels, the design of this church would correspond to that of the 'enlargement scheme' – with the sole difference that we would have here a richer columnar decoration of the domed part of the building. Instead of one column to guide our sense of direction, double columns are now placed on the longitudinal axis, so that the eye is more forcibly led to the apse. This dynamic concentration, typical of High Baroque and completely absent in buildings such as S. Salvatore, is counteracted by the features already mentioned, namely uncertainty about the domed zone for which the foremost part of the building does not prepare us, and doubt about how to relate the columns of the crossing to the walls.

These complications are further accentuated by the treatment of the transverse axis: the two large chapels correspond in width exactly to the bay before the dome, so that the barrel vaults are of equal height. Furthermore the depth is the same, and the decorative motifs, both large and small, are identical – from the free-standing columns to the coffered arches adorned with rosettes, and from the doors and the *choretti* to the arched windows. Indeed, even the third column which, placed at right angles, supports the crossing of the dome, is repeated again in the chapels, where it supports the triangular pediment. On entering the church, however, it is at first practically impossible to realize these repetitions, for one sees only one wall of each of the two large chapels displayed in full, while the bays connected with the dome are very much foreshortened.

The striking articulation of the 'transept' and its gilded vaulting strengthens the impression of a transverse axis across the nave. But the farther one penetrates into the interior, the more one notices the relation between the columns of the chapels and those of the bays and the clearer becomes the identity in design between chapels and bays. The repetition of the

64 *Tepidarium* of the Baths of Diocletian, Rome. Project for restoration by Francesco da Sangallo

65 CARLO RAINALDI. S. Maria in Campitelli. View from the choir

same kind of decoration in both parts of the church produces the impression of a single vast entity of which the structural shape as such gave no indication. We become conscious of the fact that in the elevation both parts of the church are dominated by one and the same principle, and that the two large chapels on each side counterbalance, as it were, the dynamic concentration towards the choir.

Simultaneously with this realization of the identity of chapel and bay, one becomes aware of another feature, namely that identical units

47

66 CARLO RAINALDI. Design for the titlepage of
Cod. Barb. lat. 4411, 1633
67 CARLO RAINALDI. Project for the alteration of the
façade at St Peter's with towers, 1645

are placed in completely incongruous positions:
the same type of column that supports the
arches is also used to support pediments, and
so on. In a building conceived on classical lines,
equal elements of the articulation always serve
equal purposes and thereby ensure an effect of
ease and tranquillity. In Rainaldi's buildings, on
the other hand, equal elements are given
diverse functions, producing the impression of
a bewildering enrichment.

The results of this examination of the interior
confirm our analysis of the façade. Here, as
there, we find an indivisible fusion of dynamic
Baroque with ambiguous Mannerist elements.
In contrast to Michelangelo whose *Ricetto* is a
static structure which derives its conflicting
character from the ambiguity in the treatment
of walls, orders and mouldings, Carlo Rainaldi
evolved in S. Maria in Campitelli a method of
interpenetrating a dynamic structure with a
second, ambiguous architectural system.

The development of Carlo Rainaldi

The analysis of S. Maria in Campitelli will have
shown that the classicist tendency which
appeared suddenly in the style of Carlo Rainaldi
around 1662 in the churches of the Piazza del

Popolo and in S. Andrea della Valle, and which
could be traced back to the influence of Carlo
Fontana was actually only a short interlude in
Rainaldi's long artistic career. In order to
illustrate briefly the lines along which his work
developed we may examine some material
which has not been sufficiently studied.

First a drawing which is not directly concerned with architecture. At the request of
Cardinal Barberini, Carlo Rainaldi in 1633 – at
the very beginning of his career – made drawings of those hospitals and quarantine buildings
which had been erected in Rome during the
plague scare in 1629–32.[109] This proof of papal
solicitude would be of historical and topographical interest only, if the same volume did
not contain two independent designs by
Rainaldi. We shall only mention one – the title 66
page – which was certainly not made upon some
outside suggestion but represents a completely
free invention. Worked out here by the twenty-
two-year-old Rainaldi, it was none other than
that very type of façade derived from the
triumphal arch which he was to elaborate
twenty years later in the design for S. Agnese, 14
to use thirty years later in the Vatican project
for the churches on the Piazza del Popolo, and 12
finally to repeat with new variations in the
façade of S. Maria in Campitelli. 53

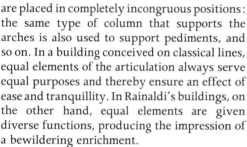

68 BERNINI. Project for the alteration of the façade
of St Peter's, 1645
69 St Peter's, Rome. Façade as built

In this architectural design for a title page the ambiguous framework of the bays is very noticeable: the inner columns are united by base and cornice with the outer columns, and must therefore be regarded as framing the outer bays, yet at the same time they are made to enclose the central blank compartment by the crowning cornice, pediment and cartouche.

We have already endeavoured to show that the impression of ambiguous movement in this kind of architecture arises from the dual function of the inner orders, and that it is not therefore a question of subjective interpretation on the part of the onlooker, but of objective guidance in the architectural design itself. I have shown elsewhere[110] that this architectural characteristic was first developed in Giuliano da Sangallo's Cappella Gondi in 1506, and it is now evident that Rainaldi carries over into the seventeenth century the tradition of those sixteenth-century architects who are called 'Mannerist' because of their 'ambiguous' structures, so fundamentally different from the buildings of both the Renaissance and the Baroque.[111]

Even when he had only to suggest alterations to an already existing building, Rainaldi pursued the same line. When Innocent X, in 1645, turned his attention to the problem of the

towers of St Peter's, Carlo Rainaldi was one of those who came forward with projects for the 67 towers and suggestions for modernizing the façade.[112] The proposed alterations submitted by various architects were all made with a view to counteracting the excessive width of the existing Maderno façade. The most important 69 part of Rainaldi's scheme consisted in enclosing the central motif of four columns by an aedicule with segmental pediment. The other alterations which he suggested, such as the separation of the lower structure of the towers from the façade, and the removal of the last outer compartments of the attic and their replacement by scrolls, are designed to the same end, namely, to lessen the impression of disproportionate width and to emphasize the vertical movement.[113] But the changes suggested by Rainaldi have also another result: because of the projection of the cornice above the columns supporting the segmental pediment, these columns lose the neutral character they possessed when they merely framed the bays, and new and ambiguous relations are thus introduced into the façade.

Nothing is more informative than to compare Rainaldi's solution with Bernini's.[114] The latter 68 attained the same end, that of increasing the impression of height by moving the outer com-

49

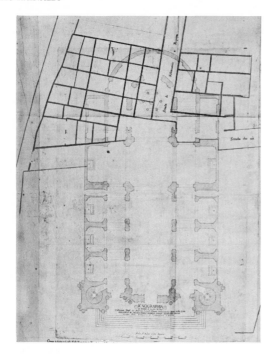

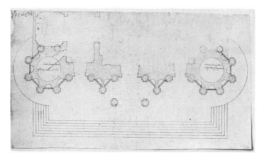

70, 71 MARTINO LONGHI THE YOUNGER. Projects for
S. Carlo al Corso, Rome

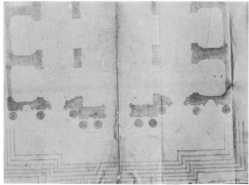

72 CARLO RAINALDI. Project for S. Carlo al Corso,
Rome

partment with the blank windows farther back. This real shortening of the façade which also resulted in an effective separation of the façade from the towers, made it possible for him to leave the rest untouched. By this ingenious solution, Bernini removed just those parts of Maderno's façade which impaired the systematic gradation of the wall units. The composition, which now consisted of only the group of eight mighty columns, is of elementary clarity. The problem, therefore, of accentuating the vertical impression of the façade, is solved by the two artists in ways which represent two fundamentally divergent architectural concepts.

During his last years Rainaldi was concerned with two extensive schemes which throw a clear light upon the final state of his development. He submitted designs for the façades of S. Carlo al Corso and of S. Marcello. The design for S. Carlo,[115] probably dating from the end of 72 the sixties, is closely connected with a design by Martino Longhi who was in charge of the 70 construction until his departure from Rome.[116] 71 Longhi intended to erect a deeply recessed façade, flanked by two towers and richly adorned with columns, similar to his façade of SS. Vincenzo ed Anastasio with its triad of free-standing, slightly forward-stepping columns.[117] The towers with *their* columns were to be clearly differentiated from the façade itself. Rainaldi's proposed alteration would have destroyed the clarity of Longhi's unequivocal, lucid design. In Rainaldi's project the triad of columns cannot be regarded as a simple triplification of one motif. Through slight variations of the original design his columns are involved in an intricate net of relationships. The two foremost columns of each triad, together with the two columns at each side of the main entrance, form a porch with six columns, so that the forward-moving effect of the triad is arrested by their being also part of the ring of columns round the portal. But this is not all. The two columns at the rear of each triad correspond symmetrically to the first columns of the towers. Together they have to be regarded as surrounds of the side portals, and, moreover, they are also part of the ring of columns around the towers.

This three-dimensional, ambiguous movement is interwoven with another principle, that of a differentiation of planes. The façade can be easily divided into three zones, each a little behind the other, marked respectively by six, again six, and two columns; these groups, though heterogeneous in function, stand each on the same level and consequently have to be regarded as equivalent in value. It is obvious that the composition of this façade surpasses that of S. Maria in Campitelli in the richness and depth of the columnar grouping as well as in an even greater complexity, and an intensification of ambiguous relations.

Rainaldi's intentions are still more strikingly expressed in the design for the elevation of S. Marcello. This project must date from about 1682 and was probably made in competition with Carlo Fontana, whose classicist Late Baroque design, however, easily won the day.[118] The first point to be noted here is that Rainaldi again starts with the idea of two aedicules. But the division of the façade into several planes is carried much further than in S. Maria in Campitelli. The cylindrical inner aedicule is enclosed in the hollow of an outer one. Further analysis shows that here, just as in S. Carlo, every order has a dual function: for the columns as well as being essential parts of the structural system, must also be regarded as a rhythmical articulation on one plane. Thus the columns which support the two small subsidiary domes (the logical three-dimensional substitutes for the outer bays of S. Andrea della Valle and S. Maria in Campitelli) find their counterpart and their rhythmic response in the outer columns of the aedicules. These, in turn, are connected in both storeys with the two columns framing the central part of the façade; for the cornice, detached from the background wall, follows the forward movement of the outer and inner aedicules. The columns at the back of the inner aedicule form, together with the foremost columns, the cylindrical oval unit, but, at the same time, they belong to those wall panels which are framed at the outside not by corresponding columns, but by pilasters. This double function of orders, tied together on the same plane, yet belonging to different spatial formations, is carried through with the strictest logic.

The design for S. Marcello is the most important example of Rainaldi's late style. However, at the end of a life spent in the service of the Church he was responsible for yet another

73 CARLO RAINALDI. Design for S. Marcello, Rome, 1682

74 CARLO RAINALDI. Project for S. Maria del Sudario, Rome

building, but so modest that it gave him little scope for expanding his ideas; it is the little church of S. Maria del Sudario, for which a design in Rainaldi's own hand has survived.[119] In keeping with his by now familiar principle of ambiguity he designed the façade so that it included the first section of the buildings on either side: this is effected by the projecting outer pilasters surmounted by a broken entablature and by the attic extending beyond the pediment. The two-storeyed façade which was eventually built in the early eighteenth century is based on Rainaldi's design but differs from it in essential points.

74

Looking back on Rainaldi's development during the course of half a century, one is surely right to say that throughout his life he remained true to the principle of permeating and overlaying Baroque structures with ambiguous elements. In his late designs for S. Carlo al Corso and S. Marcello, Rainaldi manifestly exaggerated this principle even though he followed contemporary taste in such features as Roman plasticity, expansion into depth and vertical thrust. Had these façades been built, they would scarcely have been a match for his masterpiece, the church of S. Maria in Campitelli.

75 Foundation medal of the Piazza S. Pietro, 1657

II THE THIRD ARM
OF BERNINI'S
PIAZZA S. PIETRO

The Third Arm of Bernini's Piazza S. Pietro

IN 1935–36, the *Spina* – the area in front of the Piazza S. Pietro between the Borgo Nuovo and the Borgo Vecchio – was pulled down in order to allow the monumental *sistemazione dei Borgi*. Few people then or later were happy with the result, and there have been various suggestions for redeeming the situation. None of them, however, seemed to be familiar with Bernini's own last thoughts on the planning of the piazza.

Everyone knows that Bernini intended to complete his piazza on the east side with a third arm. The effect of this would have been, of course, to enclose the piazza, because of its position on the perimeter of the oval and also because of its external structure looking towards Piazza Rusticucci. Whatever the form and nature of this arm, it would have to have been developed as a continuation of the colonnade so that it would have appeared to anyone looking at the piazza from the steps of St Peter's as a link between the two curved arms. It is so obvious that Bernini could not have thought of it in any other terms that a long discussion of this point really does not seem necessary; and yet I shall have to return to it later.

If we consider a project put forward in 1948 by Professor Polazzo,[1] we note that, looking from St Peter's towards the piazza, we would be seeing not a closure on the opposite side, nor a continuation of Bernini's columns, but colonnades running along our line of vision. The effect achieved by enclosing the piazza would immediately be lost because of the infinite repetition of arcades in the wrong direction. Their rapid diminution in perspective in the west-east axis would distract attention from the oval of the piazza, opening it out instead of keeping it as a self-contained entity.

Bernini's ideas for enclosing the piazza were quite different. In every document we possess, from the beginning to the final phase of the original plans, the third arm is shown. Its architecture always comprises a continuation of the long arms of the colonnade and, whatever Bernini's intentions may have been at various stages, this arm, in dimensions and design, was always part of the piazza and not of the street. One of Bernini's early plans for the piazza is known to us through the foundation medal struck in 1657. It shows double columns without forepart on the transverse axis of the piazza; consequently the third arm too looks like a succession of six double columns, without any forepart in the middle. The closed ring made by the colonnades is interrupted in two places, where the streets lead into the piazza.[2]

We can get an idea of what the third arm was like in this phase by looking at a drawing by Bernini's studio which is in Palazzo Chigi at Ariccia: here we find a construction with four pairs of columns, and not six as in the medal; but here, as in the medal, there is an attic which demonstrates Bernini's wish that the nature of his colonnade should be related to that of the façade of St Peter's. This was a concept which grew in importance as his plans were developed and altered.

The next important document is a print by Bonacina which is datable between April and September 1659.[3] It represents the final design for the colonnade, in which a passage, lined with double columns which protrude from the ring, is opened on the transverse axis of the piazza. The third arm, which repeats the forms and details of the long arms, consists of four intercolumniations on either side of a central passage, corresponding exactly to the passages on the transverse axis of the piazza.

After this stage, recorded in Bonacina's print, Bernini revised some of the details of his plans, without altering the essential parts. In the Vatican Library a drawing by Bernini[4] shows the third arm similar to that in the print, but with only three intercolumniations on either side. It shows however a new and important feature, a portico with four columns in front of the façade of St Peter's.

76 Falda's engraving of the Piazza S. Pietro, from Rossi's *Nuovo Teatro*, 1665

Bernini's wish to return to Michelangelo's free-standing portico is clearly proved by his original sketches.[5] It is obvious that he not only wanted to improve Maderno's façade but that he wanted to create a complement to the four free-standing columns of the third arm. Thus the same motif appears at the four ends of the two axes and indicates with the greatest clarity that Bernini planned the curved and straight parts of the piazza as a grandiose whole. But we know that the idea of altering the façade of St Peter's then had to be abandoned.

The plan represented in Bonacina's print is the same as that used in Falda's engraving in 1662[6] which, in its turn, served as a basis for Falda's well-known engraving in Rossi's *Nuovo Teatro* in 1665. This print has always been regarded as an illustration of Bernini's final plan for the piazza. In 1931 I demonstrated[7] that Bernini developed his plans beyond this stage, but since I think that this demonstration did not receive enough attention, I should like here to recapitulate my theory with new and even more conclusive arguments.

The colonnades, apart from the corridor on the south side, were built and completed between 1659 and 1667. In February 1667 demolition began of the Priory of Malta which

76

77 Project for the completion of the Piazza S. Pietro by Professor T. A. Polazzo, 1948

78 BERNINI. Design for the third arm, 1657 (Palazzo Chigi, Ariccia)

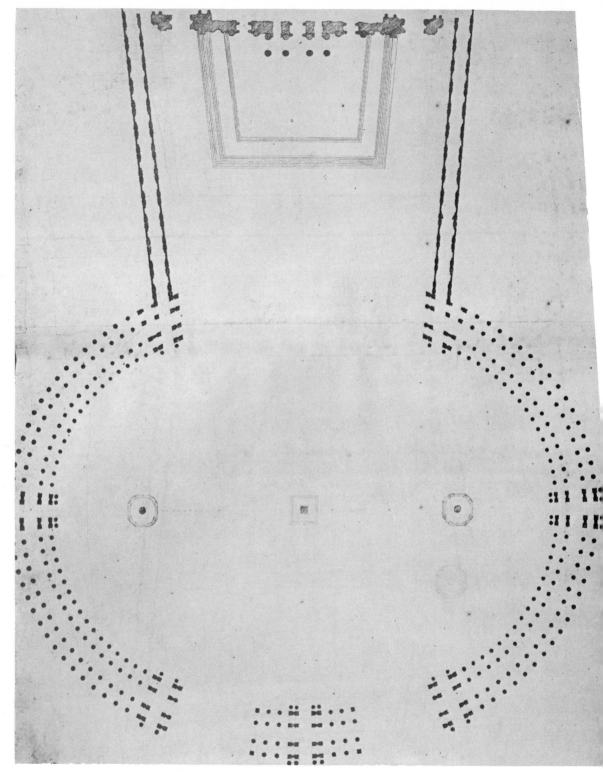

79 BERNINI. Project for the Piazza S. Pietro, 1659 (Vatican)

occupied, in Piazza Rusticucci, a good part of the site on which the third arm was to have been built. Obviously the building of this arm could not have been seriously considered before then. When Bernini at this point returned to the problem he moved the arm outside the perimeter of the elliptical piazza, pushing it back into Piazza Rusticucci. Documents relating to this phase are so convincing as to leave no room for doubt; they consist of the original drawings, already published and analysed in the work by Brauer and myself.[8] These point to the indisputable fact that Bernini now wanted to complete the third arm with a clock which would have replaced Ferrabosco's clock-tower, pulled down when the north corridor was built.

It is likely that these drawings were preceded by a phase in which Bernini thought of moving the old third arm of Bonacina's print outside the oval, taking it into Piazza Rusticucci. We have fairly certain proof of this in the plan made for the Conclave after the death of Alexander VII, i.e. in June 1667.[9] It is unthinkable that the author of this print would have altered Bernini's plan on his own initiative; he must have been aware of the development of Bernini's plans during the early months of that year. This supposition is confirmed by the small plan of Rome by Falda, dated 1667: as in the plan for the Conclave, the third arm is shown here in Piazza Rusticucci; but in this case we find a small feature, over the centre, which can be identified as the clock-tower in Bernini's sketch.[10] Falda, who was so well-informed, would never have altered his engraving of 1662 and incorporated this new project into his plan of Rome, if he had not had knowledge of Bernini's latest ideas. Thus we have two reliable witnesses who in 1667, the very year in which Bernini resumed his studies for the third arm, were informing the public of the latest stage in the plans they knew about.

But the Falda and the Conclave plans still do not represent Bernini's final conclusions. The large clock-tower in a sketch by the artist[11] probably relates to the last stage. This tower was to have been placed in Piazza Rusticucci, farther back than the third arm in Falda's plan and in the Conclave plan. Two sketches by Bernini himself indicate exactly where this construction was to have been erected.[12] Having passed through the clock-tower, one

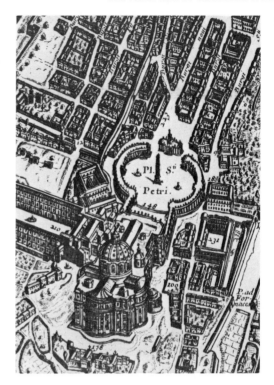

80 Detail of Falda's plan of Rome, 1667

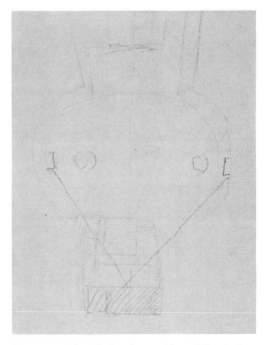

81 BERNINI. Sketch showing position of the clock tower

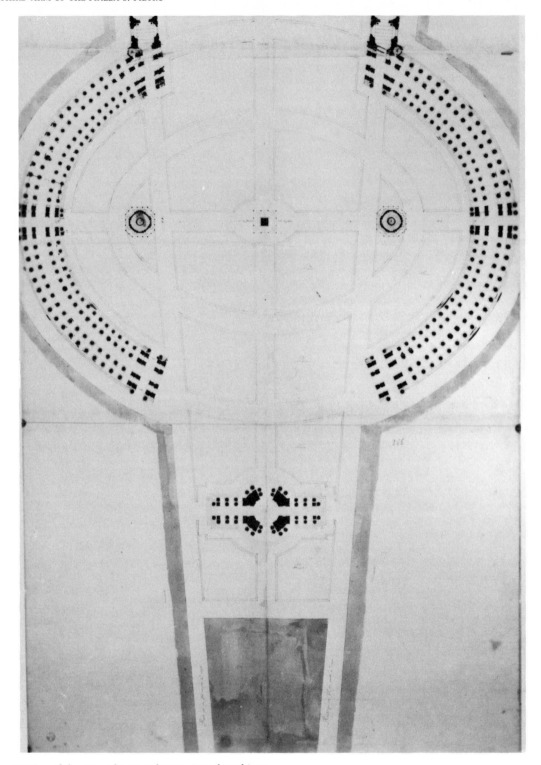

82 Plan of the Piazza by an unknown French architect

would immediately have had a complete view of the oval piazza, and the lines of vision shown in the sketches provide ample evidence of this. Since this new construction was quite far from the ring formed by the colonnades, it would have been pointless to give it the curving movement which the third arm originally had, and which is still preserved in that phase of the projects recorded in the Falda and Conclave plans.

This last phase too was known to the people close to the artist. A plan drawn in Bernini's 83 studio, for the paving of the oval piazza, in fact shows the third arm in a position set back in Piazza Rusticucci, corresponding exactly to the position indicated in the sketches.[13] Its measurements here (apparently according to instructions given by Bernini himself) are 230×90 *palmi*; that is, about 40 *palmi* wider than the measurements indicated by Bonacina. This enlargement became necessary for various reasons, one of which being that the construction now had to be regarded as an isolated building.

The paving of the piazza was begun in spring 1667, so the author of this drawing must have made use of Bernini's latest project. There is an 82 almost identical ground-plan in the Uffizi,[14] the work of a French architect and inspired by another study by Bernini,[15] as can be seen from the design for the paving, which was never carried out. Here too the third arm, 230 *palmi* wide, lies exactly on the point of intersection of two lines of vision which go to the farthest points of the transverse axis of the piazza, touching the corners of the two colonnades on the way.

We therefore have abundant material to demonstrate that in the spring of 1667, Bernini modified his earlier projects, and that he was now thinking in terms of a straight-sided piazza which would correspond on the Borghi side to the similar piazza in front of St Peter's.[16] One could say that the clock-tower which was to enclose the piazza on the east side was to serve as a counterbalance to the façade of St Peter's. The previous idea, of creating a relationship between the façade of the Basilica and the third arm, is here taken up again on a larger scale.

That the project was already well advanced is proved by the fact that Bernini submitted it to the Congregation on 19 February 1667. The

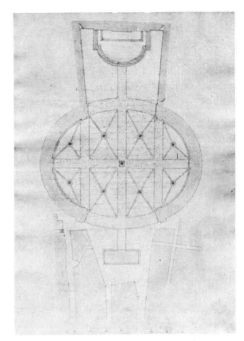

83 Plan for the paving of the Piazza

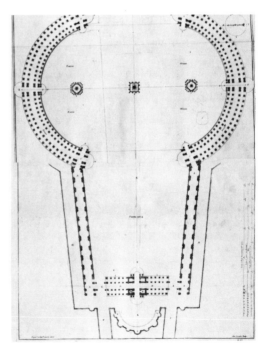

84 CARLO FONTANA. Project for the third arm, 1694 (*Tempio Vaticano*)

59

report of the session says: 'the model for the clock to be made in the Piazza S. Pietro was considered'. But the members of the Congregation decided to continue the paving of the piazza before embarking on this new work. On 22 May Alexander VII died, and with him went the power which supported the immense work of creating the piazza, now almost completed; the third arm remained on paper for ever.

Carlo Fontana, in his *Tempio Vaticano* of 1694 (p. 208 ff.), published three projects for the layout of the east side of the piazza. One of them shows a high clock-tower in Piazza Rusticucci. There cannot be the slightest doubt that Fontana had here returned to Bernini's last conception. He certainly knew the latter's work, because he had collaborated with him as a minor assistant from about 1659 onwards but, although he made use of Bernini's essential features, he varied the design in several places. As well as the changes to the clock-tower itself, which appear quite clearly when compared with Bernini's sketch, he introduced two important variations, linking the third arm with the columns by means of corridors, corresponding to those at the sides of the Basilica, and moving it much farther back into Piazza Rusticucci, thus creating a complete repetition of the rectilinear shape of the piazza in front of the Basilica, both in architecture and in depth.

With these alterations Fontana was taking Bernini's last plan *ad absurdum*. By making the two piazzas so similar, he made the clock-tower the counterpart of the façade of St Peter's. Bernini in his last project hinted at this relationship, without however making it too obvious and banal. He never thought of repeating the corridors in Piazza Rusticucci, and his ante-piazza was to have been much smaller in size than the trapezoidal piazza in front of the Basilica. Moreover, as has been demonstrated, the position of Bernini's third arm was such that, from the middle of it, the whole extent of the oval piazza was visible, while in Fontana's project the oval piazza could not be seen in its entirety by anyone coming through the central passageway in the clock-tower, and the colonnades, since only their nearest and farthest parts would be visible, would appear to the spectator like the scenery on a stage.

Later, with the idea of making the dome and its drum more visible, projects for the third arm moved it as far as possible outside the piazza, thus violating the spirit of Bernini's design, as Fontana had already done. The fact that even this would not give a much better view of the dome seems to have been forgotten. Everyone knows from their own experience, that the dome and its drum appear in their full glory only from a considerably greater distance. Bernini conceived the only possible conclusion, cutting the Gordian knot and disregarding a problem which was anyway insoluble.

As a result of this study I feel I am right to say that in Bernini's last design he placed the third arm in a position which could be reconstructed without difficulty and where any future closure of the piazza should be erected. No argument can alter this conclusion; every project should, in my opinion, start from this premise. I do not claim that this will solve all the problems arising from the present state of Via della Conciliazione, but it would be advisable to tackle them by slow degrees, starting with the one certainty among so many unreliable solutions: the construction of the third arm on the place assigned to it by Bernini in 1667.

84

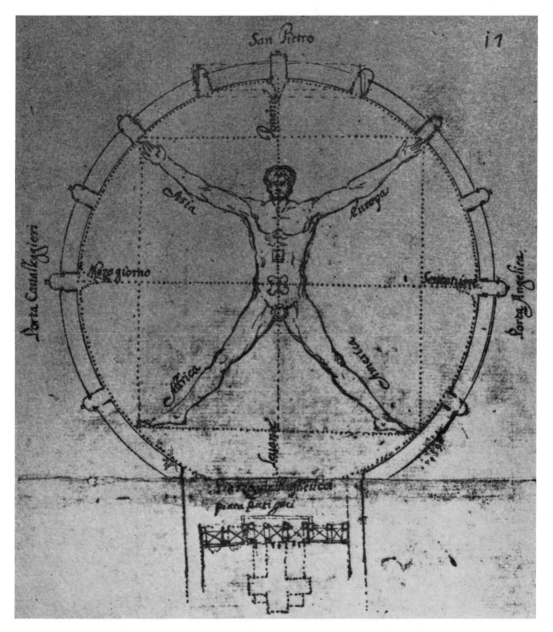

85 Drawing 17 of the counter-project. Symbolic design showing correspondence between the proposed Piazza S. Pietro, the earth and Man

III   A COUNTER-PROJECT TO BERNINI'S PIAZZA S. PIETRO

A Counter-Project to Bernini's Piazza S. Pietro

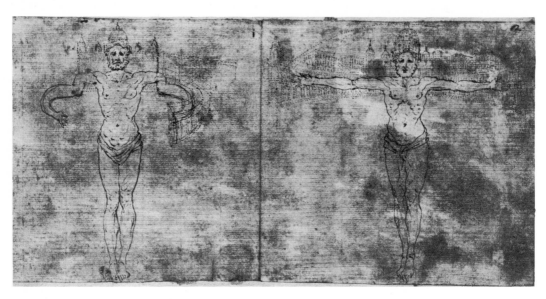

86 Drawings 1 and 2. Criticism of Bernini's piazza in terms of human proportions

BERNINI'S PIAZZA S. Pietro was such an ingenious and complicated piece of planning that it could not fail to arouse contemporary criticism. He had not only to deal with a vast number of practical architectural difficulties, he had also to provide for religious, liturgical and ceremonial requirements and last but not least to satisfy the taste of his time. Critics attacked him from all these angles according to their own points of view.

There were two religious ceremonies which had primarily to be taken into account in the planning of the piazza. First, at Easter and on a few other important occasions the Pope blesses the people of Rome, assembled in the piazza, from the Loggia della Benedizione above the central door of the church. It is a blessing which symbolically includes the whole world: it is given *urbi et orbi*. To give the greatest effect to the benediction the piazza had not only to hold the maximum number of people but also as much of it as was possible had to be visible from the Loggia. Secondly, the papal blessing of pilgrims is not given from the same spot but from a window of the private papal apartment

situated in the palace built by Domenico Fontana on the north side of the piazza. From here also as much as possible of the piazza had to come into view.

To these considerations there were others no less vital to be added. For instance, the entrance to the papal palace, situated in the north-west corner of the piazza, had to be of dignified and imposing form. The church itself had to have an approach in keeping with its position at the centre of the Catholic world. Arcades, in front, were required for certain processions, and in particular had to be suitable for the grand ceremonies which took place on the day of Corpus Christi; they were also needed as a protection against the weather not only for pedestrians but also for coaches.

But it was mostly on theological grounds that Bernini's solution of these and other minor problems met with the greatest opposition. The attack, led by a particularly ruthless critic who probably belonged to the most reactionary ecclesiastical circle of the time, can be reconstructed from a set of twenty-five drawings which have always been misinterpreted by

87 Drawings 3 and 4. Ground-plan of the counter-project with figure of Christ; and criticism of the sight-lines of Bernini's piazza

modern scholars and have even been attributed to Bernini himself.[1] It is the purpose of this article to attempt a description and explanation of the procedure and arguments of this critic. His attitude is not purely destructive; for he puts forward counter-proposals with corrections for all the supposed mistakes of Bernini's project. The best method of approaching these drawings is to discuss them in their old sequence indicated by numbers in a seventeenth-century hand.[2]

86   Drawings 1 and 2 are studies of human proportions drawn in relation to the façade and the piazza of St Peter's. In drawing 1 (left) the arms of the figure follow the shape of the piazza and are therefore broken and deformed; in drawing 2 (right) they are well made and stretch across the picture plane without following the lines of the architecture behind. The two figures are related to two different architectural projects: on the left is Bernini's piazza with the straight corridors, forming the almost quadrangular space (actually a trapezoid) in front of the church, and the oval of free-standing colonnades before it; whereas on the right the

colonnades are directly connected with the façade of St Peter's and the quadrangular space is missing. In contrast to Bernini's single colossal order the arcades here are two-storeyed and lean against buildings behind them. It is evident that this plan is a counter-proposal directed against Bernini's ideas. Since the arms of the figure in front of Bernini's project are broken exactly where the corridors join the façade on the one hand and the colonnades on the other, it is these corridors which seem here to be the main point of criticism.

It is the aim of the next two somewhat 87 enigmatic drawings to show why it was that the quadrangular space of Bernini's piazza was open to objection. Here the ground-plans of the projections of the first drawings are given. In drawing 3 (left) two segments of a circle, which the colonnades follow, join the façade and in the space between them six smaller segments are drawn in such a way that they fit exactly into it. These semicircles correspond in their pyramidal arrangement to a quartering in the coat-of-arms of Alexander VII during whose reign (1655–67) the piazza was built. Thus

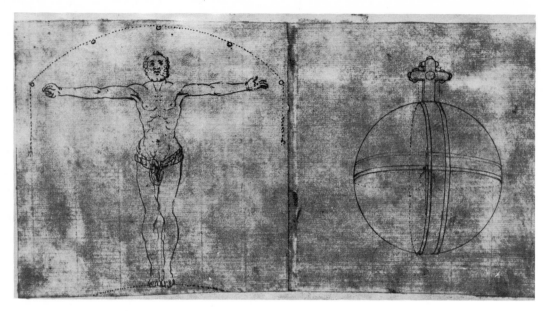

88 Drawing 5. St Peter between heavenly and earthly spheres; and the Cross above the Orb

Alexander VII is suggested by his *monti* – as the Italians call these armorial bearings. The top segment touches the wall at the entrance to the church, and on it stands in the ground-plan of St Peter's[3] the figure of Christ, bearing the stigmata, with his arms outstretched. According to tradition, the cross-shaped Basilica symbolizes Christ crucified.[4] The whole drawing now appears as a naive illustration of the words of the Psalmist (87, 1): *'Fundamenta eius in Montibus sanctis.'* The generally accepted New Testament parallel to this text is: *'Tu es Petrus et super hanc petram aedificabo ecclesiam meam.'* (Matth. XVI, 18). This rebus-like design is thus based on the addition of the pun on the Chigi-*monti* to the pun on the word Petrus.

In the colonnades, behind the small circles of the double columns, there appear, though hardly visible in reproduction, the sun on the left and the moon and stars on the right. These imply that the construction of the proposed circular piazza embraces the whole world, and the drawing should now be interpreted as representing the upper part of the globe on which the cross is erected.

Thus the idea of the critic is to show that by directly joining a circular piazza to the façade of St Peter's an ideal relationship is formed on the one hand between Alexander VII and Christ and on the other between the Pope and the world. Such an arrangement would alone be suitable for the place where the word of Christ was preached to all mankind through the medium of the Papacy.

In contrast to this the drawing opposite (4, right) with the plan of Bernini's piazza[5] dispenses with all symbolical allusions. Instead a dotted line runs from the centre of the façade past the corner of the northern meeting-point of the corridor and the colonnade to the centre of the oval part of the piazza. This line shows what parts of the piazza are not visible to the Pope from the Loggia della Benedizione, since they are screened by the protruding corners of the quadrangular space. This is the reason why this space is in dispute, and why the arms of the figure in drawing 1 are broken and deformed.

The real meaning of this figure now becomes clear. The small curly beard is a characteristic feature of St Peter, and the placing of the dome of his church like a mitre on his head makes it certain that it is he who is represented. Only in drawing 2 can he embrace humanity with his blessing. This is expressed not only by the widely extended arms, but also by the emphasis on the dome and even more by the appearance of the Loggia della Benedizione through the lines of his mouth and of the entrance of the church in the centre of his neck. The implication here is that only in this plan – and not in

89 Unnumbered drawing. View of the Piazza looking towards St Peter's

that of Bernini where neither Loggia nor doorway are drawn in – can the papal blessing be effectively given and access to the church itself be readily had. A dotted line making a wide segment connects the arcades with the top of the church to emphasize that in this project an ideal relation between the earthly (arcades) and the heavenly (dome) spheres is obtained through the successful intercession of the Pope.

The ideal combination of the three spheres is not present in drawing 1, where they are all deformed. The dome of St Peter's is dwarfed, the mouth of St Peter is distorted, and his arms are crippled. The harmony of the world is disturbed, and it is here impossible to draw an arc connecting Heaven and Earth.

86 87   The correspondence in symbolism between the critic's projection and his plan is complete. In the projection Christ, Papacy and Humanity are envisaged in the dome of the church and in the mouth and the arms of St Peter; in the plan they reappear in the figure of Christ, in the Chigi-*monti* and in the sun, the moon and the stars (the symbols of the world). This symbolism is used to show in the projection *the* ideal benediction, and in the plan its result, the raising of the cross upon Earth.

88   In the light of this interpretation the next two drawings (5) also become intelligible. The critic does not oppose a good and a bad project but

sums up in purely symbolical language the line of his argument up to this point. On the left the figure of St Peter appears again – according to Matth. XVI, 19: 'and whatsoever thou shalt bind on earth shall be bound in heaven' – as the intercessor between Heaven and Earth, which are indicated by the curved dotted lines above[6] and below. On the right the cross, which recalls the plan of St Peter's, is shown on the Orb.

After this introduction dealing with general principles, a detailed elaboration of the criticism and of the alternative scheme follows. The most important drawing of the whole series, the view of the piazza looking towards the church,[7] repeats on a large scale the projection in drawing 2. The two-storeyed arcades on double-columns are placed above a flight of steps which run round the whole piazza. At intervals the arcades are surmounted by towers, and towers also appear on the façade of St Peter's. On the right, behind the arcades, the group of buildings enclosing the Cortile di S. Damaso is visible, with Raphael's Loggie nearest the church and the square palace erected under Sixtus V to the right of them. The arcades are attached to the palaces and to their lower extensions which are added by the draughtsman. A corresponding set of palaces is proposed for the southern side of the piazza. The following drawing (6) shows a small section of the 89 86 99 90

65

90 Drawing 6. Section of preceding scheme, with alternative arrangement for the arcades
91 Drawing 7. View of the Piazza looking away from St Peter's

same project with an alternative arrangement for the arcades: the arcades of the ground floor now protrude, thus allowing for two covered passages instead of one.

91   This project is supplemented by the next drawing (7) which gives a view of the piazza facing the Borghi.[8] A systematization of the Piazza Rusticucci – the square extending towards the city – and of the Borghi is obviously intended. Two parallel streets run into the Piazza Rusticucci, and the palaces surrounding

it echo, in their arcades, the arrangement in the Piazza S. Pietro itself. In these last three drawings the counter-project is set out at length.

The next three drawings (8–10) are concerned with the entrance to the Vatican. In 1617 the old entrance to it was replaced by the monumental tower of Ferrabosco.[9] The difficulties of the site with its sloping ground prevented Ferrabosco from making a straight way through[10] from his entrance to the old staircase leading from the church to the

92
93

66

92 Drawing 8. Entrance to Cortile di S. Damaso as seen from the Piazza
93 Drawings 9 and 10. Plan and perspective of the Cortile di S. Damaso

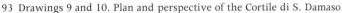

palace.[11] At the time of the critic there was only one way of entering the palace; from Ferrabosco's Portone di Bronzo a long winding passage, after branching off to the right, led to the Cortile di S. Damaso. It was obviously necessary to make alterations here. In a first design (8) the critic shows a flight of steps as seen from the piazza. In order to make his idea intelligible he draws a section of the back wall of the arcades without showing the arcades themselves. Next to the staircase is the guard-

room of the Swiss soldiers which is indicated by a gun, armour and halberds.

The plan of drawing 9 with the Cortile di S. 93 Damaso and the section of the arcades adjoining it, sets out the whole arrangement of this staircase. Half-way up, the staircase divides into two flights which turn back and lead up to the level of the Cortile. At the same time the Cortile is made square by cutting off five bays from the western palace which contains Raphael's Loggie. The regular appearance which the

67

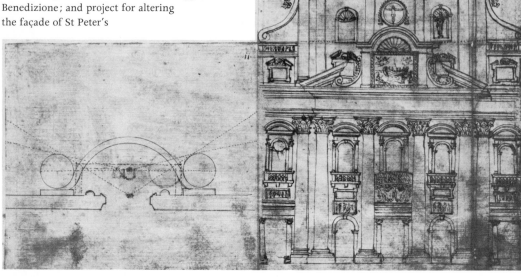

94 Drawings 11 and 12. Plan of the Loggia della Benedizione; and project for altering the façade of St Peter's

Cortile would present from within is demon-
93 strated in drawing 10. It represents a view
facing the staircase, with its one central and two
side flights. The Cortile is on a level with the
second storey of the arcades of the piazza, and
since this storey corresponds exactly in height
with the ground floor of the surrounding
palaces, the Cortile has an appearance of great
uniformity. It is to be noticed that the open
arcades[12] allow a view on to the piazza, and that
the entrance is surmounted by one of the
towers which are repeated at regular intervals
round the piazza. It is in this way that the
difficult problem of creating an appropriate
entrance to the palace was to be solved by the
critic's new plan.

The only part of the project which has not
yet been dealt with in detail is the proposed
alterations for the façade of St Peter's, and the
following two sheets of drawings are concerned
94 with them. On the right half of drawing 12 are
the five central bays, where the principal
changes are in fact suggested. It was an old
point of criticism that the façade was too wide
and therefore appeared too low in relation to
its height. For very sound reasons Bernini left
it unaltered. But his critic wished to restore

proportion to it by placing above the three
central bays a second storey[13] which was to be
connected with the original attic by large scrolls
on each side. It would serve the same purpose
to remove the attic above the last bay as is to be
seen in drawing 13. But the chief object of the 96
drawing under discussion is to deal with the
view from the Loggia della Benedizione. The
existing rectangular Loggia has been altered in
such a way as to protrude in a semi-circle
beyond the columns at each side of it. This
point is stressed in another drawing on the back
of No. 15, where the central portion alone, with 95
the projecting Loggia supported by two atlan-
tes, is shown on larger scale. Further explanation of the critic's intention is supplied by the
two accompanying plans. In No. 11 the old 94
rectangular Loggia is indicated by dotted lines,
while in the gap between the walls in the centre
there is a human eye, from which two dotted
lines radiate touching the circumference of the
columns. These lines show that in the old
Loggia the Pope, who has to sit almost in the
entrance to the balcony, cannot see those parts
of the piazza which are hidden by columns. The
new protruding Loggia would allow his throne,
actually drawn in here, to be moved forward to

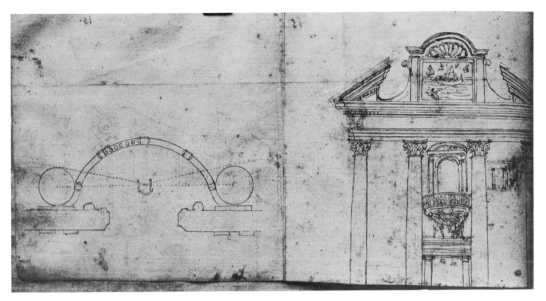

95 Verso of drawings 15 and 16. Loggia della Benedizione, plan and view

96 Drawing 13. Reduced alternative counter-project

97 Drawing 14. Criticism of Bernini's project of March 1657

a position on the central axis of the columns, and the two dotted lines radiating from another eye placed in the throne make it obvious that the problem of visibility could be overcome in this way. The same proposal is shown, again on 95 a larger scale, in the second plan without, however, repeating the point of criticism.

Allegory, which is extensively used throughout, also plays a great part in the alterations of 94 the façade. He places in the broken pediment, which he designs for the centre, the most important relic of Old St Peter's, Giotto's Navicella, showing the ship of the Church which braves every storm through the faith of the Apostles. Above it he repeats the main theme of the whole series: St Peter with outstretched arms in a circle, expressing, as before, the all-embracing power of the Papacy.

96 The next drawing (13) is a modification of the critic's own plan, apparently to demonstrate that the essential features of his project could be preserved on a smaller scale at considerably less expense. It chiefly involves making the arcades one storey high and dropping his scheme for the Cortile di San Damaso. The building, with Raphael's Loggie in it, is left untouched (though only twelve bays are given in the drawing instead of thirteen – presumably a slip of the draughtsman) and the arcades of the piazza run through the end of it. The first project is modified throughout, and among the

many changes are the reduction in size of the towers on the arcades and the omission of lateral towers on the façade of St Peter's.

The critic's counter-proposals end here and in the next three drawings (14–16) he returns to a still more detailed consideration of Bernini's project, though No. 14 does not in 97 fact correspond to Bernini's final plan. It differs from it in three respects: 1 the colonnade has only one passageway and not three, and 2 is made up of arcades instead of columns bearing a straight cornice, while 3 Ferrabosco's tower which surmounted the entrance to the Vatican between 1617 and 1659, when Bernini finally decided to demolish it, still appears above the corridor. The critic is dealing here with an earlier project by Bernini which contained all these elements,[14] and he obviously wishes to show that it was not too late at this stage to alter Bernini's plans and adapt them to his own scheme;[15] for he has drawn the outline of his circular plan in dotted lines above and behind Bernini's colonnade.

In drawings 15 and 16 Bernini's colonnades 98 appear in their final state.[16] In both cases the criticism turns to the problems of the view from the piazza of the Pope's private apartment and of the façade and the dome of St Peter's. The left-hand drawing which gives the whole arm of the colonnades shows two figures in the piazza. One of them seems to move along a line

98 Drawings 15 and 16. Criticism of Bernini's last project of 1659

towards the church, while the other looks up to the papal palace. From the head of the second figure two dotted lines lead up to the front corner of the building, one ending immediately below, the other above the end window of the first storey. This must be the window from which the Pope blessed pilgrims, and the lines indicate that a man standing even at this point in the piazza could not see it, for the upper line marks the lowest point in his view, while the lower line shows that the view of the window is screened by the roof of the colonnades through which it runs.

The figure is placed on this spot for special reasons, since it is from this point that a pilgrim, entering the piazza from the north through the central passage of the colonnades, would have his first full view of the façade of St Peter's. This is indicated by the two dotted lines crossing in front of the figure. One of the lines running from east to west starts at the beginning of the colonnades, passes the end of the corridor and finishes at the corner of the façade; the other going from north to south retraces the steps of the figure from a doorway outside the colonnade. This doorway, which is still in existence today, gives access to the quarters of the Swiss guards. The critic must have been acquainted with Bernini's scheme for planning at this point on the central axis of the colonnades a large roadway for pilgrims approaching

the church from the north. This roadway which in fact was to follow an old pilgrim's way[17] would have brought foreign pilgrims to the centre of the piazza without their having to pass through the city. Bernini's plans for this were well advanced and, in addition to sketches and other evidence, there exists a large-scale working drawing,[18] about 7 feet long, in which a straight line indicates the road and shows exactly what alterations were needed.

The problem of the view of the palace is again dealt with in the right-hand drawing (16). Here only half of the colonnade, on a larger scale, is given. As the dotted line running from left to right suggests, it is a section of it drawn on the central axis of the piazza where pilgrims were to pass through the colonnade from the new road. The figure is now placed nearer the colonnade than in No. 15, and therefore the dotted line leading up to the palace ends not at the top of the window of the first storey but below the window of the storey above it. Again there is special significance in the position of the figure; for at this point a pilgrim standing before the entrance to the palace would, according to the critic, have a poor view of the church, since it is badly obscured by the colonnade.

Another dotted line shows that the drum of the dome is completely hidden from the view of the pilgrim, and in the left-hand drawing the

98

71

99 Piazza S. Pietro, a photograph taken in 1929 showing how part of the Piazza is left empty

dotted line rising from the figure walking towards St Peter's makes the same point. While from the position of this figure, which is less than half-way into the piazza, the whole of the façade is visible, the lower part of the drum still remains hidden behind the attic of the façade.

Finally, in this drawing the critic returns to two questions which he has already raised. The dotted line starting from a very small figure – hardly visible in the reproduction – standing in front of the entrance to St Peter's, at a point where the rectangle and the oval part of the piazza meet, indicates that from here only the roof of the papal palace is visible since the corridor intervenes. Another line running from the door of the church past the corner of the corridor marks out the section of the oval piazza which cannot be seen from the doorway of St Peter's.

Considering that these drawings were made before the erection of the colonnades, it is clear that the critic was a man of considerable perspicacity and foresight. It is true that pilgrims have to go well into the piazza to have a view of the window from which the Pope gives his blessing; this is shown by a photo-
99 graph, taken at the Benediction of the Alpini in 1929, in which the right half of the piazza is empty despite the fact that the Pope appears at a window in the second storey. It is also true that at no point in the piazza is the drum of the dome completely visible, and as one approaches the church the dome sinks down from view behind the vast mass of the façade. Bernini

himself tried in vain to find a remedy for this weakness which was due to Maderno, the architect of the nave and the façade of St Peter's. The critic's solution consists in raising his second storey above the centre of the façade so that the drum of the dome would be entirely obscured.

In drawing 16 the extent of the disappearance of the façade behind the colonnade is much exaggerated; for the view here is not, in fact, taken from the position of the figure but from a point just within the piazza at the central passage of the colonnade. The fault, then, lies not in the treatment of the architecture but in the positioning of the very weakly drawn figure. Moreover, the draughtsman of the architecture with his remarkable sense of space would never have put his figure in the adjacent drawing. Here as elsewhere in this series of drawings, it can only, therefore, be concluded that two different hands were at work: probably an architect and an amateur, the one preparing the ground for the additions of the other.[19]

Whereas the last two drawings were mainly concerned with the problems of the approach to St Peter's from the north, the subject of the next two drawings, in which the critic con- 100 fronts Bernini's solution with his own scheme (not numbered), is the access to the church from the city through the main street of the Borgo, the Borgo Nuovo. In the left-hand drawing the façade of the church has been altered and the lateral tower added according

100 Unnumbered drawings. Access to the Piazza through the Borgo Nuovo

to the critic's project, while in the right-hand drawing the façade appears untouched as Bernini decided to leave it. According to the critic the tower would provide a suitable focal point in the view from the Borgo Nuovo. But this is not his principal 'improvement'. In his project, next to the façade at the far end of the street are two one-storied arcades corresponding to his 'modified' project (13); in the same position in Bernini's plan there is the entrance to the palace surmounted by Ferrabosco's tower. The key to the critic's argument lies in the two rather puzzling sketches which appear in the upper half of the drawings. His own project is accompanied by the old symbol of Eternity, the snake biting its own tail. As is the case with drawings 3 and 4 the critic on the one hand underlines the symbolism of his own project, and on the other draws attention to the 'mistake' in Bernini's plan. Thus the little drawing of the Borgo above Bernini's perspective supplies the point of his criticism, which appears to be the isolation of Bernini's entrance to the palace. The presence of Ferrabosco's tower shows that the critic has again Bernini's earlier project (14) in mind, for he was apparently not in a position to know what Bernini's final plans were to be. The critic maintained that the closed view at the far end of the Borgo gave no indication of the presence of an enormous piazza opening out between the Borgo and the entrance, nor even a hint of its form and character. But in his own plan the two co-ordinated arcades seem to be part of an endless sequence so that there is a clear suggestion of the existence of a large piazza. This suggestion is emphasized by the distance between the two arcades and the last houses of the street, whereas in Bernini's plan the entrance to the palace had perforce to be drawn nearer to the end of the street. And so the symbol of the snake stands for the continuity of the arcades of a circular piazza, the erection of which would symbolically be in keeping with the idea of the eternity of the Church.

Now that the critic has produced all his reasons for considering Bernini's plans inadequate as to the giving of the benedictions from both St Peter's and the palace, the view of the church from the piazza, and the approaches from the country and from the city, and has put forward his own project with solutions for all these questions, he sums up in a last symbolical drawing the whole trend of his ideas. Here (17) the complete circle of his piazza is drawn out with naive indications of the towers on the arcades. Inscriptions indicate not only the four points of the compass but also the positions of buildings and gates corresponding to their actual sites.[20] The ideal character of the circular piazza finds its symbolical expression in an ideal figure which, with outstretched limbs, touches the circle at four points. On the arms and legs are the names of the four parts of the world, and so the figure becomes an ideal representation of the inhabitants of the earth;

73

in this connection the four points of the compass may be taken as evidence that the circle of the piazza symbolizes the orb. Europe and Asia, together the home of the Faith, are significantly placed on the side of St Peter's, while the arm of Europe points to the entrance to the palace.

Here the symbolism, begun in the first drawings, is made complete. Whilst ideal figures of Christ (3) and the Papacy (2) illustrated the perfection of the scheme in the first drawings, now the figure of Humanity is brought in to round it off. Thus the three forces embodying the order of the world form the basis in which the critic built up his counter-project.

Attached to the series of architectural drawings is a sheet of the same size and of the same paper[21] with two designs for a sculptural group of *Religione Christiana*. The subject of the group is explained by inscriptions written by the same hand as those in drawing 17. In the left-hand drawing the representation of *Religione Christiana* slavishly follows the description in Ripa's *Iconologia*:[22] her head is surrounded by rays, one breast is uncovered and she is winged; her left arm rests on a cross, from one of the arms of which hangs a horse's bit, while she holds up a book in her right hand and treads a skeleton under foot. The four Cardinal Virtues carry a globe on which she is seated. They too are completely taken from Ripa; of Prudence and Temperance, the two virtues on the side out of view, only the symbols are indicated: stag, lance and fish belonging to the former, elephant and reins to the latter. In the right-hand drawing the alternative design for *Religione Christiana* is less closely connected with Ripa, while of the Four Parts of the World, on which the globe now rests, Africa and America are the only two visible, with their symbols again coming from Ripa.

The ground-plan (17) shows that this group was intended for the centre of the piazza. Three monuments are marked in the central axis of the human body: under the chest the obelisk is clearly indicated, with the fountain below (see pl 108).[23] In accordance with his conception, and as the key to his architectural scheme, the critic places in the centre between them a sculptural group of the Cross above the Orb.

This series of drawings was, no doubt, enigmatic even at the time when it was produced. It was only intelligible in connection

with a treatise which in all probability it was drawn to illustrate. There was, in fact, a long tradition in treatises of this kind. Whenever and wherever an important architectural work was proposed the voice of criticism was generally raised in this way. It had been used against Bernini himself about fifteen years earlier, when in 1645 Innocent X was considering the problem of the tower on the façade of St Peter's. On that occasion no less than eight different architects expressed their opinions in drawings accompanied by memoranda.[24] The same method of criticism was not uncommon in France; Colbert ordered the public exhibition of Le Vau's plans for the Louvre and asked the architects of Paris for their criticism. Perrault comments on this: '*Presque tous les architectes blâmèrent le dessein de M. le Vau, et en firent la critique dans des mémoires qu'ils donnèrent. Plusieurs même apportèrent des desseins de leur invention.*'[25]

The responsible body for the fabric of St Peter's was the Congregazione della Fabbrica,[26] a committee set up by Leo XI in 1605 and consisting of a number of cardinals who met regularly to consider the progress of work in hand, the next steps to be taken, together with counter-proposals and objections. All criticism had to be submitted to this committee and, though evidence of their proceedings is not very extensive, it provides proof that there were heated arguments over Bernini's plans for the piazza. Bernini himself read an explanation for his first project which he submitted to the Congregation on 19 August 1656.[27] And at the same meeting Cardinal Pallotto, a leading member of the body, made observations on Bernini's project in a memorandum that still exists. He objected principally to its excessive size and urged that there should not be so much expenditure on a building which had only an ornamental value.[28] Two other memoranda by unknown authors were submitted to the Congregation on 17 March 1657. One of them criticized Bernini's project at that stage – not yet the final one – above all from an aesthetic point of view, and the author's own idea for suitable arcades is added in a drawing. The other emphasizes practical and ritual considerations.[29] There are two more treatises in existence which cannot, however, be related to a definite meeting of the committee, and are to be taken

101 Two designs for a sculptured group of *Religione Christiana*

as answers by Bernini's supporters to criticisms of his plans. In the first of these[30] Alexander VII himself is made responsible in laudatory terms for the choice of the final oval plan – a clever method of flattering the Pope and silencing opponents at the same time. The second is directed against attacks on the free-standing triple colonnade, Bernini's outstanding innovation, and shows, with the familiar display of seventeenth-century erudition, that with it Bernini returns to Greek tradition.[31] To these memoranda are to be added a few drawings without text, of which those surviving have always been attributed to Bernini himself although their critical character seems to be obvious.[32] There is thus ample evidence for establishing the original purpose of the series of drawings discussed in this essay; undoubtedly at one time they formed the illustrations to a memorandum submitted to the Congregazione della Fabbrica.

It can even be shown within a few months when this took place. At a meeting of the Congregation on 17 March 1657, Bernini presented a project based on the oval plan with a *single* passageway of colonnades and preserving Ferrabosco's tower.[33] This is the project to which drawing 14 in the series refers.[34] But as the critic knew Bernini's final plan (15, 16), which did not take shape till the spring of 1659, it is evident that he was familiar with all the different stages in its development. In March 1659, the construction of the right (northern) side of the colonnades was begun.[35] At about the same time a large engraving by Bonacina illustrating Bernini's final project was published.[36] Now in this engraving there appear projecting double columns on the central axis of the colonnades, both within and without the piazza. The presence of the double columns on the outside of the colonnades at this point was reasonable as long as Bernini needed a *point de vue* for his newly planned road which was to lead up to the central axis of the piazza.[37] One detail is very instructive: the existing preparatory drawing for the engraving, passed by the

97

98

102

103

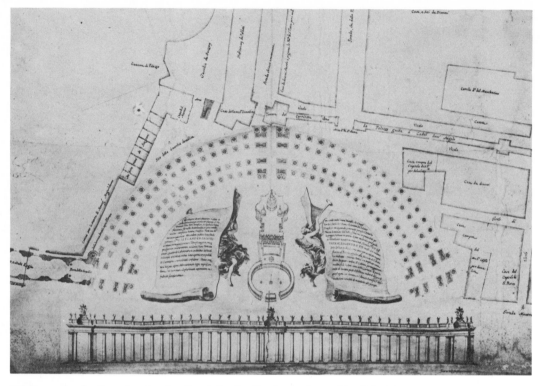

102 Engraving by Bonacina showing Bernini's plan for the northern side of the Piazza, *c.* 1659

papal censor for reproduction, does not show the columns on the outer circumference. It is, therefore, justifiable to conclude that the idea of the new road occurred to Bernini early in 1659, between the preparation and the execution of the engraving.[38] Since the critic was, as has been shown,[39] acquainted with Bernini's plan for the road, his memorandum cannot have been finished before the spring of 1659. Nor can it have appeared much later. A plan which involved vital alterations is unlikely to have been produced after the beginning of the actual construction in March of that year; moreover, it has already been noticed that the critic had no knowledge of Bernini's ingenious solution for the entrance to the palace.[40] The planning of the Scala Regia had not been begun when the Bonacina engraving was published, but it seems to have been fully developed by the late summer of 1659.[41] It is therefore clear that the critic's memorandum was intended as a last and powerful appeal to the Congregation before construction of the piazza was started in the spring of 1659.

It remains to be considered who this critic was. The answer to this question is, curiously enough, not made easier by the fact that a name appears in an inscription on one of the drawings. The right-hand drawing on the sheet with the two sculptural groups bears the inscription 101 *'Constanzo de Peris inventore'* written in the moulding at the top of the pedestal. There are reasons, which will later become clear, for believing that this artist was throughout only the executant of the critic's ideas.[42] The identity of Constanzo de Peris remains a complete riddle; his name appears neither in contemporary writings nor in any document connected with the history of the piazza.

It is, however, possible to reconstruct with more or less certainty the tradition and atmosphere in which the critic's ideas and plans originated, and thus to put forward a suggestion as to the possible *spiritus rector* of the counter-proposal.

The core of the whole problem lies in the question of the giving of the blessing both from the church and from the palace, which was,

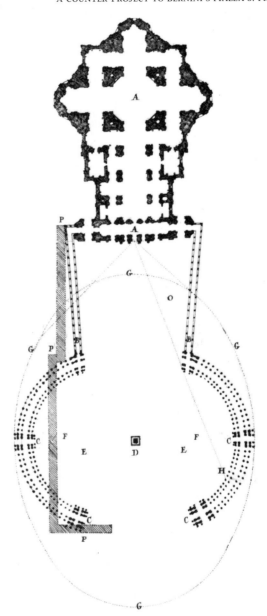

103 Preparatory drawing for Bonacina's engraving

indeed, much discussed during the planning of
the piazza. The benediction from the church
was still considered thirty years later, as is
shown in the standard work on St Peter's by
Carlo Fontana who, as Bernini's assistant, had
first-hand knowledge of all its implications. In
104 a plan of the church and the piazza[43] he marks
in dotted lines: 1 the *visuale* from the centre of
the church (*'Linea visuale della Loggia della
Benedizione'*) in order to point out the parts of
the piazza which are out of view; 2 an oval, the
longer axis of which is on the axis of the church
(*'figura elipse che haverebbe assegnato il perfetto
modo dei portici'*); and 3 *visuali* to show that
this oval would have given a complete view of
the whole of the piazza. But Fontana states that
a realization of the 'right' project was impossible because it would have involved the
destruction of the papal palace.[44] As to the
benediction from the palace, in the memorandum, written in Bernini's defence between 1657
and 1659, the rejection of his first rectangular
project, which would have given a full view of
the piazza, and the preference for the existing

104 Plan of the Piazza by Fontana showing the
sight-lines from the Loggia della Benedizione (A-H),
the oval along the axis of the church (G) and sight-
lines from the Loggia to the sides of this oval (A-G)

105 Drawing of Arcades (Bibl. Vat., Codex Chigianus H II 22, folio 94)

oval form, are explained as being due to the desire to bring the piazza as near as possible to the palace.[45] Even in one of the memoranda directed against Bernini this point is favourably mentioned.[46] Baldinucci too in his life of Bernini, which is based on direct information from the artist's circle, repeats this reason for the choice of the existing oval.[47] Finally there are two drawings which are also concerned with these problems. They show plans which are nearly identical: both are more or less octagonal, one with straight, the other with curved sides.[48] The layout of these plans is perfectly adapted to ritual requirements; for the *visuali* from the centre of the church prove that the whole of the piazza is in view, and at the same time its northern side touches the papal palace. The distinctly critical character of these projects is made evident by the abundance of *visuali* which demonstrate that here the obelisk does not obscure views from focal points as it does in Bernini's scheme.

Just as the problem of the giving of the papal blessing was a much argued question, so all the other points raised by the critic were subjects of great discussion before he produced his counter-project. A circular piazza had already been proposed in the reign of Innocent X by Carlo Rainaldi.[49] This plan, which Rainaldi seems substantially to have repeated under Alexander VII in competition with Bernini, must have strongly influenced the critic since it includes single arcades attached to buildings and the systematization of the Borgo – both features also adopted by the architect of the two *visuali*-plans.

Bernini himself had started by basing his plans on the traditional scheme of attaching arcades to palaces,[50] and criticism was naturally aroused as soon as he departed from this tradition.[51] In addition to this both aesthetic and practical arguments were brought against Bernini; isolated columns were not considered sufficiently imposing[52] and his free-standing colonnades were thought to be no adequate protection against rain and sun. The design of the specimen arcade added to one of the 105 memoranda directed against Bernini was intended to overcome these difficulties. It may be noted that the critic adopted a similar type of arcade, so that in this respect also he followed proposals made by others before him.

It is the same with the problem presented by the façade of St Peter's. Since the substruc- 69 tures[53] of Maderno's towers remained unused, they became part of the façade and gave it its unsatisfactory breadth. For two generations the best brains tried to correct this fault. The catastrophe of Bernini's tower is well known. Structural conditions made the erection of towers almost impossible. Bernini, therefore, in his project for the piazza abandoned all alterations in the façade and endeavoured to give the impression of increased height by attaching to it his long and comparatively low corridors.[54] Regardless of the structural difficulties the critic sticks to the old demand for towers. Here as with his other alterations for the façade – the heightening of the centre and the removal of the attic at the sides – he follows in the steps of Carlo Rainaldi.[55]

Even the critic's symbolism strikes a familiar note. The parallelism between the body of Christ and the church is almost as old as Christianity itself.[56] But only in the interpretation of the Middle Ages does the choir become the symbol of the head of Christ, the transept that of his outstretched arms, and the nave that of his body and legs.[57] This symbolism was always kept alive in connection with St Peter's. Manetti, in his description of the buildings planned by Nicolas V,[58] compares the plan of the new St Peter's with the limbs of the human body, and under Clement VIII (1595) the centrally planned buildings of Bramante and Michelangelo are condemned because they do not symbolize the body of Christ crucified.[59]

The use of punning in coats-of-arms is a typical feature of the Baroque age. There are frequent examples of Pope Alexander's coat-of-arms used in a symbolical setting,[60] but the most significant application of this occurs in the foundation medal of the piazza of 28 August 1657,[61] which bears the motto taken from Psalm 87: *'Fundamenta eius in Montibus sanctis.'* This verse, apparently proposed by the learned humanist Luca Holstenius,[62] was chosen by Alexander because of its special bearing on the laying of foundation stones; for bishops had to recite it on these occasions according to a tradition going back through the Middle Ages to Rabanus Maurus.[63] But it is obvious that Alexander himself realized the special connection between the 'holy Mountains' and his armorial bearings. What, therefore, the critic did in drawing 3 is no more than to use this idea, which had papal approval, as a warning to the Pope himself. The drawing then acquires a special significance; for it suggests that the Pope's own desire – that Christ's foundation is in the holy Mountains – can only find fulfilment in the scheme proposed by the critic. By this manoeuvre the critic attempts to influence the Pope himself, who was about to accept Bernini's project.

But this is not all; the critic actually intends

106 BERNINI. Sketch showing the Piazza S. Pietro in anthropomorphic terms

to defeat Bernini with his own weapons. It is well known, that Bernini was fond of comparing the façade of St Peter's with the body, and the colonnades with the arms of a man. He reveals this during his stay in Paris in 1665 in conversation about the experiments he made when planning the piazza.[64] One of his drawings of about 1667, concerned with the removal into the Piazza Rusticucci of the central portion of the colonnades, which in fact was never built, actually represents, though in a cursory way, the dome as the head, the façade as the body and the colonnades as the arms of a man.[65] In his memorandum against his critics, probably written in 1658 and not later than 1659, he even compares the oval colonnades to the motherly arms of the Church, 'which embrace Catholics to reinforce their belief, heretics to reunite them with the Church, and Agnostics to enlighten them with the true faith';[66] in a word, he suggests that his piazza is a symbol of all humanity. The critic's drawings contradict this claim.

But Bernini's language is fundamentally different from that of his critic. Whether he represents the piazza as a man or calls the colonnades the arms of the Church, his comparisons are no more than similes, meant in a metaphorical sense; this is the anthropomorphic approach towards architecture, which had existed in Italy since the time of Alberti. In order to justify his architectural design he

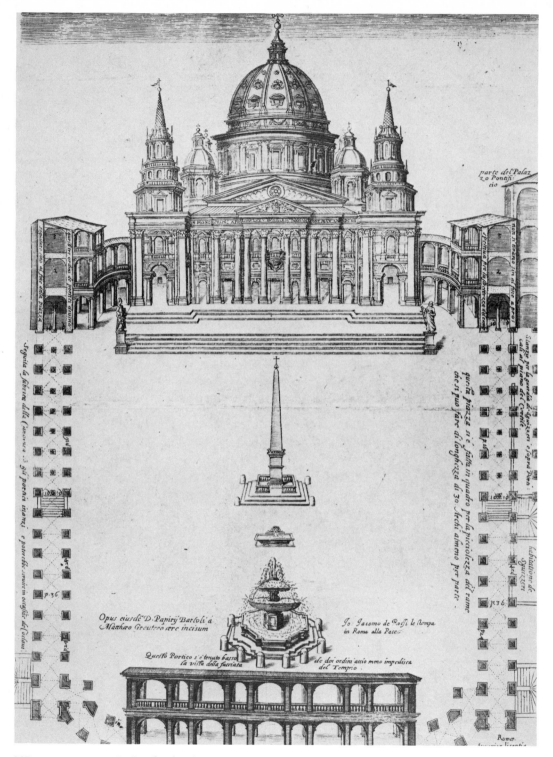

107 PAPIRIO BARTOLI. Project for the Piazza S. Pietro

108 Unknown painter. View of the Piazza looking towards the Borgo based on the counter-project

connects human proportions and features to it. The critic on the other hand is completely absorbed in medieval symbolism which implied that the arrangement of his plan is dependent on an external correspondence between the symbolical idea and the architectural form.[67]

The critic's conception consists not simply of a mosaic of various symbolical details put together to suit his own purposes; it is based rather on a much repeated theological theme which he revives in an odd manner. Medieval writers from Honorius Augustodunensis to Durandus[68] refer to two forms which are alone possible for a church: the cross-shaped and the circular. The former, a symbol of the Cross, implies that the faithful are 'to tread in the steps of the Crucified according to the word: If any man will come after me, let him deny himself, and take up his cross, and follow me.'[69] The latter would signify that the Church has been extended throughout the circle of the world, according to the Psalmist (XVIII, 5): 'And their words to the end of the world – *et in fines orbis terrae verba eorum.*' Yet this form not only symbolizes the propagation of the Faith throughout the world, but also means 'that from the circle of this world we reach forth to the crown of eternity – *quod de circulo orbis, perveniemus ad circulum coronae eternitatis.*' It is obvious that the critic intended to combine the symbolism of these two basic forms for church-building in the central monument of Christianity: the church and the piazza of St Peter's. For this he had a special justification. His piazza is the *circulum orbis*, for Christ's word is spoken from the Loggia della Benedizione *in fines orbis terrae; the circulum coronae aeternitatis* which is here symbolized by the dome of St Peter's is thus reached. The puzzling segments of circles in drawing 5 now become 88 completely clear: St Peter, speaker of the *verba eorum*, mediates between the *circulum orbis* and the *circulum coronae aeternitatis*. If final proof that the critic based his conception on these texts is needed, it is to be noted that above the head of St Peter appears in a pencil a wreath (the *circulum coronae*) and above this the outline of the dome.[70] An allusion to the relation of the *circulum orbis* to the *circulum coronae aeternitatis* appears in the symbol of Eternity in plate 100 as well as in the placing of St Peter in the circle on the façade. The crucified Christ in the 94 church had to be shown according to this text, as well as the figure of man as a symbol of those 'who come from the four parts of the world'.[71] The critic went back to medieval symbolism for the unity of conception on which he based the abstruse elaboration of his architectural scheme.

This curious visual translation of medieval thought has itself a prototype in the seventeenth century from which the critic drew

81

inspiration. At the beginning of the century an eccentric Roman dilettante, the *doctor iuris utriusque* Papirio Bartoli,[72] was engaged on plans for the church and piazza of St Peter's, on which he spent much time and even more money without any practical result. His favourite project, described in a detailed memorandum and illustrated by an engraving,[73] was to erect in the church, above the tomb of the Apostles, the realistic image of the mystical ship of the Church. In the bow of the ship appears the figure of St Paul, while St Peter is the pilot with the tiller under his arm. In front of St Peter is the Cathedra, the throne of the Popes, while above the tomb of the Apostles is the papal altar, surmounted by a huge crucifix on the upright shaft of which the whole passion is shown in the same way as the reliefs on Trajan's column. This crucifix forms the mast of the ship on which the sail is fixed. The whole theme, the symbolism of which is much more elaborate than has been suggested here, is based on the Apostolical Constitutions.[74] It is evident enough from this that the critic in his naive translation of medieval symbolism followed Papirio Bartoli.

107 Now Bartoli also left a project for the piazza in which there are a great number of features which reappear in the critic's counter-proposal. The arcades are attached to palaces, façade and arcades are joined together in very similar ways, there is also in each case the same solution for the entrance to the Cortile di San Damaso as well as the same idea for towers above the façade;[75] and finally, and above all, the semicircular Loggia della Benedizione occurs in both schemes.

Papirio had a nephew, also a doctor in the two laws, who was the faithful apostle of his uncle's beliefs in matters of art.[76] It may be suggested that the nephew is the critic behind our series of drawings, made more than thirty-

five years after his uncle's plan had been engraved. Living in the curious world of Papirio Bartoli, he must have followed with keen interest all the stages of the planning of the piazza under Alexander VII, and finally reissued the old project of his uncle, though taking into consideration all the points raised during the years preceding construction. Whoever the critic may have been, he was acquainted with the whole range of symbolical thought which had come down from the past, and therefore his proposals, speculative and fantastic though they were, were not likely to pass unnoticed in reactionary circles among the clergy.

A small picture by an unknown painter,[77] 108 which shows a view looking towards the Borgo identical with the critic's drawing 7, provides 91 proof that his project made a definite impression in his own time. There was, nevertheless, not the slightest chance of its supplanting Bernini's plans; for it was by no means practical. The extent of the critic's scheme is much larger in size than that of Bernini, and its execution would have involved not only the demolition of parts of the papal palace and certain buildings in front of it – including the small but important Cortile di Maresciallo and the quarters of the Swiss Guard – not only the erection of enormous palaces on the southern side of the piazza together with a complete reconstruction of the Borgo, but it would also have meant the removal of vast masses of earth to level out the slope on the northern side and, as a result, the risk of undermining the buildings round the Cortile di San Damaso. The subtleties of the counter-project were effective only on paper; practical issues had in no way been taken into consideration, and it was not long before the critic had been completely forgotten and his project properly shelved.

109 BERNINI. *Louis XIV*, changed into *Marcus Curtius* (Versailles gardens)

IV THE VICISSITUDES OF A DYNASTIC MONUMENT: BERNINI'S EQUESTRIAN STATUE OF LOUIS XIV

The Vicissitudes of a Dynastic Monument:
Bernini's Equestrian Statue of Louis XIV

BERNINI's equestrian monument of Louis XIV has never attracted much attention because it was taken for granted that its quality was so poor that the less said about it the better. Among the dissenting voices, however, there is one which should not be dismissed lightly, namely that of Bernini himself. He regarded this statue as his parting gift to the world – and, let it be said, the octogenarian was far from becoming senile.

The myth that the monument is a monstrosity was to a large extent created by Louis XIV, who was so shocked when he first saw it that he gave orders to have it destroyed. In the end, he agreed to have it changed into a Marcus Curtius and to banish it to the farthest part of the gardens at Versailles, where he was certain he would never see it again.

The royal displeasure was, of course, a sign of the unbridgeable gulf which separated Bernini's exalted late manner, as inimitable and personal as that of the aged Michelangelo, from the somewhat pompous, egalitarian, academic-classicist taste in France. A greater affront to the conventions of *bon goût* than Bernini's statue can hardly be imagined.

Paradoxically, the act of vandalism on the part of the King saved the monument from the axe of the vandals of 1789. Had it been put up in the heart of the city, as originally intended, it would have been the most conspicuous and most magnificent royal monument in Paris, and no power in the world could have prevented its destruction. The statue survives where it was placed in Louis's reign – at the far end of the Bassin des Suisses, about a mile outside the garden gates of Versailles on the longitudinal axis of the palace.

Leaving the disputable question of quality aside, I am here concerned with the fact that the statue is so richly documented that we can open the book of history on pages which are usually closed to us. Although the story of the monument has been told before,[1] some of the most interesting documents have never been properly evaluated, and it is precisely these on which the tale in this paper is focused.[2]

The prelude and the problem of payments

It was in 1665, during Bernini's stay in Paris, that an equestrian statue of the King was first considered for the city. But at that time the idea was rather vague. Colbert had two different projects in mind: one, a monument of staggering size to be erected between the Louvre and the Tuileries, the main feature of which would have been an obelisk or a column; the other, a monument of the King in the centre of a new square which he planned on the left bank of the river.[3] At the same time Bernini played with ideas for a monument combining elements of Colbert's two schemes; he suggested erecting an equestrian statue of the King between two colossal columns in the square between the Louvre and the Tuileries. On 12 October, eight days before Bernini and his party left Paris, the equestrian statue was only briefly mentioned, but in such a way that the initiate seemed certain Bernini would be commissioned to execute this as well as other works for the King.[4]

For over two years no more was heard about the equestrian statue. It was not until 2 December 1667 that Colbert came back to the idea. He broached the question rather carefully but emphatically, leaving Bernini an entirely free hand with regard to size; nor had he any preconceived ideas concerning where the statue would be placed. Bernini's answer does not survive, but it must have been favourable, for in a letter of February (?) 1668 Colbert makes a serious suggestion concerning the position of the monument. He now thinks the statue might be erected on a permanent stone bridge planned to replace the wooden bridge opposite the Theatines. This arrangement would have been similar to that of the equestrian statue of Henry IV on the Pont Neuf farther upstream.[5] So this was the third place proposed for the King's statue during these early discussions.

It is rather surprising that Bernini's (lost) answer to the revival of the old project was not a determined refusal, because about six months before the reopening of this matter, on 15 June 1667, Colbert had informed him of the final decision that his Louvre plans would not be carried out. Bernini's readiness to tempt fate once again – despite this almost unbearable slight – cannot easily be explained. The idea that the mightiest king on earth seemed to come begging for his co-operation surely tickled his vanity. Certainly there is no indication that he should have felt under any obligation. The King had promised to pay him a handsome annual pension of 6,000 livres (the value of which may have corresponded approximately to an equal amount of dollars at present – 1961 – purchasing power), but no strings were attached to this royal act of generosity.[6] Yet the question of money loomed large over this whole affair. To be sure, Bernini adored money. He was the highest-paid artist in Italy if not in Europe, and a proper compensation for services rendered appeared to him as no more than due acknowledgment of his outstanding worth. Even when working for such an illustrious patron as the French King, he did not see any reason why glory without financial gain should be his only reward. In his negotiations with Colbert Bernini had learned to be careful and suspicious. And who can blame him after the experience of his Louvre project?

Mirot believed that the lengthy prelude to Bernini's starting work on the statue was the result of his unspeakable avarice.[7] In his exposition of the case Colbert and Louis appear as innocent white doves who never for a moment thought of taking economic advantage of the artist. Mirot and I have examined the same documents, but our interpretation could not be more at variance. The matter is not without interest because, apart from the light it sheds on the characters of the main protagonists in Paris and Rome, it seems to supply a contribution to the relativity of historical judgments even when the documents would appear perfectly straightforward.

Let us first turn to the question of the pension, which was, after all, a contract voluntarily entered into by the King of France. The money due on 1 January 1666 reached Bernini early in 1667. This was no doubt the result of a reminder on Bernini's part, although Colbert maintained that he had dispatched the money before the complaint reached him. We may grant Colbert the benefit of the doubt, but a study of the documents shows that he was an inveterate liar. The pensions for 1667 and 1668 appear in the *Comptes des bâtiments* on 19 January and 15 December 1668 respectively. But this improvement did not last. The pension due on 1 January 1669 had not yet been paid by 13 June 1670, and only on that date and under considerable pressure did Colbert take the necessary steps.

Bernini and Colbert approached the question of the pension from diametrically opposed points of view. For Bernini its regular payment was the touchstone of the King's and Colbert's sincerity. Colbert, on his part, hated to be reminded of his obligations; it irritated him and produced angry outbursts. He had good reason for a bad conscience; in addition, he seems to have seriously felt that Bernini should be proud and happy to be allowed to serve a king of France even without special regard to material compensation. He puts on paper his surprise that 'the consideration of such a small sum as the pension can possibly make him delay a work that should be both advantageous and honourable' for him. 'However,' he goes on, 'in order not to give him a pretext for breaking his promise to execute the statue,' the pension for the previous year would now be paid.

Bernini hesitated a long time – in fact over two-and-a-half years, from December 1667 to the second half of 1670 – about whether he should embark on the gigantic enterprise of the equestrian statue. Just as he had wasted immense energy and ingenuity on the Louvre plans, so he might one day find himself with the King's statue on his hands. In April 1670 he confidentially voiced his doubt that the King was really much interested in the equestrian statue, for if he were, he would pay the pension more regularly. It is extraordinary how correctly Bernini judged the situation: throughout this time the King had been unaware of Bernini's right to a pension as well as of the plan for an equestrian monument. And in a note to his royal master Colbert, who on previous occasions had been indignant that Bernini could doubt the validity of the royal promise ('we have a King who knows how to reward merit,' etc.), did not dare to point out that to pay the pension was a moral obligation, and justified it solely as requital for Bernini's work on a royal monument. The King's answer was disarmingly straightforward: 'You have done well to pay him the pension since he is working.' Now at this moment, 16 May 1670, Bernini was not yet working on the monument and Colbert knew it; but he also knew that he had to make a false statement in order to prevent the pension from being stopped. It appears, therefore, that Colbert and his master made the regular payment of the pension dependent on the progress of the statue, or rather, regarded it as recompense in lieu of a proper fee. That this was their interpretation of their obligations is illustrated also by the fact that the pension was paid out fairly regularly as long as Bernini worked on the statue but was stopped altogether when the monument was finished.[8] Bernini, on the other hand, did not show a businessman's acumen during the negotiations. His resistance melted away once he saw a readiness to continue the pension, and after the payment of June 1670 he seems to have decided to begin work even without discussing a fee.[9] The manner in which he handled this matter at a later date is characteristic of his artistic temperament.

Some time in May 1673 he explained to Cardinal d'Estrées, the French ambassador's brother, with whom he was on friendly terms, that for the last few years he had abandoned all other work and had forgone considerable profit in order to devote himself entirely to the service of the King; now he felt the time had come for a special mark of favour and he wanted the Cardinal to communicate the request to Colbert. Meanwhile, however, the pension for 1672, dispatched from Paris on 13 May 1673, arrived in Rome, and when the Cardinal saw Bernini in the first days of June, he found the master in a very happy mood; the question of extra remuneration was never once mentioned again. Bernini himself communicated his appreciation in a rather touching letter written to Colbert on 13 June 1673. The latter's piqued answer to Cardinal d'Estrées' epistle, by contrast, was far from magnanimous. He had, so he claimed incorrectly, always sent Bernini's

pension absolutely regularly. He felt he had to warn the Cardinal that Bernini 'is a most selfish man who should be very satisfied with the royal munificence.' Nevertheless, Colbert was prepared to propose to the King that he give the artist 'une gratification extraordinaire' for the equestrian monument. Of course this démarche did not materialize once the letters of 6 and 13 June assured Colbert of Bernini's satisfaction.

From the French point of view the pension was never meant as a purely philanthropic gesture. Colbert regarded Bernini's good will as an important asset to French interests in Rome. He was expected, above all, to take an active part in the affairs of the newly founded French Academy in Rome. Bernini, on the other hand, seemed to have made up his mind to follow the maxim, 'No money, no service.' In any case, he withstood all pressure during 1666 and the beginning of 1667 and avoided the Academy. Then the 1666 pension arrived; soon after we hear that he discharged his duty with great zeal and that Colbert expressed his gratitude. In addition, Bernini's advice was sought on such matters as French purchases of classical statuary in Rome, and Colbert even took it for granted that, on the occasion of his son's visit to Rome, Bernini would act as cicerone. One wonders what Bernini said to his entourage when he received Colbert's request to show his son 'all the beautiful works in Rome'; yet even this duty Bernini did not shirk.

For the shrewdly calculating Colbert an equestrian statue of the King by Bernini had a dual attraction: it was a means not only of getting proper returns for the pension, but also of letting the students of the Academy profit. Colbert's intentions are most clearly stated in a letter of 6 December 1669, written at a moment when the beginning of the work seemed imminent. He asked Bernini to make the King's statue similar to that of Constantine, but to vary it a little so that nobody could say it was a copy; he was to execute the head himself and to use the students of the Academy for everything else; then he was to touch up the whole 'so that one can truly say that it is a work of your hand'.

110

During the intervening two years the project made comparatively little progress. In February 1669 Bernini confessed to Girardon, who was in Rome at that time, that he felt he could not burden himself with this work and mentioned by way of comparison that the *Constantine* had taken him seven years of uninterrupted labour (a statement which was almost correct). At that moment the large marble block for the *Louis XIV* lay ready for shipment in the harbour of Carrara; it had been paid for in May 1669 and taken to some storage place in Rome but not, as an *avviso* reports, to Bernini's studio.[10] Our records for 1668 are rather scanty. During that year, however, Bernini must have yielded to pressure, made preliminary studies, and determined the rough measurements of the marble block which was then quarried in Carrara. From the summer of 1669 to the summer of 1670, the block was lying ready without tempting the master into action. Colbert's direct and indirect prodding throughout 1669 and the first half of 1670 was of no avail, and one would sympathize with his irritation if less were known of the background of the whole undertaking.

Although Bernini decided to start work only after the payment of the pension in June 1670, he knew pretty well what he would do when on 30 December 1669 he answered Colbert's letter of 6 December. Having said that he himself would first make the terracotta model of the statue, Bernini goes on: 'I shall assist continually the young men who are going to copy the model telling them everything they should know. Then I shall make His Majesty's head entirely myself. And finally, *Deo volente*, for the great love and feeling of obligation I owe the King of France, I shall try to do something that I do not want to promise in so many words, but prefer to express by deeds.'[11] This sentence is somewhat mysterious. Evidently Bernini had an idea which he was anxious not to discuss in writing. He added a last paragraph rather abruptly and perhaps not without pique: 'This statue will be completely different from that of Constantine, for Constantine is shown in the act of admiring the vision of the Cross and the King will be in the attitude of majesty and command. I would never allow the King's statue to be a copy of that of Constantine.'

It must be assumed that soon after this letter Bernini settled down to making the terracotta model of which he had talked. This, as is well known, is fortunately preserved in the wonder-
111 ful terracotta now in the Galleria Borghese which is without any doubt by his own hand.[12]

110 BERNINI. *Constantine* (Rome, Vatican)

111 BERNINI. Terracotta model for *Louis XIV* (Rome, Galleria Borghese)

He used, in fact, the formula of the rearing horse of Constantine, even for such details as the wind-swept mane. This formula, established during the Baroque era for dynastic equestrian portraits, could not be improved upon.[13] But the figures of the riders in the two works are entirely different. In accordance with Bernini's own statement, Constantine appears in the act of admiring the vision of the Cross and the King in the attitude of majesty and command.

The development of Bernini's 'concetto'

Bernini's impatient reaction to Colbert's request that the King's statue should be similar to that of Constantine must be understood against the background of his ideas and beliefs as an artist. Not only would such a similarity have offended the demands of decorum (i.e., the appropriate and becoming) peculiar to each individual case, but it would also have made it impossible to apply a *concetto*, a characteristic and ingenious theme or device which epitomizes the meaning of the specific work in hand. It is needless to stress here the importance of the *concetto* as a central tenet of humanist art theory, for it was the nobility of the literary concept that allied painting and sculpture so closely to poetry.[14]

Many passages in Chantelou's diary show that, in a typical Seicento spirit, Bernini's mind was much occupied with conceits – from the quick emotive response in the course of conversation, the pointed play with words,[15] and the pun, to the intellectual penetration of a sculptural theme. Apart from his exceptional brilliance, Bernini may have shared all this with other artists of his time. Yet for him, in contrast to many of them, the *concetto* never was a cleverly contrived embroidery, but formed an intrinsic part of his work. He always chose a dramatic climax for representation – that fertile and unique moment in which the life-story of his hero culminates.[16] This is true from the beginning of his career on: the *David*, the *Rape of Proserpina* and the *Apollo and Daphne* bear witness to it. Thus the *Constantine* too is not simply an equestrian monument representing the first Christian Emperor but a dramatic history-piece illustrating a precise moment in that Emperor's life: the historically and emotionally decisive moment of conversion in face of the miraculous appearance of the Cross.

It is therefore evident that for Bernini the equestrian statues of Constantine and Louis XIV could not have much in common. And we must expect that he devised his *Louis XIV*, too, as a dynamic history-piece rather than as a purely representational dynastic monument. Yet the fact that the King 'will appear in the attitude of majesty and command', as Bernini said in his letter, proves only the adherence to the requirements of decorum without betraying an elaborate *concetto*. An event which must have happened at least three years after that letter was written confronts us with an entirely different situation. In the biography of his father, Domenico Bernini relates the following story to which he was probably an eyewitness and which, in my view, may well be essentially true.[17]

He tells us that a Frenchman once came to inspect the monument in the studio. The visitor found fault with the discrepancy between the prowess of the King in armour, enhanced by the equally bellicose horse, and the joyous expression on the King's face, which suggested that he was prepared to dispense kindness rather than to frighten his enemies. Bernini answered that his intentions were clearly expressed in the work, but since his guest was unable to discover them, he had to explain:

I have not represented King Louis in the act of commanding his armies. This, after all, would be appropriate for any prince. But I wanted to represent him in a state which he alone has been able to attain through his glorious enterprises. And since the poets tell us that Glory resides on top of a very high and steep mountain whose summit only few climb, reason demands that those who nevertheless happily arrive there after privations joyfully breathe the air of sweetest Glory. The wearier the labour of the ascent has been, the dearer Glory will be. And as King Louis by virtue of his many famous victories has already conquered the steep rise of the mountain, I have shown him as a rider on its summit, in full possession of that Glory which, at high cost, has become synonymous with his name. Since a benignant face and a gracious smile are proper to him who is contented, I have represented the monarch in this way.

Bernini concluded his speech by pointing out that his idea could very well be understood simply by looking at the monument and that it would be even clearer after the rider and horse had been placed upon a high rock.

112 BERNINI. Head of *Louis XIV* (Versailles)

113 BERNINI. Louis XIV, drawing (Bassano, Museo Civico)

Whether or not Domenico's report is a verbatim transcript, it does show that at this advanced stage of execution Bernini could talk freely and persuasively about an involved poetical *concetto* which he had in mind. If chosen with proper insight, such a poetical *concetto* contained no less intrinsic historical truth for his contemporaries than a *concetto* derived from actual historical events (as was the case with the statue of Constantine).[18] Bernini's speech also reveals a peculiar *circulum vitiosum*, for it appears that certain formal features remain unintelligible or even nonsensical if the meaning of the *concetto* is missed but, on the other hand, are necessary to make the *concetto* understood. The two features crucial for a correct 'reading' of the *concetto* were obviously the King's smile and the high rock.

Rock formations are to be found under the 111 horse's body in the model. This proves that already at an early stage Bernini planned to place the equestrian statue on a rock. I have no doubt that he was playing with this idea even

earlier and that it was this to which he alluded on 30 December 1669 in the mysterious passage which I have commented on before. But the *bozzetto* does not show the King smiling. He appears, in accordance with Bernini's own words in the letter to Colbert, in the attitude of majesty and command. Thus the development of the *concetto* entered a new phase after the *bozzetto* was finished, and it was only then that Bernini hit upon an idea that seemed to him truly appropriate to the King's greatness.

In the finished work the King certainly did look benign. Bernini's friend, Padre Gian Paolo Oliva, in an enthusiastic letter of November 1673, mentions that '*il Rè parla et aggratia*' (i.e., displays charm);[19] Baldinucci describes him as being '*in atto maestoso ed insiememente benigno*';[20] and, I believe, even after Girardon's alterations, the '*avvenente riso della bocca*' (the pleasing smile on his lips) of which Domenico 112 Bernini speaks is discernible. In spite of considerable changes in the face, it may be assumed that at least part of it remained untouched.[21]

89

114 ANTONIO TRAVANI. Louis XIV, medal

The impression of the graceful smile is mainly conveyed by the deeply cut corners of the mouth, and I hope I am right in maintaining that this part of the face was not altered by Girardon.

Finally, the smile seems visible also in a
113 drawing[22] which at the same time is the only visual documentation for the formation of the rock. There is clearly a time lag between the *bozzetto* and the drawing. The former, probably dating from the early months of 1670, was still close to the *Constantine* (which was finished in 1668). The drawing, by contrast, shows idiosyncrasies of Bernini's latest style; we find here what I would like to call a dynamic 'ornamentalization' of form, most clearly observable in the corkscrew twirls of the horse's tail and mane. It seems justifiable to date the drawing in the year 1673, when the statue was nearing completion and when Bernini turned to planning the formation of the rock. Indeed, this seems to have been the main purpose of the drawing.[23] Another feature confirms the relatively late date of the drawing – the body of the horse is no longer supported by rock as in the *bozzetto* but by band-like curled flags, symbols
114 of victory.[24] Travani's bronze medals cast after the finished monument prove that such flags were in fact executed.[25]

It seems that Bernini's final conception was motivated by the military events of the day. In May 1672 Louis had started his successful *Blitzkrieg* against Holland. Cardinal d'Estrées wrote to Colbert in July that Louis's recent conquests had already resulted in plans for ornaments and trophies to be placed at the foot of the statue and that 'such great ideas nourish Bernini's imagination'. Two months later the Abate Elpidio Benedetti, Colbert's Italian agent in artistic matters in Rome, confirmed this when he wrote to the minister that the more Bernini meditated about an elegant[26] and noble idea the more worthy of the greatness of the monarch the work would be. In sum, there is good reason to assume that, inspired by Louis's recent exploits, Bernini changed the *concetto* at the last moment when the execution in marble was far advanced. Apart from the flags, the visual expression of his new idea was the contented smile on the King's lips – technically a minor change.

The *Roi Soleil* sculptured smiling for eternity! From the point of view of French court etiquette no worse assault upon seemliness and decorum could be imagined, and the King's negative reaction was a foregone conclusion. But from the point of view of poetical truth the smile made sense; it was, in fact, unavoidable: it answered, within the terms of the *concetto* (which Louis never took the trouble to 'decipher'), the demands of decorum.

Bernini's 'elegant and noble idea'

What exactly was the meaning of the noble idea which Bernini tried to explain to his French guest? It is convenient to discuss the salient elements of his remarks one by one and to begin with the most obvious, the steep mountain. This is, of course, no other than the mountain of Virtue about which poets talk from Hesiod onward.[27] It is the mountain whose long and wearisome climb Hercules prefers to the easy path of Vice. To design a high rock as base for an equestrian monument was an unheard-of innovation. By introducing the concept of the rock, Bernini ingeniously solved the artistic contradiction presented by a rider in movement on a traditional, formalized pedestal. It is a sign of true greatness that Bernini knew how to reconcile the visual requirements of the *concetto* with the claims of personal style and artistic sensibility.

The reference to Hercules, implied in Bernini's design, presented no difficulty to contemporaries. When describing the monument, Baldinucci explained that only by the steep and precipitous path of virtue does one arrive where true Glory has its abode.[28] The Abbé de la Chambre, who wrote Bernini's obituary for the *Journal des Sçavans*, argued rather ingeniously that Hercules did not arrive at the summit until he had reached old age, while Louis is seen there in the full flower of his life.

It is not at all strange that Hercules symbolism came to Bernini's mind in connection with Louis XIV, nor that his ideas were so well understood, for all imperial allegory abounded in references to Hercules.[29] The symbolic implications were obvious and manifold: the hard path of virtue and the invincible strength of the ruler immediately come to mind. Moreover, the French kings had another and very special relationship to Hercules. Wisdom was regarded as the accomplishment of the Hercules Gallicus – an idea derived from Lucian[30] – and therefore as the attribute of his successors, the French kings, who from the sixteenth century on often appear in the guise or role of the new Hercules Gallicus.[31] The allusions to Hercules reached a climax during the seventeenth century, and in the reign of Louis XIV they were literally legion.[32] Hercules' apotheosis and associations with the sky opened another way of seeing the *Roi Soleil* in and through the Hercules image. The Jesuit Claude-François Menestrier, the most encyclopaedic emblematist in Europe and a kind of impresario and unofficial propaganda minister, demonstrated this in an engraving published in his *Histoire du Roy Louis le Grand*.[33] Hercules is shown with the slain hydra at his feet before the signs of the Zodiac, and the surrounding inscription reads: '*Je fais de mes travaux pour le ciel des trophées*.'[34] Thus the Herculean labours appear here as works dedicated to God. Under the old Hercules is placed the portrait medallion of the new Hercules, the *Rex Christianissimus*, with *Religio* and *Pietas* at his sides. The connotations are too obvious to need further comment. Bernini's monument even had more precise religious overtones; the two medals made by Travani after the monument bear the mottoes: *Hac iter ad superos* and *Victore rege victrix religio*.[35]

It may now be recalled that Bernini had already contemplated the use of Hercules sym-

115 *Henri IV as Hercules Gallicus*. Engraving by Thomas de Leu

116 The Hercules page from C.-F. Menestrier's *Histoire du Roy Louis le Grand*, 1689

115

116

114

117 *Impresa* of the Emperor Charles V, from
G. Ruscelli, *Le Imprese illustri*, 1566

118 PIETRO DA CORTONA. *Hercules at the Crossroads*
(copy) (Stuttgart, Württembergische
Landeskunstsammlungen)

bolism for his Louvre design: two Hercules
figures were to guard the entrance to the King's
residence.[36] And when Colbert first broached
the idea of the equestrian monument to Bernini
in the summer of 1665, the latter suggested its
erection between two columns similar to those
of Trajan and Marcus Aurelius, its pedestal,
moreover, to bear the inscription *non plus ultra*
'as an allusion to Hercules'. Bernini knew
exactly what he was saying, for he played with
the idea of translating into monumental art the
impresa of the German Emperor Charles V, con- 117
sisting of the two 'Columns' of Hercules and the
motto PLUS ULTRA – indicating not only that
Charles V, the universal ruler, was one better
than Hercules (for *his* realm stretched to the
New World, far beyond the 'Columns' of
Hercules), but also suggesting, as Girolamo
Ruscelli informs us in his *Imprese illustri*, the
imperial qualities of the Holy Roman Emperor,
his valour, virtue and piety.[37] By proposing to
use Charles V's Hercules-*impresa* for a monument of the French King, Bernini implied that
he regarded Louis as the real heir to Charles's
universal empire.[38]

A few years later, when Bernini began to
consider the equestrian monument seriously, he
immediately returned to Hercules symbolism
but changed the *concetto*. As we have seen, he
planned the rock at an early stage, i.e. he now
took his cue from representations of Hercules
at the Crossroads. The further development of
the *concetto* was only a refinement and elaboration of the primary idea. His reputed statement
must be used as a further guide.

According to Bernini, the poets tell us that
Glory is the reward of those who reach the
summit of the mountain of Virtue. But with the
one exception of Petrarch, the poets make no
such assertion. Erwin Panofsky has shown that
Hesiod's unforgotten verses started a long
literary tradition, according to which Virtue,
not Glory, resides there, and in representations
of Hercules at the Crossroads the Temple of
Virtue appears therefore on top of the mountain.[39] Petrarch,[40] on the other hand, anticipated
a development which came into its own in the
course of the sixteenth century. From then on
the 'modern' concept prevailed that Glory or
Fame[41] was the precious reward at the end of
the hard path of Virtue. Thus in late pictures of
Hercules at the Crossroads it is difficult or even 118

impossible to decide whether the temple on top of the mountain represents that of Virtue or Glory.[42] But a more tangible image was found to express the new concept. In his *Discorso sopra le Medaglie degli Antichi*, Sebastiano Erizzo illustrated a medal of Domitian with Pegasus on the reverse. The text informs us that 'Pegasus represents Fame, the reason being that Pegasus was born as a result of the killing of Medusa, for Virtue (i.e., Perseus) having driven out Fear generates Fame . . .'.[43] This allegorization of the Perseus myth was, of course, not Erizzo's idea; he took it straight from the medieval mythographers.[44] But through Erizzo this old tradition reached Cesare Ripa, who acknowledged his source: 'And the Roman people, to honour Domitian, had a medal struck showing Pegasus, signifying Fame, since his fame had spread throughout the world; see Sebastiano Erizzo.'[45]

Through Ripa the concept won general acceptance, and so in many representations of Hercules at the Crossroads we find Pegasus, symbol of Fame, appearing on the rock of Virtue.[46] Contrary to Bernini's own assertion, we may now claim that when he talked of 'Glory residing on a very high mountain' he had neither Petrarch nor any other text in mind but was verbalizing visual recollections. He was intimately familiar with such works as Annibale Carracci's *Hercules at the Crossroads*, then in the Palazzo Farnese, and it need hardly be said that the grazing winged horse in the left background (which puzzles the few modern beholders who happen to discover it) held no riddle for him.[47]

Thought processes in the Baroque age were the natural concomitants of visual experience: the distinction between image and word, emblem and exposition was much more tenuous than it would now appear. If this be admitted, we should go a step further and ask ourselves if Louis's horse may not contain layers of emblematic meaning; at any rate, such connotations cannot have been far from many people's minds since, like Pegasus-Fame, this horse resides on top of the rock of Virtue.

But now, by declaring that Louis himself had become the symbol of Glory, Bernini seems to transfer the notion from the horse to the rider. One is reminded of similar 'synonyms' which are not without relevance in the present con-

119 *Pegasus*, from Erizzo's *Discorso sopra le Medaglie*, 1571

120 Pegasus on the summit of the rock of Virtue, detail from Sebastiano Ricci's *Hercules at the Crossroads* (Florence, Palazzo Marucelli)

121 ANNIBALE CARACCI. Detail from *Hercules at the Crossroads* (Naples, Museo Nazionale)

122 *Bellerophon and the Chimera,* from Ripa's *Iconologia*, 1613

123, 124 *Bellerophon and the Chimera* and *Pegasus and Mercury* from Erizzo's *Discorso sopra le Medaglie*, 1571

text. Thus Natale Conti in his much-read *Mythologiae*[48] explains that Bellerophon and Pegasus are different names for the same thing: the power of the Sun. Perhaps Erizzo and Ripa may help to clarify further what might appear as a peculiar *quid pro quo*. Erizzo, followed by 123 Ripa, illustrates a medal of Lucius Vero with 122 Perseus (Bellerophon, as Ripa correctly noted) riding Pegasus and fighting Chimera, signifying Virtue exalted by Fame overcoming Vice.[49] And Pegasus led by Mercury on a medal of 124 Antinoüs is said by Erizzo to be an allegory of Bright Fame, for Pegasus means Fame and Mercury stands for the quick spreading of Fame throughout the universe by word of mouth.[50] Under the heading '*FAMA CHIARA* 125 *nella Medaglia di Antinoo*' Ripa closely follows the text and picture of his source.[51] These allegorizations are somewhat different from Bernini's, but they show that the horse and the figure express different aspects of a unified concept – and this is what I would like to claim for Bernini's monument.

A word must be added about the contented smile: according to the moralizing fable by Prodicus and the classical authors dependent on him, eternal bliss awaits those few who reach the summit of the mountain of Virtue.[52] Erwin Panofsky has shown the enormous influence of the Prodicus legend from the Renaissance onward. But in the mass of visual material published by him there is hardly an instance of Hercules at the end of his labours on top of the mountain, and there is none with an expression of happy fulfilment on his face. It is now clear that this was precisely what Bernini attempted: his Louis-Hercules was to display the gracious smile of eternal bliss.

We have seen that many different strands are merged in Bernini's 'noble idea'. Intangible aspects of the diversified tradition of Hercules allegorizations enter into it. But the core of his conception seems simple enough: by concentrating, as it were, on the rock of Virtue with Pegasus at its summit in traditional representations of Hercules at the Crossroads, he evolved a poetical *concetto* which – in his eyes – applied only to Louis and contained the quintessence of the King's life and achievement.

125 *Pegasus and Mercury*, from Ripa's *Iconologia*, 1613

126 LEBRUN. *Monument of Louis XIV*, drawing (Paris, Louvre)

A note on Pegasus and allied themes

The steed of Bernini's monument is not winged, and I may be accused of jumping iconological fences. I have, however, good reason to believe that contemporaries were aware of the Pegasus associations, for winged horses do in fact appear in monuments connected with, or dependent upon, Bernini's *Louis XIV*. Charles Lebrun in 126 one of his designs for a monument of Louis XIV, demonstrably derived from Bernini's, represented Louis riding Pegasus on top of a rock.[53] 127 A second design illustrates the close alliance between emblematic and mythological conceptions. Here Perseus is riding Pegasus, and one would surmise that this was a project for a fountain without direct relationship to the King's monument. Nonetheless the similarity of the designs is proof of their interdependence.[54] Over a hundred years later the German sculptor Karl Georg Merville was given a commission for an equestrian monument of the Empress Catherine II of Russia. The Empress was to appear on a rearing Pegasus, and four allegories were to sit at the corners of the base. The project 128 survives as a model cast in bronze.[55] It can hardly be doubted that there is a distant connection with Bernini's monument, particularly since the summit of the rock is shown. Thus the

127 LEBRUN. *Perseus Fountain*, drawing (Paris, Louvre)

128 K. G. MERVILLE. Bronze model for *Catherine II* (Vienna, Unteres Belvedere)

129 COYSEVOX. *Renommée* (Paris, Place de la Concorde)

130 *Louis XIV in the Temple of Glory*, from C.-F. Menestrier's *Histoire du Roy Louis le Grand*, 1689

abbreviated reference to the mountain of Virtue contains a faint echo of the Hercules theme. Catherine is literally carried aloft on Pegasus and allegorically on the wings of Fame; in addition, the mythological steed may here also allude to her patronage of the arts.[56]

Representations of Pegasus are of course legion,[57] and one must be careful not to construe connections where there are none. We are on safe ground with regard to Coysevox's *Renommée* and *Mercure* in the Place de la Concorde.[58] Both are riding winged horses and, although Louis is not represented, his presence is implied, since the two groups together express one idea: the announcement of the King's eternal glory.[59] While one and the same visual symbol can express many different ideas, it is the prerogative of the emblematic language to express similar ideas in many different ways. The King's eternal glory was also Bernini's theme. and his version contained at least an allusion to Pegasus-Fame. When Menestrier had the same concept illustrated,[60] he placed a huge medal of the King before an otherwise empty centralized building and on the base which supports the medal published a sonnet with the opening line: '*Louis occupe seul le Temple de la Gloire*.' The important word here is '*seul*' and

129
131

130

131 COYSEVOX. *Mercure* (Paris, Place de la Concorde)

132 *Louis XIV Ascending to the Temple of Glory,* from Benedetti's *Le Glorie della Virtu,* 1682

in this respect Menestrier's idea parallels that of Bernini who 'wanted to represent the King in a state which he alone had been able to attain . . .'.

The Abate Elpidio Benedetti, whom we have mentioned, approached the same theme from yet another angle. He belonged to Bernini's circle in Rome and was therefore familiar with the artist's aims and ideas. They even stimulated him to a production of his own. In 1682, shortly after Bernini's death, he published a pamphlet with the title *The Glory of Virtue in the Person of Louis the Great made apparent by his Coronation in the Temple of Glory.*[61] The text is accompanied by two engravings,[62] the first showing

132 the King (as the explanatory note says) riding up the mountain of Virtue, trampling Envy under foot and escorted by Prudence, Valour and Perseverance, who prepare the thorny and difficult road leading to the Temple of Glory.

133 The second engraving illustrates Louis's arrival at the top, where Glory crowns him with the laurel of immortality. Halfway up are to be seen some of those heroes who, in contrast to Louis, succumbed before reaching the summit. At the foot of the mountain appears Imitation leading the Dauphin.[63]

With these engravings we are back to the

133 *Louis XIV at the Temple of Glory,* from Benedetti's *Le Glorie della Virtu,* 1682

well-trodden path of mixed allegorical narratives: the hero and the personifications mingle on the same representational level – a method abhorred by Bernini.[64] In Bernini's monument allegory is implied, not made explicit. The naturalistic rock, the fiery horse and the heroic rider with the benevolent face combine to express in dramatic visual terms the poetic-allegorical content. Where Bernini appealed to the beholder's imagination, we now find ourselves bogged down by a trite imperial adulation. This does not necessarily result from the mixture of historic personages and allegorical figures (a method with a venerable tradition to which, among others, Rubens's Maria de' Medici cycle belongs) but from the mediocrity of the engravings: an object lesson that the same ideas expressed by different visual metaphors may strike us as lofty in one case and trivial in another.

The later fortune of Bernini's work

Between the summer of 1671 and the autumn of 1673 Bernini as a rule spent six to seven hours daily working the marble, and this was in addition to other work on which he was engaged in these years – an astonishing feat of endurance for a man in his seventies.[65] Although the statue was not entirely finished until 1677,[66] it was almost completed in August 1673. And as early as 14 September 1672 Elpidio Benedetti reported to Colbert that the head was finished and the rest well advanced.

The same letter contains the following interesting statement: 'The work will be a majestic memorial to the magnanimous qualities of this great hero, an exemplar of virtue to his royal offspring and a testimony of truth to those who will in future write his deeds of valour, the prodigious greatness of which might otherwise render doubtful the faithfulness of historical records.' This sentence (and other similar ones could be quoted) reveals how the initiate expected Bernini's statue to be viewed: for them it was truer and more convincing than history itself – a testimony of truth just because the allegoric-poetical concept transcended historical data. Despite the traditional pattern of eulogy, we get a telling glimpse here of the unbroken power of the emblematic language.[67]

Precisely the same approach to general concepts expressed by pictorial devices led Louis's Chancellor Pontchartrain to regard the allegorical imagery on the King's medals as a most effective means of political persuasion. In a circular of 1702 he made it mandatory for all 'intendants et présidents des parlements' to have Menestrier's Histoire du Roy Louis le Grand par les Médailles, Emblèmes, Devises, etc., on their writing desks handy for consultation.[68]

At the exact moment when Bernini's statue was nearing completion, the correspondence with Paris came to a sudden stop. Colbert's last letter to Bernini dates from 28 October 1673. This appears all the stranger since, up to that date, it was Colbert who had vigorously pressed to have the statue finished at the earliest possible moment.[69] Colbert's silence indicates that the same camarilla in Paris which had prevented the execution of Bernini's Louvre designs had won a new victory. There must have been constant pressure on Colbert (though, of course, we are told nothing about it) to abandon his support of Bernini's work. I take it that at the end of the year 1673 Colbert gave in and transferred his allegiance from Bernini to Lebrun.

Meanwhile it appeared that conditions in Rome were adverse to letting the monument leave the city. The worthy Abate Benedetti, whose power as Colbert's agent should not be underrated, had a vested interest in preventing the dispatch of the statue on its journey north. He would never, of course, have broadcast his intentions to all and sundry. But it was very likely owing to his insinuations that the Romans believed the statue was being made for the Scala di Spagna. Even the usually well-informed Este Ambassador in Rome mentioned in a dispatch of 30 May 1671 that Bernini had started working the King's equestrian statue 'which will be placed at the Trinità de' Monti although some maintain that it will go to France'. The area in which the Scala di Spagna was built in the early eighteenth century was French property, and as early as 1660 Mazarin had planned to have a monumental staircase erected there.[70] Under his auspices Elpidio Benedetti had projects drafted that included an equestrian statue of Louis XIV.[71] The very moment Bernini considered beginning on the King's statue, Benedetti revived his pet idea.[72]

134

134 Benedetti's project for the Scala di Spagna (Rome, Vatican)

In the summer of 1672 he seems to have been resolved to further it at any cost, for he undertook a *démarche* with the King through the pen of the French Ambassador. As is well known, Benedetti's attempt to have the stairs built remained abortive. On the other hand, it is now difficult to judge to what extent the delay in transporting Bernini's equestrian statue to Paris was also due to the Abate's machinations.

Bernini was probably unaware of all this. Nor does he seem to have been fully informed of what was going on in Paris. We know that from about 1670 on (i.e., at the time when Bernini began work on his statue) Lebrun busied himself with designs for a large monument of the King.[73] And he and his circle must have been fretting to find out what Bernini intended to do. Bernini, on his part, appears to have sensed danger. The self-imposed silence regarding his project in a letter to Colbert of 30 December 1669 is an indication.[74] He was suspicious. In spite of promises and requests, he never sent a drawing of the monument to Paris and even after his death Colbert was still

without an exact record of it. Further events justified Bernini's reticence. As early as May 1670 rumours circulated in Rome that he had been deprived of his commission and that the King had handed it over to artists in Paris. At that date the information was, of course, biased. But it is undeniable that for some years a rival undertaking was vigorously promoted in Paris. And it is also undeniable that Lebrun availed himself of Bernini's ideas. By 1672 and 1673 so many people had seen Bernini's work *in statu nascendi* that its conception was no longer a secret. Bernini had evidently expected that the naturalistic rock formation – his great innovation in the context of the equestrian monument – would hold the world spellbound. But all that happened was that Lebrun pilfered the idea (which was so foreign to French tradition), incorporated it into his project, and diluted it not only by designing a structureless rock but also by embroidering it with masses of allegorical figures. In the final design, which survives only in a copy discovered by Josephson in Stockholm, the King appears riding over Heresy and

135

135 LEBRUN. *Monument of Louis XIV*, copy of a drawing (Stockholm, Nationalmuseum)

136 Studio of LEBRUN. *Monument of Louis XIV*, drawing

Rebellion, and at the foot of the rock are personifications of the four principal rivers which Louis had crossed during his victorious campaigns.[75] By his rationalizing, narrative procedure Lebrun killed the poetical and universal quality of Bernini's *concetto*. Moreover, in contrast to Bernini's rock (which the rider has climbed from the left), Lebrun's rock is inaccessible. The elements of time, movement and dramatic climax are therefore excluded: paradoxically, Lebrun's rock formation has no other function than that of a static pedestal.

The sculptor commissioned to execute Lebrun's design was Girardon, the same artist who in 1686 changed Bernini's statue into a *Marcus Curtius*. Between 1679 and 1683 Girardon spent much of his time preparing the large models,[76] and the marble was lying in the Louvre court ready to be worked when Colbert died. Louvois, his successor and arch enemy, made it his primary concern to stop, if possible, the enterprises sponsored by his predecessor. He immediately pounced upon this scheme and, after a sharp encounter with Lebrun, brought it to an inglorious end. No wonder that Louvois now proceeded to claim the all-but-forgotten work by Bernini. In the autumn of 1684 it was on its way to Civitavecchia, whence it was shipped to France. On 10 March 1685 it arrived in Paris. For a short while the old project was probably revived of erecting the statue in a square opposite the garden of the Tuileries on the left bank of the river. But if this was at all under serious consideration, it was forgotten the very moment the Parisians had an opportunity to inspect the work. Not long before his death Bernini himself had had evil forebodings. In December 1678 he wrote to Chantelou: 'The equestrian statue of the King has been finished for some time – but when they [the Parisians?] see it, they will find little to admire. Since, however, those people are courteous, cautious, and discreet, they will be indulgent toward me'. As the event showed, even this was too optimistic. Exactly what happened in Paris we do not know. In any case, the statue was taken straight to Versailles; near the Orangerie the King saw it for the first time. The rest has been reported in the opening lines of this paper.

It is not known who first thought of changing the King's statue into the Roman hero Marcus Curtius who, according to the well-known legend, gave his life for his city by leaping into a chasm which had opened in the Roman Forum. To be sure, the trophies under the horse's belly had to be altered, and to transform them into flames was a convenient solution. But by doing this two successive moments in time were contracted into one: the jumping off and the arrival in the flaming holocaust. Such poetic licence cannot have been popular in the France of Boileau. Nevertheless the change into a Marcus Curtius was a reasonable proposition, and not only because it was practicable. A suggestion of the original allegorical concept remained alive, since Marcus Curtius was traditionally depicted as a symbol of heroism. Moreover, the original and the altered versions represent an interesting case of what we may call *coincidentia oppositorum*. Aby Warburg once observed that similar expressive formulas may serve to illustrate diametrically opposed sensations. I think the choice of the new theme was not uninfluenced by this instinctive recognition, for the rise to lofty heights and the jumping into the abyss, or in other words apotheosis and sacrifice, are like two sides of a coin. Pannini[77] understood these implications when he incorporated Bernini's design with the rock into his painting of the *Death Leap of Marcus Curtius*.

By 1690 the most important *dramatis personae*, Bernini, Colbert and Lebrun, had dropped out of the picture. Only Girardon remained, with twenty-five years still to live. The next incident of this story is connected with his name. Bernini's work, exiled to the farthest corner of the park at Versailles, seemed forfotten but, as will be seen, the ideas informing it remained alive. In 1699 the city of Paris arranged rather extravagant fireworks to celebrate the inauguration of Girardon's equestrian statue of Louis XIV on the Place Vendôme. The pageantry was devised by Menestrier.[78] A rock was built in the middle of the Seine crowned by the Temple of Glory in which a copy of Girardon's statue was to be seen. An engraving gives an idea of the contraption. The rock was surrounded by water and inaccessible from all sides in order to demonstrate – so the text informs us – how difficult the path of Glory is. A demigod occupied each of the four sides of the rock. Significantly, Perseus liberating Andromeda is to be seen in the engraving. Hercules

137 Detail from Pannini's *Death Leap of Marcus Curtius* (Northampton, Mass., Smith College)

138 *The Temple of Glory with Girardon's statue of Louis XIV*, from C.-F. Menestrier's *La statue équestre de Louis le Grand*, 1699

killing the Hydra, Theseus killing the Minotaur and Jason killing the Bull completed the series. These ancient prototypes of valour alluded to different facets of the King's virtuous accomplishments. On the same occasion an anonymous abbé published a poem with the title 'L'Apothéose du nouvel Hercule, ou le Théâtre de la Gloire de Louis le Grand'.[79] As Hercules was deified in the flames of Mount Oeta, so – we are told – the greatest king of the universe will be immortalized. The superb temple surrounded by fireworks is the Oeta of the new Hercules. This demonstrates clearly how closely connected were apotheosis and sacrifice in the minds of Bernini's contemporaries.

Long after the smoke of the stupendous fireworks had cleared, the curtain was raised for the last act. The scene shifts to St Petersburg between the years 1766 and 1782.[80] It was there and then that Falconet revived Bernini's conception in his *Peter the Great*, which may be called the last dynastic monument of the Baroque. The indirect link with Bernini can be reconstructed. Diderot suggested to Falconet the erection of a gigantic fountain with allegorical figures surrounding a rock, on which Peter on horseback was to drive out Barbarism. Without any shadow of doubt, Diderot knew Lebrun's project. Falconet rejected such a Baroque conception, but retained the key motif of the high rock. Later he recalled how on a corner of Diderot's table he had drawn his own idea showing the hero on horseback dashing over what he called the 'emblematic rock'. The rock, he explained, was the emblem of the difficulties Peter the Great had surmounted. Thus a suggestion of Hercules's hard path of

Virtue survives. And the serpent, the symbol of Envy, trampled to death by the horse's hoofs, ties the work even more closely to traditional iconography than Falconet would have admitted; he said that he was wholeheartedly opposed to Baroque allegory. He did, in fact, move far towards the philosophy of Reason and the spirit of the Revolution which spelled the doom of the allegorical mode of thinking of the Baroque: he insisted that he had represented his hero not as the man of the sword, the conqueror, but as the legislator, the wise ruler of his people. Nonetheless, long-established patterns of thought are not easily discarded. Falconet's *Peter the Great* is an allegorical equestrian statue. By virtue of the metaphor of the rock, Falconet's *Peter*, like Bernini's *Louis*, is shown at the summit of his achievement. Bernini's *Louis XIV* placed on the rock of Virtue would have been the only Baroque equestrian statue in which the formal antagonism between pedestal and rider was resolved and the contradictory intellectual requirements of a purely dynastic monument and of Baroque *concettismo* were reconciled. While Falconet's rationalism narrowed down Bernini's universalism, he still accomplished (one is tempted to say in the nick of time) what exactly a hundred years before Bernini had been prevented from doing.

But the sculptor of Peter's monument was unaware of the debt he owed to the spiritual father of his work. It is the crowning paradox of this story that he of all people should have called the *Marcus Curtius* at Versailles 'one of the worst and impertinent productions that can be seen in sculpture'.

139 FALCONET. *Peter the Great*, Losenko's drawing after the plaster cast (Leningrad)

140 POUSSIN. *Massacre of the Innocents* (Chantilly, Musée Condé)

V THE ROLE OF
CLASSICAL MODELS IN BERNINI'S
AND POUSSIN'S
PREPARATORY WORK

The Role of Classical Models in
Bernini's and Poussin's Preparatory Work

BERNINI and Poussin are the chief representatives of the two great seventeenth-century currents, the Baroque and the classical, and it is generally held that there is little common ground between them or their works. Yet we know that Bernini loved and revered Poussin's paintings. In his Paris diary, Chantelou[1] recorded such reactions of Bernini's as, 'I must capitulate before Poussin's greatness'; 'This is what I call a great man'; and 'Truly, this man has studied ancient art'; before the Chantelou series of Poussin's *Sacraments* he exclaimed, 'I could study them for six months without interruption'; and before *The Gathering of the Ashes of Phocion*, pointing a finger to his forehead, '*il signor Poussin è un pittore che lavora di là*'. When he spoke these words during his stay in Paris in 1665, Bernini's intense, dynamic Baroque was at the farthest remove from Poussin's puritanically severe style of the middle and late periods – yet Bernini never so much as hinted at the world of difference between their artistic productions. Although we do not know what Poussin thought about Bernini, we may venture a guess that the esteem was mutual.

The truth is that both artists shared a broad range of convictions. Both held that an artist should be learned, that decorum – the appropriate and becoming – must be the basis for a discriminating approach to the subject matter, that historical subjects – i.e., subjects from the Bible, mythology and ancient history – are the most worthy of representation, and that art is concerned with the expression of action and emotion. Moreover, both believed that nature was never perfect but that ideal beauty had been made manifest in ancient art and in some modern interpreters of the ancients, above all in the works of Raphael. All these are well-known tenets of the classical doctrine, the various elements of which had developed from Leone Battista Alberti's days on and had become the creed of thinking artists of all kinds of opinion.

141 The so-called *Antinoüs*, engraving after Bellori, 1672

Since both Bernini and Poussin aimed in their works at representing ideal beauty, it follows that ancient art played a predominant part in all their considerations. The question then arises why, at the same period, in the same Roman milieu, the same ideology could lead to such contrasting results.

It might be argued that Bernini, the fiery southerner, the official artist of the Papacy, produced what the Catholic orthodoxy of the Restoration period needed, the dazzling imagery of ecstasies and raptures; while Poussin, the sober Frenchman, working for French merchants and bankers, civil servants and lawyers, offered in his moral subjects and judicious classicism a pictorial realization of the most cherished ideals of a public steeped as much in

104

Descartes' rationalism as in philosophical scepticism and stoicism. This line of argument, however, begs the question, because the particular qualities of both artists were their own and were the cause rather than the result of their being chosen by their respective patrons.

Nor can it be maintained that they studied entirely different classical works: Bernini exclusively works of the ancient 'Baroque', such as the *Laocoön*, the *Marforio*, the *Borghese Warrior* and so forth, Poussin exclusively Roman sarcophagi and reliefs, perhaps as one of Cassiano dal Pozzo's draughtsmen. But even if we assume that this observation contains some truth, it would not suffice to account for the contrary orientation of the two artists. In point of fact, one can prove that the two drew inspiration from the same ancient statues. Bernini remarked in his speech before the French Academy: 'In my early youth I drew a great deal from classical figures: and when I was in difficulties with my first statue, I turned to the *Antinoüs* as to the oracle.' This very statue of *Mercury* in the Vatican (then called *Antinoüs*) also enjoyed an enormous prestige with the classical circle of Poussin, Duquesnoy and Algardi; and Bellori, the mouthpiece of the 141 classicists, published an engraving of it with the measurements taken by Duquesnoy and Poussin.[2]

Nevertheless, one might justifiably argue that although both Poussin and Bernini studied a certain number of the same ancient works, Poussin carried his researches farther afield and consequently built up an infinitely larger classical repertory. This seems to me quite incontestable, but the fact in itself is less important than the question why it was Poussin rather than Bernini who felt it necessary to control as large a quantity of ancient material as possible.

I believe that one can throw some light on this question as well as on the broader issue of the Baroque and the classical, epitomized in Bernini's and Poussin's work, by investigating the different uses these artists made of classical models in the course of their preparatory studies. Although we have but little material at our disposal, compared with what has disappeared forever, sufficient evidence does exist to allow some generalizations.

Poussin's procedure was fully developed as

142 POUSSIN. *Massacre of the Innocents*, drawing (Lille, Palais des Beaux-Arts)

143 MARCANTONIO. *Massacre of the Innocents*, engraving after Raphael

early as the late 1620s when he painted the Chantilly *Massacre of the Innocents*. All the figures of the vigorous preparatory drawing at Lille are free interpretations of figures in Marcantonio's engraving of the Massacre made after Raphael, but the composition is rearranged along forceful spatial diagonals: it has been turned into a Baroque composition. In Poussin's painting, emotion is expressed by means different from those of the drawing; the figures now occupy two separate planes parallel to the picture plane, evidently in analogy to ancient reliefs: a Baroque composition has been transformed into a classical one.

At the same time, Poussin toned down action and introduced gestures expressive of *affetti*. He changed the mother's left arm with its firm

140
142
143

105

144 Roman mosaic showing a tragic mask (Rome, Capitoline Museum)

145 Creusa and Creon, detail of a Roman sarcophagus, engraving after Bellori, 1693

grip round the executioner's waist into a pose whose gesture shows her half warding off the blow and half lamenting. For this, and for her facial expression, which derives from the type of the tragic mask,[3] classical examples are legion. Perhaps even more striking is the alteration of the figure of the mother placed farther back, in the second plane. The drawing shows her running away, her child clasped tightly in her arms and her head turned back to the scene of murder. In the painting she moves more slowly, carrying in one hand the limp body of her dead child like a bundle that needs neither care nor protection. Her head, now shown in pure profile, is thrown back; she has raised her free arm and seems to beat her head with her fist. This expression of despair and approaching madness was known to Poussin from Medea sarcophagi; in fact, he combined here the attitude of Creusa's head with the gesture of her father Creon.[4] Classical antiquity had guided him to a psychological interpretation of the scene. Instead of the transitory action of a frightened mother, he finally depicted the deeply moving condition of a frantic soul.

Similar changes from preparatory drawings to finished work recur in all those cases where the chance preservation of drawings allows us to check. My next example, Poussin's *Moses Defending the Daughters of Jethro from Unfriendly Shepherds*, dates from the 1640s. The painting is lost, but we have the evidence of some surviving preparatory drawings. A loosely constructed drawing (in a London private collection) probably represents the earliest rendering of the composition; the final design seems to be that in the Louvre.[5] The number of figures remains the same, but confusion has been clarified, action has been reduced, and the composition in depth has been changed into a relief composition with isolated statuesque figures. Their derivation from classical statues is so patently evident – a Juno served for the imposing girl with the raised arm, and Niobids for the women protecting their pitchers – that one need not labour the point.

Typologically, the daughters of Niobe were obvious models for the daughters of Jethro, but Poussin had to transform the classical exemplars in order to invest them with a new meaning. Often he carried the re-interpretation of classical

146, 147 POUSSIN. *Moses defending the Daughters of Jethro. Above:* preliminary drawing (London, private collection). *Below:* final design (Paris, Louvre)

148, 149 Juno and Niobids, engravings from antique statues after Reinach

107

150 POUSSIN. *The Finding of Moses* (Paris, Louvre)

151, 152 Details of antique reliefs, showing Dionysus leaning on a satyr. Engravings after Reinach and Bellori

153 POUSSIN. *Theseus Finding the Sword of his Father* (Chantilly, Musée Condé)

models much further than in this drawing, yet he never disavowed his source of inspiration. His first painting of the *Finding of Moses* of 1638 150 (Louvre), may serve as an example. Here Pharaoh's daughter is shown leaning languidly on the shoulder of a maidservant. This group is derived from the common ancient representations of Dionysus leaning on a young satyr and, 151, as the illustrations show, Poussin once again 152 combined motifs from two different sources.[6] In the preparatory drawings for the second *Finding of Moses*, dating from 1647, Poussin broke away from the classical model, only to return to it in the painting (Louvre), in which the group appears facing the spectator. Similar figures served him on other occasions, for instance, for the Chantilly *Theseus Finding the* 153 *Sword of his Father*; even the shepherdess in the Louvre *Et in Arcadia Ego* is still connected with this expressive formula of classical ancestry.

The *Judgment of Solomon* of 1649 (Louvre) 154 belongs to Poussin's most classical period and even the preparatory drawing in the École des 155 Beaux-Arts – admittedly representing an advanced stage – looks classical enough. Although the span between drawing and painting is less obvious than in the case of the *Massacre of the Innocents*, we find our previous observations confirmed. Instead of the space-creating exedra in the drawing, a straight backdrop appears in the painting, a change whereby the composition acquires a relief character. The guards in the background have been entirely eliminated and

154 POUSSIN. *The Judgment of Solomon* (Paris, Louvre)

the number of foreground figures has been reduced. The right-hand group of spectators consists now of five adults instead of eight, not counting the soldier on whom interest was focused in the drawing. An anonymous crowd has been turned into an assembly of individuals whose striking gestures mirror their reactions. Their emotive responses to the drama hold our attention, in place of the purely physical action of the soldier.

Once again, the language of gestures reveals the close study of classical models. In the drawing there was only one individualized figure among the spectators, the mother with the child, in a pose similar to that of the *Girl with the Dove* in the Capitoline Museum. In the painting her gestures have become more complex and more expressive. With her left hand raised and her right hand stretched out, she now expresses not only fear ('I cannot bear to look') but also disgust. Her attitude and gestures

157 follow closely those of Althaea in Meleager sarcophagi. But Althaea's action has a different meaning: she, the mother of Meleager, is burning the faggot that is magically connected with the life of her son; her raised arm expresses refusal to desist from this fateful step. A gesture with a meaning similar to Poussin's is to be

156 found in Orestes' sarcophagi,[7] and I suggest that it influenced his rendering of the studied pose in the *Judgment of Solomon*.

These examples allow us to conclude that, for Poussin, antiquity was a vehicle of catharsis

155 POUSSIN. *The Judgment of Solomon*, drawing (Paris, Ecole des Beaux-Arts)

156, 157 Details of Roman sarcophagi, after Bellori and Robert. *Left:* Orestes' nurse (reversed) *Right:* Althaea

158 BERNINI. *Pluto and Proserpina* (Rome, Villa Borghese)

159 Roman statue of Hercules (Rome, Capitoline Museum)

coming progressively into play the more the preparatory work approached the final version. It is for this reason that the pool of classical material on which he drew could never be large enough. The cathartic influence of antiquity consisted in helping to objectify and intensify subjective concepts. This state of objectivity and penetrating analysis Poussin attempted to achieve by: 1 reducing the number of figures, isolating them and characterizing them as individuals; 2 using ancient expressive formulas for the process of individualization, such formulas also supplying the raw material for new renderings of gestures which, once established, belong thenceforth to his repertory; and 3 carefully observing a principle of external and internal order: external insofar as he settled on compositions of utmost readability in which a classical relief-like deployment of figures naturally had preference, internal insofar as he deliberately painted his pictures in a consistent key. In this the famous Greek modes, which interested him so much, served as a guide. A

battle scene and a bacchanal have to be painted in different keys, and, similarly, each figure has to have its own mode of representation. This was not only a requirement of decorum but also of proportion. Thus, a heroic figure in a history painting has to have the proportions of Apollo, while peasants in everyday scenes should rather conform to statues of fauns.

*   *   *

It is well known that most of Bernini's early works are close to some ancient model. Until a generation ago the Borghese *Amalthea* was believed to be Hellenistic. His *Pluto* reveals the 158 close study of the *Hercules* in the Capitoline 159 Museum, a statue that Algardi had restored at a slightly earlier date. The *David* refers to the 162–3 *Borghese Warrior*, and the Apollo of the *Apollo* 164–5 *and Daphne* to the Apollo Belvedere.

At the time of the *Longinus*, begun in 1629, the break with antiquity would seem to be complete. However, the *bozzetto* in the Fogg Art 166

110

160, 161 Head of Bernini's *Longinus* (Rome, St Peter's) and of the *Borghese Centaur* (Paris, Louvre)

162, 163 *Borghese Warrior* (Paris, Louvre) and Bernini's *David* (Villa Borghese)

164, 165 Head of the *Apollo Belvedere* (Rome, Vatican) and of Bernini's *Apollo* (Rome, Villa Borghese)

166 BERNINI. *Bozzetto* of *Longinus* (Harvard, Fogg Art Museum)

Museum, the only surviving one of a large number, shows not only a classical stance, but also an arrangement of the mantle so obviously of antique derivation that no specific prototype need be quoted. While these classical references have disappeared in the marble, Longinus' head 160 is still dependent on a classical model, the *Borghese Centaur*, now in the Louvre. 161

Only in one later case, the *Daniel* of 1655, 170 does a sufficient number of drawings survive to allow us to follow the development of Bernini's conception. His starting point was the 'Father' of the *Laocoön* group. He drew the torso of this figure in a study now at Leipzig. 167 It is unlikely that Bernini made this copy from the Antique as a preparation for the *Daniel*, but, when he began to plan his statue, he gave his 168 life-model the *Laocoön* pose in reverse. In the next drawing, the position of the arms and legs approaches that of the marble statue, whereas the torso is still closely connected with the *Laocoön*.[8] The next two drawings show all the 169 characteristics of the statue, the elongated pro-

111

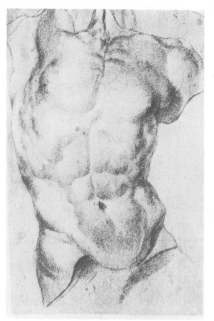

167 BERNINI. Drawing after the *Laocoön*
168, 169 BERNINI. Drawings for *Daniel*

170 BERNINI. *Daniel* (Rome, S. Maria del Popolo)

portions and the screw-like twisting of the body. But a recollection of the *Laocoön* can still be noticed in Daniel's head.

Such late works as the *Angel with the Super-* 172 *scription* of 1667–69 is, of course, utterly removed from classical antiquity in formal language, stance, proportion and sentiment. Yet a preparatory drawing of a figure in the nude 171 demonstrates to what extent Bernini relied on the *Antinoüs*, the statue that meant so much to 141 him in his early youth. In contrast to the first drawings for the *Daniel*, however, the proportions of this study differ considerably from the ancient model: they are elongated, almost Gothic. At this late phase of Bernini's career, a process of spiritualization set in at the earliest stage of preparation despite the fact that recollections of ancient statuary remain clearly traceable.

From this brief survey we can draw certain conclusions. As a rule, Bernini begins by following a classical model. In elaborating his idea, however, he ends up with an intensely personal Baroque solution. Thus Bernini's procedure may be described as a reversal of Poussin's. Moreover, one can clearly discern a development that again may be discussed as an antithesis to that of Poussin: the paintings of the early Poussin are comparatively loose, and only as he matured did they become progres-

171 BERNINI. Preparatory
drawing for *Angel with
Superscription* (Rome, Corsini
Gallery)

sively formalized; by contrast, the works of the
early Bernini are comparatively classical, and
only later in his career did they become progressively free and imaginative.

Poussin's procedure was well known to
French artists who had met the master in Rome
or Paris. They had a better understanding of his
method than is usually realized. They discussed
it often and at length, particularly in lectures
delivered at the Paris Academy. When Lebrun,
in a famous talk, traced the ancient prototypes
for the principal figures of Poussin's *Gathering
of Manna*, he acted fully in the latter's spirit.
Bourdon claimed that he had Poussin's personal
blessing for the following teaching method:
'When a student has made a drawing from the
life model . . . he should make another study of
the same figure . . . and try to give it the
character of an ancient statue.' We have no
reason to doubt the truth of Bourdon's report.

The view that Poussin's approach to painting
was rational and intellectual is supported by
the deliberate and methodical manner in which
he developed his compositions. Bernini, on the
other hand, was ultimately guided by a metaphysical concept: he firmly believed that his
inspiration came to him through the grace of
God and that in developing a felicitous idea he
was only God's tool. We have arrived at the
point where Poussin's and Bernini's ways part,

172 BERNINI. *Angel with Superscription* (Rome, S.
Andrea delle Fratte)

also theoretically, but neither Poussin's rational classicism nor Bernini's metaphysical Baroque can be divorced from the ideas that Zuccari's generation built upon Renaissance tenets.

Mannerist theory suffered from the contradiction between the *disegno interno* – the doctrine, Neo-Platonic in essence, that ideal beauty, pre-existing in man's mind, was a gift from heaven – and the *disegno esterno*, i.e., the manual work, the *maniera*, the binding rules of which guaranteed professional execution. Bernini took up the Neo-Platonic concept of Mannerist theory; but for him the idea of beauty, far from being abstract, universal, vague and speculative, became identified with the concrete spiritual requirements of each particular work. Poussin and the classicists reverted to the Aristotelian Renaissance belief that ideal beauty results from an *a posteriori*

selective process, best characterized by the well-known and constantly repeated Zeuxis legend. Yet insofar as Poussin and the classicists were concerned with evolving a code of objective rules, they are linked with the *disegno esterno* side of Mannerist doctrine. Once again, the concrete requirements of each individual task saved Poussin from the pitfalls of the *maniera*.

Bernini's and Poussin's different approaches to ancient prototypes – the one using them at the beginning and the other at an advanced stage of the creative process – reflect their ultimate beliefs as artists. Their contrasting procedures may go a long way to account for the 'Baroque' and the 'classical' trends in the seventeenth century, and yet they spring from the same faith in the eternal validity of ancient art.

173 Ruins of the Temple of Fortune, Palestrina

VI PIETRO DA CORTONA'S PROJECT FOR RECONSTRUCTING THE TEMPLE OF PALESTRINA

Pietro da Cortona's Project for Reconstructing the Temple of Palestrina

IT IS TYPICAL of the slight attention so far paid by art history to the temple of Palestrina (Praeneste) and its influence on Italian architecture since the sixteenth century that Pietro da Cortona's reconstruction scheme for its ruins has been completely overlooked, though archaeologists have always been aware of his activity in this field. The first work on the ruins of Palestrina, J. M. Suarez's *Praenestes Antiquae libri duo* of 1655, contains three engravings after Cortona, showing the whole temple area – a ground-plan,[1] view[2] and isometric projection.[3] It is these engravings which are largely responsible for subsequent ideas of the appearance of the ancient site. The view and the isometric drawing reappear as early as 1671 in Kircher's *Latium*;[4] copy engravings by Pietro Santi Bartoli appeared in 1699;[5] and in 1743 J. R. Volpi used Suarez's plates for his work *Vetus Latium Profanum*.[6] Finally all three engravings were republished by Canina[7] in poor outline reproductions.

In Volpi's work a fourth sheet is added (numbered 7): another view of the temple area, but differing substantially from those previously published in that it shows a crowning round temple instead of a free-standing belvedere. The key to the interpretation of this fourth sheet, which alone makes possible a full understanding of the others, is to be found in three drawings in the Royal Library at Windsor.[8] These drawings show the temple site in ground-plan with two differing elevations. One of them corresponds to the Suarez elevations. The other is virtually identical with Volpi's fourth sheet and is clearly its original. The ground-plan, too, unlike those of both Suarez and Volpi, corresponds to the 'round temple' view. The drawings that incorporate this feature (the Windsor plan, one of the Windsor drawings and the Volpi 'fourth' sheet) will from now on be referred to as Scheme A; those featuring the belvedere (the Suarez engravings and one Windsor drawing) as Scheme B.

The ground-plan in Windsor is accompanied by an exhaustive description. This is introduced by the following remarks: 'This plan and its elevation were found among the possessions of the Prince of Sant' Angelo, Duke of Acquasparta, Federico Cesi, Principal of the Accademia dei Lincei, who had it copied in Palestrina from a drawing which he found, made by a knowledgable person at a time when many more remains of the said temple were to be seen than are to be seen today, and the drawings of the said plan and elevation were given by the Duchess, his widow, to his Eminence Cardinal Francesco Barberini, nephew of Pope Urban VIII, in August 1631 . . .'.

One glance at the sheet shows that inscription, numbering and drawing must have been made at the same time. Therefore the remarks on the ground-plan and view cannot refer to these actual drawings but to their originals. This also appears from the final words, which mention '*i disegni di detta Pianta e Alzata*', that is, the lost originals – and it is these which came into the possession of Cardinal Francesco Barberini as a legacy from Prince Cesi.[9]

'This plan and its elevation' unmistakably refers to the ground-plan with the related view (Scheme A) – not, therefore, to the second view (B) with the free-standing belvedere. The separation of the two schemes is justified not only by such secondary clues[10] but above all by the differing character of the reconstruction of the temple. Three elements characterize the drawings of Scheme A:

1 They very clearly depend upon a reconstruction scheme made by Pirro Ligorio about 1560, known to us today in a series of copies.[11] They agree not only in the form of presentation, that curious mixture of perspective and orthogonal projection, but also in the general conception[12] and a great number of idiosyncracies.[13]

2 The drawings show that original research had been carried out at the site itself.[14]

3 They represent a revision of the Ligorio

174 The Windsor drawings: elevation. This is reproduced as pl. 7 ('the fourth sheet') in Volpi's *Vetus Latium Profanum*

175, 176 The Windsor drawings: view and ground-plan

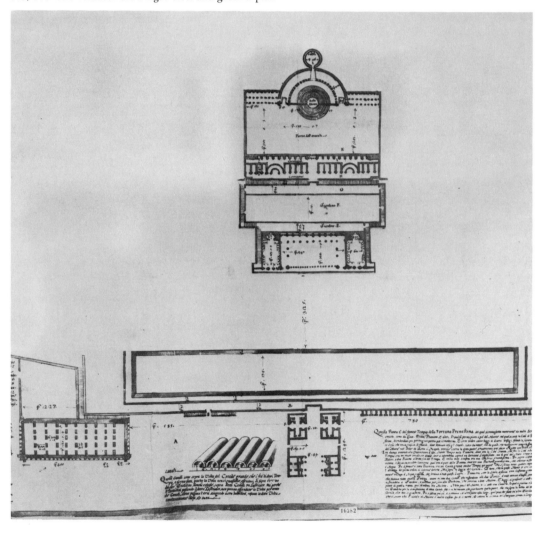

177, 178, 179 The three
engravings from J. M.
Suarez, *Praenestes
Antiquae*, 1655

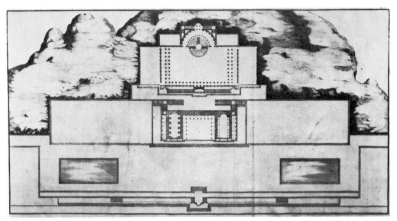

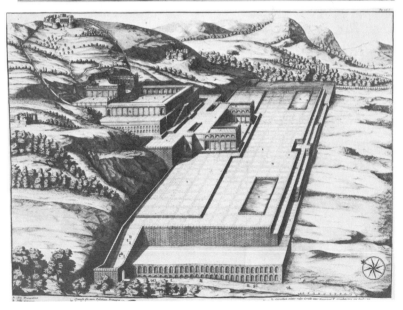

plan from the aesthetic point of view: certain simplifications and intensifications of motifs,[15] and above all the domination of the cupola motif distinctly lead one beyond Ligorio to the Baroque.

One can therefore see Scheme A as a critical, modernized version of the Ligorio project, so that the meaning of our inscription becomes clear; according to it, the original plan A was copied from older drawings, dating from a time when more remains of the temple were visible.

From its character and its relation to Ligorio one would date the origin of Scheme A to the turn of the seventeenth century. An indirect source enables us to fix the date more accurately.[16] In his *Memorie Prenestine* Pier Antonio Petrini[17] had access to a diary from the estate of Prince Federico Cesi, from which we learn that the latter had the remains of the temple at Palestrina surveyed and examined in 1614. There can hardly be any objection to connecting the information on our drawing with Petrini's observation. A second, later, survey of the temple ruins by Federico Cesi is most unlikely. It would scarcely have remained unknown. The date 1614 excludes Cortona's authorship of the reconstruction plan. He came to Rome in 1613 as a sixteen-year-old and his activities at first were purely those of a student. Who originated the 1614 scheme we cannot now say. But if it is entirely unrelated to Cortona's later scheme (A) the question arises how, in the Windsor drawings, and later in Volpi's book, it came to be combined with that scheme.

To answer this question we must look at the history of the Albani volumes, in which our drawings are to be found. Part of this collection, acquired for George III from Cardinal Alessandro Albani, Winckelmann's patron, consists of the estate of that learned antiquarian Cassiano dal Pozzo (1588–1657). Cassiano played a notable role in Roman artistic and scholarly circles in the first half of the seventeenth century.[18] He was a friend of Francesco Barberini, who was made a cardinal after the accession of Urban VIII and was soon entrusted with important foreign missions. The Cardinal and the scholar had similar scientific leanings; both were 'Accademici dei Lincei', members of the learned academy founded by the eighteen-year-old Federico Cesi in 1603. When Cesi died young in 1630, Cassiano dal Pozzo acted as his executor. He also succeeded him as *princeps* of the Accademia dei Lincei, a post he held until his death.

Cassiano's most important achievement was a large collection of material relating to classical remains, which, according to Carlo Dati, filled twenty-three volumes – probably even more. Cassiano began his collection about 1620 and went on adding to it for almost forty years until his death. He systematically had everything copied that he could get hold of, and for this task he often used artists of the first rank, notably Poussin and Pietro Testa.[19]

One of Cassiano's volumes included *Templa et arae, earumque formae et dedicatio; etc.* The Palestrina sheets fit meaningfully into this volume. If we assume that they once belonged to this material of Cassiano dal Pozzo's, all the riddles of our inscription are solved. The detailed knowledge evident in the inscription comes straight from Cassiano. He himself, when administering the Cesi estate, would have ensured that the originals of the Palestrina surveys of 1614 came into the possession of his patron, Cardinal Francesco. In 1630 Palestrina was sold by the Colonnas to the Barberinis. Don Taddeo, the Cardinal's brother, became Prince of Palestrina. So it is quite understandable that Cassiano gave the most recent reconstruction of the new Barberini estate to his friend the Cardinal, but had copies made for his own collection, which have been preserved in Scheme A, the Windor sheets.

Later, when Pietro da Cortona attempted a new reconstruction of the temple, Cassiano dal Pozzo could not deny himself a copy for his own collection. The close connection between the two men makes it certain that Cassiano followed the artist's reconstruction work with interest. It was of course Cassiano's custom as a collector to keep abreast of the latest opinions and findings. Cortona's reconstruction was naturally placed with the older plans of the temple area.[20] Volpi must then have studied Cassiano's much-used collection at Cardinal Albani's in about 1743, and relying on Cassiano's authority, must have added to the Cortona engravings an engraving which followed Scheme A. This seems a sufficient explanation of the combination of the 1614 reconstruction with that of Cortona. We now have to ask when Cortona's

180 PIRRO LIGORIO. Reconstruction scheme for Palestrina, *c.* 1560 (Vat. Cod. lat. 3439 folio 51)

reconstruction scheme was actually evolved.

The inscription on the engraving in Suarez's *Sciographia*[21] includes a dedication of the sheets by Domenico Castelli to Prince Maffeo Barberini, the heir of Palestrina. It follows from this that the engravings were made in the 'interregnum' years between the death of Prince Taddeo Barberini and the succession of his son Maffeo. In 1647 Taddeo Barberini had died in exile in Paris, whither the nephews of Urban VIII had fled after the accession of Innocent X. But his son did not succeed to the princely title until 1656, after a reconciliation with the Pope.[22] So the engravings could not have been made before 1647; most probably, therefore, they were done specially for Suarez's work. This however tells us nothing about the time when the Cortona scheme (B) came into being, for the very fact that the dedication is not by Cortona but by Domenico Castelli[23] suggests that the Cortona plans were not intended as direct models for these engravings.

We can however establish with a high degree of probability when the original Cortona drawings (for Scheme B) were made. In 1636 Cortona was commissioned by Cardinal Francesco Barberini to carry out rebuilding work in S. Pietro in Palestrina.[24] On this occasion he stayed on the site for some time. The probability that Cortona was occupied at the time with a scheme for restoring the ancient ruins is in itself very strong, especially as we know of no other extended stay by him in Palestrina; it becomes almost a certainty in the light of a passage in Suarez, saying that the engravings were made possible through the magnanimity of Cardinal Francesco Barberini.[25] We may assume that in 1636 the Cardinal commissioned not only the rebuilding of the church but a new reconstruction scheme for the temple, and that this remained in the possession of the Cardinal, who later made it available for the preparation of the engravings. The date of 1636 thus seems to be well established on external evidence. We shall come back to the internal justification of this dating.

First however we must investigate the relationship of the 1614 survey to the engraving in Suarez and of the engraving to drawing B at Windsor. We have already noted the discrepancies between them. While the engraving contains elements which cannot be explained except by reference to the 1614 plan, it in fact goes far beyond the older scheme. Typologically, the projection used in the engraved view lies between that of 1614 and the pure orthogonal projection of the drawing. In the lower half of the engraving the peculiar motif of the temple façade with high arcades has been taken straight from Scheme A, and the columned courtyard, closed on three sides, shows the same characteristics of detail as the one closed on four sides in the earlier scheme. In the Windsor drawing all these points of agreement have been eliminated. Instead of the view into the columned courtyard we find a long arcaded front,[26] which stands in a well-defined relationship to the rows of columns of the terrace higher up. The drawing (Scheme A) therefore represents a later stage of development than the engraving (Scheme B).

We are now in a position to postulate four reconstruction schemes of Palestrina, which form a clear sequence: 1 Ligorio, *c.* 1560; 2 anonymous, 1614; 3 Pietro da Cortona, scheme of the engravings, 1636 (Scheme B); 4 Cortona, scheme of the Windsor drawings (Scheme A). (To these schemes we need add only the earliest reconstruction attempt of all, a series of sheets from the hand of Palladio (perhaps about 1550), which probably remained unknown in Rome and therefore had no noticeable influence.[27])

The date of the revised Cortona scheme (A) cannot easily be established. It may either have been during the period between the publication of Suarez's book and the death of Cassiano – i.e. 1655–57[28] – or it was developed as early as 1636 and not engraved because it diverged too boldly from its ancient model. However, this is a comparatively minor issue. The main elements of Cortona's ideas for restoration are already present in Suarez's engravings.

The search for a pattern linking these four schemes as they develop will lead to unexpected insights. Since the 'rediscovery' of ancient architecture at the beginning of the fifteenth century there had been three contrasting ways of responding to it: straightforward excavating and surveying – that is, making an archaeologically correct inventory of the finds; the romantic cult of ruins; and finally the attempt to reconstruct ancient monuments from existing remains. Each of these responses sprang from the same feeling that the classical heritage

181 Rome, the Victor Emmanuel Monument, begun 1884

somehow embodied an unattainable perfection. Excavation and surveying expressed the desire of a dawning scientific age to establish measurable norms of expression even in matters of art. The cult of ruins saw in ancient remains a pregnant symbol of the Western Christian sensibility: the transience of all earthly things. The ambition actually to reconstruct lies between the two: it combines scientific research with pure imagination. The history of reconstruction thus forms a not insignificant part of the history of architecture in general. For here ancient architectural remains both stimulate revolutionary new architectonic thought, and also legitimize it. It is only when one becomes aware of this creative role of antiquity that one can see the Palestrina ruins as the starting-point for a series of architectural experiments – experiments which lead in entirely different directions, which belong to different centuries, and whose common root is hardly to be recognized.

The Quattrocento had no eye as yet for the scale and complexity of such a layout.[29] Bramante was the first to see the unity of this many-layered hillside. In the Belvedere courtyard of the Vatican he created the first large-scale terraced area of Italian architecture on the model of Palestrina.[30] The derivation is clearly from motifs like the exedra which closes the whole complex, and the staircase – a combination of convex and concave steps.[31] Palladio's plans show an instructive transition from archaeological reconstruction to purely imaginative forms, and the lessons learned from such an exercise in total planning were surely put to good use in his villas. Ligorio was the first to take over the idea of terracing on a steep gradient in the construction of villas. His scheme for the Villa d'Este, which had such a revolutionary effect on Italian villa design, is unthinkable without the thorough study of the temple area of Palestrina.[32]

In this sequence of buildings and projects one sees a pattern emerging: the progressive subordination of all the elements in a design to one dominating feature. Ligorio takes the idea of the Giant Niche, the *Nicchione*, further than did Bramante at the Vatican, where the exedra, according to his overall design, would not have risen higher than the adjoining walls. The form of the *Nicchione* actually used by Ligorio is based on his new interpretation of the one at Praeneste.[33] Pietro da Cortona adapted it to villa architecture in the Villa Sacchetti (now destroyed).[34] There were certainly substantial differences in the way the middle block dominated the composition, in the steeply built terrace, and the sideways expansion of the site, though the enclosing side walls are missing. But the outline of the structural mass is almost completely identical to Cortona's Palestrina

123

reconstruction scheme of almost ten years later.

This 1636 scheme (B) therefore has a logical place in Cortona's development. The significance of Cortona's reconstruction however lies not only in his complete mastery of the problems that faced him – the consistent organization of so complex a structural mass on successive levels crowned by a dominant motif. In this respect it was the final stage in a development beginning with Bramante. Moreover, it also led to the formulation of two elements that were new and of far-reaching importance for the future history of architecture: the free-standing, non-functional colonnade and the free-standing belvedere.[35] The belvedere, especially in the north, soon lost its monumental character and became a hackneyed component of garden architecture. But the colonnade became a main theme of the High Baroque. Cortona himself used it in his unexecuted palace designs for Piazza Colonna, the first concave façades with a giant order.[36] The effect of what he had learnt at Palestrina can be proved here in detail. The nonfunctional colonnade was used and made popular by Bernini in Piazza S.

Pietro, and the first two Bernini schemes for the Louvre have concave façades with a giant order.[37] Cortona's own Louvre scheme seems to depend directly on the colonnade motif,[38] but Perrault, starting from the Cortona-Bernini High Baroque version, returns to Palladianism, one of the sources of Cortona's style.

This sketch has allowed us to discern the outstanding importance of the ruins of Palestrina as a stimulus to new architectural thinking. The building of terraces in Italian architecture, and certain motifs of villa and palace design have their origin here. But the importance of Cortona's reconstruction scheme is not exhausted by showing its role as a link between the study of classical remains and Baroque architectural thought. The magnificent archaeological imagination shown here retained its power to fascinate long after it had been unmasked as pure invention.[39] In the 1880s the newly united nation found the symbol of its glory in a monument which, for all its bourgeois 181 overbearance, springs from that grandest architectural achievement of Imperial Rome, as seen through the eyes of the High Baroque.

182 S. Maria della Salute. Façade from the Canal Grande

VII SANTA MARIA DELLA SALUTE

Santa Maria della Salute

IT IS THE PURPOSE of this paper to discuss Longhena's conceptual approach to architecture. What were his guiding ideas when planning his masterpiece, S. Maria della Salute? What is the historical place of this church in the wider panorama of Italian seventeenth-century architecture? To what extent did Longhena take up and develop north Italian and in particular Palladian ideas; how far does his specific interpretation of architecture depend on precedence? I propose to clarify these points through a closer analysis of the church than has hitherto been devoted to it. This programme cannot be carried out without a good deal of philological research into the material relating to the planning of S. Maria della Salute. But I do not intend to give a full history of the construction, of the vicissitudes presented by the site or of the decoration.[1] We shall not lose sight of our primary purpose, namely to discover Longhena's method of procedure, by which he arrived, in my view, at a true 'scenographic architecture'.

The chronology of events

The circumstances of the commission are well known. The documents, published by Giannantonio Moschini,[2] are however incomplete and not arranged in chronological order. Other authors, among them V. Piva,[3] supplemented Moschini's material, but no serious attempt has yet been made to evaluate the documents. It is for this reason that we shall begin by charting the events in their sequence of time.

1 In 1630 the population of Venice was decimated by a frightful plague. A few months after its beginning, on 22 October 1630, the Doge and Senate decided to erect as an *ex voto* a church dedicated to the Virgin and to call it S. Maria della Salute, which has the double meaning of Health and Salvation. According to the document recording this decision, it was resolved that the cost of the church should not be more than 50,000 ducats, further, that three senators should be chosen for the purpose of selecting an appropriate site and recommending a project.[4]

2 The commission of three – Simone Contarini, Pietro Bondulmier and Zuanne Marco Molin – chose the present site; this is confirmed by a decree of the Senate, dated 23 November 1630 (Corner, p. 75, verbatim; Piva, p. 31).

3 3 December 1630: It is decreed that the church of SS. Trinità, standing close to the selected area next to the Seminary of the Somaschi (which had to be demolished), is to survive (Corner, p. 76, verbatim: Piva, p. 31).

4 2 January 1631: It is resolved to begin clearing the area of the Seminary[5] (Corner, p. 77, verbatim; Piva, p. 31 ff.).

5 18 January: It is resolved to order the wood necessary for the new foundations (Moschini, p. 6; Piva, p. 33).

6 1 February: It is resolved to lay the foundation stone of the new church on 25 March, the day of the Annunciation, which is also the legendary day of the foundation of Venice;[6] it is expected that a model will have been chosen before that date (Corner, p. 77 ff.; Piva, p. 33).

7 1 April: The laying of the foundation stone took place a week after the appointed day, on 1 April (Moschini, p. 22; Piva, p. 33 ff.). On this occasion medals were put into the foundations with the inscription UNDE ORIGO INDE SALUS – in terse words referring to the origin of Venice under the Virgin's tutelage and to the physical and spiritual health guaranteed by her patronage. The same inscription was later placed in the centre of the pavement of the 'Rotonda'.

8 Beginning of April: At an earlier date (probably in December 1630) a competition had been arranged. Eleven projects were submitted, and at the beginning of April the commission chose two for closer consideration: that by Longhena and one for which Antonio Fracao and Zambattista Rubertini were jointly re-

sponsible (Moschini, p. 7; Piva, p. 35). The latter's share, however, seems to have been inconsiderable. From then on Fracao conducted his affairs alone. He was the son of Francesco Smeraldi[7] who, much older than Longhena, was well established in his profession, and as architect of the Palladian façade of S. Pietro in Castello (1594–96) commanded considerable authority.

9 13 April: Longhena submits a memorandum consisting of twelve different points, evidently explanatory notes to accompany his model[8] (Moschini, pp. 11–13).

10 15 April: Antonio Fracao hands in a memorandum (Moschini, p. 14 ff.).

11 After 15 April: Meanwhile it must have transpired that the commission favoured Longhena's project in preference to Fracao's and Rubertini's. Fracao, therefore, wrote a second memorandum reaffirming the advantages of his design which followed by and large the pattern of Palladio's Redentore. But the main purpose of the new memorandum was by a subtle device to insinuate that Longhena's project was in many ways unsatisfactory. Fracao added a centrally planned project to his memorandum in order to demonstrate that this form of design was unsuitable for the purpose. It is likely that this project was the work of a few days, drawn in a hurry with the sole aim of combating Longhena (Moschini, p. 55 ff. verbatim, without date, but obviously datable shortly after 15 April).

12 26 April: Faced with an increasingly difficult situation the Senate must have found it advisable to broaden the original committee of three: two new names – Girolamo Cornaro and Paolo Morosini – were added to it as *aggiunti alla Fabbrica* (Casoni,[9] p. 35; Piva, p. 35.)

13 21 May: The committee decided to call upon eight experts to make sworn statements mainly about the security of Longhena's dome. Four of them voiced some criticism of his design and a fifth insisted energetically on radical alterations (Moschini, pp. 19–22).

14 13 June: It seems that the committee was unable to come to a final decision. On 13 June they appeared before the Senate with a long and well balanced report. The Senate resolved to decide by ballot whether Longhena's or Fracao's model should be chosen for execution. Fortun-

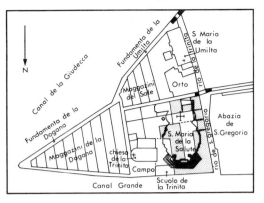

183 The site of S. Maria della Salute, with the church superimposed on the previously existing buildings

ately the senators had sufficient wisdom and taste to cast their votes in favour of Longhena's project (Moschini, pp. 7–11; Piva, p. 36 ff.).[10]

15 After 13 June: Even after the formal decision had been taken, Fracao once more assailed his successful opponent. Now in desperation, he seems to have gone over to a frontal attack. Fracao's new memorandum is not with the rest of the documents in the Archivio di Stato and may be lost, but its character can be deduced from Longhena's answer, a lengthy memorandum in which he refutes point by point Fracao's criticism. In the beginning Longhena refers to the false statements made by his adversary regarding '*la formazione del già accettato mio modello*'. This formulation makes it possible to date this episode soon after 13 June without any reasonable doubt. Longhena also mentions that eight new experts were prepared to make sworn statements to the effect that Fracao's objections were baseless (Moschini, p. 17 ff.).

16 6 September: The laying of the foundations of Longhena's structure has begun (Casoni, p. 37; Piva, pp. 40, 47).

17 9 November 1633: The foundations were finished on 8 November 1633. On the following day building above ground level was started (Piva, p. 47).

It is well known that the completion of the church dragged on for a very long time. But for the purpose of the present paper the documentation can stop here. We now have to evaluate what the documents tell us.

The stipulation of the competition

In its report of 13 June 1631 (14)[11] the committee summarized the conditions which had to be observed by the competing architects. Three specific points were made, namely: **1** that from the entrance of the church it should be possible to embrace the whole ample space of the building unobstructed; **2** that there should be an even distribution of bright light throughout the church, and **3** that the high altar should dominate the view from the entrance, while the other altars should come into full view as one proceeds in the direction of the high altar. To these main conditions, others, no less essential but of a more general nature, were added: the new building had to harmonize with the site and had to make a grand impression, in spite of the fact that sufficient ground had to be left for the erection of the monastery and that the expense should be kept within reasonable limits.

The committee followed the time-honoured and perfectly justifiable practice of squeezing the last ounce out of the competing architects. No wonder that only two of the eleven projects which had been submitted[12] were worth considering: Longhena's centrally planned church for which the report had words of high praise, and Fracao's and Rubertini's longitudinal design which, according to the jury, recommended itself by good distribution, good lighting and spaciousness. The first question that arises concerns the nature of Longhena's model. Did he submit a design corresponding to the one that was eventually built? The documents supply a clear answer.

Longhena's model

Before we let the documents speak, it is worth enquiring whether a pictorial representation of Longhena's model survives. We have noted that on the foundation day medals were sunk into the foundations. They show on the obverse the Virgin hovering on clouds over the Piazzetta S. Marco and on the reverse the Doge Nicolò Contarini (who died a day after the event, on 2 April) kneeling before the new church.[13] Desirous of beginning the church at the earliest possible moment, Doge and Senate agreed to the laying of the foundation stone two-and-a-

184 Detail from Prudenti's *Cessation of the Plague* (S. Maria della Salute)

half months before Longhena's project was accepted (Chronology, 7, 14). It is therefore evident that the elevation represented on the medals cannot be related to any of the competing projects, which came up for criticism only after the foundation day (Chronology, 8). Consequently the medals illustrate an ideal project. Nor is the model of the church carried by angels in Padovanino's *Virgin on Clouds* connected with Longhena. Painted in 1631, the work (now in the large sacristy) was placed on the high altar as a provisional arrangement. Padovanino himself was one of the eleven competitors, and one would, therefore, surmise that he painted his own model. But he certainly did not represent his final model, the plan of which was hexagonal, based on the interpretation of two equilateral triangles.[14]

By contrast, the model in Bernardino Prudenti's picture, painted to celebrate the cessation of the plague, has documentary value. The official celebration was fixed for 28 November 1631, and on this occasion Prudenti's work was exhibited in the Piazza S. Marco.[15] In spite of its large size, it must have been painted in great haste, as a cursory examination reveals. In any case, since the model here appears to be close to Longhena's executed design the picture

184

cannot have been started before the second half of June 1631. But it was not until September that the mortality began to drop very considerably, and it is therefore not unlikely that the painting was commissioned after this period. The inference seems inescapable that Prudenti copied in his picture Longhena's model of June 1631. Historical facts, however, do not always correspond to simple logic. We happen to have an eye-witness report according to which the picture was finished in four days[16] – in other words, it was probably painted late in November. Over five months had gone by since the Senate had chosen Longhena's model, so the model shown by Prudenti may well represent a project different from the one accepted on 13 June.

As we shall see, this last assumption is confirmed by certain clues contained in Longhena's memorandum of 13 April (Chronology, 9). This memorandum is a most remarkable document and requires closest attention. Longhena tells us that he had worked on his project for months,[17] and this, incidentally, makes it likely that the beginning of the competition dates back to December 1630. Some time early in the new year he had been asked to submit a model;[18] it is this model to which his memorandum of 13 April refers. Next to a detailed description Longhena supplies in the document all the important measurements of his projected building. By implication, these were the measurements shown in the model reduced in scale. A comparison between the measurements quoted by him and those of the execution will, therefore, allow us to draw definite conclusions as to the appearance of the model submitted on 13 April and accepted on 13 June. For clarity's sake I print a table giving the projected and the executed dimensions.[19]

	MODEL Finished 13 April 1631, accepted 13 June 1631. Feet are always Venetian feet[20]	AS EXECUTED	
		Diedo	Santamaria
a. Whole width of the 'Rotonda' including the walls of the chapels	118 feet	c. 126 feet	44 m.[21]
b. Diameter of the Rotonda (mentioned in Longhena's second memorandum after 13 June)	60 feet	60 feet	20·30 m. (?)[22]
c. Width of the chapels between the pilasters	19 feet	18·4 feet	6·50 m.[23]
d. Depth of the chapels, from the balustrade to the back wall	10 feet	10 (11) feet	3·80 m.[24]
e. Width of the ambulatory	no figure given	15 feet	5·25 m.[25]
f. Entire length of the church including the walls	188 feet	188 feet	c. 65·30 m.[26]
g. Presbytery (from the steps leading into it to the columns of the high altar)	37 feet	43 feet	c. 15·20 m.[27]
h. Presbytery, width within the walls	60 feet	80 feet	27·60 m.[28]
i. Depth of high altar space	no figure given	10 feet	3–3·40 m.[29]
k. Choir, length within the walls	26 feet	20·5–21 feet	c. 7 m.[30]
l. Choir, width	30 feet	c. 38·9 feet	c. 13·5 m.[31]
m. Central portal, height	32 feet	c. 37 feet	12·55 m.[32]
n. Central portal, width	15 feet	c. 14·5 feet	5·25 m.[33]
o. Steps leading up to the level of the church	13 steps		16 steps
p. Steps leading up to the high altar	6–8 steps		4 steps[34]

The data supply sufficient evidence to prove that Longhena's model was similar but not identical to the execution. The difference of 6 to 8 feet in the over-all width (a) presents the first problem. Since the diameter of the Rotonda (b), the depth of the chapels (d), and presumably also the width of the pillars (5 feet)[35] and of the outside walls (2 feet) tally, the difference of 6 feet (or, in actual fact, of about $1\frac{1}{2}$ foot more)[36] between the model and the execution must result from the design of a narrower ambulatory in the model stage. This conclusion would seem entirely convincing: if we presume that Longhena had planned the ambulatory 12 instead of 15 feet wide (e), the discrepancy in the over-all width is resolved.

But such a simple solution contradicts the facts, for it can be shown without any shadow of doubt that Longhena had incorporated an ambulatory 15 feet in width into his model. There is, however, good reason to assume that his pre-model designs to which he referred in the memorandum of 13 April[37] had a 12-foot ambulatory. It will be noticed that the width of the ambulatory (e) is the only important measure that he left unmentioned in the memorandum accompanying his model, and this may be interpreted as an indication that he did not want to draw attention to the widening of the ambulatory in the model. As we shall see, he may have had very good reasons to keep silent on this point. The hypothesis of a discrepancy between the designs and the model is supported by the fact that some of the experts in their memorandum of 21 May (Chronology, 13; Moschini, p. 21) clearly imply that the ambulatory was planned 15 feet wide, while the final report of the committee of 13 June (Chronology, 14) mentions the width as *ca.* 12 feet.[38] This contradiction can only be resolved if we suppose that the experts and the committee had different evidence before them. But the words *'piedi dodici incirca'* used in the report also indicate that the committee was somewhat puzzled and probably not unaware of the alteration. It may be assumed that in his memorandum Longhena mentioned the over-all width of 118 feet (a), as originally planned in the drawings, although it no longer applied to the model, because it was contrary to his interests to admit an increase in the over-all width of the church. I shall later demonstrate

that Longhena's decision to enlarge the width of the ambulatory was concerned with one of the most hotly debated aspects of his project. As a result of the present discussion it can be stated that in the model the Rotonda and ambulatory must have corresponded to the execution.

But the design of the presbytery and the choir differed. The figures given by Longhena prove that, compared with the execution, the model showed a presbytery of considerably less depth and width (g, h) as well as a longer and narrower choir (k, l).[39] A welcome control is at hand in the way these different units fit into the general design of the model. Since Longhena supplied the over-all length of the church in the model stage (f, 188 feet) – a length equal to that of the present building – the sum of the individual measurements must add up to 188 feet. It now becomes clear (as is demonstrated in note 40) that such correspondence depends on the assumption that in the model the ambulatory was 15 feet wide.[40] This is at variance with the over-all width given by Longhena (a), and confirms our hypothesis that he made the latter statement with his tongue in his cheek. If this premise is accepted the model chosen by the Senate for execution can be reconstructed with a high degree of certainty. The presbytery and the choir were less differentiated as regards size than they are in the execution. If a small dome was planned over the presbytery – and there is no reason for doubting it – it would have been no match for the dome of the Rotonda and would have played a less important part for the silhouette of the exterior than the present second dome. The Rotonda of the model, in other words, was considerably more dominant than that of the execution. Briefly, the relationship of the Rotonda to the presbytery in the model stage was still close to such older structures as Sanmicheli's Madonna di Campagna or even the Bramantesque S. Maria di Canepanova at Pavia.

The model in Prudenti's picture proves that Longhena's change of design must have taken place before mid-November 1631. Since the original model was ready on 13 April and still valid on 13 June, the day of its acceptance, Longhena must have worked out the revision during the intervening five months. At this period his attention was focused on the enlarge-

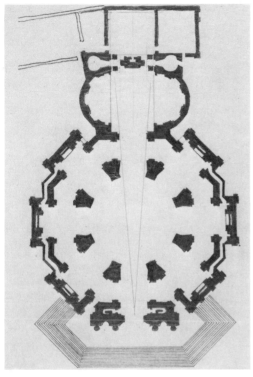

185 Reconstruction of Longhena's model (drawn by Colin Rowe)

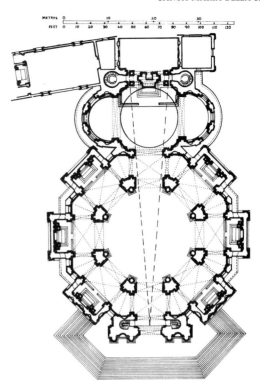

186 S. Maria della Salute, plan

ment of the presbytery. This made a reduction of the length of the choir necessary, for he had to keep within the over-all limits of the site at his disposal. After its enlargement the presby-

182, tery offered a much more striking silhouette
198 holding its own next to the dome of the Rotonda. But other reasons, too, must have prevailed upon Longhena to change the model. The final

186 plan exhibits an intrinsic beauty and logic still lacking in the model stage: now both the presbytery and the choir have their longer axes along the transverse line, and the gradual reduction in size from the Rotonda to the presbytery and the choir immediately strikes the eye as intimately related and harmonious even in the black and white of the ground-plan. In fact, it was the change of design that enabled Longhena to achieve a simple progression of ratios from one unit to the next[41] – a problem, as we shall see, to which he must have devoted a good deal of careful thought. We may sum up that the final design was the result of a slow

development and growth. It is not unlikely that he found this solution between September and November 1631, at a time when the foundations were built (Chronology, 16, 17), many months after the completion of the model.

The plan of the Rotonda

The main portion of Longhena's project – the octagon which is always called 'Rotonda' in the documents – presents a baffling problem. A centrally planned building with ambulatory is rather rare in Renaissance and post-Renaissance architecture. Well known from late antiquity (S. Costanza, Rome), the type recurs not infrequently in medieval, particularly Byzantine, baptistries and churches. S. Vitale at 188 Ravenna immediately comes to mind. It seems fairly evident, why octagons (or, for that matter, any centrally planned building) with ambulatory were almost excluded from Renaissance planning, for it is the ambulatory that renders

131

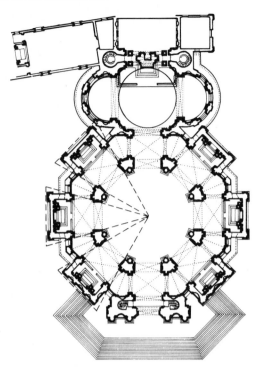

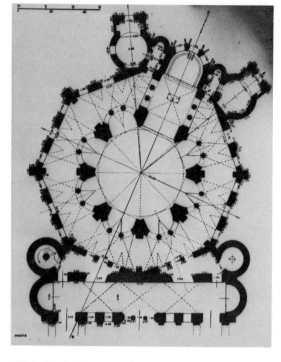

187 S. Maria della Salute, plan with lines added to show the effect of pillar-shapes determined by radii

188 S. Vitale, Ravenna, plan

it impossible to produce a design with entirely regular sub-units. If an architect with Longhena's classicizing leanings accepted this shortcoming (for such it must have appeared to him), he had important reasons for it. These reasons clearly overrode every other consideration. But before throwing light on them some characteristic features of his design must be described.

The success of the plan depended on the shape given to the pillars of the octagon. Had he chosen the obvious solution of trapezoid 187 pillars determined by the radii from the centre, he could not have avoided alternating large and small trapezoid units in the ambulatory, trapezoid chapels and acute angles at the meeting points of the chapel walls and the octagon outside. Although feasible in cases of circular design,[42] this solution was evidently not appropriate to an octagon. Longhena found a way out of this predicament by designing trapezoid pillars without relating their sides to the centre of the octagon radially: he made the

sides of two consecutive pillars parallel to each 189 other. To be sure, this was not a new idea. Following Byzantine tradition, the architect of S. Vitale at Ravenna had done the same. But in 188 order to be able to repeat the octagonal shape of the interior also outside, he returned in the ambulatory to a radial design resulting in large trapezoid sub-units and a complex system of vaulting. This was not acceptable to an architect reared in the Renaissance tradition. Longhena had to be consistent throughout, and it is precisely the parallelism of the sides of 189 adjoining pillars, logically carried over into the ambulatory, that enabled him to give the visually important units of the ambulatory as well as the chapels regular geometrical shapes. Owing to this procedure the irregularly shaped sections of the ambulatory behind the pillars and between any two chapels are reduced to insignificance.

This is, however, not the full story, for Longhena also incorporated radial relationships in his design. The radii not only determine, as

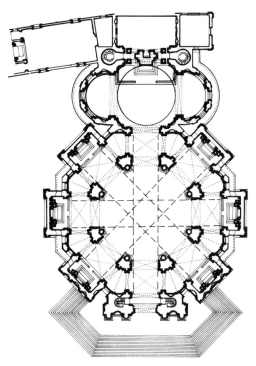

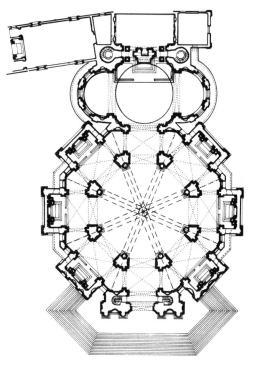

189 S. Maria della Salute, plan with lines added to show the parallelism of the sides of adjoining pillars

190 S. Maria della Salute, plan with lines added to show the radii which determine the bases of the columns

one would expect, the angles of the octagon and the broken faces of the pillars, but also the bases of the columns inside the octagon. Thus within the compound design of each pillar the geometrical loci of the sides of the pillar and of the basis of the column differ. Analytical enquiry then leads to an important result: while it is the openings between the pillars, and not their sides, that correspond across the octagon, the opposite is true regarding the bases of the columns; here it is solid form, and not open space, that corresponds. Longhena's handling of the pillar and column motif was new and ingenious. This will be realized when its effect is interpreted in terms of optical impact. Seen from the centre of the octagon the units of pillar and column reveal their dual function: while the sides of the pillars are space-limiting, the columns with their bases are space-absorbing.

Instead of a further verbal exposition I refer to pl. 191: the columns push forward into the central space, and as one is more or less consciously aware of their radial arrangement,

191 S. Maria della Salute, view from the centre of the Rotonda

133

they suggest rotation or, better, they support the enclosed centralized character of the octagon; the small orders of the piers, by contrast, face sideways, carry the arches of the octagon, and link up with the corresponding order of the chapels. We begin to see what fascinated Longhena in the plan with ambulatory.

Criticism of the model

Longhena's model contained features which his contemporaries could not accept unchallenged. Current criticism found expression in the memoranda submitted by the experts (Chronology, 13). The statements of the brothers Comin were most explicit. They explained that the opening between two pillars of the octagon as well as the entrance to each chapel is 'at least 18 feet'[43] and the width of the ambulatory only 15 feet. The arches inside the ambulatory would therefore have to be lower than those between the pillars. They could not agree to this and regarded it as necessary to increase the width of the ambulatory by 3 feet so that the arches encompassing each ambulatory unit could be made equally high. Such treatment was, according to them, not only a requirement of correct design, but also a technical necessity because, they maintained, the ambulatory as planned by Longhena would not give sufficient support to the dome. Moreover, for reasons of proportion they advocated that externally the ambulatory should be raised at least 5 feet. Other experts summarily agreed with these stipulations.

The overall width of Longhena's design was just, and only just, inside the permissible limits. By incorporating the experts' recommendations the area of the Rotonda would have to be enlarged, and this was not possible because the building would have come too close to the church of SS. Trinità and would also have encroached on the site reserved for the monastery. The impasse seemed almost insoluble. The brothers Comin made a clear statement to that effect. And the expert Pietro Zambon opined laconically that the arches of the ambulatory were disproportionate in relation to those of the octagon, but that the restriction of the narrow site did not allow the present limits to be exceeded. Girolamo Oti, finally, repeated the same criticism and held

that the replanning of the entire Rotonda was unavoidable.[44]

These views are reflected in a passage of the final report of the committee (Chronology, 14), where the whole argument is reiterated with reference to the experts' opinions. The deadlock created by the supposed necessity of enlarging the area of the Rotonda and the impossibility of doing so, is summarized in one lapidary sentence: 'a manifest defect [of Longhena's model], unsurmountable, known to one and all, affirmed by experts, a defect which we felt we had to bring to the attention of the Senate as of most urgent importance'.[45]

All this was, of course, very much on Longhena's mind. It now becomes clear why he mentioned in his memorandum (Chronology, 9) the width of the Rotonda of the pre-model designs instead of the increased width of the model stage. By incorrectly quoting 118 feet rather than 124 feet as the greatest width of his model he hoped to avoid discussion of this critical point. In addition, the greatest width of Fracao's project was 120 feet (Moschini, p. 16), and Longhena must have felt it necessary to score against his competitor in this matter of vital importance. We have come to the conclusion that between his first set of designs and his model Longhena widened the ambulatory from 12 to 15 feet. This was not a concession to criticism, for the experts pounced upon him long after the change had been made. Once he had made up his mind that he had found the right solution he was prepared to defend it tooth and nail, even at the risk of having his project rejected.

In the end Longhena carried his point. He was a better technician than the experts, for his ambulatory remained 15 feet wide, and the church stands as firm as a rock. Nor was he unduly worried by the offence against uniformity in the height of the arches in the subunits of the ambulatory. He adjusted the arches inside the ambulatory by stilting them slightly, but their apex is about 60 cm lower than that of the arches of the octagon. He must have been convinced that this irregularity would remain unnoticed because the arches of the ambulatory belong to an optically neutralized area. This has proved so true that Diedo's section, which shows the octagon and ambulatory arches as of equal height, has always been accepted as

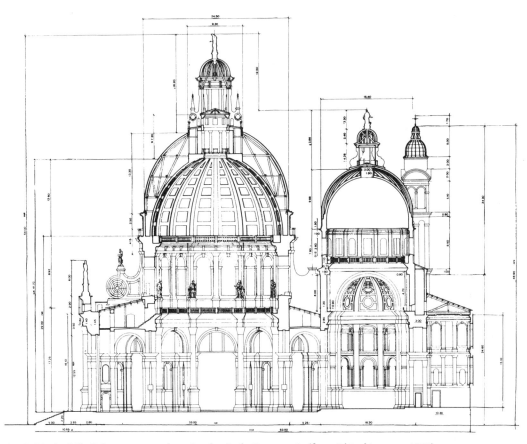

192 S. Maria della Salute, measured section by Carlo Santamaria (from *L'Architettura*, 1955)

correct.[46] Only recently have the real facts been revealed by Santamaria's measured drawings, 192 published in *L'Architettura*, 1955.

As regards the exterior Longhena had no intention of yielding to the expert's recommendation. An increase of the height of the ambulatory wall would have had serious repercussions on the carefully balanced internal design. Moreover, he had many other reasons for keeping the ambulatory wall low. On the other hand, the magnificent scrolls optically form part of the body of the church, which 182 seems, therefore, higher than it really is.

The criticism of the experts was focused on the discrepancy in the height of the ambulatory arches. The points they made may seem to us somewhat spurious; we may feel that the argument was taking place in the thin and unrealistic atmosphere of academic finesse. But this would be misjudging the situation. After all, the criticism came from men well versed in the practice rather than in the theory of architecture. These experts had certain standards with which they had grown up and which they regarded as unimpeachable. The tradition of Renaissance aesthetics was part of their intellectual equipment, and to them it was, therefore, an article of faith, almost a law of nature, that a spatial unit must be encompassed by arches of equal height. Longhena, on the other hand, introduced new optical standards, and it is these that enabled him to transcend the limitations of the earlier approach. Yet he was far from throwing tradition overboard.

135

193 S. Maria della Salute, view from main entrance

194 PALLADIO. S. Giorgio Maggiore, Venice, interior

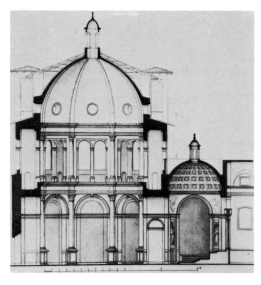

195 S. Maria di Canepanova, Pavia, section

Traditional aspects of Longhena's design

In his two memoranda Longhena himself proudly points out the novelty of his design (Chronology, 9, 15), and his view is echoed in the final report of the committee (Chronology, 14). Nevertheless his grammar of forms is firmly based on precedent. In a hundred direct and indirect ways S. Maria della Salute shows links with Palladio's architecture. Such features as the high pedestals of the columns, the 193 breaking of the entablature above them, and the combination of the small Corinthian and the large Composite order derive from S. Giorgio 194 Maggiore. Moreover, although it is less obvious, the attentive student cannot fail to discover the impact of a distinct older group of buildings. A number of Bramantesque Lombard churches, for which S. Maria di Canepanova at Pavia 195 (begun 1492?) may serve as an example, are designed as octagons with columns on high pedestals in the re-entrant angles. The similarity to S. Maria della Salute is evident. These churches also have as a rule the high drum with the two round-headed windows to each wall section – a clear indication that Longhena knew this class of works.[47] But instead of continuing the columns of the octagon into the architecture of the drum – the rule in Bramante's circle – Longhena placed large wooden figures of 196 Prophets above the projecting entablature of the columns. He therefore strengthened the impression that each column with its figure is a unit in its own right; at the same time, the coherent sequence of these 'monuments on columns' supports the self-contained, centralized character of the octagon. It may be mentioned at once that the addition of an almost independent centralized presbytery to the centrally planned main body of the church is common in the North of Italy;[48] again, the closest parallels to S. Maria della Salute will be found in Bramante's circle.

Among the Palladian detail used by Longhena the segmental window with mullions deserves mention. Palladio first incorporated this type of window, derived from Roman thermae, into ecclesiastical architecture in S. Giorgio Maggiore and Il Redentore. He found the type eminently suitable because it supported and repeated the form of the arches, so that he was able to avoid introducing a new shape for the lights into an otherwise homogeneous design. The same applies to Longhena's chapel windows: within the logic of his design it was absolutely indispensable to give the windows 191 the form of the arches of the chapels.

Palladio's influence on Longhena is so obvious that it needs no further elaboration. We shall see that it can also be traced in the architectural motifs of the presbytery, the high altar zone and choir as well as in important aspects of the exterior. Moreover, even on far more fundamental matters Longhena turned to Palladio for guidance. He owed to Palladio his basic, conceptual approach to architecture, and this is a point which we shall later discuss in some detail.

It seems hardly possible to reconcile with our analysis the view, often expressed, that the design of the Rotonda was dependent on the 197 famous woodcut in Colonna's *Hypnerotomachia*, first published in 1499, which shows a section through a centrally planned building with ambulatory. Although slight affinities between the woodcut and S. Maria della Salute cannot be denied, the romantic idea that the former supplied the basis for the planning of a real structure must be abandoned once and for all. To regard Longhena's project – as has been done – as a literal plagiarism from the Quattrocento source,[49] is only proof of the blinding effect of preconceived notions. Yet one motif Longhena may possibly have owed to the graphic representation: the figures above the columns. There is, incidentally, no reason to doubt that the *Hypnerotomachia*, well known to every Venetian, had a certain impact on the direction of his thought.[50] For the actual planning, however, he turned, as we have seen, to Byzantine and Bramantesque ideas and wedded them to the Palladian tradition.

The Rotonda as symbolic architecture

When he decided on a centrally planned design, Longhena was, of course, guided by a great variety of considerations. He had to reconcile the spatial limitations dictated by the 183 restricted site at his disposal with the request for monumentality, and his choice of a centralized plan was not independent of this aspect. He knew that a centralized church looks larger

196 S. Maria della Salute, view into dome

197 The Temple of Venus, from *Hypnerotomachia Poliphili*, 1499

137

198 S. Maria della Salute from the air. The Canal della Giudecca is on the left, the Canal Grande on the right

200 S. Maria della Salute from the air

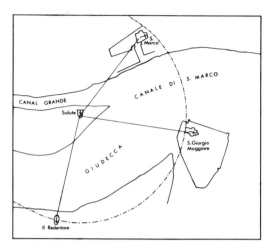

199 Plan showing relation of S. Maria della Salute with San Marco, S. Giorgio Maggiore and Il Redentore

than it is, and this was also observed by the members of the committee who mentioned in his favour (Chronology, 14): '*ricerca spaziosità e larghezza per goderla non meno al di dentro che a fuori, eguaglianza di parti, principalmente grandezza, più che ordinaria*'. The urban setting, too, almost required a centralized solution. It was most appropriate to crown the tip of the 198, island between the Canal della Giudecca and the 200 Canal Grande, near the point where the two merge into the broad Canal di S. Marco, with a compact building and a widely visible, high dome. In addition, chance had given this exposed setting a particular significance, for the new church was to rise in the centre of a semi-circle with San Marco and Palladio's S. 199 Giorgio Maggiore and Il Redentore at about equal distances on the periphery. Although we cannot prove it, it seems more than likely that Longhena was fully aware of the fact that only a centrally planned church would establish an ideal relationship to the arc of these great churches. Whether he was conscious of it or not, this intangible harmonizing of the design with the monumental buildings in the vicinity testifies to the susceptibility of a master who had his ear close to the heart-beat of his city. By introducing the conception of the centre, the radii and the periphery of the circle Longhena superimposed on the varied and picturesque sky-line of Venice the kind of urban order that was in line of descent from the town-planning ideas of the Renaissance – but the scale and extensive sweep of his scheme has a truly Baroque quality.

No practical, utilitarian or technical considerations could possibly have dictated Longhena's choice of a centralized project. But the artistic reasons, just stated, would seem amply to justify his decision. The centralized design, therefore, has the quality of a powerful symbol in so far as it must be regarded as the formal sublimation of a visionary responsiveness to the *spiritus loci*. This is, however, only one side of the story, for Longhena felt the need to suggest a distinct literary concept by the specific form of his design. The centrally planned church was the symbol of a sublime mystery for him. He expressed it himself with these words in his first report (Chronology, 9): 'The mystery contained in the dedication of this church to the Blessed Virgin made me think, with what little talent God has bestowed on me, of building the church in *forma rotonda*, i.e. in the shape of a crown.'[51]

The crown alludes to the Queen of Heaven whose help was implored in the Venetian litany which was recited during the processions at the time of plagues.[52] And the Virgin as Queen of Heaven appears twice in the building, first over the pediment of the main entrance, elevated above the host of angels,[53] and a second time on 205 the high altar under an enormous crown hanging from the vaulting. Longhena's own words seem to suggest that he also thought of the crown of stars of which the twelfth chapter of *Revelation* speaks: 'a woman clothed with the sun, and the moon under her feet, and upon her head a crown of twelve stars'. Indeed, the Queen of Heaven over the altar is an *Immacolata*; in addition, the large figure of the 201 *Immacolata* with the crown of stars raised high above the dome proves without a shadow of doubt that at some time during the construction the passage from *Revelation* had unequalled authority. The iconographical programme contains, moreover, a further important reference to the *Immacolata*: the Apostles, who were always thought of as the Virgin's companions[54] and, since St Augustine, were symbolically identified with the twelve stars of her crown. Characteristically, they appear as large figures on the scrolls of the exterior.[55] Longhena's image of the crown takes on a new dimension,

201 S. Maria della Salute, the dome

202 S. Maria della Salute, rear view from the air

139

203 S. Maria della Salute, an apse in the presbytery

204 PALLADIO. Il Redentore, Venice, the crossing

for it does not seem idle speculation to interpret his words more literally than we are nowadays inclined to do and compare the figures with the points above the rim of the Virgin's crown. 196 Inside the Rotonda, corresponding to the Apostles, over-life-size figures of Prophets are placed before the re-entrant angles of the drum, below the area where the octagon is transformed into the round of the dome. Like the sibyls in the spandrels of the entrance it was they who by their prophecies foreshadowed the coming of the reign of Grace.[56] Thus the pointed contrast between the bizarre scroll-brackets – the realm of the Apostles – and the calm silhouette of the dome of Heaven is taken up inside as a contrast between the octagonal drum – the realm of the Prophets – and the divine roundness of the domical vault. The mystery of which Longhena speaks finds its human-made echo in the perfect symmetry of the 'crown-shaped' church,[57] and even the choice and distribution of the decoration plays a part in illuminating the symbolism expressed by the structure itself.

Longhena's symbolic interpretation of the Rotonda looks back to, and is superimposed on, a very old tradition. Already at an early period

the Virgin was glorified as the Queen of Heaven and the protector of the whole universe, owing to the accretion of ideas around her burial, assumption and coronation.[58] The martyrium erected over her tomb, the heaven in which she is received, the crown of the heavenly Queen and the crown of stars of the *Immacolata*, the roundness of the universe over which she presides – all these interrelated concepts played their part in determining the centralized planning of so many sanctuaries and churches dedicated to the Virgin. The Italian Renaissance was particularly responsive to this symbolism, since Renaissance architects were attuned to the 'divine harmony' which they found expressed by the perfect geometry of centrally planned churches with dominating domes.[59] Buildings such as S. Maria della Consolazione at Todi, S. Maria di Canepanova at Pavia, the Madonna di Campagna near Verona and many others immediately come to mind. The Incoronata at Lodi retains in the name the reference to the crown. Like all these older churches, Longhena's design was deeply rooted in ancient religious symbolism. Moreover, he fully harmonized artistic considerations with the demands of the iconographic tradition.

140

Presbytery and choir

Our discussion so far has been mainly focused on the Rotonda. A closer inspection of the presbytery and choir is now necessary. A few steps separate the Rotonda from the presbytery. This domed area with apsidal endings in the transverse axis is only loosely connected with the octagon – a manner of combining isolated spaces known from Roman antiquity.[60] Adopted at an early date in northern Italy, the type – as we have seen – served Longhena as model. But in an important respect Longhena's solution 195 departs from similar spatial groupings of the Renaissance. Instead of maintaining the homogeneity of wall treatment in the main and subsidiary units, neither the form nor the articulation of his presbytery has much in common with the Rotonda, as a cursory glance at the 192 section demonstrates.

203 The giant pilasters of the apses are the principal motif in the presbytery. Between them are two tiers of windows, the lower ones in the shape of the so-called Venetian window, the upper ones rectangular and framed by columned aediculae. There is nothing in the Rotonda to prepare for this arrangement.[61] But Longhena took his cue from Palladio[62] who in 204 Il Redentore had performed a similar change of system between the nave and the centralized domed unit. In spite of the evident similarities, however, the break does not appear as radical as that carried out by Longhena. The comparison between the two sections speaks for itself and makes further analysis superfluous. Only one point requires special comment. In Il Redentore all the horizontal divisions are carried over from the nave into the domed area; in S. Maria della Salute, on the other hand, there are in this respect significant discrepancies between the Rotonda and the presbytery. The high common base of the pilasters does, in fact, rise to the height of the pedestals of the columns in the octagon; but the Venetian windows of the presbytery begin and, consequently, end at a higher level than the ambulatory windows; the broad string-course between the two tiers tallies only at the upper edge with the cima (top profile) of the entablature of the small order in the Rotonda; the pilasters of the presbytery are slightly longer than the columns of the octagon;[63] and the main entablature lies

205 S. Maria della Salute, the high altar

about 50 cm above that of the octagon. When looking at the section, it is this lack of elemen- 192 tary unification between the two spaces that one registers long before analysing its cause. It would not have been difficult for Longhena to avoid such inconsistencies. They are, of course, deliberate and must, therefore, have a special reason for which we shall try to account in a later context.

The rectangular choir is separated from the presbytery by a broad arch resting on pairs of free-standing columns;[64] between them stands the large high altar crowned by Le Cort's sculp- 205 tured group of the Queen of Heaven with the personification of Venice in devotional attitude kneeling at her feet, while Venice's counterpart, the gruesome allegory of the Plague, takes to flight. The whole area of the high altar and choir is raised one step above the level of the presbytery.[65] Once again, the articulation changes inside the choir: two small orders of pilasters are placed one above the other.[66] And once again, the horizontal divisions in the presbytery and the choir do not entirely correspond. The string-course is carried over from one unit to the next, but in the choir the base is higher than in the presbytery, and the

141

206 PALLADIO. S. Giorgio Maggiore, Venice, the high altar

windows of the upper tier are on a higher level than those of the presbytery.

206 Pairs of columns framing the high altar, and functioning as a screen through which the choir is seen, were used by Palladio in S. Giorgio Maggiore for the first time. In spite of important changes, Longhena had recourse to this solution. In the choir of S. Giorgio Maggiore Palladio switched to a small-scale system, and this is precisely what Longhena did in S. Maria della Salute. And as in S. Giorgio Maggiore, the beholder views an entirely new type of articulation behind the area of the high altar.

In making such changes from unit to unit Palladio as well as Longhena were, of course, guided by the rational consideration that rooms with different functions and of different shape and size require different architectural treatments, whereby they are given their specific and autonomous character. One may be tempted to conclude that Longhena not only used retrogressive Palladian detail, but also grouped together isolated spatial units in an additive Renaissance-like manner. This, however, would be a serious misinterpretation of his intentions. It is a misinterpretation from which the older pragmatic history of art knew no escape.

The mathematical concept

Longhena employed, in fact, a dual method of unification and integration: an objective-mathematical and a subjective-optical one. Both procedures will have to be investigated in turn. It is they and their relationship to each other that supply the key to Longhena's ideas. To begin with his objective-mathematical approach, it is hardly necessary to emphasize that his method of establishing arithmetical ratios throughout the entire building is derived from the Renaissance conception of proportion. He worked mainly with the ratios of small integers, and it may at once be said that his specific procedure reveals a thorough and intelligent study of Palladio's work, on a level that leads deep below the surface of patent influences and straight-forward borrowings of motifs.

Fortunately, we have Longhena's own quotations of measurements as a guide to the system of proportion underlying his model of S. Maria della Salute. As we have seen, not all the figures given by him were incorporated into the final design. But the measurements of his model are sufficiently illuminating to allow us to draw certain conclusions regarding the ratios he was aiming at. The key is contained in five notations of our table (b, d, h, l, n); they show that in the model the size of the diameter of the Rotonda (without ambulatory) – 60 feet – was repeated in the width of the presbytery, halved in the width of the choir (30 feet), quartered in the width of the central portal (15 feet) and divided by six in the depth of the chapels (10 feet). If one regards the width of the piers of the Rotonda as the module (5 feet),[67] the following simple series results: 5 (piers) – 10 (chapels) – 15 (entrance and ambulatory) – 30 (choir) – 60 (Rotonda and presbytery).

It is clear now that within this system of continuous ratios there was no room for an ambulatory of 12 feet width,[68] and it is reasonable to assume that in the model Longhena enlarged the width of the ambulatory not only for spatial and structural reasons, but also on grounds of proportional symmetry and coherence. Similarly, after the stage of the model, the change of the presbytery and the choir seems to have resulted as much from a maturing of Longhena's architectural conception as from the desire to integrate the entire structure fully

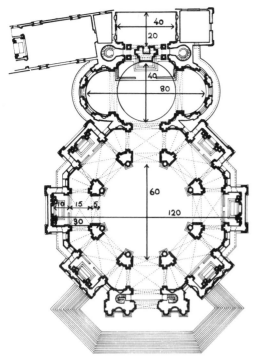

207 S. Maria della Salute, plan with principal
measurements added

into an unbroken series of arithmetical ratios.
In the model neither the 37 feet of the presbytery (g) nor the 26 feet of the choir (k) have a
place in the simple progression discussed above.
These unsatisfactory figures must be regarded
as the by-product of the integrated widths h
and l. One would expect Longhena to have
striven to bring the length as well as the width
of presbytery and choir into line with his series
of continued ratios.

207   His final result is as ingenious as it is simple.
First it should be noted that the over-all width
of the church is related to its over-all length
(a:f) as 1:1½. This was not the case as long as
he planned an over-all width of 118 feet. The
final measurements of the domed spaces are 60
(Rotonda) and 40 feet (presbytery),[69] and the
length of the choir is 20 feet; in other words,
the relation between these three spaces follows
the decreasing progression of 3:2:1. A similar
co-ordination of ratios he achieved along the
transverse axes. The series runs: 120 feet
(measured across the whole Rotonda from
chapel wall to chapel wall),[70] 80 feet (presby-

tery), and 40 feet (choir).[71] Once again, we find
a decreasing progression of 3:2:1, and the first
series to the second is related as 1:2.

One is on less firm ground as regards the
ratios intended for the height of the structure,
since Longhena himself supplied no figures. But
it is a reasonable hypothesis that he applied a
similar system of proportions to the vertical
dimensions. This view is supported by the fact
that the interior of the Rotonda is about 120 feet
high,[72] corresponding to the entire interior
width, while according to Santamaria's inscribed measurement the whole exterior height
from the street level to the top of the Immacolata
is 64 m (182·4 feet) and is, therefore, close to the
entire outside length (f). Moreover, the height
of the arcades of the octagon corresponds to the
height of the dome, and the whole area between
the arcades and the dome repeats the same
measurement. Thus the interior height is built
up of three times 40 feet,[73] but units of 30 and
60 feet are also significant.[74] The most important large unit outside seems to be once
again 40 feet. The height from the level of the
entrance to the entablature of the giant order
and from there to the top of the entablature
above the drum is twice 40 feet,[75] and the same
measure recurs in the height from the foot of
the scrolls to the top of the attic and from there
to the foot of the lantern.

The same unit appears also in the elevation
of the presbytery, first, in the height from the
floor to the entablature above the giant order
and, secondly, in the combined height of drum
and dome. This analysis could easily be carried
considerably further,[76] but I am well aware of
the danger of deception presented by a pair of
dividers in the hands of the historian. Enough
has been said to show that a unifying system of
arithmetic ratios informs the whole structure in
all three dimensions. I have confined myself to
the demonstration in detail of the all-pervading
logic of the system of proportion in the plan,
where Longhena's own measurements can be
used as a guide.

My analysis shows – I trust – that he endeavoured to bring a variety of exigencies into
line with what he regarded as a harmonic
mathematical development of his design. This
was for him a pre-condition of successful
planning. Still heeding Alberti's recommendation and warning that a building dedicated to

143

208 S. Maria della Salute, view towards the high altar

God did not permit of the slightest liberty in proportion, Longhena must have regarded an immanent mathematical structure as a *sine qua non*. And for an architect who had studied Palladio so closely, it was the musical ratios of the small integers[77] that attuned the building to universal harmony.

The optical concept

The second method of unification which Longhena employed, attunes the beholder to the optical relationships suggested by the handling of the design. A detailed description of his procedure will show clearly the extent to which he transcended the procedure of the Renaissance. On entering the church, the spectator 208 sees in his field of vision the columns and arch framing the high altar, and it is essential to note that, looking straight ahead, his view of the altar is not interfered with by any distracting features. Thus the beholder's attention is immediately directed to the spiritual centre of the church; its importance is emphasized by the framing function of a contracting series of arches, one behind the other, from the arch of the octagon to those of the ambulatory and of the altar and, concluding the vista, to the arched wall of the choir. Originally, this wall contained the apogee of the composition. Before

it was blocked up, the central window, opening to the south,[78] shed an aureole of light around the head of the Virgin on the altar.

So, in spite of the carefully calculated centralization of the octagon and in spite of the autonomy of spatial entities, unification is achieved in terms of a scenic progression. More thoroughly than the selection committee could ever have expected, Longhena had complied with the demand that the high altar should dominate the view from the entrance.

Only when the optical factor is taken into consideration can the meaning of Longhena's design be fully understood. Whichever way one looks from the centre of the Rotonda, entirely homogeneous perspective views open: an arch of the octagon, an arch of a chapel and of the mullioned window appear set one into the other, and even each altar pediment consists of a segment with the same curve. From the ideal standpoint in the centre the trapezoid sectors behind the pillars are completely invisible; Longhena evidently knew what he was doing when he refused to respond to criticism.

The question which we have been asking throughout this study, why Longhena clung so stubbornly to a design with ambulatory, despite the criticism and the overwhelming difficulties it created, can now be answered. His passionate interest in determining the beholder's field of vision was surely one of the major factors which made him concentrate on his problematical project instead of choosing one of the more traditional centrally planned designs common since the Renaissance.[79] It cannot be emphasized too strongly that no other type of plan allows only carefully integrated views to be seen; it is the plan with ambulatory that prevents the eye from wandering off and making conquests of its own.

In his first memorandum (Chronology, 9), Longhena himself pointed out that one can enjoy the full view of all the chapels and altars from the centre of the church.[80] In a precise and unexpected sense he thus fulfilled the stipulation that the altars should come into view as one walks into the church. Indeed, they are all visible from the same point from where no other distracting views are possible – apart from that toward the high altar. One may argue that the uniform 'pictures' here described are not effective unless the beholder takes up certain

191

pre-selected standpoints. This does not invalidate our conclusions: Longhena's own words prove that he had such fixed viewpoints in mind, and they recommend themselves to the sensitive spectator by the character of the design.

Once again, for his method of optical unification Longhena followed Palladio's lead. In Palladio's Redentore the hall-like nave and the centralized domed area – objectively entirely separate entities – form an optical unit for the view from the entrance.[81] The visual lines which I have drawn on the plan show that from the entrance the beholder sees a half-column coupled with a pilaster at the far end of the crossing – a precise repetition of the motif that closes the nave. Walking along the central axis, one perceives more and more of the farther supports of the dome, until, from the centre of the nave, one sees a grouping of half-columns and niches very similar to the bays at the end of the nave. That such an optical rapport was new and unusual, may be exemplified by reference to the most important and most progressive Roman structure, the Gesù. Here the unification of the nave and the domed area is accomplished by the repetition of the same order of giant pilasters around the entire building, without any of Palladio's scenic effects. The comparison demonstrates all the more clearly to what an extent Longhena was indebted to Palladio's principle of optical unification of separate spaces. But S. Maria della Salute shows that the disciple went far beyond the master in the application of this method.

It is often said that Baroque architecture owes a great deal to the contemporary stage. This assertion requires considerable modification when applied to Roman High Baroque buildings. Short of divesting the term of any precise meaning it is difficult to detect scenographic concepts in such a church as Borromini's S. Carlo alle Quattro Fontane, begun in 1634, three years after S. Maria della Salute. It can easily be demonstrated that S. Carlino was conceived in terms of a sophisticated arrangement of interlocking rhythms, which determine the poignancy of the unified spatial impression. Once the implications of this procedure have been understood, a generalization seems inescapable: on the whole, the architects of the Roman Baroque aim at dynamic spatial effects,

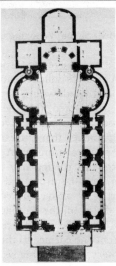

209, 210 PALLADIO. Il Redentore, Venice, view from the entrance, and plan with sight-lines added

and their structures are, therefore, intrinsically non-scenic. With Longhena, it is quite another matter: in the case of S. Maria della Salute the relation to the stage is real and specific. Here scenery appears behind scenery like wings on a stage. Instead of inviting the eye – as the Roman Baroque architects did – to glide along the walls and savour a spatial continuum, Longhena constantly determines the vistas across entire spaces.

It is also reminiscent of the stage that in S. Maria della Salute the floor rises with the perspective, first at the transition from the octagon to the presbytery and then at the junction of the presbytery and the high altar.[82] By contrast, in none of the Roman Baroque churches is the continuity of the floor space interrupted by steps.[83] In contrast also to

145

211 S. Maria della Salute. View into the dome

Roman churches, and even to those of Palladio, in the different units salient features such as entablatures and windows are not on the same level; as we have noted, they lie higher from space to space. It is such diversions from objective alignments that guarantee the impression of optical continuity. A study of the exterior makes this particularly obvious. The cornice separating the drum and dome of the presbytery is 1 m. above the cornice which crowns the drum of the Rotonda, with the result that, from a distance, there seems to be continuity from one cornice to the next.

182, 192

All the observations of this section make it apparent that the judicious grouping of almost self-contained Renaissance-like units rather than the Roman concept of dynamic unification was the pre-condition for a strictly scenographic architecture. This also explains why the architecture of the Late Baroque (which may be said roughly to begin with Carlo Fontana), in spite or just because of its classicizing tendencies, was essentially a scenographic style.

Taking Palladio's architectural principles as his starting point, Longhena evolved an alternative to the Roman Baroque. His Venetian Baroque was, in fact, the only high-class alternative Italy had to offer. It is hard to resist the temptation of seeing, on a different plane, a renewal of the contrast between Venice and Rome, Titian and Michelangelo. But just as this old contrast between *colore* and *disegno* cannot simply be stated in terms of freedom versus law, illusion versus truth, optical refinement versus representational honesty, irrationality versus intellectual sobriety, so Longhena's architecture should not simply be interpreted as arbitrary, 'painterly' and 'picturesque', as has been done from Selvatico to the recent monograph by Semenzato.[84]

Without going further into the semantic problem, I would claim that the term 'scenographic' rather than 'picturesque' helps to define Longhena's intentions. In its specific stylistic sense, the term 'picturesque' should be reserved for a late eighteenth-century trend, the promoters of which stood for asymmetry in theory and practice and were violently opposed to all Renaissance values.[85] In contrast to this purely sensorial style, Longhena's scenographic approach to architecture implies a precisely construed relationship between the object to be viewed and the viewer; space is organized with reference to him in such a way that from the right standpoint he always perceives coherent perspective images. Longhena, therefore, drew the logical consequences of the Renaissance conception of space and its corollary, central perspective.[86]

But for Longhena this subjective, scengraphic space would have lacked the quality of finality, were it not anchored in, and superimposed on, an objective mathematical space ordered according to absolute ratios and existing in its own right, independent of the beholder. It is this interweaving of the objective mathematical and the subjective optical concepts that gives the planning of S. Maria della Salute its singular character and makes the church one of the most important buildings of the entire seventeenth century. And nobody can deny that it needed a master of rare ability to be stimulated by the strictly defined requirements into conceiving a design with flawless absolute proportions beneath the scenographic surface.

Although Longhena's problem was to a certain extent still that of Brunelleschi, he had moved far from the position of the founder of modern architecture. To Brunelleschi central perspective was the intellectual vehicle for perceiving metrical harmony and order in space.[87] The metrical organization of his structures and the perception of their harmonic mathematical quality may be likened to two sides of a coin. In Longhena's case this unity was broken. The ratios of the series 5, 10, 15,

20, 40, 60, 80, 100, 120, on which his design is based, have little, if any, bearing on the perspective images revealed to the beholder inside the church. If I talk of the interweaving of the mathematical and optical concepts, it should be understood, therefore, that I mean the process of thought informing Longhena's design rather than the duality between the hidden metrical scheme and the obvious perspective effect.

A recognition of this duality invites a further reflection. It appears now that little would be said about a structure like S. Maria della Salute by only noting certain proportional relationships. All too often enquiry breaks off at that stage. But proportion as such is rarely meaningful. Our question should be: proportion for what purpose and in what context? I have attempted to supply an answer.

The colouristic concept

A study of Longhena's sophisticated handling of colour will throw more light on the relationship of mathematical to optical devices in the church. The whole interior is conceived in terms of the contrast between grey stone and whitewashed areas. Once again, the method was derived from Palladio. But it is well known that it was neither Palladio's invention nor speciality. It had, in fact, a medieval pedigree, was taken up and systematized by Brunelleschi, and, after him, resorted to by most architects who in one way or another took their cue from the Florentine Renaissance. The architects of the Roman Baroque avoided this method of differentiation, the isolating effect of which would have interfered with the dynamic rhythms of their buildings. Thus, in a very important respect Longhena was tied, via Palladio, to the tradition of the Florentine Renaissance.

It is even more important to notice where he departed from Florentine usage. Tuscan architects were consistent in applying grey stone to the structural parts and whitewash to the rest. Longhena abandoned this logical procedure. For him colour was an optical device, which enabled him to support or suppress elements of the design, thereby directing the beholder's vision. The grey stone columns of the octagon rise before the whitewashed pilaster shafts of the piers, and this gives emphasis to the homogeneous 'reading' of the eight columns. On the other hand, the pilasters of the piers and the orders of the ambulatory and the chapels form a visual unit not only because of their equal height but also by virtue of their whiteness. Thus the colouristic treatment helps to isolate the octagon from the radiating spaces and, in addition, supports the impression of scenographic entity of the latter. Yet the position is somewhat more complicated, for the capitals, entablatures and arches of the small orders are of the same dark grey stone as the columns of the Rotonda;[88] and so is the lower part of all the shafts of the small orders to the height of the pedestals of the large columns. It is these dark stone features that re-establish a tangible link between the radiating spaces and the enclosed space of the octagon.

In S. Giorgio Maggiore Palladio had placed the half-columns of grey stone against white-washed pilasters,[89] whereby he pulled the nave together as a rhythmically divided unit and contrasted its longitudinal direction with the transverse direction of the aisles and chapels; among other things he also made the lower part of the pilaster shafts of stone. Longhena's acceptance of this not entirely agreeable device – which incidentally was also dictated by obvious practical reasons – shows to what extent he relied on the older master. But he went far beyond his model and experimented with infinitely more complex colour arrangements.

The colouristic handling of the drum and dome is a case in point. In the past, purists attacked Longhena for having placed above the Composite order of the columns of the octagon a Doric order of pilasters along the walls of the drum.[90] Yet these pilasters are not meant to be a structural and logical continuation of the columns; this is indicated not only by the function of the columns as bearers of 'monuments', by the intense break between the body of the church and the drum caused by the gallery, and by the flatness of the pilasters, but, above all, by their warm beige colour which contrasts with the cool grey of the columns.[91] The beige pilasters rise before window surrounds – arches resting on pilasters – of grey stone, so that the colour relationship between the columns and the pilasters in the octagon is very nearly reversed in the drum. By virtue of their colour

211, 196

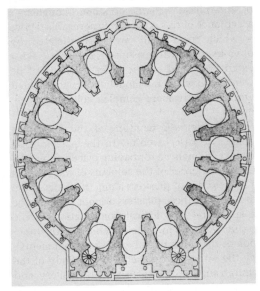

212, 213 ANTONIO DA SANGALLO. Project for S. Giovanni de' Fiorentini, Rome (from Labacco's *Libro di Architettura*, 1558)

the window surrounds establish an unexpected link with the body of the church; unexpected, because the grey stone pilasters of the drum correspond to the whitewashed pilasters of the pillars below. The reversals in the colour scheme show that Longhena wanted to treat the drum as an area existing in its own right. He, therefore, did not hesitate to introduce another 'licence': he also placed pilasters above the voids of the octagon – an unforgivable sin against the letter and the spirit of classical precepts.[92] The round vault of the dome, boldly placed upon the octagonal drum, is structurally again conceived as an isolated unit, but optically drum and dome belong together owing to the sixteen beige-coloured, band-like ribs which continue, also colouristically, the hexadecagonal articulation of the drum.[93] Finally, with the eight columns of the lantern Longhena returned to the number of supports in the lowest tier – thus resolving the contrast between the octagonal and hexadecagonal dispositions.

Colour reversals more telling than those in the Rotonda are to be found in the presbytery. 203 Here the shafts of the giant pilasters are whitewashed and what remains of the walls between the pilasters is grey stone. In other words, the entire colour scheme of the octagon has been reversed. This subjective play with colour was for Longhena primarily a means of supporting the autonomous character of adjoining spaces. In terms of visual experience, such colour reversals present the beholder with a whole range of new sensations, for one might almost say that the plastic solids (grey areas) and the flat fillings (white areas) have exchanged places. No further comment is needed to illuminate the essential contrast between the Florentine colouristic procedure which sustains a coherent metrical system and Longhena's which operates with large optical fields.[94]

A word should be added about the light. Strong contrasts of dark and brightly lit areas as a means of dramatizing architecture belong to the repertory of the Roman Baroque. Longhena's S. Maria della Salute, however, is anything but dramatic. He worked with an evenly distributed bright light using, in the wake of Renaissance procedure, individual sources of light for each spatial unit; even the trapezoid sectors of the ambulatory have their own windows. Since studied light effects would have interfered with the clear perception of scenographic views and, implicitly, of unified or contrasting colour areas, he had to make no concessions in complying with the request of even distribution of bright light throughout the entire church. Thus Longhena's approach to colour and light supplements each other. The upshot of all this is that his specific use of colour, rare or even unique at the time,[95] further obscured the mathematical harmonic structure of the design, while supporting the perception of 'pictures' defined by optical laws.

The exterior

It remains to investigate to what extent sceno-graphic principles apply to the exterior of S. Maria della Salute. Without losing sight of our main quest, some observations about the exterior may find a place here. In designing the church, Longhena had to take into considera-tion the different requirements concerning the far and the near view. This old problem of monumental building needed closest attention since the church was to rise in one of the most exposed and busiest parts of the city. The high dome and the rich silhouette were intended for the view from afar. Technical wizardry was needed to make this dome possible. Even from a fair distance the beholder cannot avoid [182, 198] noticing the 'functional' quality of the design. The scroll-brackets take the place of Gothic buttresses, and their thrust is conducted further, along the projecting side walls of the chapels. In this way Longhena created an extremely lucid system of abutments to the dome.

It has been maintained that this design closely [212, 213] followed Labacco's engravings of 1558[96] after Antonio da Sangallo's project for S. Giovanni de' Fiorentini in Rome.[97] A sober study reveals, however, that this opinion cannot be accepted without considerable reservation. In Labacco's plan the walls of the chapels which serve as abutments to the dome are placed entirely inside the containing circular wall of the church. His design is essentially a 'wall structure' with an uninterrupted sequence of subsidiary units. Longhena's church, by contrast, is a rhythmic-ally arranged 'skeleton structure' where the static problem is solved by way of an intricate system of pillars and arches.[98] In Labacco's

214 S. Maria della Salute, scrolls

project neither the dome itself and its relation to the drum nor even the triumphal arch motif of the façade show more than the vaguest analogies with S. Maria della Salute. On the other hand, one will not hesitate to agree that Longhena seems to have been attracted by the uncommon motif of the large scrolls. But while Labacco's engraving shows the traditional S-shaped scrolls and giant figures placed before them, Longhena entirely transformed the scroll-brackets, crowning them with the figures as stabilizing weights. It is the bulging circles of [214] the bracket ends with their decorative spirals that introduce the luxuriant note into an other-wise austere design.

The dome of S. Maria della Salute has an [192, 201] outer and an inner vault, the outer one consist-ing of lead over wood, in keeping with the Venetian tradition. The use of double shells for domical structures had, of course, a long pedigree: it was an ingenious Byzantine device, revived in the Renaissance, of making an effective external silhouette possible. By treat-ing the outer shell as a separate vault, only connected with the inner shell by a system of wooden supports, Longhena departed from central Italian technique as practised from Brunelleschi's dome to Michelangelo's and beyond, and returned to the structural method of San Marco. But he accepted the 'false' inner lantern, placed between the two shells and therefore not visible from outside – a type which was not rare after the dome of S. Spirito in Florence and which even Michelangelo incorporated into his model of the dome of St

149

215 S. Maria della Salute, rear view

216 PALLADIO. Il Redentore, rear view

217 PALLADIO. Church of the Zitelle, Venice

Peter's. Longhena's external lantern, an airy structure, designed for the far view, has at its base a simplified version of the scrolls on which are perched Scamozzesque obelisks instead of the figures. Continuity of design is further emphasized by the repetition of similar scroll-brackets at the lantern of the subsidiary dome as well as by the corresponding small domes 202 over both lanterns and their echo in the two domes crowning the towers.

The most striking motif of Longhena's main dome is the transformation – inside and outside – of the octagonal drum into the round. Outside, this resulted in the hiatus between drum and dome for which Michelangelo's very different dome of St Peter's established a precedent. If the design of the principal dome ingeniously blends a variety of stimuli from Byzantine, Renaissance and post-Renaissance sources, the subsidiary dome with its stilted form over a simple cylindrical drum is in direct line of descent from Byzantine-Venetian models. Palladio himself had followed this tradition and in the Redentore had placed a Byzantine dome 216 between two round belfries. It is this grouping that Longhena accepted for the south end of the 215 Salute.[99] In spite of such acceptance of the local tradition, it remains a fact that never before had the silhouette of a church been so varied and never before had such entirely different types of domes been combined into a unified 'picture'.[100] One can hardly doubt that for the panoramic view Longhena deliberately brought into play perspective effects[101] – but not scenographic principles of the kind discussed in this paper.

Quite different problems are posed by the near view which had to be designed for the approach from the Canal Grande. The area in 182 front of the church is necessarily shallow, and it was, therefore, a wise decision to make the body of the church as low as possible and, moreover, to emphasize the relationship to the human scale in the subsidiary fronts. It was also an imperative requirement to create, for the view from the Canal Grande, a rich and diversified façade of which the two conspicuous chapel 218 fronts right and left of the main entrance had to make part. Longhena treated them elaborately like small church façades in their own right; they are, in fact, clever adaptations from Palladio's small church of the Zitelle. The entire 217

218 S. Maria della Salute, front of chapel to the right of the portico

tripartite front may be compared to an altar-piece with two wings, with a decisive emphasis on the central portion. We notice that once again Longhena applied the principle of treating each part as an isolated unit; nevertheless some important horizontal divisions tally, and the small order of the chapel fronts is carried over into the large triumphal arch motif of the main entrance.

It is the centre motif that sets the seal on the entire composition. The central arch with the framing columns corresponds to the interior arches of the octagon and the width of the side bays to that of the bays in the presbytery. In addition, the small order conforms with the one inside, and the niches for statues in two tiers echo the two rows of windows in the presbytery. The façade, therefore, combines the principal motifs of the octagon and presbytery.

There is even more to this integration of outside and inside. Clearly, the façade is devised in analogy to a *frons scenae*, to which the platform over the staircase forms the proscenium. A contemporary engraving shows the central door thrown wide open.[102] It is then that the consecutive sequence of arches inside the church, contained by the triumphal arch of the *frons scenae*, conjures up a proper stage setting. It is then, too, that the triumphal concept is thrown into full relief, for encompassed by arches – projections, as it were, of the triumphal arch of the front – appears the Queen of Heaven above the altar like a distant vision.

When talking of a *frons scenae* in connection with the façade of S. Maria della Salute, I am not thinking of the contemporary Baroque theatre which, after Aleotti's Teatro Farnese at Parma (erected between 1618 and 1628), always shows a wide open proscenium arch. Longhena's architectural *frons scenae* with the perspective appearing through the central opening points to an older prototype, namely Palladio's Teatro Olimpico. One can hardly doubt that this

building had an important formative influence on Longhena's design. It is the conceptual analogy rather than the similarity of detail that proves the point.

As a rule, architects of the Renaissance designed their church façades as isolated structures without organic relationship to the interiors behind them; this resulted from the Renaissance practice of interpreting each problem on its own merits. Most Roman Baroque architects, on the other hand, endeavoured to interpret exterior and interior as an organic whole. In consequence, Baroque church façades in Rome differ widely among themselves. They have at least one characteristic in common – that they are in a variety of ways linked with their respective interiors by dynamic devices. This is as true of Cortona's SS. Martina e Luca and Borromini's S. Carlino as of Bernini's S. Andrea al Quirinale, where patently the façade reverses the inside movement and design.

Longhena, too, interpreted the relationship of inside and outside in organic terms. In his case, however, the integration is derived from perspective contrivances borrowed from the stage. Though both should be termed Baroque, the Roman and the Venetian approach are worlds apart.

It seems to us that S. Maria della Salute is the most distinguished scenographic structure of the seventeenth century – at once a pioneering work and a culmination. Imbued with Palladio's ideas, but carrying them a decisive step further, Longhena made an important contribution to European architecture. In the last decades of the seventeenth century a remarkable *volte-face* can be observed in Italy: in their search for new values many architects turned from Rome to Venice and embraced Longhena's scenographic concepts. It was then that S. Maria della Salute came into its own. The aftermath can be found not only in Italy but also in countries as far apart as Spain, Poland and England.[103]

219 Portrait of Borromini from *Opus architectonicum*

VIII FRANCESCO BORROMINI, HIS CHARACTER AND LIFE

Francesco Borromini, his Character and Life

Paradoxically, we are more fully informed about Borromini's last days than about any other period of his life. During the summer of 1667 the aging artist was plagued by a virulent fever and by alarming signs of a nervous disorder. He must have felt that he was suffering from a serious or even fatal disease because on 1 August he began to write his will. Exhausted, he spent a restless night; his condition worsened owing to his doctor's orders to keep him quiet at all cost and not to allow him candle-light after dark. During those sleepless hours he became obsessed with the idea of ending his misery and in a moment of extreme despair pierced himself with his sword. Though mortally wounded, he survived long enough, the clarity of his mind unimpaired, to sign his properly drawn up and witnessed testament, to dictate and sign a full account of his night of suffering, and to receive the Sacraments. Immediately after his death a full inventory of the contents of his house was made. All three documents – his will, the description of his suicide and the inventory – have been preserved and are an invaluable addition to the meagre facts known about him.[1]

Suicides are rare among artists and Borromini's self-destruction has given rise to some speculation. Was it the result of a sudden impulse, a crisis brought about by months of debilitating fever, or was it the last act of a melancholic with latent suicidal tendencies? Was he, in short, plagued by a physical disease or did he show signs of a mental disorder? Most students of the history of architecture prefer not to probe into these questions. But at least one art historian, Professor Hans Sedlmayr, has given them much thought.[2] Using Kretschmer's psycho-physical typology, he argues that Borromini was a 'schizothymic' type, that is a type whose schizoid condition remains on the whole within the bounds of normality; but he finds in Borromini's late work, from about 1650 onwards, indications of a growing schizophrenia,[3] in other words, of a serious patho-

logical condition, and he based his view on the exotic character of some of the master's late structures such as the domes of S. Ivo and S. Andrea delle Fratte. Moreover, he assures us that, by all accounts, Borromini's behaviour in the last decade of his life supports his assumptions.[4]

It may be true that in present-day clinical terms Borromini was a schizoid type, for in daily life he showed – as we shall see – its acknowledged characteristics: he was unsociable, eccentric, hypersensitive and easily excitable. Yet, so far as we know, neither in his youth nor his age did he ever suffer from abnormal thought processes and the kind of emotional disturbances nowadays regarded as symptomatic for the various forms of schizophrenia.[5]

Apart from imaginative and creative ideas, a successful work of architecture demands a clear mind, cogent thought and unimpaired technical abilities, and nobody will deny that Borromini displayed these qualities to the very end. It may even be claimed that the thoughtfulness of his planning outshone all his competitors. Surely, such faculties are incompatible with a progressive schizophrenia. That Borromini was a difficult, unhappy and eccentric man is another matter. He probably shared traits of character and behaviour with other eccentrics in the history of art. Thus, Professor Argan[6] has pointed out similarities between Caravaggio and Borromini and emphasized that their character limitations had a bearing both on their peculiarities and their intensity as artists. But the reciprocity between an artist's emotional life and his work remains highly debatable, and as regards Borromini I shall later offer conclusions diametrically opposed to those of Sedlmayr.

The biographers help us to form a fair idea of Borromini's appearance, personality and habits. According to Passeri[7] he was good-looking ('*di buona presenza*'), but attracted attention because he always appeared in the

220 BORROMINI. Cupola of S. Ivo della Sapienza, Rome

221 BORROMINI. Spire of S. Andrea delle Fratte, Rome

same old-fashioned Spanish garb, to which the younger Pascoli (probably informed by Borromini's nephew Bernardo) adds that he was 'tall, large-limbed, and muscular; that he had black hair and a bronze-coloured face; that he lived chaste and pure and always dressed in black'.[8] Though briefer, the well-informed Baldinucci supports this description; he calls him 'a man of tall and fine appearance with large and strong limbs' and also points out 'that he was temperate with his food and went through life chaste'.[9]

Other remarks by Baldinucci and Passeri fill in this picture: he lived entirely for his work; inordinately suspicious, he burned many of his drawings shortly before his death in order to prevent them from falling into the hands of his enemies 'who would either publish them as their own or would alter them'; he was equally jealous of his freedom and, as Baldinucci writes, 'did not want to take money so as to be able – as he said – to work exactly as he liked'.[10] Baldinucci is also explicit about his inclination to self-torment and depression: 'He normally suffered from a melancholic disposition or, as

some nearest to him said, from hypochondria; on account of this infirmity, allied to continuous speculations about his art, he found himself in the course of time so immersed in, and obsessed by, perpetual thought that he avoided as far as possible social intercourse remaining alone at home solely occupied with endlessly turning over his gloomy thoughts.'[11]

By combining all this information, we may now say that Borromini was an athletic type, a high-minded man of great integrity and self-discipline (witness his love of freedom, his disinterestedness in money and his temperance), while at the same time he was a brooding introvert, alienated from his environment, inclined to fears of persecution (his enemies are after his drawings) and perhaps disposed to exhibitionism (his dress!)[12] which may have been a compensation for his inhibitions. But later we shall see that his exhibitionism was rationally motivated.

The meeting of Borromini and Bernini, the two giants of the Roman Baroque, led to a human problem of historic proportions. Borromini could never forget their unequal rivalry and at times must have been obsessed by feelings of frustration and heart-breaking disappointment. Bernini was the scourge of his life. Both artists were born within less than a year of each other, Bernini in 1598, Borromini in 1599. Both followed initially their fathers' professions, Bernini that of a sculptor, Borromini that of the more humble stonemason.[13] But whereas Bernini was a prodigy, who soon blossomed out in all conceivable directions and won general acclaim not only as a sculptor but also as a painter, playwright, stage-designer, actor and architect, Borromini developed slowly, methodically and tenaciously towards the one goal he had set himself: to rise from the ranks and become an architect.

Bernini was clearly in line of succession of the *uomini universali* of the Renaissance, an all-round talent, an all-round man, who would have found Alberti's whole-hearted approval. Borromini represented a different, newer tradition: he belonged to the brotherhood of professionals coming down from Antonio da Sangallo through Vignola, Giacomo della Porta and Maderno – all architects associated with St Peter's. Small wonder that Borromini regarded Bernini as an amateur in the field in which he himself excelled by training and vocation. The professional, who aimed at some clearly circumscribed objectives, versus the universally endowed, whose genius acknowledged no limitations: this lies at the bottom of Borromini's antagonism to Bernini. In this light, Borromini typifies or at least foreshadows the rigorous mould of modern man, while Bernini belongs to or at least recalls the humanist tradition of past Renaissance culture.

Both were young men in their early twenties, when Urban VIII ascended the papal throne in 1623. Bernini, firmly established as the most prodigious talent Rome had seen after Michelangelo's death, was immediately given dazzling papal commissions which assured a brilliant career. At the same time, unknown to the public, Borromini, still as Francesco Castelli – his family name – discharged his lowly duties as stonecarver and stonemason in St Peter's.[14]

Bernini, despite his unparalleled success, despite his many gifts, his wide interests, his close connection with the great and the learned, remained at heart a simple, straightforward man, untroubled by frustrating problems. He had the egotism, self-confidence, pretensions and virtues of the aspiring bourgeois. He is easily decipherable. We would expect from such a man orthodox devotion, a craving for social recognition and respectability and an enjoyment of conviviality. Before his marriage an ardent lover, he later became an exemplary husband and father, who in time accumulated considerable wealth and lived nobly with his large family in a grand palace, a centre of social intercourse.

In all and every respect Borromini was the precise opposite. A shy and misanthropic recluse, beset by psychological complexities, this eternal bachelor never knew the love or companionship of women; and there are indications that he had eccentric religious ideas.[15] He lived modestly near S. Giovanni de'Fiorentini[16] with only one assistant and a serving woman. According to the inventory his rooms were sparsely furnished, but he was an avid collector of all sorts of objects which were pressed into drawers and piled up on tables and shelves.[17] Also crammed on shelves and into drawers he kept his remarkably large library of almost a thousand volumes.[18] Only a relatively small part of this number can have been concerned with architecture and allied subjects such as geometry and perspective.[19] It is tantalizing that not a single title is mentioned in the inventory. But one can hardly be mistaken in assuming that a large part of the library consisted of books on science, philosophy and theology.[20] Passeri calls Borromini a man of erudition and intelligence possessing thorough knowledge. And his bibliomania is attested to by Don Camillo Pamfili's attorney ('*procuratore*') who complained that the architect, instead of attending to the work in S. Agnese, 'browsed in the bookshops in Piazza Navona without entering the building'.[21]

What else can we learn from the inventory? The clothes he left were few; his plate was mostly tin; his kitchen almost bare. He obviously spent little time and money on his person and his comforts. Moreover, the inventory reveals that the objects assembled in his house were of specific and very personal relevance to him. A number of items makes this quite clear. There were two portraits of Innocent X, the only Pope who took a liking to Borromini and singled him out as his favoured architect; there was a portrait of his influential patron and friend, Virgilio Spada, to whom Borromini owed perhaps more than to anyone else. These portraits were mementos of gratitude, signs of the devotion Borromini felt for those men. There was the plaster cast of a bust of Michelangelo bearing witness to the great veneration Borromini had for him whom he regarded as the 'Prince of Architects',[22] and, finally, there was a plaster cast of a bust of Seneca. Why Seneca? Before I attempt an answer, a few words must be said about some of the stipulations of the testament.

The testament too bears witness to Borromini's feelings of gratitude, affection and forethought towards the few people within his narrow circle; but one is mainly struck by a number of strange provisions. He requested to be buried in S. Giovanni de' Fiorentini in the tomb of his beloved master Carlo Maderno and left a fairly large sum of money to Carlo's daughter Giovanna for the inconvenience caused to her by this request.[23] Among generous legacies to the priests of S. Giovanni de' Fiorentini, there was also a gift of a hundred large candles, but if his body (or, I suppose, rather coffin) were exhibited in the church, the candles should be presented to another church.[24] He provided for his assistant, Francesco Massari 'in recognition of his great troubles and the work done for him'.[25] (In a sense, Massari was responsible for Borromini's death, because it was Massari who refused to light candles during the fateful night.) Omitting many other legacies, I only mention that he made his nephew, Bernardo, son of his brother Domenico Castelli,[26] his universal heir, but attached the condition that he marry Giovanna Maderno's daughter, Carlo's granddaughter.[27] As he himself longed to be united in death with his master, so he fervently wished to see their closest descendants united in life. One may regard this as an obsessive idea, an idea resulting from a somewhat morbid sensibility. I believe, however, that there is more to it.

In this strange life everything was meaningful and to the very end his reasoning found expression in actions of symbolic import. We recall his Spanish dress. In 1548 the duchy of Milan had become a Spanish enclave in Italy[28] and thus during the most impressionable years

of his life – the years in Milan before he was twenty – Borromini was exposed to strong Spanish influence and his Spanish attachment must have gone deep. I believe that he dressed Spanish as a symbolic expression of his convictions and that his dress was implicitly a protest against the French orientated society and politics in Urban VIII's Rome[29] as well as against the anti-Spanish bias of the Roman public.[30] Not by chance did his first independent commission, S. Carlo alle Quattro Fontane, come from Spanish Discalzed Trinitarians; not by chance was he commissioned to rebuild the Palazzo di Spagna, the Spanish ambassador's residence; not by chance were some of his best friends Spaniards and people with Spanish inclinations;[31] and not by chance did he come into his own under Innocent X whose policy and taste tended towards Spain rather than France.

It has been suggested that King Philip II's 'fondness for wearing black was motivated by astrological considerations',[32] an appropriate colour for the saturnine temperament. Similarly, I have little doubt that Borromini wore black because he regarded himself as a child of Saturn: his melancholy and associated temperamental qualities such as sensitivity, moodiness, eccentricity, his yearning for contemplation and solitude – all prove it.[33]

This is the moment to return to Seneca's bust. Seneca stands for sublime contemplation and stoic wisdom, for temperance and purity, for the freedom of the spirit and the tranquillity and constancy of the soul in face of the ills of the world and the hazards of blind Fortune. Both the saturnine temperament and the stoic meet in their focus on contemplation. But beyond this, for Borromini Seneca's philosophy seems to have been a sane corrective of, and an antidote to, the sinister gifts of Saturn. It is worth mentioning that Seneca's message had always fascinated the post-Antique world,[34] particularly because Christian connotations were soon interpreted into his philosophy. Borromini's interest in Seneca is in line of succession to the stoic revival brought about by Justus Lipsius[35] and his enthusiasm may have been kindled by the Jesuits who, throughout the seventeenth century, published treatises entitled *Seneca Christianus*.[36]

We now understand certain contradictions

in the texts of Borromini's biographers who report the dark sides of his character and at the same time praise his stoic qualities, his 'strong mind full of lofty and noble concepts', his healthy temperament and the nobility of his conduct, his temperance and chastity, and his disinterestedness in worldly treasures; Passeri even goes so far as to talk of his solitary life lived in freedom and with tranquillity of mind[37] – a passage that could come straight out of Seneca. We can now also understand why Bernini once likened Borromini to a *'buon Heretico'*.[38]

Of course, throughout his life Borromini's daily contact with his environment was beset with conflicts. Passeri and Baldinucci report – and we have no reason to disbelieve them – that the young stonemason in St Peter's, instead of sharing his leisure hours with his fellow-workmen, spent his lunch and dinner time in solitude making many detailed drawings of the church,[39] a practice that can hardly have endeared him to his more sociable companions but that recommended him to his kinsman Carlo Maderno, the architect in charge of the building.[40] The correctness of the literary tradition is confirmed by a few surviving drawings made by Borromini after details of the architectural orders in St Peter's (now in the Albertina, Vienna). We do not know the precise date of these studies,[41] but we do know that Maderno used Borromini as draughtsman for the dome of S. Andrea della Valle as early as 1622;[42] and in 1623–24 we find him making drawings for Maderno in St Peter's,[43] an activity not normally within the purview of a *scarpellino* or *intagliatore*, the two denominations interchangeably given to Borromini in the documents of the 1620s. In time Maderno advanced him to what we would nowadays call chief designer both for the work in St Peter's and the Palazzo Barberini.[44] According to Baglione,[45] Borromini supervised (*soprintendeva*) Maderno's projects for the palace, which was in the planning stage between 1625 and 1627 and began in 1628.[46] In other words, in spite of his continual activity as a stonemason, in 1627/8 Borromini must have felt well on the way to being approved as a professional architect, at least in the eyes of the man who meant more to him than anyone else.

Meanwhile a situation arose in St Peter's of far-reaching consequences for the history of art and for Borromini in particular. In the summer of 1624 Urban VIII conferred the commission for the Baldacchino upon Bernini. Maderno was still vigorously alive and should have designed this work of supreme importance in the course of his duties as 'Architect to St Peter's'. So far as I can see, it has never been stated that the Pope's action constituted a declaration of no confidence in the ability of the aged master. Though Maderno's reaction is not recorded, he must have been deeply hurt; nor do we know what Borromini's feelings were. But since he identified himself completely with Maderno's interests, we may safely assume that he regarded Bernini as the prime cause of the unpardonable slight. I believe that the aversion he took to Bernini dates back to this early event. But more was to come.

In 1627 Borromini was assigned some modest mason's work for the Baldacchino,[47] his first direct involvement in one of Bernini's enterprises; and this happened at the precise moment when – as we have seen – Borromini must have felt well on the way to holding his life's ambition in his grasp. At that time and for the next few years Borromini had to eat his pride and live silently with the conviction of being more than a match for the bustling intruder. A symbolic act was his only means to remonstrate: he changed his name. Significantly, Francesco Castello appears as Francesco Borromino fairly regularly in the documents from April 1628 onwards. Critics have always been mystified by this step,[48] but we now know that the name 'Boromino' belonged to his mother's family and that the combination 'Castelli-Boromino' was occasionally used. Borromini himself followed this custom once in 1619, probably immediately after his arrival in Rome. But from then on and through the 1620s he remained Francesco Castelli. It seems to me that in 1628 the name Boromino attracted him, first, because it recalled the great Milanese S. Carlo Borromeo and his cousin, Archbishop Federico, the outstanding figures in Milan's Counter-Reformatory period and almost synonyms for the Milan he had been living in;[49] and, second, because of the strange alliteration 'Boromino-Bernino'. The name Boromino may have meant to him something like 'Bernini's rival come from the North'. All this is, of course, entirely hypothetical, but would tally with Borromini's craving for symbolization as I have described it before. In any case, his specific character traits exclude the possibility that he assumed the name on utilitarian grounds.[50]

Maderno died on 30 January 1629 and Bernini succeeded him both as Architect to St Peter's and to the Palazzo Barberini. He was obviously glad to have Borromini at his side, a gifted designer and trained technician who, moreover, was fully conversant with Maderno's intentions. Passeri's account of the situation that arose is so circumstantial that we must assume information had reached him directly or indirectly from Borromini. Bernini, we are told, made Borromini generous promises, all of which he broke. Passeri adds that Bernini cunningly played mason's work in St Peter's into the hands of a certain Antonio Radi (whom he mistakenly calls Borromini's brother-in-law),[51] implying that by robbing Borromini of regular wages Bernini intended to tie him permanently to his personal service. The charge is fantastic, for Bernini used Radi as early as 1624 in S. Bibiana,[52] and Radi and Borromini worked together on many occasions before Bernini took command and continued working together after Bernini's appointment.[53] Borromini, Passeri carries on, became belatedly aware of Bernini's double-dealing and of Radi's being a party to it and broke with both of them.[54] Only Borromini's brooding imagination can have construed this story: the documents prove that it is untrue.

In a MS *Life* of Borromini in the Biblioteca Nazionale in Florence, (usually wrongly regarded as a draft by Baldinucci, but I have good reasons to believe from the pen of Borromini's nephew Bernardo and therefore a reliable guide to Borromini's views), we are informed that Bernini, who was absolutely inexperienced as an architect, attended to his sculpture and as regards architecture left all the work to Borromini.[55] This insinuation, equally contradicted by the documents, throws a clear light on Borromini's biased conception of the part he played in the collaboration with Bernini during the years 1629 to 1632.

Yet there is a grain of truth in all this. Although Borromini continued, together with Radi and others, to carry out some mason's work in the Vatican and the Palazzo Barberini until the summer of 1632, Bernini used him more and more as architectural draughtsman from the late 1620s onwards.[56] In a document of 10 February 1631 Borromini appears for the first time as *assistente del architetto* in the Palazzo Barberini,[57] and other documents mention that between April 1631 and January 1633 he made large drawings of all the details of the crowning portion of the Baldacchino.[58] It has always been acknowledged that Bernini was thoroughly impressed by his unusual assistant; but, on the other hand, all our evidence goes to show that he remained firmly in charge and allowed Borromini only a strictly limited amount of freedom.

On 15 September 1632 Borromini was appointed 'Architect to the Sapienza', the later University, for life. There is good reason to accept the tradition that Bernini himself recommended him for the vacant post:[59] he had apparently set his mind on 'lauding away' his uncomfortable collaborator at the first suitable occasion. Shortly after, Borromini's negotiations with the Procurator General of the monastery of S. Carlo alle Quattro Fontane (S. Carlino) must have begun, for the first stone of the dormitory was laid on 15 July 1634.[60]

At last Borromini had achieved the dream of his life. His ingenious and unorthodox handling of the almost insoluble problems presented by the monastery and church of S. Carlino immediately gave his name a special aura. Soon other commissions followed, and in 1637, four years before the church of S. Carlino was finished, he won the competition, open to architects from all over Italy, for the vast complex of the Oratory of St Philip Neri.[61] Fortunately, Borromini's friend and patron, Virgilio Spada, a member of the Congregation, was constantly at the architect's side, and Borromini also had Spada's support in giving a full account of his plans and ideas. Spada acted as perhaps the first 'ghost-writer' for an architect and did so with eloquence and skill, but the work, usually quoted as *Opus architectonicum Equitis Francisci Borromini*, was not published until 1725.[62]

In 1644 Virgilio Spada had to resign from the Congregation because Innocent X appointed him papal Almoner (*elemosiniere segreto*).[63] As long as Spada was in charge of the building activities, Borromini's affairs went comparatively well, but reading the *Opus architec-*

224, 225

tonicum one gains the impression that his relationship to the Fathers had been an uneasy one throughout. In the Preface the 'benign readers' are asked 'to consider that I had to serve a Congregation consisting of such timid minds that I was tied hand and foot as far as decoration goes and in consequence I often had to obey their wishes rather than the demands of art.' These 'timid minds' kept a sharp eye on the accounts and insisted on strictest economy: 'and if I exceeded somewhere even by a little the law laid down for me, I had to listen to complaints for quite some time'.[64] After Spada's exit an open break was a foregone conclusion. In 1650 Borromini resigned his office as 'Architect to the Congregation'.[65]

The history of other commissions shows that the hypersensitive master could only co-operate with congenial patrons. In S. Carlo alle Quattro Fontane he had found friendly response from the Procurator General and from such devoted friends as the Marchese de Castel-Rodrigo. Like the monastery and church of S. Carlino, the restoration of the Lateran Basilica – one of Borromini's greatest tasks entrusted to him by Innocent X in 1646[66] – was carried out with the greatest precision and speed, because Virgilio Spada had been appointed super-intendent[67] and acted as moderator and arbiter.[68] The construction of S. Agnese in Piazza Navona made rapid progress between August 1653 and December 1654, that is, from the moment Borromini assumed responsibility to the fatal illness of Innocent X, whom the architect venerated profoundly. The Pope himself had given Borromini his full support. After his death on 7 January 1655 events took a catastrophic turn.[69] The meddlesome Donna Olimpia, the Pope's sister-in-law, who had always been hostile to Borromini, immediately took charge and showed her hand, but soon requested her son, Don Camillo Pamfili, to act as superintendent to the building.[70] In an atmosphere of mutual dislike and distrust Borromini grew desultory and despondent, Don Camillo exasperated, the workmen restive. They grumbled about his irresolute directives. In January 1657, the 'Procurator to the Fabric' reported that it was 'over a month that Borromini had not come and given orders'. 'He does not work' – we are told – 'and others get the blame'.[71]

(margin notes: 222, 223; 15, 16)

Everyone requested Borromini's dismissal. The Congregation turned for advice to Cardinal Imperiali, Pope Alexander VII's Treasurer. His answer of 3 February 1657 was devastating: he recommended dismissal because it seemed impossible to finish the building so long as it was in the hands of that architect; he also expressed admiration for Don Camillo's endless patience with Borromini, for the nature of that man was intractable.[72] This was the last straw. Four days later 'Borromini was dismissed since it was impossible to continue with him because of his difficult, obstinate nature'.[73]

Adversity in human relationships, lack of sympathy and understanding transformed the most alert, the most concentrated, scrupulous and punctilious expert into an inconsistent, bewildered, sloppy and even lazy bungler.[74] Or so it seems.[75] His intractable nature may well have resulted from a conscious endeavour to tame his unhappy temperament and triumph over humiliation. To keep aloof was the lesson he had learned from Seneca. His visit to the bookshops of Piazza Navona, recorded at the time when the affairs of S. Agnese went from bad to worse, may well be interpreted as a symbolic gesture of defiance: in full view of the men on the building, he displayed openly the spirit of stoic tranquillity. The crisis at S. Agnese, which so dramatically exposed Borromini's isolation and psychological problems, had been long in preparation. In the eyes of his detractors his character must have appeared in a particularly unfavourable light during the affair of Bernini's ill-fated bell-towers of St Peter's. Borromini's old grievances against Bernini were rekindled by his rival's technical miscalculation which endangered Maderno's façade. Infuriated also by the assertion of the Bernini party that Maderno's foundations were not as solid as had been expected, Borromini rose in his master's defence. In June 1645 at a meeting of the Congregation of the fabric of St Peter's he lashed out mercilessly against Bernini. His attack was courageous, but it was not good diplomacy. It earned him additional black marks for ingratitude and jealousy.[76] A few years later, an unfortunate incident in S. Giovanni in Laterano threw a most unfavour-able light on his irascible temperament. In December 1649, while building in the Basilica was proceeding at a rapid pace, he surprised a

222 BORROMINI. St John Lateran, Rome, nave

man 'in flagranti damaging some ornament and in particular smashing up, spitting on and disfiguring some slabs of stone'. He had the man beaten up so severely by his workmen that he died the same day. In his defence Borromini pleaded 'his fatigue sustained in the construction of the noble Basilica' and craved the Pope's pardon which he obtained.[77]

Moreover, toward the middle of the century the classical faction in Rome gathered strength and as more and more of Borromini's buildings were exposed to the public eye – most notably S. Carlino, the Oratory of St. Philip Neri and much of S. Ivo – he encountered increasing opposition. The time was not far when Bellori, the all-powerful mouthpiece of the classicists, described S. Carlino as an 'ugly and deformed building' and its builder as 'a most ignorant gotico and a corruptor of architecture'.[78]

There are indications that the growing hostility, real and imaginary, directed against him, moved Borromini to organize his defence.

37, 38

223 BORROMINI. St John Lateran, detail of aisle

224 BORROMINI. S. Carlo alle Quattro Fontane,
Rome, view into the dome

Not long before Innocent X's death Fra Giovanni
di S. Bonaventura, the Procurator General of
the monastery of S. Carlo alle Quattro Fontane,
wrote a history of the structure and no one who
reads it attentively can fail to discover the
poignant self-defence which Borromini voiced
through Fra Giovanni's words.[79] I will mention
only the following points: the high praise of
that most excellent architect, Carlo Maderno,
whose example his relative had followed in S.
Carlino;[80] the extreme cheapness of this as well
as all his other structures which proves those
wrong who maintain 'that his buildings are
beautiful but too expensive'; the universal
admiration for S. Carlino expressed by Germans,
Flemings, French, Italians, Spaniards and even
Indians, who continuously trouble Borromini
with requests for the design;[81] his extraordinary
disinterested liberality ('*senza interesse nessu-*
no')[82] brought to bear upon all his works; the
conviction of the *conoscenti* that there is no
better architect than he ('no person of real
understanding intent on building is satisfied
unless he has Signor Francesco as architect');[83]
the circumstantial description of how he had

won the commission of the Oratory of St Philip
Neri by his own valour and not as a result of
recommendations by influential people; his
election by Innocent X for the rebuilding of S.
Giovanni in Laterano in preference to all other
Roman architects; and finally the admiration
for his planning skill and for his professional
expertise; 'he himself' – says the text – 'directs
the bricklayer's trowel, teaches the stucco-
worker how to use his knife, the carpenter his
saw, the stonemason his punch, the slate-
worker his hammer and the blacksmith his
rasp' and he shows all these artisans how to
work better and faster.[84] All these as well as
other arguments attest to the polemical nature
of the text: the Procurator General must have
incorporated into it the gist of Borromini's
comments.

Turning now to the *Opus architectonicum*,
written in close collaboration between Borromini and Virgilio Spada: its text was written in
1648[85] and at that time was probably intended
as a justification of the master's procedure in
order to counter mounting difficulties. But the
manuscript remained lying about for years.
Significantly, Borromini returned to it less than
a year before his dismissal from S. Agnese. He
dated the dedication to his faithful friend and
patron, the Marchese de Castel-Rodrigo, 10 May
1656, a sure sign that he wanted to bring out
the work at this precarious moment.[86]

I therefore submit that Borromini at a critical
time in his career, when hostile opposition to
both his character and his architecture was
rapidly growing, decided to parry the blows
aimed at his integrity as a man and as an artist
by promoting two expert publications while he
still enjoyed Innocent X's protection and
patronage. The one, a eulogy written by a quasi-
neutral patron dedicated to Borromini, would
have countered in general terms all the objections raised against him; the other, the most
detailed and most professional analysis made
up to that time of a single building, written in
the first person, might have silenced the
envious whispering campaigns of colleagues
and moreover, convinced amateurs of his
outstanding qualifications.

I further submit that it was the tragedy of
February 1657 that made him abandon these
projects. By then they must have appeared to
him entirely futile. More than ever he retired

225 BORROMINI. S. Carlo alle Quattro Fontane, interior looking towards the altar

226 BORROMINI. Oratory of St Philip Neri, Rome, façade

227 BORROMINI. Oratory of St Philip Neri, section at right angles to the façade showing the oratory, cortile, sacristy and arcade of the garden

into himself and presented to the world the image of the solitary recluse so well described by Baldinucci.

Both texts, that of the *Opus* and to a lesser extent that of the story of S. Carlino open up unparalleled insights into Borromini's mind. The *Opus* is focused on a penetrating analysis of purpose and needs, taking into account even the minutest eventualities. We are, for instance, informed of a novel system of making windows burglar proof; or of the elaborate, modern sanitary installations and the precautions taken to protect the silken and brocaded ceremonial robes from humidity.

226–
228
As one reads the *Opus*, one discovers that his approach to the vast project of St Philip Neri was unencumbered by theoretical considerations and speculations. And the finished work makes it equally evident that he transcended the empirical programme by artistic sublimation of a boldness rare in the annals of architectural history. He himself referred to this process of artistic sublimation by such expressions as '*bizzaria*', '*scherzo*', '*disegno vago*' and '*fantasticare*',[87] by which he meant not simply an uncontrolled wandering of the imagination, an easy and wilful play with forms, but rather the thoughtful elaboration of daring concepts, the growth of which can often be followed in the fascinating corpus of his surviving drawings. '*Fantasticare*' implied the break with

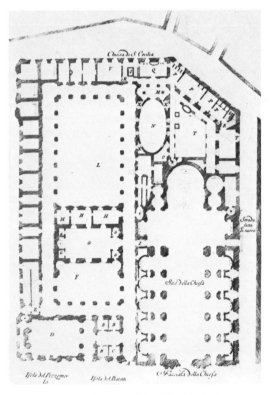

228 BORROMINI. Oratory of St Philip Neri, plan

229 BORROMINI. Collegio di Propaganda Fide

230 BORROMINI. S. Carlo alle Quattro Fontane, façade

tradition, the investigation of new and un-charted artistic solutions, and he referred to Michelangelo as witness for the insight that 'one can gather only late the fruits of one's toil'.[88] His relentless empiricism conjoined with his independence of judgment and his un-fettered freedom of invention set him apart from all the other architects of his time. These traits are the hall-marks not only of his great-ness but also of his modernity. Thus his work would appear as a projection of the positive aspects of his character or perhaps as a reversal of its darker sides: in his work self-assurance has conquered diffidence, self-discipline des-pondency, rationality obsession.[89]

His last ten years, from the dismissal at S. Agnese to his death in 1667, were extremely busy ones and some of his most remarkable
229 designs such as the façades of the Collegio di
230 Propaganda Fide and of S. Carlino and the
221 campanile and dome of S. Andrea delle Fratte

belong to this period. This burst of energy and creativity may seem unexpected, but I think that the complexity of his character makes it intelligible. He purged himself of the humilia-tion of 1657 by an extraordinary release of all his creative faculties. The late works resolved profound repressions; they were the catharsis after the abyss. The drama and density of these structures recall the works of that other great solitary, Michelangelo, Borromini's idol. It was only Borromini who resuscitated late in life Michelangelo's proverbial *terribilità*, tempered by a more restless imagination.

In paying homage to his genius and the towering greatness of his work today, three hundred years after his death and after a long period of oblivion, I am reminded of the prophetic words of the Procurator General of S. Carlino: '*Il tempo darà notizia per li effeti della Valentia del suo sapere et scienza*' ('Time will show the results of the excellence of his learning and the precision of his knowledge').

Appendix I

The Life of Borromini in the Codex Magliabechiano II II 110 (folios 170r–171v), Biblioteca Nazionale, Florence

Following Hempel in his *Borromini* (1924, p. 6, note 1) critics have almost unanimously accepted this *Life* as an early draft by Baldinucci; see J. Hess in his Passeri edition, p. 361, note 2; Ugo Donati, *Artisti ticinesi a Roma*, Bellinzona, 1942, p. 195, note 14; A. Blunt, in *Journal of the Warburg and Courtauld Institutes*, XXI, 1958, p. 264; J. Schlosser Magnino, *La letteratura artistica*, Florence-Vienna, 1964, p. 473. Portoghesi writes on p. 37 of his *Borromini*, 1964, *'non sicuramente autografa'*, but on p. 99 discusses the *Vita* as Baldinucci's *'prima redazione certamente anteriore al 1680'*. So far as I can see only Sergio Samek Ludovici in the Introduction to his edition of Baldinucci's *Vita di Bernini*, Milan, 1948, p. 22, noticed that the Magliabechiano *Vita* must have been written by 'one of Borromini's admirers'.

The MS text has never been critically examined. The following points may help to clarify its relationship to Baldinucci.

1 The text is headed (f. 170r): *'Adi 10 Giugnio 1685 Nottitia'*. This is the date when the present text was written, but it might be argued that it need not necessarily be the date of its composition.

2 The handwriting is not Baldinucci's. Again, one can maintain that this is no final argument against Baldinucci's authorship because the handwriting may be that of a scribe or of a later copyist.

3 There cannot be any doubt about the close connection between the MS text and Baldinucci's printed *Vita*. We have therefore to test three possibilities: whether the MS *Life* can be a draft by Baldinucci; whether it can have been written by someone who had access to Baldinucci's *Vita* before it was published, for in 1685 it had not yet appeared in print; or, conversely, whether Baldinucci based his own *Vita* of Borromini to a large extent on this text.

4 The MS *Life* must date from after 1680 because Bernini's death (28 November 1680) is mentioned. Thus even if the text were a copy of another, perhaps older MS the four and a half years between 28 November 1680 and 10 June 1685 is the maximum span of time during which it can have been written. This incontestable fact is crucial because the post-1680 date of the text excludes Baldinucci's authorship. The manuscript of his *Vita del Cavaliere Gio. Lorenzo Bernino* was ready for the press as early as 14 October 1681 (date when the MS reached the Jesuit Vicar General for approbation). This work was written with a strong pro-Berninesque bias and contains some remarks extremely critical of Borromini (see notes 54, 76). The author of the Magliabechiano text, by contrast, was a dedicated partisan of Borromini's cause and described the relationship of the two men from a most tendentious Borrominesque point of view (see notes 44, 55). It is impossible for Baldinucci to have written both *Vitae* at the same time; nor can he have written the Magliabechiano text – if we accept the date 1685 as that of the composition – within three years of the publication of Bernini's *Life*. There was certainly no *volte-face* of his opinions between the end of 1681 and the summer of 1685 (see below, **6**).

5 If Baldinucci's printed *Vita* of Borromini was written in about 1680, as is usually maintained following O. Pollak's statement in Thieme-Becker, or even if it was written between 1681 and 1685 the author of the Magliabechiano *Vita* would have used and transformed Baldinucci's manuscript. In order to resolve this problem an attempt must be made to establish a more correct date for Baldinucci's *Vita* of Borromini. Baldinucci began writing the *Notizie* before the death of Cardinal Leopoldo de' Medici (d. 1675); he interrupted the work while he was writing the *Life* of Bernini (1681) and continued *'a buon passi'* after this book was finished (see Baldinucci's *Life* written by his son Francesco Saverio, published by S. Samek Ludovici, *op. cit.*, pp. 47, 52). The first volume of the *Notizie* appeared in 1681, the second in 1686, the fourth in 1688; the remaining three volumes appeared posthumously: the fifth in 1702 and the third and sixth (with Borromini's *Life*) together in 1728. In other words, at the time of Baldinucci's death (1696) the material of three volumes was not quite ready for the press. Baldinucci worked on these volumes during the last decade of his life and we can therefore be fairly certain that Borromini's *Vita* dates from this late period. (Since Baldinucci refers in his *Life* of Borromini to his book on Bernini, which had appeared in 1682, the old date 'about 1680' is in any case untenable.)

6 If my contention that Baldinucci did not write his *Life* of Borromini until the end of the 1680s is correct, it must have been Baldinucci who based his text on that of the Magliabechiano *Vita*. Baldinucci, I suggest, made use of the factual material in it, but purified it of its anti-Bernini bias and incorporated into his *Vita* some criticism of Borromini, though considerably less than in Bernini's *Vita* of 1682.

7 Now that my revised dating of both *Vitae* suggests what I believe to be the correct relationship between the two texts much else falls into place. Baldinucci's *Vita* contains a great many intimate details – considerably more than Passeri's, although the latter lived in Rome while Baldinucci lived in Florence, which must have come to him from a source close to Borromini. The assumption that this source was the Magliabechiano *Vita* is supported by what we know about Baldinucci's working procedure. He assembled much of his material by personal enquiry. The Magliabechiano codex contains the outline of a *questionnaire* sent by Baldinucci to living artists, their friends, relatives and pupils; it also contains some of their answers followed by Baldinucci's own annotations (see Ludovici, *op. cit.*, p. 22; Cesare D'Onofrio, in *Palatino*, X, 1966, p. 204). Thus we find in the codex the *Life* of Buontalenti written by Gherardo Silvani (who was married to one of Buontalenti's grand-daughters) in response to Baldinucci's request (V. Giovannozzi, in *Rivista d'Arte*, XIV, 1932, pp. 505–24). Again, for his *Vita* of Silvani, who had died in 1673, Baldinucci used the *Life* written by Giovanni di Francesco Sini (*c*. 1645) that was brought up-to-date, evidently for Baldinucci, by Pier Francesco Silvani (R. Linnenkamp, in *Riv. d'Arte*, XXXIII, 1958, pp. 73–111). Moreover, for his *Life* of Bernini Baldinucci made

ample use of the material sent to him upon his request by Bernini's son, Domenico (D'Onofrio, *op. cit.*, p. 202 ff., believes that Domenico sent his complete manuscript which he himself did not publish until 1713).

Paralleling these cases, the Magliabechiano *Life* of Borromini would seem to be a statement elicited by Baldinucci from a person who had known Borromini intimately. Seen in this light, the heading of the text '*Adi 10 Giugno 1685 Nottitia*' means exactly what it says, namely, a report written on that day. In all likelihood it was written in answer to Baldinucci's request, at a moment when the latter felt that the time had come to start preparing the material for the last volume.

The author of the Magliabechiano *Vita* was not a man of the pen. Baldinucci was an excellent stylist and even in a draft would not have sunk to a level that occasionally is somewhat illiterate. As an example of Baldinucci's transformation compare the first sentence:

Magliabechiano *Vita*	Baldinucci's *Vita*
Il Sig.re Francesco Boromino nacque l'anno 1599 nella terra di Bissone al lago di Lugano diocese di Como il suo padre si chiamava il Sig.re Gio. Domenico Castelli di detto locho. Stava al servitio di Architett. a delli Sig.ri Visconti di Milano.	Francesco Borromino, figliuolo di Gio. Domenico Castelli Borromino, che si esercitò in cose d'architettura per la nobil famiglia de' Visconti, ebbe i suoi natali nella terra di Bissone al Lago di Lugano nella Diocesi di Como.

8 Who was the author of the Magliabechiano *Vita*? Before answering this question, it should be mentioned that in J. Hess's view the author – for Hess, Baldinucci – had used a MS text of Passeri's *Life* of Borromini (see *Wiener Jahrbuch für Kunstgeschichte*, V, 1928, p. 47, note 244 and Passeri, ed. Hess, p. 361, note 2). If the entire passages, of which Hess juxtaposes brief extracts, are compared, his demonstration is not convincing. It seems to me that superficial similarities are due to the fact that both authors had information from the same source: Borromini.

It seems not unlikely that the Magliabechiano *Vita* enjoyed a reputation of being especially well informed. The editor of the first printed Passeri edition of 1772, Gio. Lodovico Bianconi, may have used it. He replaced the description of Borromini's clothing habits in Passeri's MS text (as printed by Hess, see note 7) by the remark that Borromini always went about *'in abito antico'* (p. 389), which may have been derived from Magliabechiano fol. 171v.

In 1685 Baldinucci could not ask Borromini, eighteen years after his death, for autobiographical material. I venture to suggest that Baldinucci did the next best thing and turned to Borromini's nephew Bernardo. In any case, the writer not only had an intimate knowledge of correct facts (used by Baldinucci, see notes 17, 25, 26), but also wrote down what seem to be Borromini's more fanciful recollections of events. If my attribution is correct, many passages of the Magliabechiano *Vita* would echo the voice of Borromini himself.

It could be argued that the marginal note *'questo delli denari cosi mi fu detto cosi io lo dico ma io non lo so di certo'* referring to the writer's report of the young Borromini's departure from Milan speaks against my attribution. This rather unsavoury story according to which Borromini cashed money in his father's name without the latter's knowledge must, if it was true, have weighed heavily on Borromini's conscience and he would hardly have talked about it to his nephew.

Baldinucci incorporated the episode in his *Life* (p. 132 ff.) with the proviso *'se pure è vero ciò'*, thus taking into consideration the marginal note in his informant's text, and added that he had the story from one of Borromini's confidants (*'da un suo confidente'*) – the only hint at his source of information.

Appendix II

Volume 77 of the Archive of the Monastery of S. Carlo alle Quattro Fontane

For a description of the MS the reader may be referred to Pollak, *Kunsttätigkeit*, I, p. 477. Pollak used the volume extensively, but one does not get a full idea of its character. Much of the following supplements Pollak's publication.

By far the largest part of the MS was written by Fra Giovanni di S. Bonaventura who was Procurator General of the monastery from 1647 to 1650 and again from 1653 to 1656; he died on 8 November 1658.

Sequence of topics and chapters contained in the MS

Fols. 1r–2r Index: *'Titoli delle Cose che si contengono in questo libro.'*
Pp. 1–60. *'Relatione del Convento di S. Carlo alle 4° fontane di Roma . . .'*
Begins with the history of the Order and continues with the history of the present building. This well written comprehensive history is the one to which I refer in the text. It was partially published by Pollak, pp. 36–51 (with some minor errors). He omitted some interesting passages, particularly pp. 45–48, because they do not contribute to a clarification of Borromini's structure.
Pp. 61–66. Blank.

Pp. 67–194. The Dormitory: *'Fabrica del Quarto del Dormitorio.'*
Contains copies of payments, all ordered under individual craftsmen (bricklayers, stonemasons, carpenters, etc.). Expenses until 8 September 1650.
Pp. 195–98. Blank.
Pp. 199–201. Spanish list of priests and procurators general from 1612 to 1686. Written by a different hand.
Pp. 202–62. Blank.
Pp. 263–316. The Cloisters and adjoining Rooms: *'Fabrica del Claustro et stantie adherenti.'*
Documents and payments paralleling the Dormitory section. Expenses 6 February 1635–4 June 1636 when this part of the structure was finished. Borromini is mentioned as 'Sr. francesco Castello Borromino' and next to him appears Domenico Castello *'Architetto et misuratore della Camera . . .'* (see note 26).
Pp. 317–20. Blank.
Pp. 321–488. The Church: *'Fabrica della Chiesa.'*
Copies of contracts and payments, as above. Expenses run from 23 February 1638 to September 1654. On p. 342 a payment of 1

March 1655 is added by a different hand. Pp. 343–52 are left blank, evidently to allow room for later payments. On p. 485: *'Spese per la chiesa sc. 11.678 b. 53 sino alli 8 sett.e 1650 che fu scritto il conto della fabrica.'*

P. 489. Spanish *résumé* of costs, written by a different hand.

Pp. 492–542. Blank.

Pp. 543–44. Sacristy.

Additions to the settlement of 8 September 1650, p. 485. On p. 543 documents of 1651 and 1652; on p. 544: *'Questo anno 1652 si fece un Baldachino per il Tabernacolo del Altar mag.re',* etc.

Pp. 546–60. Blank.

Pp. 561–683. The Vineyard: *'Relatione della Vigna fuor di porta Pia.'*

Purchased on 28 February 1643 by the Procurator General Fra Giovanni dell'Annunziazione. On p. 607 statement that for the *Vigna* no architect was needed and that designs were made by Fra Giovanni di S. Bonaventura himself. *'Li disegni presente nelle pagine che segue fatti da me fra Gio. di S. Bonaventura.'* On p. 679 summary of costs until 8 September 1650 *'che si scrive questo libro, fatto da me fra Gio. di S. Bonaventura Presidente di questo Convento . . .'*

Pp. 684–700. Blank.

P. 701. A note about the *Vigna*.

Pp. 702–44. Blank.

Pp. 745–58. Concerns a garden *'appresso l'Antoniana'* that has come to the monastery from the estate of the Signora Prudentia Crescenti. On p. 758: *'27 Aprile 1654'* and the signature: *'fr. Gio. di S. Bonaventura Ministro'.*

Pp. 759–67. Expenses for two houses belonging to the monastery, dated 25 March and 30 October 1655 respectively and signed *'fr. Gio. di S. Bonaventura Mn.o et Proc.e'.*

Organization of the book and its date.

This list clearly shows that Fra Giovanni left ample blank spaces between the end of one section and the beginning of the next so as to be able to fill in additions and keep the book up to date. Such additions were supplied rather sparingly, partly by him and to a lesser extent by others (pp. 199–201, 342 and probably the previous pages, 489, 543–44, 701). The last sections, after the end of the Vineyard (p. 683), had not originally been planned. All the parts belonging to the original scheme were written

in 1650 (see pp. 485, 679) and Fra Giovanni's own additions were carried on until 30 October 1655.

Thus the *Relatione* (pp. 1–60), the section of interest in the present context, was written in 1650. This date is confirmed by the mention (on p. 40) of sc. 11.678 b. 53 as the entire expense for the church *'come si vede di questo libro pag. 480'.* (Page reference filled in later. The sum appears on p. 480, but I have quoted from p. 485 because of the date *'sino alli 8 sett.e 1650'.*)

Comment

After the introductory *Relatione* there are long sections dedicated to a full documentation of each part of the monastery. As shown above, the *Relatione* and the later sections are interrelated. From the beginning Fra Giovanni planned to bring together in one volume all the material concerning building operations; hence the section on the vineyard and the later additions about a garden and houses. Taking all this into consideration, the argument has some force that Fra Giovanni compiled the volume only for use inside the monastery.

However, there are definite indications that he wrote the first part with a view to publication. On more than one occasion he went to the trouble of translating simple Latin quotations. One example from p. 6: discussing the foundation of the Order, he refers to Pope Innocent III's pronunciamento *'quelle misteriose parole con impulso più divino, che con motione humano:*

> *Hic est Ordo approbatus,*
> *Non de' i Santi fabricato,*
> *Sed a Solo Summo Deo*
> *che vol dire:*
> > *Questo è un Ordine approvato*
> > *Non de' i Santi fabricato,*
> > *Ma da un Solo et Summo Dio'*

Surely, it would have made no sense thus to enlighten the monks of his Order.

In addition, there are, of course, the many passages referring to Borromini's habits and his work elsewhere. None of this had a place in a history of the monastery unless one regards it as propaganda material aiming at a wider public. As the *Relatione* stands at present, it is somewhat rambling and there are also repetitions. I therefore assume that for publication a second more polished MS would have been necessary. In any case, excepting an occasional reference to other parts of the MS, which could easily be omitted, the *Relatione* stands on its own.

On p. 45 ff. Fra Giovanni develops a theory of the psychology of vision (omitted by Pollak) that appears to be his rather than Borromini's. He quotes SS. Peter, Thomas Aquinas and Gregory the Great for the desire of angels to live in the presence of the Holy Spirit; they never tire to contemplate the divine essence.

On the other hand, the repeated contemplation of mundane things causes annoyance. As examples of mundane art he mentions St. Peter's, S. Maria Maggiore, S. Andrea della Valle, the Gesù and S. Carlo ai Catinari, observing (p. 47): *'E' vero che sonno edificij magnifici, ma visti la prima volta non resta apetito di vederle 1a 2a'*. By contrast, the repeated contemplation of S. Carlino *'mai da fastidio, sempre pare che sia nova'*. Thus, it is evident that Borromini's church partakes, as it were, of the imitation of the Divine (*'tenga qualche cossa di imitatione – in quanto si puo dire – di Divinità'*).

Appendix III

The Marchese de Castel-Rodrigo and Borromini

Hempel (pp. 37, 62) has mentioned the various occasions on which the Marchese entered Borromini's life. Castel-Rodrigo was an early admirer of the latter's architecture: on 21 September 1637 he contributed a considerable sum (2,383 scudi) to the expenses of S. Carlo alle Quattro Fontane and later he wanted to have the façade executed at his expense; he was prepared to spend 25,000 scudi for this purpose, as we learn from the Procurator General's history of the building (Appendix II; see Pollak, I, p. 44).

In his dedication to Castel-Rodrigo introducing the book on the Oratory of the Filippines (usually referred to as *Opus Architectonicum*) Borromini makes the following points: it was the Marchese who had encouraged him to prepare such a work for the press; he calls the Marchese a patron who had loved him, Borromini, as a son rather than a servant; and he refers to designs he had made in the Marchese's service for 'the Royal Palace begun by your ancestors and the tombs of your heroes' (*'fui onorato di servirla in questa Città* [i.e., Rome] *nel disegno della Regia Fabrica cominciata da' suoi Antenati, e de i sepolchri dei suoi Eroi'*). (At the time of writing no Borromini specialist had paid attention to these projects. I can here only suggest that the *'disegno della Regia Fabrica'* was probably for a palace built by Castel-Rodrigo's father, the Viceroy of Portugal.) The address to the readers following the dedication

begins with the statement that the Marchese had requested a full report on the fabric; that he, Borromini, had written it as best he could and that the Marchese had now directed him to see it through the press (*'Avendo voluto l'Eccellentissimo Signor Marchese di Castel Rodriguez mio Signore una piena relazione della Fabrica . . . ed essendomi ingegnato di scriverla al meglio, che ho saputo, mi comanda ora, che procuri darla alle Stampe . . .'*). These various statements contain problems which have hitherto been left unrecorded and are not easily resolved.

In spite of Castel-Rodrigo's distinction, we know relatively little about him. A few data relevant to Borromini's activity have here been assembled from diverse sources. The Marchese's family was probably of Portuguese origin. Castel-Rodrigo's father, Cristobal de Moura, first Marchese de Castel-Rodrigo, was appointed Viceroy of Portugal on 27 October 1607, crowning a long diplomatic career. He died on 28 December 1613. His son, Don Manuel de Moura y Cortereal, second Marchese de Castel-Rodrigo, was, after holding various offices, appointed Spanish Ambassador Extraordinary to Rome and Germany. He arrived in Rome at the end of May 1632 (Pastor, XIII, 1, p. 451). On 24 November 1643 King Philip IV appointed him Lieutenant General for political affairs of the Spanish Netherlands under the Governorship of Juan of Austria (Albert Waddinton, *La république des Provinces-Unies, la France e les Pays-Bas espagnols de 1630 a 1650*, Paris, 1897, II, p. 10 ff.). At the time of the appointment he was no longer in Rome but resided in Vienna. He left Vienna on 8 May 1644 *en route* to Flanders. After his retirement in 1647 he returned to Madrid where he arrived on 14 January 1648 and where he spent the last three years of his life. He died on 28 January 1651 (not 1652 as usually maintained). His son, the third Marchese, had a career similar to his. In 1651 he was sent to Vienna as Spanish Ambassador; from 1664 to 1668 he was Governor General of the Spanish Netherlands and he died in Madrid in 1675.

Borromini's patron, the second Marchese, was surely still in Rome on 8 May 1641, the day of completion (without the façade) of the church of S. Carlino. He also saw the Oratory and refectory of the Filippines finished (1641), but not the library (1642 to the end of 1643) and he did not know the late portion of the structure extending in the direction of Monte Giordano. Nor can he have had a hand in commissioning Borromini with the rebuilding of the Palazzo di Spagna, as Hempel (p. 37) believed, because the palace was not acquired by the Spanish Crown until 25 January 1647 (Hempel, p. 129).

Internal evidence, adduced by Hempel (p. 61), proves that the text of the *Opus Architectonicum* was written in 1648. Hempel's dating is confirmed by Borromini's reference in the text to the very recently finished staircase of the Palazzo di Spagna, which was executed after January 1647 ('. . . *ed io ultimamente ho pratticato nel Palazzo dell'Eccellentissimo Sig. Ambasciadore di Spagna . . .*'). Having established this date, we can answer the question what Borromini implied by writing the above quoted '*mi commanda* ora' – he asks me *now* to publish. The phrase surely suggests that some time had passed between the initial planning of the work and a later stage in its development, the *now*. But it may still be asked whether 'now' was the year 1648, the date of the composition of the text, or 1656, the year of the dedication appearing directly above '*mi commanda ora*'. As we shall see, 'now' must refer to 1648 and it is not impossible that at this time Castel-Rodrigo inquired from Flanders why the appearance of the book was so long delayed. On the other hand, the '*mi commanda ora*' may simply have been a rhetorical turn of phrase

to provide a plausible reason for the publication planned at this moment, i.e. in 1648. I am led to assume that Don Manuel discussed the book on the Oratory in 1641/2, before he left Rome. About six years passed until Borromini settled down to this task and – as I have suggested in this paper – his active return to the project in 1648 was in all probability stimulated by reasons of self-defence rather than by the entreaties of his patron.

Even more puzzling than the problems so far discussed is the date of the dedication to Castel-Rodrigo, 10 May 1656, over five years after the Marchese's death. The form of the dedication leaves no doubt that Borromini is addressing a man who must be presumed to be alive ('*ALL'Illustrissimo ed Eccellentissimo Signor Marchese di Castel Rodriguez. Se i cenni de i pavi di V. Eccellenza hanno forza di commandamenti . . .*'). How can this strange contradiction be explained?

1 One has to enquire whether the date can be Sebastiano Giannini's, the editor's, invention. Following Hempel (p. 62), it has always been believed that the MS in the Archive of the Congregation of the Filippines (C.II.6) with Virgilio Spada's note on the fly-leaf ('*Questo libro fu fatto da me, Virgilio Spada, in nome del Cav.r Borromino . . .*'; see also Incisa della Rocchetta and note 64) is the clean copy later used for publication. In the MS the dedication to Castel-Rodrigo is not dated. This fact would seem to clench the issue. However, an examination of the MS convinced me that Giannini must have worked from a different MS text. Giannini himself maintained that he had used Borromini's original MS ('*Relazione Della presente Opera, composta dal medesimo Cavaliere Francesco Boromini per commando del Signor Marchese di Castel Rodriguez, e copiata dal suo originale inedito*'). Had Giannini used Virgilio Spada's MS he could not have made such a claim, or else one would have to charge him with a deliberately false statement. Moreover, since the Spada MS is illustrated with a large number of drawings – admittedly most of them by a weak hand – one would have expected some use of, or at least reference to, them. (One of the drawings may be by Borromini; the rest was probably copied from originals. Five of the drawings have been published by Incisa della Rocchetta; see note 62.)

Giannini's statement by itself may not carry sufficient weight, but it takes on importance in conjunction with the fact that there are minor divergencies between the Virgilio Spada MS and the printed text and that, moreover, the printed dedication contains some major revisions. (In addition, the MS text contains an important passage about the altar of the Oratory omitted in the printed text. This passage has been discussed by Incisa della Rocchetta, p. 20.) Giannini was a most conscientious editor and it seems rather unlikely that the alterations are his. It is also intrinsically improbable that he would have pulled out of his hat an imaginary date. There was no conceivable reason for it. Nor is it permissible to assume a printer's error. Not only is this splendid publication free of careless oversights but also the date 1656 cannot be a misprint for 1648; the only misprint imaginable would be 1656 for 1646. If this were true, the dedication would have been dated two years before the writing of the text was taken in hand, a conjecture too implausible to be seriously considered. The conclusion seems to be inescapable that Giannini had before him a text with a dedication dated 10 May 1656.

2 If the date of the dedication has to be regarded as Borromini's own, one may offer four different explanations for it, three of which are equally unacceptable. First, one might posit that he was unaware of his patron's death. Such an assumption has little to recommend it. I cannot believe that the news of the death of this man who was so close to Borromini's heart, would have escaped him. Secondly, it could be argued that Borromini had transferred his allegiance from the father to the son (no first name appears in the address of the dedication), whom he probably knew quite well; the son and heir was twenty-one or twenty-two years old when the family left Rome. Content and tenor of the dedication, however, do not admit of such an explanation. Thirdly, one may want to postulate another Marchese de Castel-Rodrigo as Borromini's patron, perhaps an undistinguished brother of the ambassador, who would perforce have been in Rome concurrently with Don Manuel, who would have stayed on after the latter's departure and would still have been alive in 1656. This phantom person can safely be buried without much ado.

3 At the end we are forced to accept the fourth alternative, namely that Borromini addressed his old patron long after his death as if he were still alive. Such an attitude was possible within Borromini's phantom world: the dedication took on the character of a symbolic address.

If this, the only possible, explanation appears acceptable, the story of the *Opus Architectonicum* can be reconstructed as follows: in 1641/2 Castel-Rodrigo, still in Rome, urged Borromini to publish a report on the Oratory. But only in 1648 Borromini's own difficulties made him responsive to this enterprise; at this time the text was written with Virgilio Spada's active support, and the possibility cannot be excluded that Don Manuel, resident in Flanders, now prodded the master not to delay publication any longer. But lack of time or flagging interest on Borromini's part prevented the book from appearing. For weighty reason of his own (above, p. 162) Borromini made a new, determined attempt at publication in 1656: he treated the project as if time had stood still and his guardian angel, Don Manuel, were still at his side. The dating of the dedication indicates that this time publication plans had reached a critical stage, but once again they were abortive. In 1725, finally, publication was realized by Giannini, who used a manuscript that is no longer extant or has not yet been retrieved. Although this reconstruction must remain largely hypothetical, it resolves the contradictory evidence. The correctness of my assumptions depends, of course, on the correctness of the sequence of events here submitted.

Appendix IV

Borromini and Stoicism

So far as I know Jesuit interest in Seneca and stoicism has not yet been studied. A few random remarks may indicate the existence of the problem. The Jesuit Ignatius Bompiano (1612–75) from Frosinone, who taught at the Collegio Romano in Rome, published a book entitled *Seneca Christianus*, first in 1638 (?); later editions: 1658, 1680, 1693, 1714. See Carlos Sommervogel, S.J., *Bibliothèque de la Compagnie de Jesus*, Brussels-Paris, I, 1890, col. 1686 (I have been unable to find a copy of Bompiano's book). Other Jesuits published similar works, e.g., J. B. Schellenberg, *Seneca Christianus*, Augsburg, 1637, and later Luzern, 1645, 1660, 1696, etc. To the Jesuits Seneca was the great classical exemplar of virtue. Professor Ernst Gombrich acquainted me with a book by Daniello Bartoli, S.J., *De' simboli trasportati al morale*, Bologna, 1677, in which this aspect is fully expounded (p. 554): '. . . in the writings of Seneca: everything is the declaration of war, taking up weapons, arming, going out into the field, joining battle, fighting to the last breath, face to face, breast to breast, against all the enemies of virtue . . . he laid bare pomp, chained up anger, wrenched the teeth out of the mouth of greed, cut off the head of ambition, the hands of avarice, and broke the tendons of lust; he attacked and routed fears, he challenged death and slew it; and this fighting of his was all winning, because it was all philosophizing: and representing to himself the deformity of vice, then the beauty of virtue, was a pleasure to him.'

I have suggested that Borromini may have been led to Seneca by the Jesuits. While this is, of course, a mere hypothesis, it may be recalled that he had close contacts with the Jesuits through his work in the Propaganda Fide (1646 ff.) and that in his will a legacy of 500 scudi *'per qualche adornamento dell'Altare di S. Ignatio'* in the Gesù confirms his attachment to the Jesuit cause.

At first one feels inclined to disassociate Borromini from the secular neo-Stoical movement that swept through France in the seventeenth century and found a dedicated adherent in Poussin during the 1640s and 1650s (M. Alpatov, 'Poussin Problems', *Art Bulletin*, XVII, 1935, pp. 22–24; Anthony Blunt, in *Journal of the Warburg and Courtauld Institutes*, VII, 1944, p. 158 ff.; Walter Friedlaender, *Nicolas Poussin*, New York, 1965, p. 37 ff.; the fullest discussion is now in Anthony Blunt's *Nicolas Poussin*, New York, 1967, chap. IV: 'Poussin and Stoicism'). Poussin's themes of that period were concerned with the control of the passions by will power and reason and, as we have seen, this was the central problem in Borromini's life. We have no record of a direct connection between Poussin and Borromini and yet, contrary to expectation, more than one link between them can be construed.

Borromini was a friend of the sculptor Orfeo Boselli, his exact contemporary (c. 1600–67). Boselli's hitherto unpublished treatise entitled *Osservazioni della Scultura Antica* (Corsiniana note 1391, collocaz. 36-F-27; see Michelangelo Piacentini, in *Bollettino del R. Istituto di Archaeologia e Storia dell'Arte*, IX, fasc. 1–6, 1939, pp. 5–34), a transcript of which was graciously put at my disposal by Mrs Phoebe Weil, is a work of extraordinary interest: the author's impressive learning, his familiarity with ancient and post-antique literature, philosophy, art and science (he quotes, among many others, Vitruvius, Plato, Aristotle, Ovid, Virgil, Livy, Plautus, Terence, Petrarch, Ariosto, Tasso, Dürer, Daniele Barbaro, Erizzi, Ripa, Athanasius Kircher, Serlio, Palladio and Vignola) is matched by the originality of many of his observations, and it is revealing for Borromini that he liked to associate with this kind of man. Boselli mentions (fol. 119 v) that he had made a portrait bust of Borromini (which has not so far been traced) and the fact that Borromini was prepared to sit for him indicates that their relationship was rather close. Boselli acknowledges his admiration for Borromini by calling him *'eccelente Architetto'* throughout the *Treatise*, once in connection with an antique nymph restored by Boselli and, when he wrote, in Borromini's collection (fol. 80 v), again when mentioning the Filomarino Chapel in Naples (fol. 124 v), and again on the occasion of their joint inspection of an ancient find in front of S. Luigi dei Francesi (fol. 154 r). Boselli was a pupil of Duquesnoy, for whom he had the greatest veneration and whom he regarded as equal to antiquity and Raphael (fol. 71 v); he called him '*scultore incomparabile*' (fol. 124 v), '*l'angelico scultore*' (fol. 131r), '*vera Fenice de nostri tempi*' (fol. 146r). (It is likely that the Christ at the Column in Borromini's collection (see note 26) was Duquesnoy's original model for the bronze, known in several casts, now usually wrongly attributed to Algardi.) Small wonder that Boselli's counsellors and friends belonged to the classical camp. He singles out Sacchi and Mignard (fol. 156 v). The latter lived and worked in Rome for the better part of twenty years (between 1636 and 1657) and there 'formed his style mainly on the study of Annibale Carracci, Domenichino, and Poussin' (Blunt). Mignard was probably also Borromini's friend; their relationship dates back to the early 1640s when Mignard painted the high altar picture and the Annunciation over the entrance of S. Carlo alle Quattro Fontane. In any case, of the Annunciation (destroyed) Borromini said that no other angel expressed equally well his mysterious mission (Pollak, *Kunsttätig-keit*, I p. 104 ff.: '*come dice il Sr. Francesco Borromino nella Europa crede che non sia Pitura di Angelo che sprima così il mistero et la sua embasciata come questa . . .*').

All these admittedly tenuous points, if considered together, permit us to approach with an open mind the possibility of Borromini's exposure to philosophical ideas discussed in the circle of Poussin. Before submitting a different kind of argument in favour of such a connection I think it worth while reminding the reader that there existed constitutional similarities between Poussin and Borromini. With advancing years Poussin became an obsessed misanthrope, '*seul, étranger et sans amis*', as he said of himself (Jacques Bousquet, '*Poussin et le milieu romain*', in *Colloques N. Poussin*, ed. A. Chastel, Paris, 1960, pp. 13, 16). Walter Friedlaender has pointed out that Poussin suffered from an 'anxiety complex' and one can well imagine that Borromini would have fully subscribed to the following assessment of the contemporaneous world by Poussin: '. . . I am afraid of the malice of this century; virtue,

231 Antique bust of Seneca, of the type probably owned by Borromini

232 POUSSIN. *Suicide of Cato the Younger* (Windsor, Royal Library)

conscience and religion are banished among men. Only vice, deceit, and self-interest now reign. All is lost – I despair for the good. Everything is filled with misery' (Friedlaender, *Poussin*, 1965, p. 88).

To return now to Borromini's suicide, one may be tempted to regard the very act of self-destruction as an expression of his stoic convictions. But the documentary evidence of his behaviour shortly before and at the moment of the deed forces us to conclude that, in any case at the time of ultimate calamity, he did not deliberately contemplate a death *all'antica*. According to his own account, given verbally and written down by a city official (see note 1), he acted in a state of desperation. When his servant Massari answered his request for light with the definite *'Signor no'* Borromini responded as follows: 'And when I heard the reply, impatience took possession of me' and later in the same statement he reaffirmed 'as impatience at not having a light grew in me even more, in despair I took up the sword . . .'.

On the other hand, there is no denying that his manner of death is extraordinarily similar to Cato the Younger's stoic suicide as reported by Plutarch (*Life of Cato the Younger*, LVIII–LXX). There are a thousand different ways of ending one's own life. As Cato himself said: 'I have no need of the sword to despatch myself; for if I do but hold my breath awhile, or dash my head against the wall, it will answer the purpose as well'. But, in fact, according to Plutarch, he did use his sword and while in bed 'stabbed himself under the breast'. Borromini placed the hilt of his sword on his bed and threw himself upon it and, like Cato, fell out of bed on to the stone-floor.

It is probably more than a hypothesis that Borromini had long contemplated Seneca's meditations on death, a recurrent theme in the latter's *Epistles*; it is even possible that Borromini intended 'to depart with a tranquil mind' (Seneca, *Epist.* 36) when he turned to writing his will during the vigil before the morning of the suicide. This assumption is supported by the fact that soon after the fatal blow he regained absolute composure, as evidenced by the tenor of the physician's protocol; it is a simple, factual and entirely unemotional statement of events without a single word of complaint or remorse on Borromini's part. One is reminded of Seneca's own behaviour while he was slowly bleeding to death.

With all these criteria before us we may feel convinced that Borromini imitated Cato's method of suicide by an act of subconscious rather than conscious identification. But there is one little flaw in the argument. Plutarch reports that Cato 'could not strike hard enough owing to the inflammation in his hand', in other words, Cato inflicted the wound by striking his body and not by throwing his body on to the sword; nor did he transfix himself entirely as Borromini did. At this point we have to come back to Poussin. He was deeply stirred by Cato's suicide: diverging from Plutarch's text, he rendered a moving and dramatic interpretation of this stoic self-destruction in a drawing at Windsor, which shows Cato after 232 having thrown himself on his sword with such force that the sword has gone right through the body. Poussin's drawing, dating from about 1640, prefigures with haunting accuracy Borromini's fate, and his account of his suicide reads like a description of the drawing: 'I placed its [the sword's] handle into the bed and the point against my side and then I threw myself on the sword, and with the force with which it entered my body, I was pierced from one side to the other.'

Is it coincidence or did he re-enact Poussin's version of Cato's suicide? I tend to believe the latter if only because it would end the symbol-laden circuit of his life on a note true to his character. If he was fascinated by Poussin's drawing, perhaps many years before, it would suddenly have emerged from his subconscious and announced its vitality with compelling force at the supreme moment of his life.

A word may be added about the cast of the bust of Seneca in Borromini's possession. There can hardly be any doubt that his cast was taken from one of the so-called 'pseudo-Senecas', known in many replicas, which show an expressive head of a bearded, haggard looking 231 philosopher with strands of hair hanging loose over the forehead (J. J. Bernoulli, *Griechische Ikonographie*, Munich, 1901, II, pp. 160–77, lists no less than thirty-three which include, of course, those found in the nineteenth century; see also M. Bieber, *The Sculpture of the Hellenistic Age*, New York, 1955, p. 143). These heads were wrongly identified as Seneca for 300 years from the late sixteenth century onwards. The type was often used by Rubens for renderings of Seneca (Rooses, *L'oeuvre de Rubens*, 1890, IV, p. 27 ff., nos. 812, 813; V, nos. 1305–7, etc.) as well as by many other masters (see J. R. Judson, *Gerrit van Honthorst*, The Hague, 1959, p. 103 ff., and the list in A. Pigler, *Barockthemen*, Budapest, 1956, II, p. 409 ff.).

233 Portrait of Guarini from *Architettura Civile*

IX
GUARINI THE MAN

Guarini the Man

IN MY student days, back in the early 1920s, Guarini's name was completely unknown. At that time he was a tangible figure to hardly more than one in a hundred art historians outside Italy. Not even Borromini's *'fortuna'* suffered such an eclipse. The hostility of the Neoclassical generation fell upon him with a severity that is almost without precedent. Milizia, naturally, found in his work 'extravagant forms . . . and every kind of caprice' and concluded: 'Good luck to anyone who likes Guarini's architecture – but count him among the cranks.'[1] Even a man as moderate as Ticozzi expressed the opinion that Guarini had been appointed architect to the Duke of Savoy 'because every notion of good taste had been lost in that age . . . [Various] cities had the misfortune rather than the luck to possess buildings by him. . . . Everything about them is arbitrary, without rule, contrived. He died, to the benefit of art, in 1683.'[2] Yet about half a century later a few sensitive and judicious scholars began to reverse these established values. I have in mind mainly Sandonnini's excellent paper on Guarini published in 1888[3] and Gurlitt's chapter on him in his *Geschichte des Barockstiles in Italien* (1887). Thereafter silence for more than a generation, in fact until after the First World War. I think, modern criticism of Guarini begins with Michel's *Histoire de l'Art* of 1921,[4] where Guarini is recognized as one of the most original and most interesting masters of the whole history of architecture who opened a new epoch. The later twenties and thirties witnessed the Guarini revival with studies by such men as Bricarelli, Chevalley, Rigotti and, above all, Oliveri, Brinckmann and Argan.

Guarini's period of generally acknowledged pre-eminence was relatively brief, that of his oblivion long, of his resurgence and recognition painfully slow. Let us recall that art and architecture was not his original calling. A bird's-eye view of his life would show it divided into three major periods. Born at Modena on 17 January

234 GUARINI. Dome of the Chapel of the SS. Sindone, Turin

1624 he entered the Theatine Order in 1639, went to Rome the same year and returned to Modena only in 1647, where he was ordained priest, aged twenty-three. The first phase of his life, the formative years, the years of study, had come to an end. Rome had given him unlimited possibilities to delve into the many fields which attracted his insatiable intellectual curiosity; apart from theology, he studied philosophy, mathematics, astronomy and, of course, also military, civic and ecclesiastical architecture.

During the next phase of his life, which lasted almost twenty years, we find him teach-

235 GUARINI. View into the dome of the Chapel of the SS. Sindone, Turin

ing philosophy and mathematics at Modena and Messina, staying at Parma and Guastalla, probably travelling a good deal and finally teaching theology in Paris;[5] and all this time he is also engaged on architectural work. But this busy period looks now like a preparation for the last seventeen years of his life spent in Turin where Carlo Emanuele II appointed him 'Ingegnere e Matematico Ducale' in 1668, two years after his arrival. If he had died in 1665, at the age of forty-one, he would now hardly be recalled.

The last seventeen years – between his forty-second and fifty-ninth – saw an unbelievable burst of energy, a release of pent-up creative powers almost unparalleled in the history of art. In quick succession we witness the design and execution of one great project after another, all those great buildings so well known to us: S. Lorenzo, the Chapel of the SS. Sindone, the church of the Immaculate Conception, Palazzo Carignano, the Collegio dei Nobili (to name only the most important ones) – all buildings of a revolutionary character, each posing new and unexpected problems. And at the same time as all the great buildings in

234, 235

236 GUARINI. S. Maria della Divina Providenza, Lisbon, section

237 GUARINI. Church of the Madonna d'Oropa, exterior and section

238 GUARINI. Sainte-Anne-la-Royale, Paris, façade

Turin, his designs were much in demand else-where, at Casale Monferrato, Racconigi, Oropa, 237 Vicenza, Modena and, much farther afield, in Lisbon and Prague. 236

In Modena and Messina he had begun to make a name for himself as an architect of originality mainly within the sphere of his Order, and it was therefore not by chance that the Theatines of Paris invited him in 1662 to 238 come and build their church, for the erection of which Cardinal Mazarin had left a consider-able sum of money at his death in 1661. This great church was demolished in the early nine-teenth century.[6] At this time Guarini's reputa-tion was apparently still rather limited. When Bernini spent six months in Paris in 1665, his faithful guide, the Sieur de Chantelou, does not record a meeting between the prince of artists and the Theatine architect, but on 14 June Bernini inspected the church, then in course of construction, without Guarini being present. The Theatine Fathers were hanging on Bernini's lips; they seemed to have felt uneasy about their adventurous building. He probably shared their feelings, for he only said, 'Credo che riuscirà bella'.[7]

At the same moment a young English scientist, Christopher Wren, was in Paris, then aged thirty-three. Like Guarini he had come to architecture rather late and in 1665 he visited Paris to gather information about the Con-tinental architectural panorama. He tried hard to meet Bernini and study his Louvre design. When the meeting came about, it was not a success. Wren wrote: 'Bernini's design of the Louvre I would have given my skin for, but the old reserved Italian gave me but a few minutes view. . . .' There are valid reasons to assume that Wren also inspected Guarini's Sainte-Anne-la-Royale, but no word by him is recorded about the church and its architect.[8]

In the light of Guarini's relative obscurity in 1665, his being summoned to Turin the following year with extraordinary executive powers appears all the more remarkable and prodigious. Suddenly, an aura of greatness began to surround him and the enormous responsibilities he carried stimulated him to accomplish more than one intellectual *tour de force*.[9] His career as a writer and playwright had started in 1660 with a moral tragicomedy entitled *La Pietà trionfante*.[10] Five years later – in 1665 – he published his next book in Paris, the *Placita philosophica*, an immensely learned folio, in which he defended, rather surprisingly at this late date, the geocentric universe against Copernicus and Galileo. Now, strangely enough, after he had settled in Turin, the tempo and range of his publications increased. Despite his full-time occupation as a practising architect, he managed to continue his studies in geometry, fortifications and architecture, and almost every year a new work came from the press: in 1671 *L'Euclides adauctus . . .*; in 1674 *Del modo di misurare le fabbriche*; in 1675 the *Compendio della sfera celeste*; in 1676 the *Trattato di fortificare*; in 1678 the *Leges temporum et planetarum*; finally, in 1683, the year he died, the planetary tables *Caelestis mathematicae. . . .* His great architectural treatise, the preparation of which must have taken him many years, was, however, never completed. In 1686, three years after his death, the plates without text appeared as *Disegni di architettura civile ed ecclesiastica*, a fact of the greatest importance for the early diffusion of Guarinesque architectural principles. Guarini's text – at his death probably in some confusion and, I have reason to believe, not quite finished – was edited by Vittone and published together with the plates in 1737.[11]

Apart from his almost unbelievable burden of work as architect and author Guarini remained dedicated to his calling as a priest. His standing in his Order is demonstrated by the fact that in 1655 – aged thirty-one – he was appointed provost to the Theatines at Modena,

239

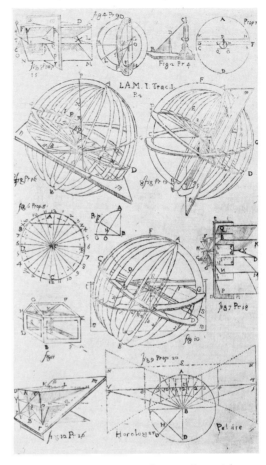

239 Page from Guarini's *Caelistis mathematicae,* 1683

240 GUARINI. S. Lorenzo, Turin, interior

though the opposition of Duca Alfonso IV d'Este forced him to leave the city. Twenty-three years later the same honour was conferred upon him again: he was elected provost of the Theatines at Turin. In 1680, the year Guarini celebrated the first Mass in S. Lorenzo – probably a unique case of the alliance of architect and priest in the same person – Emanuele Filiberto Amedeo, Principe di Carignano, appointed Guarini his '*teologo*'. In the revealing document of appointment the Prince mentions the 'ingenious and extraordinary principles' applied in S. Lorenzo, the Palazzo Carignano and the Castello di Racconigi and continues that these 'unusual qualities are combined with the most excellent knowledge of the philosophical, moral, and theological sciences as befits a zealous and worthy member of a religious Order.'[12] These words seem to me to describe most aptly Guarini's special case: the triple union of priest, scholar and artist – though perhaps not entirely unique – was never more fully and more harmoniously reconciled. And the recognition that he led three lives in one, being completely dedicated to each of his pursuits, helps us to understand a good deal

240
242

about him, his success and even the character of his architecture.

The text of the *Architettura civile* gives us a good measure of this man. I want to comment briefly on four striking features of the treatise. First, there is its immaculate structure, to a large extent Guarini's own and independent of architectural treatises, and throughout he displays an extraordinary common sense and open-mindedness. Right at the beginning – 'the architect must proceed with discretion'[13] – he warns against overspending and later returns to the same point: – 'one must do everything with the least possible expense'.[14] When he gives eleven rules for the construction of staircases he concludes: 'I know that it is difficult to fulfil all these conditions in every staircase.'[15] Reference to the demands of 'custom' and to the subjectivity of judgment recur throughout the treatise. 'Architecture can modify the ancient rules and invent new ones'.[16] The Romans themselves, he assures us, did not follow Vitruvius closely nor do the moderns always follow the ancients. Architecture changes with the changing habits of men.[17] It is therefore obvious that – in his words – 'the symmetries of architecture can be varied without causing disharmony between the parts'.[18] This relativity of judgment can be applied, of course, also to the classical orders of architecture. They are pleasing to the eye, but 'it is very difficult to know how this pleasure arises – just as difficult as to understand the pleasure we get from a pretty dress. Nay, more – not only are men constantly changing their minds, and hating that as deformed which they used to admire as

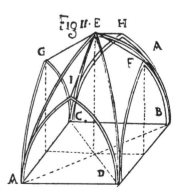

241 Diagram from Guarini's *Architettura Civile* showing a Gothic vault

242 GUARINI. S. Lorenzo, Turin, view into the dome

beautiful, but what one whole nation likes another will dislike. In our own subject, for instance, the architecture of the Romans was 241 despised by the Goths, just as Gothic architecture is despised by us.'[19] He concludes that the architect's inventions cannot be applauded by everybody; not only are there people 'blown up with self-esteem', the envious and ignorant 'who can do nothing but speak ill of them', but there is also habit which influences our likes

and dislikes, and there are even physical constitutional characteristics which condition some people to prefer excessive ornamentation to simplicity and vice versa.[20] While such ideas have a French rather than Italian pedigree, I do not think that they were ever so clearly stated and they attest, in any case, that Guarini himself was broad-minded, open to typical seventeenth-century rational argument, and that he was neither a fanatic nor an eccentric.[21]

183

My second point reinforces these impressions. The learning Guarini displays in his treatise is staggering and though he does not accept any authority as binding his criticism and controversy are reserved and temperate. He may criticize Palladio by briefly stating 'what Palladio believes is wrong';[22] in his frequent polemics against his contemporary, the Spaniard Juan Caramuel, he likes to use a subtle form of irony. In one case, for instance, he refutes his opinion as 'in my modest view a joke rather than a sensible instruction',[23] or in another case: 'He [Caramuel] corrects one fault by making a greater one, and to get rid of one error he commits many others.'[24]

Thus Guarini appears as an agile, dexterous and spirited writer and disputant who presents his enormous learning gracefully and approaches tradition with the assurance of one who has left no stone unturned in order to form his own judgment. This takes me to my third point. The same spirit of scrupulous exploration which he applied to the literary tradition, he also applied to the visual tradition. The number of monuments he uses to exemplify his points is very remarkable. To mention only his celebrated chapter on Gothic architecture: he reveals a familiarity with, and appreciation of, the cathedrals of Seville, Salamanca, Reims, Paris, Milan and Siena, among many others.[25]

Finally, he incorporated, in long chapters of his treatise, the great lesson he alone among Italians had learned from advanced French mathematics. The theme is given in the introduction to Trattato IV, entitled 'Dell ortografia gettata', where he explains that the method is 'absolutely necessary to the architect, even though little understood in Italian architecture, but splendidly utilized by the French on many occasions'.[26] Large parts of his treatise are dependent on Desargues's projective geometry – obviously causing great excitement in learned circles at the time of Guarini's stay in Paris – and no doubt Guarini himself enriched the new doctrine by theorems of his own. As we now know, it was this new geometry that supplied the scientific basis for Guarini's daring structures, particularly of domes. He also treats the problem in other publications, especially in Modo di misurare le fabbriche, where he is concerned with the precise measurement of incommensurable surfaces, parabolas, cones,

spheroids and so on, and where he observes 'the parabola and the hyperbola are scarcely, if at all, known to architects' though they 'could very well serve in dome construction'.[27]

In any case, every section of the treatise shows that for Guarini theory and practice were two sides of the same medal and that there is the closest alliance between his treatise and his architecture. We have therefore also to trust him when he pronounces the hedonistic judgment that 'architecture has for its aim the pleasing of the senses'[28] or when he tells us that 'although architecture is based on mathematics, it is nonetheless an art that delights[29] . . . so that, if the eye should be offended by the adherence to mathematical rules – change them, abandon them, and even contradict them.'[30]

I have discussed certain characteristics of the treatise primarily to throw light on what kind of man Guarini was and specifically to demonstrate that a whole world separated him from Borromini, whose early work he had studied in his youth in Rome and which he had never wholly discarded from his mind. It has been said that Guarini, 'a tormented genius who suffered from near paranoia, constantly complained of being mistreated, misunderstood and unappreciated.'[31] But I cannot find any evidence that he suffered from a pathological, obsessive, hypochondriac condition similar to that which led to Borromini's suicide. On the contrary, the image of Guarini's personality that emerges from a study of his writings as well as his life suggests equilibrium, moderation, constancy, broad-mindedness – qualities which seemed to have belonged to him as a gift of nature and been nurtured by his wide learning and his priestly calling. Even though – as Portoghesi rightly points out in his Guarini monograph – the engraved portrait at the front 233 of Architettura civile shows 'an image of absorbed sadness', he found in Guarini's character 'the strength of an exemplary open-mindedness, a capacity to adapt and to learn, which made him truly European both as a man of culture and as an architect.'[32] It was this very balanced man who created an architectural language so original, so fantastic and strange that, in historical perspective, he defies any attempt at classification.

Methodical study and procedure, new mathematical insights, an exceptionally wide and

243 GUARINI. Palazzo Carignano, Turin

receptive visual experience and memory, religious zeal – all these ·have somehow fused within a passionate imagination to produce works of infinite variety and mysterious attraction. Upon first visiting Turin, anyone with sensibility will be impressed and excited by the encounter with Guarini's buildings. To face the Palazzo Carignano and the Collegio dei Nobili after having seen the Piazza S. Carlo and other serene, elegant works of the first half of the seventeenth century means stepping into a turbulent world, a world of concentrated energy, dramatic contradictions and fascinating foci, a world that forcefully engages the beholder and keeps him spell-bound. I think everybody will agree that Guarini's appearance in Turin transformed an ambitious but still provincial capital into a centre of truly international importance. And once Turin had, through him, gained that key position she maintained it for a hundred years.

It is also revealing to see Guarini within the all-Italian situation. Significantly, he does not belong to the generation of the great Baroque masters: Bernini, Borromini, Cortona, Fanzago, Longhena were all born in the 1590s and so were Algardi, Sacchi and Duquesnoy. They all established themselves in the 1620s and those who were still alive in the 1660s, at the time of Guarini's beginnings, were entering the last phase of their careers. Their work does not offer any definite clues to the Guarini phenomenon. Nor does any of his central Italian contemporaries show a development similar to his. Take the slightly younger Carlo Fontana, whose architectural career, like Guarini's, began in the 1660s. But Fontana is explicable in terms of his own Roman experience: Fontana, not Guarini, was the legatee of the great Roman masters. His manner – learned, academically limited, classicizing and with a tendency towards scenographic rather than dynamic solutions – is the quintessence of this age.

Internationally speaking, the closest parallel to Guarini is, strangely enough, Sir Christopher Wren to whom I have referred before. He started

185

his career in 1657 as Professor of Astronomy and, like Guarini, never lost interest in purely intellectual and scientific pursuits. When, in the 1660s, he turned to architecture, he – again like Guarini – applied his mathematical training and genius and his scholarly empiricism to planning; the structural principles to be found in many of his London churches built from 1670 on are new and bold and anti-authoritarian in spirit. But this is as far as the similarities with Guarini go, for Wren's repertory of architectural forms is conventional and the cool reserve of his manner exactly corresponds to the Baroque classicism of the second half of the seventeenth century throughout Europe.

It is against this background that we have to assess Guarini's work. In the last quarter of the seventeenth century the international classicism, to a large extent imposed by the French Academy, lost its attraction. We witness, almost miraculously, a new spirit, anti-dogmatic, vigorous and enthusiastic, a new Baroque dynamism discernible in the marvellous resurgence in Venetian painting, the birth of luxuriant Baroque decoration in Genoa and of a great architecture in southern Italy and Sicily; we witness the unexpected bloom of a German and Austrian Baroque, the turn to a virile and dramatic Baroque architecture in England and to an exuberant decorative style in Spain. Guarini is one of the fathers, and probably the most important one, of this extraordinary inter-European movement. But most of the great masters of this new revolutionary era were not born until the time of Guarini's death.

Endowed with an exceptionally lively and original mind and with almost superhuman stamina, each task Guarini set himself engaged the whole man: his *Placita philosophica* is a *summa* of philosophical doctrines brought into a coherent system; his *Euclides adauctus* was planned and written as a complete corpus of mathematical knowledge compressed into one large volume, just as his *Caelestis mathematicae* aims at astronomical and his *Architettura civile* at architectural omniscience. This searching,

encyclopaedic mind handled each architectural task as if he had to elucidate a bewildering maze or an infinite series of specific problems: comparable to his literary production, every one of his buildings is like an architectural *summa* dictated by particular requirements. Because of this, progress at his buildings stopped without his personal supervision. Thus when the dome of the SS. Sindone was rising, Madama Reale had to request his urgent return from Modena; she wrote 'It is absolutely impossible to proceed without the father's assistance, since he alone knows how to direct the work.'[33]

Just as his various literary productions are closely related as integral parts of a great seventeenth-century encyclopaedia of knowledge, so his architectural structures reveal many common properties (despite their variety); paradoxes and seeming contradictions, deliberate incongruities and even dissonances belong to his architectural language; his celebrated interpenetrations of different spatial units, the placing of unrelated tiers one above the other, his operating with sections of ellipsoids and with parabolic ribs, his delight in apparent structural miracles, the juxtaposition of doughy, Mannerist ornamental forms with extremely austere crystalline shapes, the density of motifs (such as the endless repetition of the star pattern in the court of the Palazzo Carignano) – all these as well as many other characteristics recur in his work, as has often been noticed. One would very much like to understand his apparent vacillation between a hedonistic approach to architecture and the suggestion of infinity in his diaphanous domes – or, to put it differently, between his rationalism and mysticism. Let me suggest that for him intellect and emotion were not divorced. Even mathematics, the firm and solid basis of architecture, he regarded as an incredible, wonder-working science. He gave this secret away in *Euclides adauctus* where he writes: '*Thaumaturga Mathematicorum miraculorum insigni, verèque Regali architectura coruscat*'[34] – 'The magic of wondrous mathematicians shines brightly in the marvellous and truly regal architecture.'

244 JUVARRA. Titlepage and dedication of the Chatsworth volume

X
A SKETCHBOOK OF
FILIPPO JUVARRA
AT
CHATSWORTH

245 Chatsworth volume, folio 1
246 Chatsworth volume, folio 2

247 Chatsworth volume, folio 3
248 Chatsworth volume, folio 4

249 Chatsworth volume, folio 5
250 Chatsworth volume, folio 6

251 Chatsworth volume, folio 7
252 Chatsworth volume, folio 8

253 Chatsworth volume, folio 9
254 Chatsworth volume, folio 10

255 Chatsworth volume, folio 11
256 Chatsworth volume, folio 12

257 Chatsworth volume, folio 13
258 Chatsworth volume, folio 14

259 Chatsworth volume, folio 15
260 Chatsworth volume, folio 16

261 Chatsworth volume, folio 17
262 Chatsworth volume, folio 18

263 Chatsworth volume, folio 19
264 Chatsworth volume, folio 20

265 Chatsworth volume, folio 21
266 Chatsworth volume, folio 22

267 Chatsworth volume, folio 23
268 Chatsworth volume, folio 24

269 Chatsworth volume, folio 25
270 Chatsworth volume, folio 26

271 Chatsworth volume, folio 27
272 Chatsworth volume, folio 28

273 Chatsworth volume, folio 29
274 Chatsworth volume, folio 30

AMONG the treasures at Chatsworth House belonging to the Duke of Devonshire is a small book of sketches by Filippo Juvarra, the existence of which for long passed unnoticed.[1] It comprises a title page with dedication and thirty drawings of architectural fantasies, numbered by Juvarra himself in the top right corner. The drawings are all on the same kind of paper and they measure, with some slight variations, about 22·5 cm high by 33·5 cm wide. They were executed in Juvarra's familiar manner, in pen and ink, with bistre and sepia, and in some of them the preparatory pencil drawing is visible. They are mounted on larger pages (30·5 cm × 43 cm) and bound in red morocco. Their subjects are Roman ruins, bold reconstructions of ancient monuments, sarcophagi, triumphal arches and famous masterpieces of ancient sculpture, placed in an idealistic pseudo-classical setting, a fanciful combination of imaginative romanticism, archaeological realism and architectural *jeux d'esprit*.

We know other architectural fantasies of this kind carried out at various times during Juvarra's career. The first is perhaps the one dedicated in 1705 to the Roman sculptor Lorenzo Ottoni,[2] followed in 1706 by similar drawings in an album which is now in the possession of Count Adriano Tournon in Turin.[3] Two further groups of drawings of architectural fantasies belong to a much later period. One is a group of eleven drawings preserved in a volume in the Museo Civico in Turin, almost all signed and dated 1728 or 1729,[4] which seem to be rather more free in their treatment than the Chatsworth drawings. The second, much larger group, is in a volume of forty-five folios which is in Dresden and which opens with a letter of dedication to Augustus the Strong of Saxony, dated 1732.[5] The themes of these drawings are very close to those at Chatsworth, but the execution is more careful and more finished, and no doubt Juvarra intended to make engravings from them.

It seems unnecessary to analyse each drawing of the Chatsworth book separately, but a couple of observations may be set down here. The last ten folios (nos. 21–30) are over-all of a more archaeological nature than the first twenty. There is also a slight difference in technique between these two groups. The drawings of the second group are all washed with bistre, as is the frontispiece; those of the first group on the other hand are for the most part washed with sepia. I should like to begin with a few remarks on the archaeological group at the end.

No. 21: Juvarra places in the middle ground 265 an interesting version of the Arch of Constantine, with open arches also on the two shorter sides. Picturesque transformations of triumphal arches appear frequently in the pages of the Chatsworth sketchbook. They show that the triumphal arch was one of the starting points from which Juvarra developed his own style.

On folio 22 the personification of the Nile at 266 the base of the Palazzo Senatorio in Rome is placed against an Egyptian background enclosed by two pyramids and by an arched tower with a spiral stairway.[6] This tower – similar to the dome of S. Ivo by Borromini – was supposed to represent the lighthouse of Alexandria.[7] No. 23 shows in the foreground a 267 triumphal arch with a single archway, closer in design to the Arch of Caracalla at Tebessa in North Africa than to any of the arches erected in Italy, and an extraordinary three-storey bridge which takes up the entire width of the page. The drawing incorporates reminiscences of the Pont du Gard near Nîmes, of Roman aqueducts and of the drawing by Palladio for the Rialto Bridge.[8] This type of pseudo-Roman monumental bridge had a special attraction for Juvarra: he produced different versions of the same idea, on folio 22 of the Chatsworth sketchbook, in a volume in the Turin National Library[9] and in the Dresden sketchbook.[10]

On folio 24 the extraordinary motif of huge 268 serpents entwined round Roman columns appears prominently in the foreground. As far as I know, no classical model exists for this motif. However, this was not Juvarra's own idea. It was the principal emblem in the coat-of-arms of Cardinal Biscia engraved on the title page of the 1638 and 1684 editions of Giovan Battista Montano's *Architettura con diversi ornamenti*. In the right middle ground of the same drawing there is the façade of a church, the unfinished top part of which is made to look like a Roman ruin. A Roman ruin on top of a Christian church: certainly a fantastic combination.

269   No. 25 represents a scene of an ancient harbour with, in the foreground, the rostral column erected to honour the naval victory of Caius Duillius Nepos over the Carthaginians.[11] Since only a few fragments survive of the original column, Juvarra must have been familiar with the reconstruction presented in the *Opuscula in Columnae Rostratae . . .* of Ciaconius (1624) or at least some of the illustrations derived from the reconstruction by Ciaconius, which were fairly frequent in the seventeenth century.[12]

271   On folio 27 Juvarra returns to the theme of
272 the triumphal arch. No. 28 is a rich archaeological composition, representing in the foreground a monumental group derived from the Farnese Forum, and a section of the famous frieze with gryphons from the temple of Antoninus and Faustina, while a building reminiscent of the Temple of Saturn in the
273 Forum appears in the background. Folio 29 shows in the centre an almost exact copy of the group of the horse and lion in the Palazzo dei Conservatori,[13] placed on a high plinth against a background of architectural structures which vaguely recall the Capitoline palaces. Fittingly, the last folio represents the Capitoline wolf against a background of magnificent, vast architecture[14] which is clearly derived from the Arch of Constantine, and is crowned with four horses in an obvious reminder of the façade of St Mark's in Venice.

In the first twenty drawings archaeology also plays a fairly important part, but much less so than in the second group. I shall just make some isolated observations on a few particu-
250 larly interesting points. Folio 6 attempts a new and evocative setting for the Dioscuri.[15] The old fountain by Domenico Fontana, standing between them, has been replaced by Juvarra

with another, to which he has given great importance; and both figures and fountain are seen against the background of a palace of huge dimensions. The theme of a new arrangement for the Dioscuri was fresh in everyone's mind, because between 1721 and 1724 Alessandro Specchi had erected the Papal Stables on the south side of the Piazza del Quirinale. Juvarra's drawing, though it is not to be understood as a criticism of the arrangement given by Specchi, shows that he realized that the latter had let slip the opportunity for a grandiose monumental solution.

Folio 8 gives prominence to a ruined temple   252
which, like the one in no. 28, is derived from the Temple of Saturn in the Forum. The importance of this drawing lies in the fact that the classical ruin rises against the background of a Gothic church, whose façade is clearly based on memories of the cathedrals of Siena and Orvieto. A similar Gothic church appears in a drawing in Volume I in the Turin Museo Civico. Brinckmann[16] has already commented on this phenomenon; and he thought he could detect English Gothic influence in it. But in 1720 when Juvarra was in London, interest in Gothic was at its lowest ebb, especially in Burlington's circle; and what is more, no English cathedral shows the slightest resemblance to Juvarra's drawing. On the other hand it should be remembered that the taste for Gothic had been reawakened by Guarini and, although his *Architettura civile* was not published by Vittone until 1736, certainly Juvarra would have known the manuscript. The appreciation of Gothic buildings which Guarini expressed in about 1680, and his definition of the contrasting aims of the structural principles of the classical Roman and the medieval Gothic style, reveal an acute understanding of Gothic which no one else attained at that time, either in Italy or elsewhere.[17]

The remaining folios are also of course rich in archaeological reminiscences. For example, folio 15 contains certain features taken from the   259 wide niche in the temple of Venus and Rome in the Forum; and drawing 18, in the style of   262 Piranesi, represents the Arch of Constantine, the Colosseum and the Pyramid of Cestius. Over-all, however, the importance of these drawings lies in the richness and fertility of the new architectural arrangements rather than in their archaeological reminiscences. It should be remembered that in many cases Juvarra drew inspiration from modern architecture and buildings, but it is not always easy to discover the starting point for the idea he developed. The most interesting case is perhaps to be found on folio 20. Here we see in the middle ground a church of considerable height, standing in isolation in a piazza. Looking at the corner where two of the four identical façades meet, we see that on top of the first storey there is the coat-of-arms of Alexander VII, Pope Chigi, set against the concave wall of the attic. This fact alone proves that here Juvarra was inspired by a building erected during the papacy of Alexander, and the motif is so rare that its original is easy to find. As far as I know, it occurs only in the corners of the little church of San Biagio e Santa Rita, built by Carlo Fontana in 1665 and rebuilt in 1940 in Piazza Capizucchi. But other ideas from buildings constructed under Alexander VII have also been incorporated in the drawing by Juvarra. The semi-circular porticos derive from Santa Maria della Pace by Cortona; and so too the high drum, the almost imperceptible curve of the dome itself and the heavy lantern. However, the exaggerated height given to the church obscures its derivation from seventeenth-century buildings.

Instead of tracing further Roman Baroque sources I should like to mention a case in which Juvarra was influenced by French impressions. The picturesque placing of an equestrian monument on folio 5 against a background of concave colonnades with pavilions in the centre and at both ends, is an arrangement derived from Hôtel Mazarin, built by Le Vau in Paris, and now the seat of the Institut de France.

There are also drawings which relate closely to architectural plans which Juvarra was busy composing during this period. The most impressive example is no. 16 which accords with the preparatory plans which Juvarra completed in 1729 for the Duomo Nuovo in Turin. It matches almost exactly the plan reproduced on plate 212 in the *Teatrum Novum Pedemontii* by Brinckmann,[18] and no other surviving drawing gives such a complete representation of Juvarra's grandiose conception of this building which was never constructed.

The Chatsworth volume, however, has noth-ing very new to offer in the way of either invention or style. The dedication, on the other hand, is of particular interest. The drawing, with a wealth of bases, capitals, vases, sarcophagi, Roman ruins, etc., bears the inscription: 'PROSPETTIVE DISEGIATE DALL' CAVAL DON FILIPPO YUVARRA E DEDICATE All' Eccellenza di Riccardo conte di Burlington MDCCXXX' (Views designed by Cavaliere Don Filippo Juvarra and dedicated to his Excellency Richard Lord Burlington MDCCXXX). Most of the thirty drawings which follow, bear the date 1729 and Juvarra's signature.

No information has come down to us about any personal contact between Juvarra and Burlington; so now we are faced with the interesting problem of the nature of the relations between these two men. Lord Burlington died in 1752, without a male heir, and all his possessions, collections and papers went to his daughter Charlotte. She married Lord Hartington, who later became the fourth Duke of Devonshire. This is how the small sketchbook by Juvarra came to be in the Chatsworth collection. But among Burlington's numerous papers at Chatsworth there is not the slightest clue as to any relations which might have existed between him and the great architect from Piedmont. The dedication of 1730 is therefore the only valid proof that such relations did in fact exist. We are left to speculate on the place and the date of their meeting, if ever there was one, and why Juvarra deemed the English lord worthy of such a gift. Obviously, without documents, we can never arrive at a precise answer. We must talk in terms of likelihood rather than of certainty.

When he was twenty, Lord Burlington spent a year in Italy, as was the custom for an English gentleman desiring a complete education. Extremely rich, belonging to a family known far beyond English shores,[19] he travelled in great style. He was received by the Italian aristocracy and certainly met all the most renowned personalities of the day. It would be easy to assume that he also met Juvarra, whose reputation as architect of the first order was already established by then. However, an analysis of the itinerary of the two men shows us there was little likelihood of such a meeting. At Chatsworth there is the account book of Lord Burlington's Italian journey,[20] which enables us to follow all his movements, day by day. He was at Modane on 8 September 1714, at Susa on the 9th, Turin from the 11th to 13th. He slept at Alessandria on the 14th and arrived in Rome on the 28th. Juvarra, who was travelling from Sicily in the entourage of Victor Amedeus II, came ashore at Savona on 15 September,[21] and after a short stay at Govone, he set off for Turin. Thus he could not have met Burlington, who had left several days earlier.

Burlington left Rome on 5 February 1715, to return to London at a leisurely pace via Florence, Venice, Milan, Turin and Paris. He stayed a couple of days in Turin about the middle of March, before continuing to Susa and Modane. Juvarra had not stayed long in Turin. On 18 December 1714 he was sworn in as Victor Amedeus' chief civil architect,[22] but it appears that shortly afterwards, with special permission from the king, he went off to Rome, where he had been invited to take part in the competition for the sacristy of St Peter's. We find that already on 15 February 1715 a payment on account was sent to the carpenter Francesco Piccolini for a wooden model of the sacristy. This means that the architect must have arrived a few weeks before that date.[23] But since he had such an important work on hand as the design of the sacristy, it seems unlikely that he met Burlington before the latter's departure on 5 February, for only when the execution of the model was begun could Juvarra have been free to move around.[24]

In Rome Burlington met William Kent,[25] the English artist from Yorkshire, who had settled in Rome in 1709 and who was then working in the studio of Benedetto Luti. Kent, a genial man, was a very versatile artist and fanatical admirer of all things Italian. With his excellent knowledge of Roman art, artists and society, he enjoyed acting as guide to English travellers. I believe, though I have no proof, that Kent met Juvarra at the time when the latter was working in Rome as scene-painter and architect to Cardinal Ottoboni. However, it is still doubtful whether, at the end of January or the beginning of February – the only period in which they were both in Rome at the same time – Burlington would have tried to meet Juvarra. During his Grand Tour in Italy, Burlington studied art and architecture with keen interest, but he still did not have a clear concept of his vocation. His career as patron and architect began only after he had returned to London.

At that time in England a vigorous revival of interest in Palladio was just beginning. The summer of 1715 saw the appearance of the first part of the magnificent English edition of Palladio's *Four Books of Architecture*, published by Giacomo Leoni,[26] and also of the first volume of Colen Campbell's *Vitruvius Britannicus*. Burlington was attracted by this movement. A man of high principles and admirable strength of character, he set himself to study architecture with Campbell and in a short time became the greatest exponent of the movement.[27] By 1717 he had already built his first small building from his own drawings. In 1719 he left again for Italy, going directly to Vicenza, where he concentrated exclusively on Palladio. He returned to London towards the end of the year. His reputation as an expert on architecture was by now firmly established and, moreover, his hospitable residence, Burlington House, had become the principal meeting place in London for anyone with artistic interests.

We know that Juvarra spent most of the year 1720 in Portugal. On his return he went through London and Paris.[28] He stayed in London as guest of the Portuguese ambassador for about a month at the end of the year. Although we lack documents relating to his stay in England, certain conclusions seem to be inevitable. There can be not the slightest doubt that he was welcomed with enthusiasm in the Italianate circle of Burlington House, and by William Kent, an old acquaintance of Roman days. Burlington would have seen Juvarra as the most eminent representative of Italian architecture, and a man of international fame, while Juvarra must have felt flattered to find so much sincere devotion at Burlington House for things Italian. It would be idle to ask to what extent Burlington agreed with Juvarra's architectural ideas or what Juvarra's reaction was regarding the ideal of classical renaissance propagated by Lord Burlington. They were certainly both moved by the art of the ancients. Burlington's architectural principles had much in common with the classical-late-Baroque taste of Carlo Fontana, Juvarra's teacher; and Juvarra showed the deepest devotion to Fontana right up to his death.

Between 1720 and 1730 Burlington's fame as

an architect reached its peak. He built a considerable number of important buildings, including the Dormitory at Westminster School; General Wade's house in London; Petersham Lodge in Surrey, residence of Lord Hartington; Tottenham Park in Wiltshire, belonging to Lord Bruce; the school and almshouse at Sevenoaks; the Assembly Rooms at York and above all his Palladian villa at Chiswick. Thanks to his initiative, during the third and fourth decades of the century, a homogeneous style, which the textbooks call Palladian, spread through many counties of England.

His followers were influenced not only by Burlington's personality, but also by the collection of books and architectural drawings which he had assembled for his own and their instruction. In addition to numerous drawings by Inigo Jones, he acquired from various places a vast collection of drawings by Palladio and his school. This collection is still the most extensive and important source for the study of the great architect from Vicenza.[29] He must have had the idea of forming and publishing it quite early on, because already in 1719 Burlington had bought, in Villa Maser, the reconstructions of Roman *thermae* which Palladio had prepared for publication. In 1730 Burlington brought out at his own expense a magnificent facsimile of Palladio's drawings of Roman *thermae* with a preface in Italian, thus realizing a task which death had prevented his favourite artist from completing.[30]

There is no doubt that he distributed this book among his friends and that a certain number of copies were sent to Italy in order to renew contacts there. Cicognara owned the copy 'presented by the publisher to Count Algarotti'.[31] It is tempting to think that a copy was likewise sent to Juvarra, and it is perhaps not too fanciful to suppose that Juvarra expressed his gratitude by dedicating the little volume of architectural fantasies to Burlington. In order to support this theory I should like to draw the reader's attention to the difference between the date written on the frontispiece (1730) and that written on the drawings (1729). The date 1729 coincides with that of the group of architectural sketches already mentioned, in the first volume in the Turin Museo Civico. It may well be, therefore, that the thirty drawings in the sketchbook given to Burlington were first drawn without any specific aim in view, and that the frontispiece was added a year later, when the occasion arose to make a gift of them. If it were not for the coincidence in the dates of Burlington's publication of Palladio's *thermae* and of Juvarra's dedication, one might simply think that the latter was a belated thank-you from Juvarra for the hospitality he had enjoyed at Burlington House.

Dedications are a useful barometer of a man's fame. In the years preceding 1730 and up to 1740, not a year passed without Burlington receiving some flattering dedication or other, and this sign of public recognition was not limited to his own country. In 1728 the famous doctor and writer Antonio Cocchi under the pseudonym Sebastiano Artopolita dedicated to him his edition of the *Vita di Benvenuto Cellini*.[32] Scipione Maffei, man of letters from Verona who published the first biography of Juvarra in 1738, sent Burlington the volume by Alessandro Pompei, the *Cinque Ordini dell' Architettura civile di Michele Sanmicheli*, Verona, 1735, with the characteristic dedication: 'To My Lord Burlington, the Palladio and Jones of our times.'[33] These words are a clear indication of the role which Burlington wanted to play. A portrait painted by George Knapton which hangs at Chatsworth, shows Burlington in the foreground, holding his own edition of Palladio's drawings and, in the background, a bust of Inigo Jones. Burlington was represented as heir to the architectural legacy of Palladio and Jones. It is worth reproducing here an anonymous dedication, undated, found at Chatsworth in a translation of Alberti by Cosimo Bartoli (Florence, 1550).[34] In it an Italian admirer makes the book itself speak in terms which might seem somewhat excessive:

> *Al gran Lorenzo, nel sermon romano*
> *e quindi nel Toscano*
> *a Cosmo, Medicei Lumi, fui dato:*
> *poi che al Conte Riccardo, amico Fato,*
> *al Palladio Britannico mi diede;*
> *posso dire: Mi possiede*
> *un terzo Eroe, pari in Idee sublimi*
> *ma molto più Conoscitor de' primi.*

(To the great Lorenzo, in the Roman tongue, and then in the Tuscan to Cosmo, Medicean luminaries, was I given: then Fate my friend gave me to Lord Richard, British Palladio; I can say: I am possessed by a third

275 NICHOLAS HAWKSMOOR. Steeple of St George's, Bloomsbury, London

276 Details of Chatsworth volume, folios 2 and 10

Hero, equal in sublime Ideas but a far greater Connoisseur than the other two.

The extent to which Burlington's influence was widespread and acknowledged emerges from the fact that just before his death in 1751, Count Algarotti, then guest at the court of Frederick the Great, warmly recommended his architectural style as an example to be imitated.[35]

The *Catalogo dei disegni fatti dal signor cavaliere ed abate don Filippo Juvarra . . . compilato dal suo discepolo G.B. Sacchetti* ('Catalogue of drawings done by Sig. Cavaliere and Abbé Don Filippo Juvarra . . . compiled by his disciple G. B. Sacchetti'), though compiled with great precision, makes no mention of the drawings dedicated to Burlington. However, in the list for the year 1716, Sacchetti notes 'Drawings of several ideas made for various English Lords'.[36] It may be that earlier than 1714, in Rome, Juvarra had had contact with people like Thomas Coke, who later became Lord Leicester. This great classical scholar was a friend of Burlington, and he built one of the most extravagant Palladian buildings, Holkham Hall, in Norfolk. To date, however, it has been impossible to trace any drawing by Juvarra among the papers of old families of the English nobility. We know only the Chatsworth sketchbook.

Finally let me turn to two special problems arising from the relation between the Chatsworth drawings and English architecture. In the background on the left of folio 10 there is a 276 vast monument crowned by a stepped pyramid. A similar one is used for a bell-tower in folio 2, and in addition the same idea returns in two drawings in the National Library in Turin.[37] It is an odd idea, certainly out of the ordinary. But a similar stepped pyramid was built by Nicholas Hawksmoor as the steeple of St 275 George's in Bloomsbury in London. Hawksmoor was here translating into stone Sir Christopher Wren's ideas about the original form of the mausoleum of Halicarnassus. The description of the mausoleum which Wren made probably around 1715 has come down to us, together with an attempt at reconstruction in the form of a pyramid with steps.[38] Hawksmoor's church was executed between 1720 and 1724. Therefore one might be tempted to believe that

277 HAWKSMOOR and BURLINGTON. Mausoleum at Castle Howard

Juvarra got his idea from one source or the other, when he was in London in 1720. This theory does not hold, however, because one of the drawings with a stepped pyramid in Volume VI in the National Library bears the date 1719;[39] in other words, it was executed before the journey to London. It must therefore be concluded that, in this case, Juvarra, Wren and Hawksmoor drew on a common source which I have been unable to discover.[40]

The second problem offers a more satisfac-278 tory solution. In the centre of folio 14 a large building with circular ground-plan, a kind of enlarged *tempietto*, has been drawn beside a structure resembling a pagoda, which had never been seen before in Italy. It was apparently the outcome of the taste for things Chinese which was then just beginning.[41] But what interests us is the *tempietto*, which influenced English architecture. In 1729 Hawksmoor composed a design for a mausoleum of vast dimensions at

278 Detail of Chatsworth volume, folio 14

209

Castle Howard, seat of the Earl of Carlisle.[42] He envisaged a large building with circular ground-plan surrounded by a colonnade. In about 1732 preparations were sufficiently advanced for execution to begin. Sir Thomas Robinson, Lord Carlisle's son-in-law, who belonged to the new generation and firmly supported Lord Burlington's ideas on architecture, insisted that the design for the mausoleum should be submitted to Burlington for his opinion. The latter suggested a number of alterations and from that moment took over control of the plan. We know that in 1734 he disapproved of the base of the monument and that in 1736, after Hawksmoor's death, Sir Thomas Robinson managed to hand over the continuation of the building to Burlington, who entrusted its execution to one of his protégés, the architect Garrett. Burlington's main innovation was the great stairway which leads to the platform on which the mausoleum stands; and it is impossible to overlook how closely the form of this stairway resembles that in Juvarra's drawing.

277

But let us complete the story. In January 1737 Sir Thomas Robinson wrote to Lord Carlisle: 'The staircase is the same as Ld. B. at Chiswick and I think very well adapted to this Building, in short I think the whole is according to the antient taste.' The same type of staircase was in fact used by Burlington for his villa at Chiswick, constructed to his design shortly after 1720. The plan for Burlington's villa derives from plans by Palladio and Scamozzi, but the staircase had a Piedmontese genealogy. During his Grand Tour, Burlington would have seen the staircase which descends from the Castle of Racconigi into the garden, and its grandiose appearance must have led him later to introduce something like it into English architecture. However, the idea of using that complex design for a staircase in connection with a circular temple at Castle Howard was almost certainly taken from Juvarra's drawing.

Since Burlington's wish was to build in the manner of the ancients, he must have regarded the drawing by Juvarra as being in tune with the 'antient taste', to quote Sir Thomas Robinson. Burlington saw in Juvarra's drawings exactly what the latter wanted him to see: a modern realization of ancient grandeur.

279 VITTONE. Dome of the Santuario della Visitazione di Maria, Vallinotto

XI
VITTONE'S DOMES

Vittone's Domes

It is as a builder of churches that Vittone claims a place among the giants of Baroque architecture, as a man truly obsessed by new and sublime visions. His few palaces are by comparison of marginal interest; they would never have gained him the eminence that he now enjoys. Fortunately, his contemporaries understood where his strength lay. The clergy with whom he had to deal – often simple people without much artistic education – were enlightened enough (or modest enough) to give him a free hand, and to allow his genius to plot its own strange course. That course was, moreover, remarkably consistent and direct. Almost all his churches are centrally planned: his passion as a designer was dedicated to, one may even say exhausted by, that most noble theme in Italian architectural history, to which all her greatest masters – Brunelleschi, Alberti, Bramante, Michelangelo, Palladio, Bernini, Borromini, Guarini, Juvarra – had devoted so much of their creative energy.

I recall very vividly my first acquaintance with Vittone's churches. The initial impression was one of wonderment and almost incredulity. I had seen nothing like them in Italy. Where did these extraordinary structures stem from, what did they signify, where did they lead to? Some answers were not difficult to find: the specific Piedmontese character of some of his buildings was evidently due to the synthesis of Guarinesque and Juvarresque elements. These elements, however, supplied no more than the raw material for his own novel solutions. Clearly, Guarini and Juvarra fertilized his mind and his imagination more than any other architects. But as one went from church to church, one began to develop a vivid feeling for and understanding of Vittone's specific idiosyncratic architectural language. Soon one realized that the magic of his structures rested, above all, in ever new, highly personal re-formulations of the dome. Thus the visitor to Vittone's churches immediately looks up and scans the dome in expectation of surprises that Vittone has in store for him. Even without rational analysis, everyone

is aware that the dome is always the focus of Vittone's creations. It is significant that in his *Vittone*,[1] Portoghesi found it necessary to reserve two-thirds of the illustrations of his *introduzione visiva* to whole and partial views of domes in order to do justice to (I am using his own words) 'the primacy which Vittone gave to the dome as the key element in the whole design'.

Knowing the importance Vittone must have attached to domes, one would expect to find his views revealed in his writings. So let me clear this point first. Vittone's two books, the *Istruzioni elementari*, published in 1760, and the *Istruzioni diverse* which appeared in 1766 are by now well known. Although these treatises are long, or even very long, they contain no chapter on domes. Vittone liked to put down his ideas in the form of treatises and in this respect, as in others, he was in the tradition of humanist architects. Apart from his two published works, he had other literary plans – we know the subjects of six of them – and some of his material was apparently ready for the press.

As he himself announced in the Preface to the *Istruzioni diverse* (p. xiii), a manuscript 'in preparation' contained a compilation of the laws set down in Justinian's *Corpus Juris Civilis* regarding buildings in town and countryside and regarding the supply of water: '*Una raccolta, che già tengo in appresto, di quelle leggi, che nel Codice, ne' Digesti, e nelle Novelle di Giustiniano disperse si trovansi, concernenti le servitù si civili, che rustiche, gli Edifici, i fondi campestri, e la condotta dell'acque; come altresi delle sentenze più essenziali de' Giureconsoli, e specialmente del Dottore Bartolomeo Cepolla sovra le dette servitù . . .*' He is referring here to the various parts of Justinian's *Corpus*, namely the *Codex constitutionum*, the Digest or *Pandectae*, and the *Novellae constitutiones*. That this manuscript really existed is attested by an inventory entry after Vittone's death[2] which mentions five notebooks entitled: *Leggi e Dottrine Legali concernenti gli Edificj, i Fondi, e la condotta delle acque*. The same inventory mentions a second manuscript entitled: 'Discourses on theatres and the arrangements of the things most necessary to perform in them and on the method of making them.' In addition, Professor Pommer[3] has published a document of 6 December 1773 concerning a dispute of Vittone's heirs in which four more literary enterprises by him are listed, which, it is claimed, were 'omitted' from the inventory. These four manuscripts are specified as 'A treatise on the nature of the local movements of heavy bodies'; 'A description of the various considerations regarding the valuation of real estate'; 'A treatise concerning the resistance of wood against breaking'; and finally a possibly more rewarding topic: a manuscript 'On the rules regarding the curvature of the ribs for the construction of domes'. All these manuscripts, we are told, were left out of the inventory because they were at that time with the architect Gianni Battista Galletto di Carignano who was supposed to assist with the preparation of their publication. Galletto had contributed the '*Istruzioni armoniche, o sia Breve Trattato sopra la natura del suono*' to Vittone's *Istruzioni diverse* and for twenty years (from 1750 to 1770) had been Vittone's devoted assistant.

I have given you this list of 'publications in preparation', because they tell us a great deal about Vittone. From our point of view their topics may sound disappointing. But their limited technical nature and their strictly scientific orientation fit the picture of a typically eighteenth-century mind committed to rational investigation. We know from the *Istruzioni diverse* that Newton was one of his heroes. The lost manuscripts prove beyond doubt that Vittone's interest – while concerned with clearly circumscribed problems – was broad and varied and not at all wholly concentrated on purely architectural matters or even domes. When we at last discover that he had written a special piece on domes, it was, if I interpret the recorded title correctly, a treatise on the statics of various domical curvatures. From the titles of these lost treatises a clearer view emerges of Vittone, the technical expert, the '*ingegnere*' as he liked to call himself. Portoghesi summarizes the position by pointedly stating that 'he subordinated aesthetic considerations to a strict technical inquiry'. We

280 VITTONE. Santuario della Visitazione di Maria, Vallinotto

would give much to recover his treatise on domes as well as his other lost treatises and I cannot reconcile myself to the idea that they should be lost for ever.

A little more and rather illuminating information about Vittone's views can be gained by studying the descriptions of his own works in the *Istruzioni diverse*. Although these descriptions are, as a rule, of a purely pragmatic nature, they yet contribute significantly to our special problem. I think it is only once that Vittone allows us a glimpse behind the iron curtain of his emotive or, if you like, symbolic reasoning for a specific domical structure. I have in mind his early masterpiece, the Santuario della Visitazione di Maria at Vallinotto near Carignano, built between 1738 and 1739. Vittone writes that

279
280

the interior [of the church] consists of one single storey surmounted by three vaults, one above the other, all perforated and open; thus the eye of the visitor to the church roams freely from space to space, and, with the help of the light which enters through the windows invisible from inside, enjoys the gradually increasing variety which is offered by these vaults and which culminates in the little cupola [of the lantern] where one sees a representation of the Holy Trinity.

213

This description makes it clear that the unprecedented triple vault cannot simply be explained as an experimental fusing of two types of Guarinesque domical structures, the transparent dome of intersecting ribs and the solid, spherical shell, indirectly lit and wide open at the top. The *raison d'être* of Vittone's solution was the equation of the triple vault with the Trinity. The triple structure was chosen by him because it symbolized the mystery of the Trinity that appears painted in the little cupola of the lantern. The triple vault, illuminated by invisible sources of light, was a vehicle for producing the illusion of immense height – an illusion that only worked by virtue of the painted hierarchy of angels, which – Vittone tells us – he had wanted to appear in diminishing perspective ('but the hurried execution . . . prevented the desired effect of this work from being entirely successful'). In this early work, therefore, the domical structure and the painted decoration cannot be separated. The frescoes constitute an essential complement to the intrinsic meaning of the triple dome.

No other description published by Vittone tells us as much as that of the Sanctuary at Vallinotto. But in the case of the church of S. Chiara at Brà, datable to 1742, we are given at least some interesting insights. Vittone explains briefly that from the galleries above the chapels the nuns of S. Chiara were able to 'enjoy a view of the church from every part. There is a double vault and through the four large openings which have been provided in the four main fields of the lower vault, the visitor to the church can see the paintings in the upper vault.' In a sense, S. Chiara, an acknowledged climax among many masterpieces, logically continues the technique of Vallinotto. By devising two vaults, one above the other, Vittone was able to create a symbol of the infinity of the heavens where saints and angels dwell: this is the verifiable concept that made him choose this particular structural form. But without the paintings on the upper vault perceived through the four large openings of the lower one the meaning of the architectural invention could not be realized by the beholder. It is important to note that the normal beholder has not the slightest idea that two vaults and a sophisticated system of lighting were necessary to bring about the desired effect. Looking up, he

will feel, however, that a very thin, almost diaphanous shell seems to separate the constructed space from the infinity of the sky. Thinking back to the few words Vittone devoted to the practical organization of the vault and its effect, we cannot help concluding that he shied away from trying to explain the rather intangible qualities of his design – his symbolic, emotive and sublime intentions. True to the spirit of precise rational enquiry to which he was dedicated, he gave no clue to what was going on in the depths of his mind and left it to us, two centuries after his death, to try to discover and formulate it.

It hardly seems necessary to give further quotations from Vittone's *Istruzioni diverse*. Let me only point out that often he does not mention the dome at all in the description he gives of a building. One cannot, for instance, read his observations on the church of S. Gaetano and the Theatine convent at Nizza without a reaction of surprise. In the splendid church, built in 1744, he developed the idea of the galleries first used in S. Chiara, but while he talks a great deal about the clever organization of the plan of the convent, the church receives the laconic comment: 'a small, but convenient church, with five altars, and presbytery and choir in proportion'. Finally, even more revealing seems to me his discussion of S. Croce at Villanova di Mondovì, erected in 1755.

We hear that his patrons, the Confratelli Disciplinanti, expressed the wish 'that a building of originality and gay charm be erected for them without, however, involving them in too heavy expenditure', and this, he says, 'was the reason for me to omit any sort of dome [*cupole*]'. He then goes on to describe the various new devices which together 'form the principle vault [*volta*] of this church'.

So Vittone calls the domical feature of this church '*volta*' and contrasts it with '*cupola*'. From the point of view of his time Vittone was, of course, correct. In his formative years he had imbibed the Roman interpretation of the *cupola*. For him as for all other Italian architects of the seventeenth and eighteenth centuries the great exemplars of churches with *cupole* were St Peter's, S. Agnese in Piazza Navona and SS. Martina e Luca, plus a few hardly less exalted structures.

One is familiar with Vittone's various exer-

285, 286

294, 295

214

281 VITTONE. Project for the Accademia di San Luca (from *Istruzione elementari*)
282 VITTONE. Project for a large cathedral (from *Istruzione elementari*)

283 VITTONE. Dome of S. Chiara, Turin

284 VITTONE. Dome of S. Michele, Rivarolo
Canavese

cises in the grand Roman tradition. They have
been reviewed in Carboneri and Viale's *Catalogo*[4] and, more fully, in Werner Oechslin's
paper in the *Bollettino d'Arte*.[5] Characteristically, the church design that in 1732 formed part
of Vittone's victorious project in the Concorso
Clementino of the Accademia di San Luca
belongs to this tradition and so does the project
which – as Oechslin was able to establish – was
Vittone's *saggio d'abilità* delivered on 6 April
1733 'as a condition for being admitted, as he
desired, to the rank of Accademico di merito'.
Oechslin recovered the original project in the
Accademia di San Luca; apart from some
stylistic adjustments the drawn elevation agrees
with the well-known engraving which Vittone
published in the *Istruzioni elementari* and which   281
had defied precise dating and identification. I
do not believe that Vittone made these designs
with tongue in cheek – only in order to make
sure that he would conform to academic
propriety.

In fact, his mind turned again and again to
the St Peter's – S. Agnese – Superga solution.
There are drawings harking back to it in the
volumes of the Musée des Arts Décoratifs (see
pp. 223–234); and there is, above all, the project
for the large cathedral that has been associated   282
with the church of S. Giovanni at Carignano as
well as with the Cathedral of Turin despite the
fact that Vittone explicitly states that the idea
of this cathedral was 'devised by me purely for
my own satisfaction'. (I think, by the way, that
Portoghesi correctly recognized in this project
an influence from St Paul's in London: even the
idea of the portico of giant Corinthian columns
may stem from there. Vittone knew this church
from Colin Campbell's *Vitruvius Britannicus* in
his library.) We are justified in concluding that
when Vittone thought in monumental terms he
kept within the tradition that still carried unparalleled prestige.

Fortunately, Vittone never had to face the
problem of having to create a church of
monumental size; he could thus free himself
from the enticing power of tradition, turn his
energies away from the conventional type of
dome and concentrate on new and revolutionary solutions of vaulting. In a certain sense, his
early structures before and about 1740 are
preludes to his great discoveries of the mid-
1740s. But they are remarkable enough. Let me

285, return to S. Chiara at Brà for a few specific
286 observations. The vault seems precariously
balanced on the four piers which rise extraordinarily high, through two storeys. On the
lower level the piers are faced with linked
Corinthian wall strips, on the upper level by an
order of columns and these find a continuation
in the broad twin ribs of the vault. Thus an
uninterrupted movement sweeps through the
entire height of the church along the face of the
piers right up to the summit of the vault. Little
is left of the vault itself: it is reduced to four
thin shells which are almost 'eaten up' by the
four high arches of the galleries and the four
large apertures.

Structurally, this building is entirely dependent on the four strong piers; it would
stand even if the thin shell of wall containing
the four segmental chapels of the ground-plan
were dismantled. This kind of 'skeleton' structure was scarcely used in Italy, but had its home
in Germany, and I believe that this is where it
ultimately stems from. The break with the
time-honoured Italian tradition is to be found
in Juvarra's works – not yet in the church of
the Venaria Reale and the basilica of the
Superga but soon afterwards in the design for
S. Raffaele and later in those for the Duomo
Nuvo and for the *gran salone* at Stupinigi. In all
these Juvarresque designs the vault had been
devalued in favour of an emphasis on the
framework of the 'skeleton' structure, the
verticalism of which is reminiscent of Gothic
concepts. During these years Vittone was also
fascinated by the Juvarresque formulation of
galleries, another feature that belonged to the
German rather than the Italian structural
repertory. But the perforated dome through
which one perceives paintings was Vittone's
own contribution. There seems to exist a close
connection between Vittone's formulation of
this idea and the *quadratura* frescoes in the
dome of the Consolata by Giambattista Alberoni
from designs by Giuseppe Bibbiena with
figures by Crosato; they were executed in 1740,
just before Vittone planned his church. It is, in
fact, not rare to come across *quadratura* painting on vaults with *feigned* perforations through
which one looks at illusionistically painted
Biblical scenes. In the church of S. Giuseppe at
287 S. Damiano d'Asti, in Piedmont, the construction of which was finished in 1715, the frescoes

285, 286 VITTONE. Two views of the dome of
S. Chiara, Brà

217

287 Ceilings of S. Giuseppe, S. Damiano d'Asti, by G. B. Pozzo

288 Ceiling of the chapter house of S. Marta, Genoa, by Revello and Boni

of the cupola, executed a little later probably by Giovan Battista Pozzo, illustrate my point; or, outside Piedmont, the chapter house of S. Marta at Genoa, with *quadratura* by Giovan 288 Battista Revello and figures by Jacopo Antonio Boni. By translating such contemporary *quadratura* effects into structural reality Vittone transcended current conventions, a characteristic sign of the fearless independence of his searching mind.

Vittone's direct or indirect connections with the north seem to me undeniable. Germany never developed a taste for the high Italian dome rising above a drum. I believe, however, that the flat 'German' vault organically capping the supporting piers reached Vittone via Juvarra. So despite the structural affinities between northern examples and S. Chiara at Brà, Vittone's perforated vault and double shell solution has a distinctly Italian pedigree. Moreover, Vittone's later realizations of vaults lead further and further away from the northern development. The new problems formulated by Vittone from the mid-1740s onwards ripened slowly. At a relatively early date it occurred to him that any radical change in vaulting had to start with a rethinking of the pendentives, the real hub of traditional domical structures. It was the development of the pendentives, those solid pieces of masonry in the shape of concave triangles, that made an easy transition from the square of the crossing to the circle of the drum possible and was thus vital for the creation of the Renaissance and Baroque dome.

Borromini in S. Carlo alle Quattro Fontane 224 essentially returned to Brunelleschi's Old Sacristy when he queried the validity of tradition by placing bas-reliefs in heavy oval frames on the pendentives. A generation later, Guarini in the Chapel of the Santissima Sindone, where 235 contradictions abound, opened the pendentives into large circular windows, and it is from this daring idea that Vittone took his inspiration. We find this motif in some of his churches and designs of about 1740, as Portoghesi has already observed: in the Guarinesque church of S. Luigi Gonzaga at Corteranzo, in the project for the church of S. Chiara at Alessandria (which 289 was never built) and in S. Bernardino at Chieri.

In S. Bernardino, Vittone was handicapped 290, by the existence of an older Greek cross church 291 and the structure has therefore a more tradi-

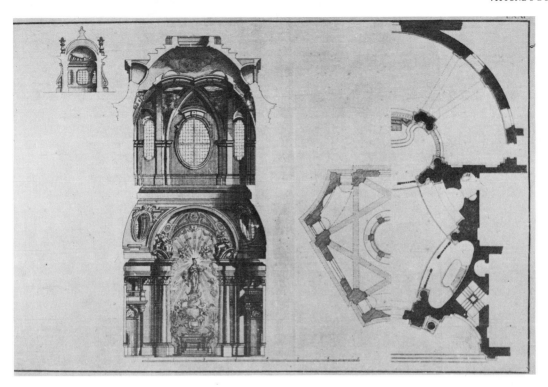

289 VITTONE. Project for S. Chiara, Alessandria

290, 291 VITTONE. S. Bernardino, Chieri. *Left:* façade and section. *Above:* view into the dome

219

292 VITTONE. S. Maria di Piazza, Turin

293 VITTONE. Ospizio di Carità, Turin, detail of dome

tional appearance than we are used to from Vittone. But by opening the pendentives (through which brilliant light streams into the church in an area that is normally rather dimly lit) and by raising the vaults over all four arms of the Greek cross considerably above the arches of the crossing the dome seems to hover weightlessly in space.

The year 1744 marked an entirely new departure, superseding the earlier experiments. From that year dates the design of the Ospizio di 293 Carità a Carignano, completed in 1749. The chapel in the centre of this large project still has a traditional crossing with pendentives between the arches, but the normal uninterrupted ring (*anello*) above the pendentives is not maintained: the upper parts of the pendentives are hollowed out, forming cavities that contain large windows; and prolongations of these strange features reach through what may be called a 'dwarf drum' area into the dome. It is obvious that this new motif opened up not only entirely new possibilities of pouring light into domes, but also gave rise to a hitherto unknown unification of the pendentive, drum and cupola zones. It had magnificent properties that allowed solutions never before dreamed of.

294 VITTONE. S. Croce, Villanova di Mondovì

295 VITTONE. S. Croce, Villanova di Mondovì,
detail of dome

296 VITTONE. S. Maria Maggiore, Mondovì, ruins in
1945

This feature is so central in Vittone's later work that attention must always be focused on it. We may rapidly glance at three final 292 examples. The presbytery of S. Maria di Piazza at Turin, datable 1751 to 1754, is more complex than the chapel of the Ospizio, although here too the original shapes of the pendentives and the ring are still recognizable. The organization of the windows of the *tiburio* repeat the quadrangular form of the crossing and since two windows at right angles appear over each pendentive there are twelve windows in this zone, while the piers between them form a regular octagon leading over into the regular octagonal star-shape of the vault.

296 My next example is S. Maria Maggiore at Mondovì which was bombed during the last war. I photographed the ruins shortly after the war. The little that was then standing allows the conclusion that here each of the originally eight zones (in the diagonals, pendentives, drum and dome) had been unified by means of a coherent recessed field. The most mature manifestation of this idea is S. Croce at Villanova 294 di Mondovì erected in 1755. The crossing 295 carries extremely high and wide arches. By broadening and widening the completely hollowed out area of the pendentives, their original character and meaning is made almost unrecognizable. Vittone once again found a new way of transforming the square of the crossing into the octagon of the dome. The regular shape of the vault stretches, as it were, protective tentacles over the structure beneath. The old notions of arch, pendentive, drum and dome have lost their meaning. Such buildings carry their measure within themselves; they are without peer both in Italy and abroad.

297 VITTONE. Copy of a design by Carlo Fontana for the catafalque of Pedro II
(Paris, Musée des Arts Décoratifs, no. 114)

XII VITTONE'S DRAWINGS IN
THE MUSÉE DES ARTS DÉCORATIFS

Vittone's Drawings in the Musée des Arts Décoratifs

WHEN Bernardo Antonio Vittone died in Turin on 19 October 1770, he left behind not only a very large *oeuvre* of most extraordinary buildings but also two printed works, the *Istruzioni elementari* of 1760 and the *Istruzioni diverse* of 1766. These treatises, now extremely rare, will have to be referred to time and again in this essay. An inventory made after his death, moreover, lists many other items, including further manuscripts ready for the press which have been described in more detail in the preceding essay. These have never been traced, nor do we know what happened to the bulk of the material mentioned in the inventory. But – to anticipate the result of my investigation – I believe that at least some of it has come down to us in two volumes now in the library of the Musée des Arts Décoratifs in Paris.[1]

The pedigree of the volumes does not go far back. In 1903 they were presented to the library by the painter Albert Besnard, who had bought them in Rome, and this is virtually all we know about them. It seems that the drawings were not bound when they entered the museum. In any case, their present arrangement and binding date from 1903.[2] At that time many of the drawings were mounted on modern paper and numbered (usually with one, but sometimes with two and occasionally with three or even four sheets to a mount).

The numbers in the first volume run from 1 to 132, but since nos. 4, 11, 55 and 63 are missing, the volume contains only 128 sheets of drawings. The second volume begins with no. 133 and ends with no. 237, containing 104 sheets.[3] Thus at present there are altogether 232 old sheets with drawings in the two volumes.[4] The discrepancy between the actual number of drawings and the numbering from 1 to 237 – thus including five lacunae – is satisfactorily explained by a note on the fly-leaf, according to which the museum's librarian transferred some drawings from the Vittone volumes to a volume entitled '*Etranger XVIe au XVIIe s.*, because they were signed 'Andrea Cattaneo'.[5]

It seems that, with the exception of the Cattaneo drawings, no drawings were taken out of the material that reached the museum in 1903, but it is evident that the present arrangement played havoc with the original condition and also with the original organization of the drawings: many sheets of the original series were cut, and often carelessly cut, in order to separate, whenever possible, unconnected designs and put together similar subject matter. Even though the drawings seem originally not to have been bound, they formed a continuous series, for, in addition to the numbering of 1903, there are on many sheets two sets of older numbers, one in dark ink, the other in red crayon. The old ink numbers appear on 111 sheets[6] and the red numbers on 118 sheets,[7] but only seventy-nine sheets carry both sets of these numbers.[8]

The number-game is worth pursuing because the older numbers offer some clues to the original character of the whole group of drawings. In the first place, both types of old numerals appear on some of the Cattaneo drawings and, since these drawings can be dated in the mid-1790s,[9] the collection cannot have been formed until after that date. Thus post-Vittone material formed part of the collection when it was ordered and numbered twice in succession at least twenty-five years after Vittone's death.

The old double numbering makes it likely that two different groups of material were united after 1795. This assumption finds support in the fact that the ink numbers 8, 14, 16, 19 and 28 appear twice.[10] In addition, not all the old ink numbers are by the same hand; on some sheets one finds a smaller and more spidery type of number than usual, and there are even sheets on which both types of ink numbers appear.[11] The red numbers, always centred at the top of the sheet, would appear to have superseded the ink numbers, at a time when the whole collection had come together. Now the highest old ink number is 199 and the highest red number 214, and it therefore has to be asked whether drawings were added to the collection at some time in the nineteenth century. This must be denied categorically. Where the original sheets were left more or less intact, both old numbers are regularly found.[12] Since, as I have mentioned, many old sheets were cut when preparing them for their present mounting, the old numbers were lost – sometimes the ink numbers, sometimes the red numbers and often both. Moreover, by dismembering large sheets, the number of sheets was ostensibly increased. Finally, two unconnected drawings on one large sheet, left intact, now carry two modern numbers but only one old number.[13] The discrepancy between the number of drawings in the post-1795 and the present collection is therefore fictitious rather than real.

We have seen that the Cattaneo drawings originally belonged to the present volumes and that for reasons of chronology these drawings cannot have been in Vittone's estate. This discovery invites us to enquire what the reasons are for attributing the drawings in these volumes to Vittone, as has traditionally been done. In fact, the volumes contain a great deal of extraneous material which one cannot easily associate with Vittone's name. There is a ground-plan which Michael Petzet has recognized as a project for the Kajetanerkirche at Salzburg by Kaspar Zuccalli.[14] The German inscriptions on this prove that it is an original design and, since the old numbers appear on the sheet, it cannot be a later addition to the collection. Petzet also found among the drawings a plan and section of Chiaveri's Hofkirche in Dresden; once again the old numbers guarantee the pedigree of these drawings, but Petzet is surely wrong in attributing them to Chiaveri himself.[15] They are copies after a Chiaveri project[16] and belong together with many other copies in these volumes. Hellmut Hager informed me verbally that the large project of a church with an adjoining palace, of which the volumes contain the elevation and plan,[17] is copied after Pompeo Ferrari's prize-winning project in the Accademia di S. Luca, dated 1678; he also noticed that the elevation and section of a centrally planned church[18] are copied from a project of 1704 by Pietro Paolo Scaramella, the originals of which are also in the Accademia di S. Luca. Furthermore, there are copies in the volumes of the plan of S. Carlo al Corso in Rome and of the plan of S. Lorenzo in Milan.[19] I believe that more copies after miscellaneous projects are still hidden in these volumes and await identification.

The bulk of the identifiable copies were, however, made after drawings by Carlo Fontana. I have been able to trace no fewer than 70 sheets copied from Fontana drawings now in the Windsor Royal Library and the Soane Museum.[20] In addition, six sheets were copied from the Fontana volume now at Modena.[21] The copyist used at least 138 originals, sometimes telescoping parts of three, four, five and even six originals on one sheet. In addition, 23 sheets have drawings entirely or partly derived from Fontana, the originals of which I have so far been unable to find.[22] Another 19 sheets are probably copied after Fontana.[23] Thus Fontana originals were used for at least 99, and possibly for 118 sheets. Add to this the other 8 copies previously mentioned, the Zuccalli drawing and the five certain Cattaneo drawings, originally belonging to this material, and we have 132 sheets (possibly more) out of 237 which are not original contributions by Vittone.[24]

Nevertheless, Vittone's name is justifiably associated with the two volumes. Eleven drawings bear his signature,[25] 43 drawings are more or less closely related to illustrations in the *Istruzioni diverse* of 1766[26] and at least 4 (possibly 7) to the *Istruzioni elementari* of 1760.[27] Furthermore, 13 drawings can be attributed to him without reservation.[28] Thus, without counting twice nos. 3, 50 and 206, which are signed as well as connected with his published work, 68 (71) sheets of drawings are certainly by Vittone's hand. In addition, 3 sheets with altar designs,[29] 20 sheets with portals, doors and windows and 3 sheets with towers[30] can almost certainly be given to him, while another 13 drawings may or may not be by him.[31] The Vittone group, therefore, consists of 94[32] and, more probably, 107 (110) sheets, and this number may possibly be increased to 111 (114) by the inclusion of 4 more sheets.[33]

We have now accounted for most of the numbered sheets and it so happens that the Fontana group of 118 sheets and the Vittone group of at least 107 (and perhaps 114) sheets are fairly evenly divided. But 18 sheets belong to both groups[34] and this is a phenomenon which will occupy us further.

298 CARLO FONTANA. Design for the catafalque for the memorial service for Pedro II of Portugal, 1707 (Windsor, Royal Library)

299 VITTONE. Engraving of a catafalque from the *Istruzione diverse*, 1766

It is these 18 sheets that provide the key to attributing the copies after Fontana to Vittone. *Prima facie*, everything militates against Vittone's authorship. Vittone, probably born in 1705, was nine years old when Fontana died in 1714. One is at first inclined to assume that the copies were made in Fontana's studio and that a late eighteenth- or early nineteenth-century collector united them with a group of Vittone drawings; and the old ink numbers would seem to support such an assumption.[35] Is it imaginable that a man like Vittone, the highly strung creator of extremely imaginative and daring dome structures, would have wanted to turn to the pedantic sobriety of Fontana's work for study and inspiration? Moreover, when and where could Vittone have copied Fontana drawings in such numbers, long after the master's death? The character of a great many sheets leaves no doubt that the copyist had full access to Fontana's drawings.[36] Bound in many volumes, the latter reached the collection of Pope Clement XI Albani (1700–21) from Fontana's estate and left Italy for good in 1762 when they were acquired by King George III.[37]

Now, unexpectedly, a number of sheets containing copies after Fontana were used by Vittone for illustrations to his treatises, particularly the *Istruzioni diverse*.[38] As to the close connection between the drawings and these engravings there cannot be any doubt; as a rule the engravings reverse, as they should, the design of the drawings. As an example I illustrate the catafalque designed by Fontana in 298 1707 for the memorial service for Pedro II, King of Portugal, in S. Antonio dei Portoghesi (Windsor 9379), together with the Paris copy 297 (no. 114) and the engraving on plate CIII of the 299 *Istruzioni diverse*. In actual fact, the engraving is even closer – in almost every detail, including the architectural setting – to Fontana's drawing 300 9381. Furthermore, this engraving distinctly incorporates minor elements from Fontana 9382 and 9383. The latter Fontana drawing is copied in the centre of a composite sheet of studies in Paris (no. 93),[39] while Fontana 9381 and 9382 301 are not among the copies. Since Vittone must have had copies of these drawings at his disposal when preparing the design for his engraving, we have definite proof that the copies

300 CARLO FONTANA. Another design for the same catafalque as in pl. 298 (Windsor, Royal Library)

301 VITTONE. Sheet of studies after Fontana (Paris, Musée des Arts Décoratifs, no. 93)

preserved in the Paris volumes are only a part of a once fuller collection of copies.[40] It may be noted that in the example under review, as elsewhere, Vittone does not mention in his text (p. 200) that his design was cribbed from Fontana.

It has become clear that, at the time of the preparation of his treatises, Vittone had in his collection copies after Fontana drawings, and the old numbers on many of these copies, which also appear on those not used for publication, support the assumption that he owned all the copies in the Paris volumes and, as we now know, probably many more. But this in itself does not mean that he was the copyist, and my question as to when and where would he have had the opportunity to copy Fontana drawings has still to be answered. Vittone was in Rome only once, as a young man between the end of 1730 and the spring of 1733,[41] and on this occasion he might conceivably have come into possession of copies made in Fontana's studio. I believe, however, that the old tradition is correct and that it can satisfactorily be demonstrated that Vittone himself was the copyist.[42]

To make this hypothesis acceptable, we have to presume, first, that in his youth he was passionately interested in Fontana's work and second, that he had free and prolonged access to the papal collection.

Fontana's great reputation survived unabated, particularly in the circle of the Accademia di S. Luca where Vittone studied during his Roman years. Now, it is a fact to which some attention has recently been given[43] that Vittone's early work abounds with Fontanesque reminiscences. They are fully in evidence, even before his visit to Rome, in his designs for the parish church at Pecetto Torinese of 1730,[44] in his prize-winning project at the Accademia di S. Luca in 1732,[45] in his competition design for the façade of S. Giovanni in Laterano, also dated 1732,[46] and even in his later work such as the façade of SS. Vincenzo ed Anastasio at Cambiano, constructed in 1740. In the *Istruzioni elementari* (p. 285) Vittone calls Juvarra 'his master'. Insufficient attention has been paid to this claim, and it is usually maintained that he 'discovered' Juvarra only after his Roman journey. This seems, however, unlikely, not

227

302 VITTONE. Design for the *coretti* at the side of the
high altar of the Oratory of the Decollazione di
S. Giovanni Battista, 1728 (Paris, Musée des Arts
Décoratifs, no. 230)

only because Vittone was an independent
architect before he went to Rome, but above all
because definite proof of his pre-Roman attachment to Juvarra is furnished by a hitherto
unnoticed project in the Paris volumes showing
the elevation, section and plan of the new *coretti*
at the side of the high altar of the Oratory of the
302 Decollazione di S. Giovanni Battista, which is
dated by Vittone's own inscription 13 April
1728.[47] The Juvarresque character of this
project is immediately evident and confirms
Vittone's early apprenticeship with Juvarra. It
is well known that the latter always held his
master Carlo Fontana in the highest esteem, and
it must have been he who directed Vittone's
attention to Fontana's work as the source and
embodiment of good classical precepts in
architecture. Without Juvarra's mediation,
Fontana's influence on the pre-Roman Vittone
(e.g., at Pecetto) would be difficult to explain.
We may even go a step further and suggest that

it was Juvarra who impressed on the young
man the importance of a thorough study of
Fontana's work, best accomplished through the
established academic method of copying after
drawings. Juvarra was in Rome early in 1732,[48]
concurrently with Vittone; at that time the
older master enjoyed an immense reputation
and he – the most distinguished of Fontana's
pupils – may well have intervened on behalf of
his own pupil and negotiated Vittone's entry
into the Albani collection,[49] which then contained the Fontana drawings. This is, of course,
an unsupported speculation on my part, but it
seems to me a hypothesis that makes a situation
intelligible for which it would otherwise not be
easy to find a plausible explanation. In any
case, Vittone's authorship of the copies, which
at first appeared so unlikely, is not precluded
by circumstances. It remains to show that the
style of the copies is his.

To determine stylistically whether a copy
made after an architectural design is by one
hand rather than by another is almost impossible, particularly when measured drawings are
the object of study. It is true that the Paris
copies after Fontana have certain idiosyncrasies
in common which distinguish them clearly
from Fontana's originals. Thus, in spite of close
adherence to the originals, Vittone, as a rule,
increased the area of shadows in his copies or
even supplied shadows where there were none
in the originals; in other words, he tended
somewhat to dramatize Fontana's sober academic statements. His figures, too, differ
slightly from the originals; they display a
tendency to contraction and simplification. But
all this would hardly suffice to attribute the
copies to Vittone with any degree of certainty;
in fact, a number of the copies look remarkably
like the signed Cattaneo drawings.[50]

There exists yet another approach to the
question of authorship. Many of the copies
after Fontana drawings exhibit strange associa-
tory tendencies. Parts or even fragments lifted
from different original projects are often copied
on a single sheet and made to run into one
another; elevations and plans may be unrelated,
and a sheet may present a peculiar medley of
designs undecipherable without the aid of the
originals. Of course, Vittone made the copies
for his own education and exercise and not with
an eye to art-historical analysis over two

303 VITTONE. Sheet of studies after Fontana (Paris, Musée des Arts Décoratifs, no. 88)

hundred years later. Nevertheless, the method he employed subconsciously seems quite his own; occasionally it calls to mind an almost schizophrenic associative mentality. A few examples may help to explain what I mean. On three sheets by Vittone are to be found copies after details of Fontana's designs for the decoration of S. Maria dell'Anima on the occasion of the memorial service to Leopold I of Austria.[51] No. 8 (red 110) combines on one sheet Fontana 9842, 9843 and 9846. No. 88 (old ink 62, red 109) – a less straightforward case – shows on the left a column with hangings behind it. Fontana's original, corresponding exactly to this design, does not seem to be extant; but there is a close connection with Fontana's sketch 9837 (reversed in Vittone's design). The hanging is to be found in Fontana's sketch 9840. The column in the centre of the sheet may be based on Fontana 9836 or possibly on a less sketchy original that has not survived.

The plan on the right conflates Fontana's two plans of the catafalque, 9833 and 9834. Even more obscure is the design above the plan showing a seated *putto* with his feet resting on a half-moon; at one side of the *putto* is a cannon lying on a curved wall, at the other a segmental line with a cannon next to it. The design merges the view and the plan of the same motif which appear separately on Fontana 9854.[52] Another sheet belonging to this series, No. 89 (old ink 64, red 108), is similarly based on six originals, namely (from top left to right) Fontana 9851, 9848 (bottom), 9850 (top), 9849 (bottom), 9840 and 9845. Sometimes entirely unconnected designs are united on one sheet. no. 216 (red 114) shows at the top a section and plan from the palace on the Isola Borromeo after Fontana 9751 and, underneath, the decoration of the *stanze nobili* in the same palace after Fontana 9752, while on the right of the sheet appears half of the organ, set in a rock design in the

303

304 VITTONE. Design for the altar in the Santuario di Sant'Ignazio, Monte Bastia, near Lanzo, probably 1727 (Paris, Musée des Arts Décoratifs, no. 38)

Quirinal gardens copied from Fontana 9753.[53] On the upper half of no. 147 (old ink 111, red 68) there are part of the façade of the Casa Cantonale, S. Michele a Ripa (1704), after Fontana 9730 and two plans of the same building after Fontana 9732 and 9753, the upper one irrationally turned through 180 degrees. On the lower half of the same sheet, Vittone gave in one design the elevation and section of an unidentified palace by Fontana, contracted from the two Fontana drawings 9351 and 9347. Even stranger than such conflation is the fact that the upper and lower designs are copied from two different Fontana volumes.[54] This is not at all an uncommon occurrence[55] – a further proof, if it were needed, that the copyist was in a position to use freely the major part of Fontana's legacy of drawings.

Now a number of plates in the *Istruzioni diverse* show miscellaneous designs which are as badly co-ordinated or as crowded as the

sheets of copies.[56] Indeed, it can be maintained that there exists a 'structural' similarity between some of the sheets with copies after Fontana and some of the plates in Vittone's treatises, and it is this that excludes any doubt as to the authorship of the copies. We may conclude that the copies after other architects' projects – enumerated above – are also by Vittone. They, too, were made at the time of his stay in Rome, with the exception of the copies after Chiaveri's Hofkirche project which must be dated at least ten years later.[57] The copy after S. Lorenzo at Milan probably also belongs to the later period.[58] In any case, it is revealing that the spatial complexity and sophistication of this late antique structure attracted Vittone; this copy focuses attention on a source of his mature style.

If the foregoing analysis and reconstruction of events is acceptable, there remains the surprising fact that Vittone returned to his early studies of Fontana when he began to prepare his two publications. During the interval of more than two decades he had become the acknowledged master of his generation in Piedmont. He had passed through a Rococo phase without relinquishing his attachment to classical principles, but in his late period he favoured more conventional designs with distinctly Neoclassical overtones and so he moved once again closer to Carlo Fontana and to the Roman experience of his youth. It is for this reason that both publications clearly reveal Fontanesque and other Roman reminiscences.[59] However, only one strictly architectural project, of which Vittone published the large plan and elevation, is a straightforward copy after Fontana.[60] All other cases of direct copies are to be found among the plates showing catafalques, tombs and memorials,[61] rather than buildings. Vittone had to include this material in his *Istruzioni diverse* for the sake of completeness. But as an architect in the modern sense of the word he was a stranger to this type of design, and this seems to have been the reason for his almost total reliance on his archive of drawings.

Vittone's original drawings would require a discussion of considerable length, but I can hardly do more in this paper than put down a few miscellaneous observations. The Paris volumes contain two different classes of such drawings; first, preparatory designs for actual buildings and, second, study sheets the purpose of which seems to have been to bring together a large collection of models, ultimately for publication.

A survey of the first group shows that the designs belong to all periods of Vittone's career. 302 I have already mentioned the project of 1728; even earlier is his design for the picturesque 304 altar, with the sculpted vision of St Ignatius, in the Santuario di Sant'Ignazio on Monte Bastia near Lanzo, traditionally dated 1727.[62] Vittone described the altar at great length in the *Istruzioni diverse* (LIII–LV) and discussed it in 305 plate XCIII. It is evident that the drawing served as basis for the engraving, which reverses it. Two designs for canopies, one empty, the other with the Virgin and Child, both on the same sheet (no. 3), were clearly intended for the altar of S. Chiara at Alessandria, planned before 1740, but never executed.[63] In the mid-1740s Vittone must have designed the church and college of the Chierici Regolari Ministri degli Infermi in Turin, a work that also remained unexecuted. He attached great importance to the project, for he gave it three plates in the *Istruzioni diverse* (LIII–LV) and discussed it in great detail (p. 177 ff.). The Paris volumes contain three plans of the church and adjoining building, a proof of the care he took over the preparatory stages (nos. 138, 160, 165); no. 160 comes closest to the published plate LIII, but differs in a few minor though significant details. To the same, or possibly even a slightly earlier period, seem to belong a number of extremely important plans for S. Chiara at Vercelli (nos. 143, 206, 206v, 207, 208). Common characteristic features leave no doubt about the identification, namely a broad sacristy with rounded-off corners and the marking of existing buildings into which the church had to be fitted.[64] The pencil sketch 206v, which returns to the plan of S. Chiara at Alessandria, 306 appears again in the clean pen and ink drawing 207. No. 143 is reminiscent of the plan of the Santuario del Vallinotto (1738) and the church of the Chierici Regolari Ministri degli Infermi. 307 No. 206 recalls the plan of S. Bernardino at Chieri (1740) and no. 208 is close to the published plan (*Istruzioni diverse*, plate LXXII). Thus, in the course of developing the plan of S. Chiara at Vercelli Vittone recapitulated a number of solutions he had used around 1740.[65]

305 VITTONE. Engraving in the *Istruzione diverse*, based on pl. 304

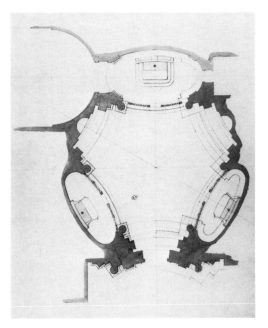

306 VITTONE. Plan for S. Chiara, Vercelli (Paris, Musée des Arts Décoratifs, no. 207)

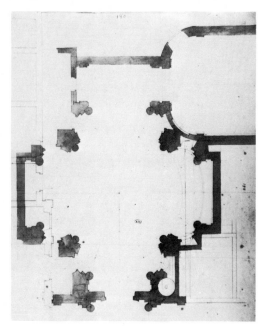

307 VITTONE. Alternative plan for S. Chiara,
Vercelli (Paris, Musée des Arts Décoratifs, no. 206)

308 VITTONE. Sheet of studies (Paris, Musée des
Arts Décoratifs, no. 130)

A longitudinal and a cross section (nos. 198, 199) certainly belong to an early project for S. Maria Maddalena at Alba built in 1749.[66]

Very similar to the plan of this church is Vittone's project for the unexecuted parish church at Spigno Monferrato, published in the *Istruzioni diverse*, plate LXI; no. 145 represents an annotated '*pianta abozzata*' for it and should be dated about 1750. Nos. 56 and 57 show the plan and longitudinal section of S. Maria dei Servi at Alessandria with notes and the signature: 'Torino, li 17 marzo 1756 Ing.e Bernardo Vittone'. These drawings are the only surviving testimony of this unexecuted project; they are of particular interest because of their dependence on Juvarra's Chiesa del Carmine in Turin (1732–36). Finally some designs of altars can be related to executed works: no. 12 to the two side altars in the Chiesa dello Spirito Santo at Carignano datable 1750–52,[67] no. 23 to the altar of the Capella del Crocifisso in S. Francesco, Turin (1761);[68] no. 18 perhaps to the altar of S. Valerico in the Consolata, Turin (1764).[69] The free sketch of an altar, no. 40, so far unrelated, may be added to this list because it has on the verso the draft of a letter the date of which seems to read 'Aug. 2 – 1764'.

The drawings so far discussed belong to four decades of Vittone's professional life and it is apparent that none was made with publication in mind. Nor can it be maintained that the other class of drawings – the study sheets – were all made for this purpose. A few study sheets contain numerous miscellaneous 'notes' not destined for publication, although individual motifs could be used when the occasion arose. On nos. 42 and 44, which originally formed a large sheet cut in two in 1903 and reunited in our pl. 309,[70] there are assembled no less than sixteen designs in pen and ink and one in crayon covering a wide range of subjects: altars, cartouches, doors and *sopraporte*, a capital, a holy-water stoup and two tabernacles. This study sheet is of particular interest because of its link both with Fontana and the *Istruzioni diverse*; the double door with the picture-frame above it is copied from the first chapel on the left in S. Maria di Montesanto in Rome,[71] while the strange door with the ram's head decoration and the realistic eagle holding an inscription-scroll in its beak and talons recurs in reverse on plate XXIII of the *Istruzioni diverse*.[72] Other study sheets with

232

309 VITTONE. Sheet of studies (Paris, Musée des Arts Décoratifs, nos. 42 and 44)

310, 311 VITTONE. Two alternative designs for a tabernacle (Paris, Musée des Arts Décoratifs, nos. 16 and 29)

well-arranged altars, tabernacles, windows and
doors were probably made with publication in
308 view. The example reproduced here, no. 130,
shows six doors incorporating twelve alternative designs. Strangely, Vittone used in his
books little of the material assembled on this
type of study sheet. The possibility cannot be
excluded that he planned yet another publication, apart from the two published works and
the manuscripts which were ready for the press
when he died.

I have mentioned above that forty-seven
drawings are related to the illustrations in
Vittone's books and that many of the engravings
reverse the drawings. In spite of this, none of
the drawings served the engravers directly.[73]
In preparing his publications Vittone consulted
his archive of drawings, lifted out what seemed
to him suitable and had clean copies made for
the engraver's use. In a number of cases Vittone's procedure can be reconstructed. My
310, examples are the two tabernacle drawings, nos.
311 16 and 29, which served for the two tabernacles
on plate XCV of the *Istruzioni diverse*. Originally,
he probably designed these tabernacles as
alternatives: in both drawings the altar and the
angels with the Crown of Thorns and the Sudary
are identical. In the engravings the altars were
omitted; otherwise no. 29 was exactly followed
and reversed, while the angels of no. 16 were
changed to kneeling ones in the engraving.

Fortunately, the clean copy from which the
engravings were made survives in the Royal
Library at Turin.[74] A number of points regarding this copy are worth noting. There is a title-
page that corresponds neither with that of the
Istruzioni elementari nor with that of the
Istruzioni diverse; the date of publication is
given as 1760;[75] and, by and large, the 135
plates of the manuscript combine the illustrations of both printed works. In other words, the
material Vittone had singled out for publication,
including that for the *Istruzioni diverse* of 1766,
was ready at the time the *Istruzioni elementari*
appeared. It is for this reason that, with the

exception of a very few added plates,[76] no
designs of the 1760s were included in the
Istruzioni diverse.[77] We may therefore conclude
that the bulk of the study sheets made in preparation for publication have to be dated some-
time in the 1750s.

The foregoing analysis of the volumes in the
Musée des Arts Décoratifs has shown that they
contain four different classes of material: **1**
Vittone's copies after Fontana's and other
architects' works datable mainly to 1732; **2** preparatory studies for a number of Vittone's own
architectural works covering the long period
from 1727 to 1764; **3** study sheets, many of
which were made in preparation for his publications and date from the 1750s; **4** a sprinkling
of drawings by other hands, above all by
Andrea Cattaneo.

Cattaneo was probably born shortly before
Vittone's death. We know that in 1788 the
University of Turin conferred on him the title
'architetto civile' and that he was still alive in
1831.[78] If the late eighteenth-century parish
church at Favria[79] is by him, he started his
career as a Vittone enthusiast. A later work,
however, S. Dalmazzo at Cuorgnè (1805–10),[80]
shows that he had swung towards acceptance
of the prevalent Neoclassical taste.

Since Cattaneo's drawings originally formed
part of the collection, I am tempted to conclude
that it was this somewhat obscure architect who
had acquired the Vittone material from the
latter's heirs. Thus, to find Cattaneo's own
exercises in Vittone's manner intermingled
with Vittone drawings would need no further
explanation. It is likely that Cattaneo did not
come into possession of all the Vittone drawings
at the same moment and this would account for
the inconsistencies in the numbering to which
I have alluded at the beginning of this paper.

At the moment we cannot go beyond such
hypothetical reconstructions. But I hope that
my analysis of the two Paris volumes has solved
some riddles, though many more still await
clarification.[81]

312 PIRANESI. Titlepage of *Osservazioni sopra la Lettre de M. Mariette*, 1765

XIII PIRANESI'S ARCHITECTURAL CREED

IN 1761 Piranesi published his *Della Magnificenza ed Architettura de' Romani*, a book with 200 pages of text and 38 plates. It contains his view on art in a polemical form directed against two works: *The Investigator* by an anonymous English writer (actually the painter Allan Ramsay) published in 1755,[1] and *Les Ruines des plus beaux Monuments de la Grèce* published in 1758 by the Frenchman Le Roy. The latter was much the more important adversary, for he was the first to bring home to the West the Greek architecture of Athens, an event of far-reaching effect. In the text accompanying his engravings Le Roy explains that architecture is a Greek creation, from which all Roman buildings derive. As the Romans are only copyists, their architecture is decadent compared with that of the Greeks.

These principles, similar to those formulated by the English writer,[2] awakened Piranesi's opposition. Hitherto he had lived in a purely archaeological world, and had not attempted any speculative theorizing or criticism. But now his answer burst forth with satirical violence. It consists of three different arguments. In the historical field he claims that the Etruscans are an older race than the Greeks, that they developed the arts to a high degree of perfection before the Greeks really began and that for a long period they were the sole masters of the Romans. His second point is concerned with the natural gifts of the Etruscans. He emphasizes that they were much more talented than the Greeks. They invented and brought to perfection sculpture, painting, mathematics and the technical arts. This is proved by their remarkable constructions, such as the waterworks of the Lake of Albano, the Cloaca Maxima, aqueducts, circuses, road-building, etc. His last point stresses a still more extravagant aesthetic theory: the Etruscans did not adorn their buildings; their grand style in architecture is comparable to the Egyptian. The Greeks for their part adhered to a vain prettiness and not to a grand style; they thought mainly of the ornaments, of the treatment of details, but not of the architecture as a whole; they took almost all the liberties that they wanted.[3] In the later Roman empire, when reason was replaced by caprice, architects accepted many things from the Greeks, but even then they corrected a great many of the Greeks' faults.[4]

The plates accompanying Piranesi's text can only be understood on the background of his theoretical views, for they do not only show examples of which he approved. Many of them represent bad specimens opposed to reason and grandeur, and are criticized in the text.[5] On a number of plates one finds engravings after Le Roy's work.[6] Thus bases, columns and capitals from Greece are compared with those of Rome, always in order to demonstrate the superiority of the Roman. The full sharpness of his sarcasm becomes evident on plate XX, where, amongst other examples from Le Roy, the Ionic capital of the Erechtheion is compared with a great number of Roman capitals. The Greek capital bears a quotation from Le Roy: '*Chapiteau Ionique dont on n'a eu jusqu'ici aucune idée et supérieur a plusieurs égards aux plus beaux chapiteaux de cet ordre.*' For Piranesi the two rows of Roman capitals framing the Greek one are witnesses of the greater wealth and beauty of the Ionic style in Rome. But above them he quotes from the same author: '*Les chapiteaux Ioniques que l'on voit à Rome paroissent pauvres et défectueux.*'

In their historical conceptions Le Roy and Piranesi are only exponents of two much discussed general tendencies of the eighteenth century. The Pan-Grecian theory was first developed in France, Le Roy's country. For artists and writers Greek superiority became an indisputable axiom. A few quotations may illustrate the trend of ideas. In one of the most important books of the mid-half eighteenth century, Goguet's *Origin of Laws, Arts and Sciences*,[7] the name of the Greeks calls forth romantic enthusiasm: 'It was from the Greeks that architecture has received that regularity, that order, that entireness which are able to charm our eyes . . . We owe to them, in a word,

313

236

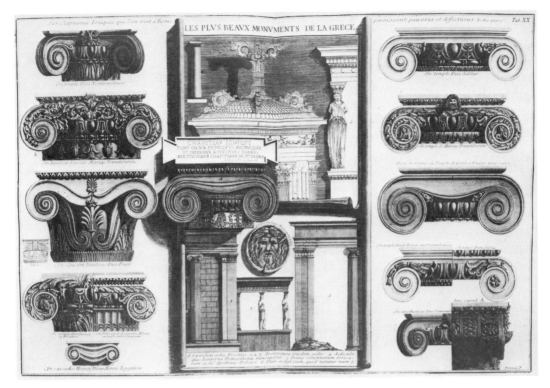

313 PIRANESI. *Della Magnificenza ed Architettura de' Romani*, 1761, pl. XX

all the beauties of which the art of building is capable. In this sense we may say that Greeks have invented architecture.'

The next step lay with the Comte de Caylus. An enthusiastic dilettante and collector, Caylus published the seven volumes of his immensely influential *Recueil d'Antiquités Egyptiennes, Etrusques, Grecques, Romains, et Gauloises* over a period of fifteen years, from 1752 to 1767 (the last volume appeared posthumously). He used and adapted for the history of art the old historical theory of the succession of world empires and postulated that the arts had been carried from one empire to the next while changing their basic character from empire to empire. The essence of Egyptian art, he maintains, is massiveness, bareness and grandeur; from Egypt this style was passed on to the Etruscans who added to it *'des parties de détail'*; from the Etruscans it reached Greece where, based on the achievements of the Egyptians and Etruscans, the arts attained their greatest perfection;[8] Roman art, finally, derived

from Greece, was in Caylus' eyes an anticlimax and decline: *'à Rome, où sans briller autrement que par des secours, après avoir lutté quelque temps contre la Barbarie, ils s'ensevelissent dans les débris de l'Empire.'*[9]

Even Caylus, therefore, accepts the historical views of the great age of Etruscan civilization, which the Etruscologists put forward, partly as a nationalist endeavour to show the antiquity, importance and continuity of culture on Italian soil. But he differs from them in that, whereas they saw in the art of Etruria the high point in the development, he regards it as a mere preliminary stage, far excelled by Greece. Curious though it may appear, research on Etruscan art begins with the work of a Scotsman, Thomas Dempster.[10] In the course of the eighteenth century more and more Italian scholars were attracted by the history of their ancestors. Etruscan academies and museums were founded; fieldwork was undertaken in places like Volterra, Corneto (Tarquinia), Chiusi; innumerable volumes appeared filled with the treasures

237

of what purported to be Etruscan art. The outstanding scholars in this fight for the rehabilitation of the Etruscans were A. F. Gori, G. B. Passeri and M. Guarnacci. Piranesi mainly quotes Gori and Dempster, but Guarnacci seems to be his real stimulator. He lived in Rome until 1757, and before 1743 was in the service of Cardinal Rezzonico, later Pope Clement XIII, whose close relations with Piranesi are well known.[11] Guarnacci's scholarly work[12] actually appeared a few years after Piranesi's *Della Magnificenza*, but one finds in it, supported by an enormous wealth of material, all the artist's axioms about the great antiquity of Etruscan civilization, its creative power in the arts, crafts and technical sciences and its priority over Greek culture.

Piranesi's aesthetic categories, too, are not his own. From many quotations it is evident that he was well acquainted with Caylus' works. He accepts the latter's analysis of the grandeur of Etruscan and the elegance of Greek style – but reverses the valuation. The supremacy of Roman art is a conception belonging to the arsenal of national Italian historians ever since Vasari's days. The latter had already interpreted the development of art as an ascent from Egypt through Greece and Rome, and, with a gap for the Dark Ages, right up to modern times. For him the early stages prepare the perfection of Roman art. Vasari is even conscious of the peculiarity of Etruscan art, but it does not yet find a final place in his system.[13]

The axiom of Roman superiority was not limited to Italian authors and artists. Sir William Chambers, who is animated by the same hatred of the Greeks as Piranesi, summarizes the situation:[14]

All that has been said, respecting the superiority of the Roman architecture, was written a considerable time ago, when the Grecian had been extolled into repute; and structures were erecting in different parts of England, after Attick designs. Fortunately, the sight of these first specimens excited no desires for more: after a few ineffectual struggles, the Roman manner obtained a complete victory. There seemed, at that time, no farther necessity to fight its cause; and these observations intended for the second edition of this work (1768), were then suppressed. But latterly, the *gusto Greco* has again ventured to peep forth, and once more, threaten an

invasion. What therefore was omitted in the second edition, it has been judged necessary to insert in this, as a caution to stragglers.

Although the different camps in which Le Roy and Piranesi stand are thus clearly defined, and the principal barriers between them seem to be insurmountable, below the surface there are very important points of contact. Both of them believe in objective laws, both fight for reason, necessity, truth and simplicity in architecture. These are the central points of the classicistic doctrine of the Age of Enlightenment, in which the two have their roots. Le Roy seems to derive his ideas from Cordemoy[15] and the Abbé Laugier,[16] whereas Piranesi was certainly under the spell of Padre Lodoli[17] (1690–1761), who must have been one of the decisive influences on him during his early years in Venice. From him comes not only Piranesi's rationalistic approach to architecture in general, but also the way in which certain problems presented themselves, for instance that of the development from wood to stone construction in Greek architecture. Certain pages and plates of *Della Magnificenza* follow Lodoli's ideas in showing this process as illogical, unreasonable and opposed to nature.

Piranesi's polemical book could not be left unanswered by the 'Grecians' and nobody will be astonished to find a Frenchman taking up the pen. In 1764 Mariette published a letter against Piranesi in the *Gazette Littéraire de l'Europe*.[18] His point of view is essentially identical with that of his compatriot Caylus. But for him the Etruscans are Greek colonists; all Roman art had its origin in Greece, was mainly executed in Rome by Greek slaves, and declined under Roman patronage: '*Il n'est alors aucune production qui ne se charge d'ornements superflus, et absolument hors d'oeuvre. On sacrifice tout au luxe, et l'on se rend à la fin partisan d'une manière qui ne tarde pas à devenir ridicule et barbare.*' Greek art on the other hand pursues '*une belle et noble simplicité*'. This is a complete reversal of Piranesi's view about the styles of simple and ornate architecture.

Piranesi, in a fury, prepared an answer at once. It appeared in 1765 and consisted of a title-page, twenty-three pages of text and nine plates. The actual title-page already contains a programme and an attack. The greater part of 312 it is filled with an example of the Tuscan order. For Piranesi the Tuscan order is an invention of the Etruscans, independent of the Greek orders. Peculiar as it may seem to us, the discussion about the originality and merit of the Tuscan order was of central importance in the battle of the 'Grecians' and 'Romans'. For Le Roy and architects like J. F. Blondel the Tuscan was a degenerate Doric order. But the camps are not rigidly divided. The learned D'Hancarville, for instance, who published the Hamilton Collection in 1766,[19] though by tradition and as an admirer of Winckelmann a 'Grecian', accepted a great deal of the 'Roman' theory. He not only assumed the antiquity and inventiveness of Etruscan civilization and the Etrusco-Roman development, but he applied this view to architecture, and believed that the Tuscan order was the model for the Doric. He asks: 'May not the Doric order be nothing more than the Tuscan to which Greece added ornaments which make it appear different?'[20]

Robert Adam, on the other hand, a friend of Piranesi,[21] in whose circle in Rome he certainly acquired much of his historical education, acknowledges only three orders 'for as to the Tuscan, it is, in fact, no more than a bad and imperfect Doric'. And the Composite – also a purely Roman order – is for him a 'very disagreeable and awkward mixture of the Corinthian and Ionic, without either grace or beauty'.[22]

Thus, for every contemporary onlooker, Piranesi's title-page had a topical quality, which was increased by two enigmatical designs on the left hand side. Above appears Mariette's hand,[23] writing the letter to the *Gazette Littéraire*, under the motto: '*aut cum hoc*'. Below is the outline of a Tuscan column filled with artists' tools and the motto: '*aut in hoc*' – a symbol for the scorn of the practising artist for the theorist.

Piranesi's text consists of three parts. The first with the title *Osservazioni di Gio Battista Piranesi sopra la Lettre de M. Mariette* is merely a repetition of his arguments in *Della Magnificenza*; he tries to refute Mariette sharply, sentence by sentence. The next part with the title *Parere su l'Architettura* is written in the form of a dialogue between a friend and an opponent of Piranesi. The discussion begins about certain designs by Piranesi. Protopiro,

the rigorist, attacks them because they are overloaded with ornament. He condemns Piranesi as illogical, for in *Della Magnificenza* he was against ornament. And he concludes that with these inventions Piranesi '*si è dato a quella pazza libertà di lavorare a capriccio . . .*' Didascalo, Piranesi's man, defends his designs with unexpected arguments. He denies that severity, reason and adherence to rules are to be pursued for their own sakes. Not only Greek architecture, but also the rules of Vitruvius and the classicism of Palladio are rejected. If one carries the principles of Vitruvius to their logical conclusion the result will be a primitive hut: '*Edifizi senza pareti, senza colonne, senza cornici, senza volte, senza tetti.*' The Grecians, Vitruvians, rigorists and purists dictate laws of architecture which are never inherent in it. The accusation that Piranesi had imposed laws on architecture in *Della Magnificenza* and attacked *capriccio* is refuted. In this book, he argues, Piranesi had actually shown that there was something fundamentally wrong with Greek architecture, and that the Romans had tried to mitigate its inherent evils. If one follows the laws of the rigorists, architecture becomes terribly monotonous. Without variation art is reduced to the mason's craft. But the liberty advocated by Piranesi is not the same as confusion. The parts should be in harmony with the whole; ornament has its own laws of gradation and mass ('*i gradi, le preminenze, il più, e'l meno dignitoso*') which make the whole appear elegant and delightful.

In his final words Piranesi turns directly towards Mariette asking him how one should keep to '*une belle et noble simplicité*' (Mariette) without reducing architecture to '*un vil métier où l'on ne feroit que copier*' (Le Roy). To elaborate the possible variations implicit in architecture and to give way to creative impulse leads according to Mariette to '*une manière ridicule et barbare*'. If one thus condemns the wealth of invention, one condemns not only ancient architecture but also what is being produced in modern Europe.

In conclusion Piranesi declares that he is preparing a large new work in which all his ideas will be further explained. But the introduction to it which follows (and the work was never developed beyond this) with the title: *Della introduzione e del progresso delle Belle Arti in*

Europa ne' Tempi antichi is rather disappointing, since it merely resumes his old thesis of the priority of Italy over Greece.

If one takes care not to be misled by Piranesi's attempt to bring his different opinions into line with one another, the decisive break between his ideas in *Della Magnificenza* of 1761 and those expressed in the *Parere* of 1765 cannot be overlooked. In the earlier book Vitruvius enjoys unchallenged authority, in the later the ancient author is rigorously criticized. Though Piranesi tries to find a way out by sophistry, he now recommends as indispensable those ornaments which he condemned before. But above all the principles of law, reason and simplicity are now ridiculed.

What can have caused the change in Piranesi's views? The words in Mariette's letter, *'une belle et noble simplicité'* show the way. This is already the language of Winckelmann whose approach to antiquity had conquered Europe since the early sixties. Piranesi could no longer ignore the fact of the simplicity of Greek and the ornate character of fully developed Roman architecture. For the sake of continuity he tries to prove, in strict contrast to his earlier views, 314 that even Etruscan architecture was ornamented.[24] Therefore, he switches over to admiration for ornate architecture and condemnation of simplicity. And, curious as it may sound, Winckelmann himself recommends ornate architecture. In his book *Anmerkungen über die Baukunst der Alten* (1762) one finds the source of Piranesi's theory of monotony. The essay of Winckelmann consists of two parts which he calls *das Wesentliche* (the essential) and *die Zierlichkeit* (meaning: *'Verzierung'* – ornament). To the 'essential' belong material, the way of building (construction), the form of the building (including orders), the parts of the building. But an 'essential' building without *Zierlichkeit* would be monotonous: *'das Einerley oder die Monotonie kann in der Baukunst . . . tadelhaft werden'* (p. 50). So far Piranesi follows Winckelmann. He is, however, blind to the conclusion which Winckelmann draws. For the latter decoration, although theoretically desirable, coincides historically with the decline of architecture.[25]

But, apart from a desire to vindicate Roman architecture, there are still other and more important reasons for Piranesi's change of attitude

which can be only understood by taking into account his entire development. Up till 1761 his activity was primarily archaeological. His publications contain no aesthetic confession, they consist mainly of volumes of engravings – the type of antiquarian book which ever since the sixteenth century had been common in Rome. In his first work, *Prima Parte di Archi-* Fro *tetture e Prospettive*, of 1743, he strives to pie reconstruct – on Palladian principles but in a completely fantastic way – the main types of ancient buildings. His *Antichità Romane* of 1748 consists of a collection of views of Rome dedicated to his tutelary genius, the antiquarian Giovanni Bottari. In *Le Antichità Romane* of 1756, a vast collection of Roman antiquities contained in four volumes, he is more explicit: he states in the preface, that his intention is to make known the relics of Roman greatness for the benefit of amateurs and architects. *Della Magnificenza*, though a historical work, pursues by virtue of its polemical character a thoroughly pedagogic aim. Thus he shows an ever increasing interest in the demands of actual architecture.[26]

But his talents were not in keeping with his classicistic theory as formulated in *Della Magnificenza*. Therefore, when he wanted to indulge in inventiveness, he escaped into a field outside every-day architecture. His *Carceri* 315 (1750) are imaginative creations without the use of traditional architectural forms. No rules of any kind can be applied to them.

Mariette, familiar with Piranesi's leaning towards extravagance, only took into account the evidence of the plates of *Della Magnificenza*, ignoring the fact that the author's aesthetic theory cannot be deduced from the engravings alone,[27] and concluded that Piranesi was advocating *'une manière ridicule et barbare'* – which at that date was certainly not true. It is not until the *Parere* – after the change in Piranesi's theoretical outlook – that Mariette's criticism becomes justified. The anti-Vitruvian, anticlassical theory expressed in the *Parere* is now not only in keeping with the character of much of the architecture which Piranesi had previously engraved, but coincides with his own pictorial interpretation of these monuments.

His new views on architecture no longer permit him to illustrate them with engravings

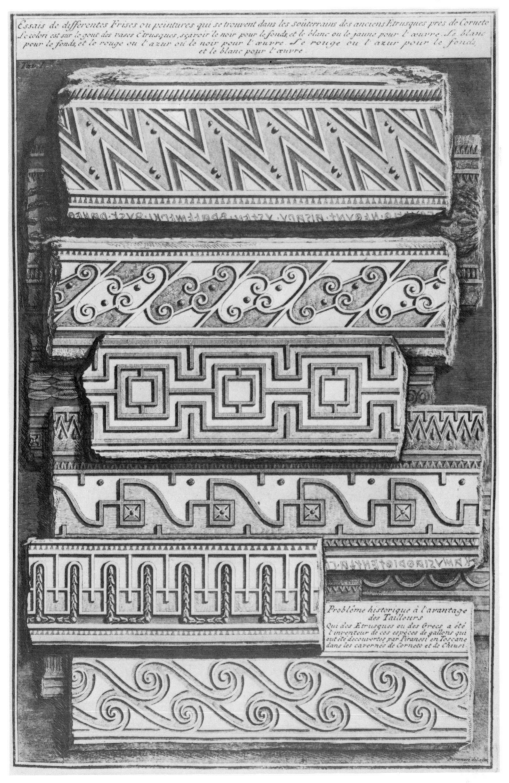

314 PIRANESI. *Osservazioni sopra la Lettre de M. Mariette,* 1765, pl. I, showing ornamental motifs from Etruscan tombs

315 PIRANESI. *Carcere d'Invenzione*, 1750, pl. XVI

316–
318 of ancient buildings, but he uses designs of his own invention which are now in complete accordance with his theory. These are the plates which are discussed by Protopiro and Didascalo. Their designs are, indeed, more surprising than any others in Piranesi's *oeuvre*, and their fantastic appearance could well supply an illustration to the characterization of Piranesi in Chamber's *Treatise on Civil Architecture* (1791).[28] They show sections of monumental buildings covered with exceedingly rich ornament. All the rules of the Vitruvian-Palladian rigorists are trampled upon. There appears no proper order; no entablature, no cornice; no moulding is correctly applied or in its traditional place; sculpture used as an architectural feature, and in this capacity condemned in Piranesi's text to *Della Magnificenza*, is freely distributed over the building. His selection of motifs is taken from Roman and mostly from late Roman architecture and sculpture, from

Egyptian sculpture and sarcophagi, and from Etruscan and Greek vases. He shows how the whole heritage of antiquity should be used to develop new variations and to promote creative forces.

Four of these designs bear inscriptions, set in the architecture, in which Piranesi's intentions are expounded in aphoristic form. The first[29] is 318 a quotation from Terence's *Eunuch* and reads: 'It is reasonable to know yourself, and not to search into what the ancients have made if the moderns can make it.'[30] Here is a justification for independence in contemporary creations. Next follows a quotation from Ovid's *Metamorphoses* (XV): '*Rerumque novatrix Ex aliis alias reddit natura figuras.*' Nature renews herself constantly – to create the new out of the old is, therefore, also proper to man. On the next building a sentence from Le Roy, which we already know, discourages the literal copying of ancient art: '*Pour ne pas fair de cet art* 317

242

316, 317, 318 PIRANESI. *Parere su l'Architettura,* 1765, pls. IX, VIII and V

sublime un vil métier où l'on ne ferait que copier sans choix.' This is exemplified in the design which is fantastic instead of imitative. In the last inscription all the bitterness of polemic breaks through and Piranesi becomes personal: 'They despise my novelty, I their timidity.'[31]

Thus, Piranesi proclaims himself in favour of novelty, that is, of a free transformation as against a literal rendering of ancient models. His *Parere* represents the conscious transition from archaeology to imaginative art. Archaeological material now becomes a weapon in the hands of a revolutionary modernist.

But Piranesi is not alone in his views. Many others now attack the copyist who rigidly abides by the ancient rules, and recommend variety and individual transformation of the ancient heritage. Even traditionalists like J. F. Blondel turn – though not whole-heartedly – against the classical doctrine that art consists of rules which can be taught and learned with such statements as: *'Quelquefois on peut et l'on doit s'affranchir de certaines règles. Ne vouloir jamais s'en écarter, c'est risquer de tomber dans la sécheresse et la stérilité.'*[32] Others are much more explicit. The brothers Adam state that the great masters of antiquity themselves did not keep scrupulously to the rules: 'Rules often cramp the genius and circumscribe the idea of the master.' From the liberty which is permissible to genius they take for themselves permission 'to transfuse the beautiful spirit of antiquity with novelty and variety through all our numerous works.'[33] These views are in complete accordance with Piranesi's. In France Clérisseau accompanies his publication of the antiquities of Nîmes with the challenge: *'Apprenons des Anciens à soumettre les règles mêmes au génie. Effaçons cette empreinte de servitude et d'imitation qui déparent nos productions.'*[34]

In these writings – and also in the *Diverse Maniere* – the word 'genius' appears with the new significance applied to it in the eighteenth century. Piranesi and his fellow architects participate in a world-wide movement, the battle-cry of which is a call for originality and unfettered development of the personality.

Starting from England a new conception of the artist as creator spread all over Europe in the course of the eighteenth century. As early as 1711 Addison opposed imitative art based on

rules to the work of the genius who invents 'by the mere strength of natural parts and without any assistance of art or learning'.[35] Winckelmann expresses the axiom of the copyists – creation by imitation – with his famous words: *'Der einzige Weg für uns, gross, ja, wenn es möglich ist, unnachahmlich zu werden, ist die Nachahmung der Alten.'*[36] It is still the result of a classical heritage when Piranesi and many others[37] demand a firm basis of historical knowledge to justify individual liberties. From here to the romantic conception of the genius as conceived in Germany – *'Naiv muss jedes wahre Genie seyn, oder es ist keines'*[38] – is still a long way. But Piranesi has gone further in this direction than any contemporary artist because of his intensity of purpose and his singularly sanguine fervour.

To return to Piranesi's designs, it must be said that in spite of his negation of hard and fast rules he does not advocate complete liberty. But the rules, already mentioned, concerning the harmony of the parts and the whole, the prominence and degree of ornament, etc., are rather vague. One thing, however, is certain. The principle on which his designs are based is anything but new. In his search for originality the artist unconsciously hit upon a method which is deeply rooted in the Italian mentality. He reverses the traditional meaning of architectural structure in general and of the single parts. A pediment, on which the structural emphasis of the building is usually laid, is degraded by him to a decorative detail; ornamental frames, on the other hand, became structural features; one architectural feature is placed in front of another in such a way that the different planes of the building are confused; columns in the same row are fluted differently and stand on framed panels instead of on bases; even vegetable ornament which should grow upward is turned upside down. The spectator is plunged by these contradictory methods into constant unrest and conflict. In short, we are faced with the principle of an earlier style, in which originality and individuality replace an objective doctrine – that of sixteenth-century Mannerism.[39] With his designs Piranesi continues a tradition which has been taken up by more than one independent artist since Michelangelo's days.

Piranesi's *Parere* is an act of liberation from

319, 320 PIRANESI. Three designs for fireplaces from *Diverse Maniere d'adornare i Camini,* 1769

traditional fetters, and from the ideas with which the artist had grown up. His theoretical standpoint now conforms with his intuitive artistic purpose.[40] The splitting up of his personality into doctrines opposed to his actual talents comes to an end and he can now freely produce his thoroughly individual inventions.[41]

The principles laid down in the *Parere* guided Piranesi in his later activity. In 1769 appeared his *Diverse Maniere d'adornare i Camini ed ogni altra parte degli Edifizi.* The dedication to Monsignor Giovanbattista Rezzonico, nephew of Pope Clement XIII and Piranesi's patron, is signed '7 January 1769'; but the majority of the plates must have come off the press in the autumn of 1767, for in a letter of 3 October 1767, now in the Morgan Library, William Hamilton, the British Consul in Naples, thanked Piranesi for a consignment of prints of the fireplaces.

The title of the book 'Various Manners . . .' contains a programme and a challenge, announced in the Dedication in sentences like the following: 'I have noticed, Signore, how unsatisfactory modern manners of beautifying works of architecture are, and recommend that our architects make use in their works not only of the Greek manners, but also of the Egyptian[42] and Etruscan and select wisely and judiciously from such monuments desirable and beautiful parts. I therefore intend to show how much decorative variety the Egyptian, Etruscan and Greek manners can supply to the exterior as well as the interior embellishment of our buildings.'

In keeping with this programme the publication contains mainly fireplaces in a variety of styles. Even a superficial glance shows that they all, whether designed in Piranesi's so-called Etruscan, Greek, Roman, mixed or Egyptian manner, exhibit the same stylistic idiosyncrasies which we have previously observed in the exterior designs published in the *Parere*. Piranesi's long-winded explanatory text – let me make this quite clear – contains excellent passages and they help to understand not only the direction in which his mind moved, but also the specific stylistic character of the designs.

By doing what he does, he claims to have ancient authority on his side. He needed it to justify his own licence; the fact is that he was unable to pry himself loose from the classical doctrine. 'After having used Etruscan architecture through several centuries' – he assures us – 'the Romans also had recourse to the Greek manner and united both. Similarly the modern architect must not be satisfied with being a faithful copyist of the ancients, but based on the study of their works must display an inventive and – I am tempted to say – creative genius; and by wisely combining the Greek, Etruscan and Egyptian styles, one must give rise to the discovery of new decorations and new manners.' He is now willing to accept and even to admire Greek art. As he is now free from doctrines there is no reason to despise them any more. He even goes so far as to adopt Mariette's opinion that the Tuscans had been a colony of Greeks, but adds that this is not adequately proved. 'Certain elegances and graces' have now become for him a reason for admiring Greek art.

But the demand for originality is strongly stressed: 'Let us borrow from their stock, not servilely copying from others, for they would reduce architecture and the noble arts to a pitiful mechanism.' This spirit of adventurous creativity entitled Piranesi to use in his own personal way and for his own purposes the entire heritage of antiquity – as he says 'of medals, cameos, intaglios, statues, reliefs, paintings and other ancient works.' Moreover, in combining all this material 'the architect may be as capricious [*bizzaro*] as he likes', but there is one condition: 'he must not deform the architecture and each member must have its proper character'. An injudicious 'multiplicity of ornaments' is equally objectionable. He demands 'a certain variety of degrees' in the application of ornament: in other words, a principal theme and its accompaniment. If this advice is followed 'the multiplicity of ornament will not present a confusion to the eye, but a pleasant and delightful arrangement of things'.

These then are the stylistic principles that guided him: a search for fancies (*bizzarie*) controlled by clear definition of form and motifs, and clear qualitative gradation of multiple decoration. In the spirit of these principles both the *Camini* and the façades in the *Parere su l'architettura* of 1765 are carefully considered compositions. As he had shocked before, in the *Carceri* and elsewhere, by virtue of the excessive contrasts of scale, so he now shocked by virtue of the bizarre assembly of motifs. But, however fantastic the result, it is obvious that the new principles of framed containment and gradation – demands he never failed to satisfy in his designs – show his taste developing in the direction of Neoclassicism.

With his rejection of theoretical rules which were opposed to his gifts and with his transition to original creations with which he was able 'to get out of the old monotonous track', Piranesi's pugnacity was mitigated to such an extent that at the end of his life he visited Paestum and left behind engravings of the Greek temples on Italian soil.[43]

321 PIRANESI. S. Maria del Priorato, Rome, façade

XIV
PIRANESI AS ARCHITECT

Piranesi as Architect

To DISCUSS Piranesi as a practising architect means commenting on the church of S. Maria del Priorato in Rome, the only building of importance which came his way. He was then forty-five years old and, although he styled himself *architetto veneziano* from the beginning of his career on, one may well ask whether he ever had any serious intention of 'wasting' his time on such traditional activities of an architectural practitioner as scale drawings, specifications, negotiations with workmen and clients, and so forth. Even relatively late in life, when he did build and even welcomed the opportunity offered him, he was probably not attracted by the by-products of the career of his choice. It is necessary to point this out because it is sometimes maintained that it was a lack of architectural commissions which drove him into etching.

Of course it is true that in 1740, when Piranesi first arrived in Rome from his native Venice, the building boom which saw the rise of such extraordinary structures as the Spanish Staircase, the Fontana di Trevi, the Palazzi della Consulta and Corsini, the façades of S. Giovanni de' Fiorentini and S. Maria Maddalena was just beginning to ebb. Ferdinando Fuga, the most accomplished master in Rome, perceived the situation astutely and soon looked outside the Eternal City for more rewarding opportunities. Piranesi, by contrast, after a brief journey home, settled in Rome for good in 1744 or 1745. In retrospect, with his life's work before us, this decision would appear a foregone conclusion. But it is also clear that an 'architect' who was resolved to stay in Rome even during the meagre years after 1750 was not seriously interested in developing an architectural practice.

Evidence to the same effect can be derived from Piranesi's published works. His first volume of etchings, the *Prima parte di architetture e prospettive* of 1743, reveals him as an imaginative scenographer in the tradition of the Bibiena but already with a bias towards classical antiquity stronger than customary among the

Frontispiece

rank and file of the *quadraturisti*. Many of his designs show extraordinarily fanciful reconstructions of Roman buildings with emphasis on colossal dimensions and ample articulation.

After such beginnings no prophet could have predicted the next step in his development. There appeared, probably in 1745, the first edition of his *Carceri*. He discarded the entire ballast of learned *quadratura* tradition and ignored the classical paraphernalia which were the basic material of the *Prima parte*. The fantastic architecture of these etchings – 'capricci', in Piranesi's own diction – has no possible relationship to reality, painted or physical. Haunted by his fantasies and bursting into an unparalleled paroxysm of creativity, Piranesi gave expression here to a romantic megalomania a generation in advance of his time. Clearly, at this moment he could not have been further removed from a willing acceptance of the drudgery of architectural practice.

Then his restless energies took a swing away from inner fantasies: he became absorbed with the physiognomy of Rome ancient and modern. Soon he developed into the foremost topographical artist of his age and a devoted antiquarian. It need hardly be pointed out that such activity does not appear to pave the way to an architectural career. In 1748 he published the *Antichità romane de' tempi della repubblica*; the same year saw the first engravings of the *Vedute di Roma*, on which he worked to the end of his life; at about this time the surveying and drawing for the four tomes of the *Antichità romane* of 1756 must have been begun. All this goes to show that he was full to the brim with images of Rome, his only interest and only love in these years. Nevertheless there are sufficient indications that the temper of the artist of the *Carceri* did not lay wholly dormant. One finds strange outbursts of an unfettered imagination and energy – the phantasmagoric frontispieces of the second and third parts of the *Antichità* 322 *romane* are telling examples. Moreover, he never ceased producing drawings which remind us that the dreams of the theatrical

248

322 PIRANESI. *Antichità Romane*, frontispiece of Volume III

designer and scenographer were not just a thing of the past. Nor does he seem to have lost the wish to activate the antiquarian world of Roman buildings and ruins as a challenge to contemporary art and life.

The first indication in that direction will be found in one of his less bulky productions, the *Trofei di Ottaviano Augusto* of 1753, in the following words added to the title: *'utili a Pittori Scultori ed Architetti'*. This pedagogic advice may be interpreted as a first attempt to close the gap between antiquarianism and modern artistic production. He was even more explicit in the preface to the *Antichità romane* of 1756, but it was only with the *Della magnificenza ed architettura de' romani* of 1761, his first work with a long polemic text, that he entered the arena as a champion of the supremacy of Roman architecture against those who believed that Rome was far excelled by Greece. All over Europe the battle between the supporters of Rome and those of Greece was joined with growing fury, and Piranesi soon found himself in the role of the prime defender of the Roman cause.

His *Parere su l'architettura*, which appeared in 1765, marks a climactic event in these discussions and is also significant for Piranesi's own development (see preceding essay, pp. 235–246). With vigour and persuasion he now advocated that the great variety found in Roman buildings should not only encourage a free and imaginative use of ancient models but should also lead to an unfettered blossoming of a novel and personal manner. Now the circle was closed: Piranesi discovered that his immense labours as an antiquarian could be brought to fruition in a personal contemporary style. I think it is not fortuitous that he received the commission for S. Maria del Priorato in 1764 – at the critical moment of his intellectual and emotional preparedness for such a task.

Critics in the past have held diametrically opposed views on Piranesi's contribution to the Priorato. But W. Körte's historically sound and carefully argued paper on the church,[1] pub-

249

lished in 1933, clarified most of the basic problems and silenced further controversy. He established that the church and adjoining palace erected in 1568 by the Knights of Malta on a promontory of the Aventine, high above the Tiber, were left practically intact by Piranesi in so far as their structure was concerned. The old church had fallen into a bad state of repair; Piranesi's restoration and redecoration gave it a new vault and a new façade.

Such were Körte's essentially correct findings although at the time of writing he was un-acquainted with the two major groups of evidence which have since come to light. In the first place, there exist five meticulously exe-cuted original drawings for details of the church. They once belonged to Mrs J. P. Morgan and, with far over a hundred other Piranesi drawings, are now on deposit in the Pierpont Morgan Library. Felice Stampfle's model catalogue[2] brought these drawings to the attention of a wide public. Secondly, some time ago James Grote Van Derpool had the good fortune of being able to purchase for the Avery Library, Columbia University, a hitherto un-known account book covering Piranesi's res-torations of the area of the Priorato.

This book, a quarto bound in vellum (28 cm high), contains no less than 762 specified entries on 384 closely written pages. It is wholly con-cerned with the work of the *capomastro mura-tore* Giuseppe Pelosini, the 'foreman' who was responsible to Piranesi and had probably been selected by him. It was Pelosini who determined the quantities of all the materials needed, delivered them at a price agreed to by the architect, had control of manpower and super-vised the execution. His duties may perhaps be compared with those of a modern contractor.

What is preserved in this book are not the original specifications, but records of every detail of the entire building programme after its completion. This is ascertained from the follow-ing observations: 1 all the entries are written in the characteristic hand of an eighteenth-century scribe who seems to have covered many pages without a break; 2 the book is headed by the dates '2 November 1764 to 31 October 1766', the period in which expenses were incurred in regard to the restoration, and is followed by a summary description of all the work done with the remark that the undersigned architect (i.e.,

Piranesi) has examined and approved the quality and quantities of the materials men-tioned in the entries; 3 at the bottom of each page the sums spent are added up and carried over to the next page, and on the last page appears the entire sum spent on the restoration, $10,947 \cdot 29\frac{1}{2}$ scudi, this sum being confirmed as correct on 10 April 1767, under Piranesi's own signature; 4 on the back of the last page is a note written by Giuseppe Pelosini, who on 30 October 1767, drew an *a conto* payment of 300 scudi from the Banca di S. Spirito.

The wording of many entries also reveals that the Avery volume was intended as a clean presentation of the day-to-day accounts, of the payroll, and of every aspect of the work within the purview of the 'contractor'. The question arises why Piranesi had arranged for this clean copy to be made. Endless trouble was taken over it and a scribe must have worked for weeks to complete it. Obviously the copy was required to satisfy immaculate standards of book-keeping, for while the work was in progress expenses had been paid by the contractor. Now the time had come to settle the accounts with the patron. As the architect responsible for the entire undertaking, Piranesi had the copy made in Giuseppe Pelosini's office to be put before Giovanni Battista Rezzonico, nephew of Pope Clement XIII, Grand Master of the Knights of Malta and great admirer of Piranesi.

We are most probably correct in assuming that the majority of the entries was worded by Pelosini rather than Piranesi. For instance, Entry 122 describes the erection of a scaffolding near the fourth arch of the church and Entry 151 the building of the foundations upon which the high altar was to stand; these, as well as a large number of other entries, leave no doubt that they were based on the daily work sheets. If this be so, one wonders to what extent the contractor determined the actual work of restoration. There is, of course, no reason to doubt that Piranesi was sufficiently well equipped to handle work of this nature. He must have had a fair technical training in Venice in the studio of his uncle Matteo Lucchesi, who was mainly engaged on engineering tasks. If we can trust Giovanni Lodovico Bianconi's report of 1779, written a year after Piranesi's death, he also studied architecture with Giovanni Antonio Scalfarotto, the distinguished architect of SS.

323 PIRANESI. Design for the central panel of the
vaulting of S. Maria del Priorato, Rome (New York,
Pierpont Morgan Library)

324 PIRANESI. Central panel of the vaulting of
S. Maria del Priorato, Rome

Simeone e Giuda in Venice. Taking Piranesi's
whole career into consideration, however, one
is not easily prepared to admit that the un-
interesting task of saving S. Maria del Priorato
and the adjoining palace from complete ruin
would have fired his imagination: this was
indeed a task for a *capomastro*. The reinforce-
ment of all the foundations and the replacement
of old walls, the filling in of cracks in the
vaulting and façade of the church, the raising
of the upper part of the walls and their preparation for the beams of the new roof – all this and
much else of this order needed a practical
builder and could very well have been handled
by him alone.

Nevertheless there are entries which could
not have been written by the contractor with-

out the most detailed directives on the part of
the architect. This is true for the entire decoration of the church. The relevant entries contain
everything down to the minutest detail. Entry
269 referring to the four Ionic capitals of the
façade, for instance, informs us, among other 321
things, that there is a cherub's head under each
corner and that the spirals of the volutes have
been filled by sphinxes resting with one front
paw close to the tower with rusticated corners
which is placed in the centre of each capital. Or
take the long description (Entry 460) of the
large central panel of the vaulting; it begins: 323,
'The decoration of the central panel of the 324
ceiling in relief consists of an equilateral
triangle in the centre, representing the Trinity,
made up of garlands of roses arranged as nose-

251

325, 326 PIRANESI. Early sketch and finished
drawing for the high altar of S. Maria del Priorato,
Rome (New York, Pierpont Morgan Library)

gays all around the triangle; the festoons are
connected at the angles with bands fastened in
loops. In the middle of the triangle is the Cross,
formed by simple bars. Under the triangle
passes a long shaft . . . with (on top) the shirt of
the Holy Order of Malta worked with carved
sleeves . . .'

Such texts could only have been written if
Pelosini had had Piranesi's full notes and working drawings before him. Fortunately, the
drawings in the Morgan Library give an excellent idea of Piranesi's scrupulous preparations
for the decorative parts. These drawings show
that the master of the sparkling sketch, rapidly
drawn with pen and wash, could also be the
most irksome disciplinarian. The two drawings
for the high altar reveal something of the chasm
in Piranesi's personality as an artist: the early
sketch (some years ago with a New York dealer   325
and now also in the Morgan Library) and the
finished drawing seem to reflect his dual gift as   326
a fiery creator and as a dispassionate antiquarian.

Only two of the drawings may be regarded as
actual working drawings. Both are for sculptured panels of the decoration of the little piazza,   334
which was entirely Piranesi's work (the entrance gate, however, incorporated an older
one). The finished drawings for the central   323,
panel of the vaulting and for the high altar, by   326
contrast, cannot have been used as working
drawings because they do not correspond closely enough with the execution.[3] In spite of their
precision it must be assumed that they were
followed by other, still larger and more detailed drawings which served the contractor,
the stonemasons and the sculptor Tommaso
Righi, who was responsible for the execution of
all the figures on the vault and the high altar as
well as for the medallions of the Apostles in the
nave and the apse.

Our analysis of the character and purpose of
the account book and of the relevant drawings
may appear to point in one direction, namely,
that Piranesi's contribution to the church was
mainly that of a decorative designer. But any
such conclusion would be fallacious. To be sure,
the building remained unaltered as a structure:
it still has all the characteristics of a late
sixteenth-century church, consisting of a simple
nave with four shallow chapels to each side, a
hardly emphasized transept, and a slightly con-

252

tracted apse. Contrary to Körte's assertion, not even the vault was changed; the roof was raised only for purely technical reasons. But the present church does not strike the beholder as an older building to which – incongruously – eighteenth-century decoration has been added. It seems all of one piece and has an unmistakable style of its own. What is even more astonishing, perhaps, is that it has exchanged its specific Roman quality for one which can only be described as north Italian. To achieve so much with so little and in spite of the handicap which the preservation of the old structure presented is a remarkable feat that should long have elevated Piranesi to the rank of a resourceful architect.

In Rome, as a rule, the area reserved for divine function is slightly elevated above the rest of the church; one or two steps and the Communion rail usually separate choir and apse from the transept, and the high altar is placed 328 at the far end of the apse. Piranesi's high altar, by contrast, projects considerably into the transept, the Communion rail is moved from its traditional position and is placed above three steps, between the third and fourth chapels of the nave. In addition Piranesi also elevated the apse three steps above the transept. This dual change of level within a church is quite un-Roman. In Roman churches the nave and transept, I think without exception, form an undivided area. Spatial continuity was regarded as a *sine qua non* for the expression of a unified architectural concept. In Venice, however, such changes of level are common, although a caesura rarely occurs within the unit of the nave.

327, A study of the articulation inside the church 329 leads to even more revealing results. The articulation of the sixteenth-century church is not known; yet one can hardly doubt that it was similar to such a church as S. Maria dei

328 PIRANESI. High altar of S. Maria del Priorato, Rome

329 PIRANESI. S. Maria del Priorato, Rome, view into south transept

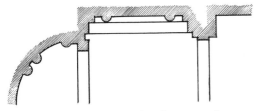

327 S. Maria del Priorato. Plan showing wall articulation of crossing and choir apse

330 PIRANESI. S. Maria del Priorato, interior looking towards the high altar

Monti, even though there was never a dome over the crossing. Corresponding to many late sixteenth- and early seventeenth-century structures, the original choir of S. Maria del Priorato was slightly narrower than the nave. A study of the plans of the Gesù, S. Maria de' Monti, S. Maria in Vallicella, and many others will show the same phenomenon. Now in all these churches a coherent articulation, as a rule of single pilasters, is carried around the entire building, and the treatment of the four corners under the crossing is of course always identical. In my view, it cannot be doubted that Piranesi also found four equal corners under the crossing of the old church. He changed this Roman tradition in two respects. First, the character of the order varies: instead of the single pilasters of the nave, there are double half-columns in the apse and single half-columns in the transept. Secondly, the four corners of the crossing are not equal: on the side of the nave they are formed by imposts corresponding to those on which the arches of the chapels rest; on the far side of the crossing there are double pilasters of which only the outside one is answered across the transept. Here the corners are formed by full pilasters which carry the arch separating the apse from the rest of the vault. The vaulting of nave and crossing is consistent in height up to the point where the arch at the far end of the crossing is met. To formulate this problem differently: we are faced with a situation where only three arches of the crossing are identical and the fourth – that at the far end of the principal axis – is made dissimilar.

No clearer sign of Piranesi's contempt for structural logic in the Roman tradition is possible. In a Roman church the beholder feels stimulated to notice and appreciate the element of continuity, but the system of articulation is deployed without optical or illusionist concessions. Piranesi, by contrast, breaks the traditional continuity because he has primarily the subjective optical experience of the beholder in mind. Once again this points to Venice, to Palladio and Longhena who were intent on scenographic relationships from space to space. 330 Upon entering S. Maria del Priorato, the visitor is immediately attracted by the 'image' he views at the far end: the highly decorated, luminous apse seen through the framing arch with the picturesque high altar placed under it.

Now it would be wrong to conclude that Piranesi sacrificed architectural logic to picturesque appearances. Even the first impression of his severe and precise detail seems to exclude such an assumption. What in fact happened is that he replaced one type of architectural logic by another. This is revealed by a closer study of the orders in the transept and apse. The double pilasters under the crossing are not an isolated motif: each of the two pilasters is joined across the corner by another pilaster – a half-pilaster in the transept, a full pilaster in the apse. The latter pilasters form a unit with the adjoining half-columns. Furthermore in the depth of the apse there are two double half-columns. In other words Piranesi, working in the transept and apse with variations of the duplication of orders, displayed the full range of possibilities: double pilasters, half-pilaster plus column, full pilaster plus column, and double columns. The strongest accents are actually reserved for the apse, but the optical emphasis is on the liturgical and emotional centre of the church, the high altar, which, for the view from the entrance, appears encompassed by double pilasters as well as double columns.

Add to this the decoration of the semi-vault of the apse by the sharply chiselled coffers on which a large shell and, in turn, the Rezzonico arms are superimposed; add the large window in the centre of the apse, an utterly un-Roman feature, and the lantern in the crossing, both opened into the fabric by Piranesi (so that the high altar is not only silhouetted against the apse but also receives light from above); add finally the extravagant size and shape of the 328 altar itself – and it must be admitted that no similar apse and high altar exist in Rome. Obviously Palladio's Redentore and S. Giorgio Maggiore come to mind; one also recalls the high altar of S. Maria della Salute, framed by columns and originally silhouetted against a window in the choir. The north Italian parallels can easily be multiplied, but it may suffice to mention Juvarra's Chiesa della Venaria Reale near Turin, where once again the columns are reserved for the apse and where we also find the tall, complex altar with a window illuminating it from behind.

About this north Italian character of Piranesi's transformation of the Priorato there

331 PIRANESI. S. Maria del Priorato, entrance gate

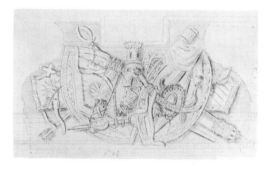

332, 333 PIRANESI. Panel in the garden wall of
S. Maria del Priorato, Rome, drawing (New York,
Pierpont Morgan Library) and executed work

cannot be the slightest doubt. But, in addition, his individuality is everywhere most effective. In its present state the façade, which lost Piranesi's high attic in the first half of the nineteenth century, consists mainly of a temple motif with pairs of pilasters carrying a large pediment. The outside pilasters are doubled across the corners. We have here, therefore, a group of three pilasters which corresponds in reverse to that at the entry of the apse. The theme of the façade is taken up and re-interpreted on the inside at the far end; the central area of the façade also prepares in a subtle way for the design of the high altar. Nobody who has a feeling for the cogency of architectural themes will remain unimpressed by the way Piranesi handled them here.

We ought now to discuss other no less important matters; in the first place, how he brought his antiquarian knowledge to bear on the design of the detail. The Piazzale is the *locus classicus* for this. Furthermore we would have to investigate his often strange interpretation of individual motifs: the sometimes confusing superimposition of architectural elements, the play with different planes, the unpredictable breaking up and reversal of familiar

331–
334

256

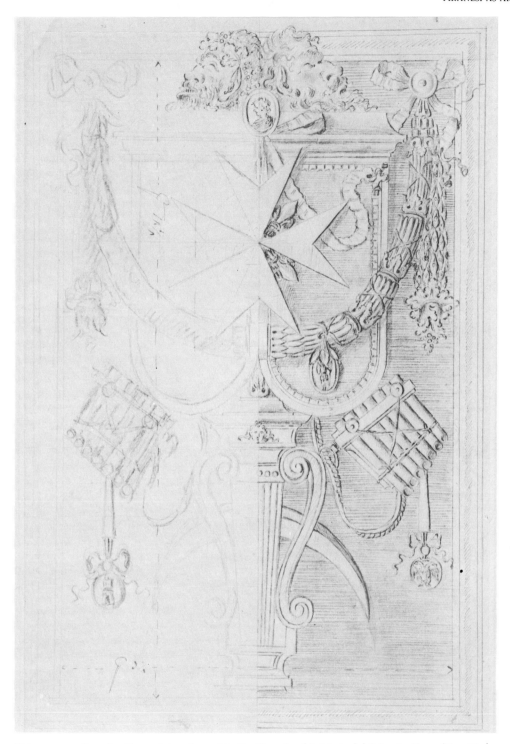

334 PIRANESI. Drawing for sculptured panel in the Piazzale of S. Maria del Priorato, Rome (New York, Pierpont Morgan Library)

257

features, the wilful combination of traditional ornamental detail and, indeed fascinating, his introduction of an ornamental language till then unknown. All this would suggest that he apparently had recourse to the principles of Roman Mannerist architecture of the sixteenth century. This is true to such an extent that Giuseppe Fiocco[4] even attributed to Piranesi the façade of S. Nicola in Carcere, a work indubitably by Giacomo della Porta. The problems of the antiquarianism and Mannerism of Piranesi's architectural designs have been touched upon in Körte's paper and in one of my own.[5] Here I shall do no more than note the emblematic quality pervading his entire design

– expressed in the ornamental usage of the elements of the Rezzonico arms in the Piazzale, on the façade, and inside the church on the vault and in the apse, in the capitals of the pilasters and of the columns. This cryptic iconography ties Piranesi's conceptual architecture firmly to the Baroque age.

S. Maria del Priorato was a test case of Piranesi's theory that a vital style displaying an immense variety could arise from a meaningful digestion of the architectural styles of the past. He must be judged by the result. He himself firmly believed that he had passed the test and, as the pages of this essay show, I am inclined to agree with him.

335 PIRANESI. Sculptured panel above one of the side chapels of S. Maria del Priorato, Rome

336 PIRANESI. Detail of a design for an Egyptian fireplace from *Diverse Maniere d'adornare i Camini*, 1769 (see pl. 349)

XV PIRANESI
AND EIGHTEENTH-CENTURY
EGYPTOMANIA

Piranesi and Eighteenth-century Egyptomania

THERE HAVE been some excellent studies on the influence of Egypt on European thought and art. The founding father of this field of study was of course Karl Giehlow, whose *Hieroglyphenkunde des Humanismus* (published in 1915) I have always regarded as one of the most creative and remarkable achievements of our discipline. But he as well as those who followed him such as Ludwig Volkmann[1] and George Boas[2] were only concerned with the Renaissance. It was only more recently that some scholars – Erik Iversen,[3] Siegfried Morenz[4] and Jurgis Baltrušaitis[5] – also paid attention to later periods. But much remains to be done. I think, eighteenth-century events cannot be properly assessed without at least a fleeting consideration of 'Egypt and Europe' in previous centuries.

So let us start in antiquity. After the Battle of Actium in 31 BC Egypt became part of the Roman empire, and the thought and art of that ancient country of mysterious wisdom immediately aroused Roman interest and admiration. The cult of Isis and Osiris gained a firm foothold in Italy. Large temples to Isis were built in the very centre of Rome and portable objects reached Rome in a steady stream. The Romans stopped at nothing. Obelisks were ferried across the sea; in the course of time Rome had more than forty-two, thirteen of which survive to this day.

After the collapse of the empire, contact with Egypt was sporadically interrupted and no pre-Christian Egyptian works seem to have reached the West for over a thousand years. But Rome remained a repository of ancient Egyptian art, even though most of these treasures were buried with the ancient city deep in Roman soil.

Nevertheless, in the course of the thirteenth century Rome had a first Egyptian Renaissance, an indication that sufficient material was available to stimulate such borrowings. Sphinxes turned up in stylistically remarkably correct adaptations and, for the first time, pyramids were incorporated in Christian tomb monuments.

337 Sphinx from an Italian late thirteenth-century tomb, signed Fra Pasquale (Viterbo Museum)

The thirteenth-century Egyptian revival was of comparatively brief duration. When interest in Egypt was once again awakened in the course of the fifteenth century, it had come to stay. Elements of Egyptian art – above all, pyramids, obelisks and sphinxes – were absorbed by, and incorporated in, Renaissance and post-Renaissance styles. These Egyptian paraphernalia carried funerary associations and soon became an important part of tomb structures. But my example (the Contarini tomb, Santo, Padua; 1544–48, designed by Sanmicheli) clearly demonstrates that pyramids were used in an entirely un-Egyptian way. This tomb is a typical Renaissance monument: the pyramid here is a mere funerary emblem, a symbol of immortality, and no one would ever claim, that stylistically it gives the tomb an Egyptian character.

The lesson we learn here can safely be generalized: Egyptian features lose their connotations with ancient Egyptian art when they become part and parcel of a Renaissance or post-Renaissance stylistic entity. With rare exceptions this remains true right into the eighteenth century.

While Egypt had no influence to speak of on the *styles* of works of art between the fifteenth

260

338 Pyramid on an Italian thirteenth-century tomb, monument to Rolandino de' Passeggeri, Bologna

339 The Contarini tomb, Il Santo, Padua, 1544–48, designed by Sanmichele

and eighteenth centuries, it yet had a profound influence on the *minds* of an élite. The Florentine Neo-Platonists believed that Plato and the pre-Christian revelations attested to the truth of Christianity by means of veiled mysteries and that these mysteries were enshrined in hieroglyphs. From their misinformed late antique sources they learned that hieroglyphs contained a secret code. Plotinus taught them that the Egyptian sages, instead of using discursive arguments, had found a way of embodying whole concepts in images; from Plutarch they learned that Greek philosophers had gone to Egypt to study the mystic teachings of old; and from Clement of Alexandria that 'the mysteries of the word are not to be expounded to the profane' and that 'all things that shine through a veil show the truth grander and more imposing'. If one could decipher hieroglyphs, one would have access not only to many ancient mysteries, but above all to the secret of how to express the essence of an idea, its platonic form (as it were), perfect and complete in itself, by means of an image.

Horapollo's *Hieroglyphica*, a Greek AD fourth-century manuscript brought to Florence after 1419, explained close to two hundred hieroglyphs and seemed, therefore, to answer the quest. For two hundred years it was never seriously doubted that this work contained the much coveted answer to the Egyptian riddle. In their search for expressive pictographs, Renaissance scholars and artists had, next to Horapollo, the hieroglyphs on Roman obelisks and such works as the *Tabula Bembina* (a 340 tablet found in Rome in 1525 and called after its first owner, the Cardinal Bembo). As early as the mid-fifteenth century the great Leon Battista Alberti publicized the opinion that not only the Egyptians, but other nations too, among them the Romans themselves, had made use of the Egyptian language of symbols.

261

340 Tabula Bembina, detail

Naturally, the Romans had expressed their veiled truths in terms of their own style. An 341 innocent temple frieze with sacrificial implements (at that time in S. Lorenzo fuori le mura), for instance, enjoyed the reputation of conveying a message in hieroglyphs. From such interpretations the humanists took their licence of creating pictorial hieroglyphic symbols in their own style. But although Egyptian hieroglyphs were the starting point of their search for the lost wisdom, they never for a moment regarded it as necessary to use Egyptian pictographs.

Eventually an enormous 'hieroglyphic' material accumulated, among which medals, emblems and *imprese* must be counted. This material was incorporated into mythological and iconological manuals and eagerly used by artists. Throughout the seventeenth century and even in the first half of the eighteenth century the symbolic language of pseudo-hieroglyphs was still practised and fully understood. But in the early eighteenth century we can discover the beginnings of a new attitude toward Egypt.

One began to see Egypt in an entirely new light. Precise on-the-spot observation and investigation, hardly known before the eighteenth century, now became a real challenge. Travelling to Egypt became fashionable and many travellers published scholarly reports. I

will only mention the important publications by Paul Lucas in 1705, Dr Pococke in 1743, 342 Ludvig Norden in 1755, Carsten Niebuhr in 1774. Of these Norden's is the most impressive achievement. His archaeological material is uncommonly reliable, but there was still a long way to go to render the specific characteristics of the Egyptian style (as his plate with the great sphinx near the pyramids at Gizeh shows). 343

These books, which for the first time supplied trustworthy descriptions and pictures of Egypt, were avidly studied. Also Piranesi knew some, if not all, of them. They helped to correct many misconceptions about Egypt and stimulated an interest in Egyptian architecture.

Parallel with the growing number of field studies in Egyptian history, topography, art and archaeology, went the research into Egyptian treasures at home. Egyptian antiquities were accumulated. The greatest among the collectors of the seventeenth century was Athanasius Kircher, who was also the greatest Egyptologist of his time and enjoyed international reputation (Museo Kircheriano, Rome). Next to him other collectors shrink in stature, such as the Grand Dukes of Tuscany, the Conte Lodovico Moscardo in Verona and even the remarkable Peiresc in Paris who had agents working for him in Egypt and the Levant. The task of sifting, ordering and discussing in a new

341 Part of a temple frieze formerly in S. Lorenzo fuori le Mura

342 Plate from Paul Lucas' *Voyage au Levant*, 1705

263

343 Plate from F. L. Norden's *Travels in Egypt and Nubia*, 1757, showing the Sphinx and Pyramids

344 Plate from Montfaucon's *Antiquité expliquée*, 1719–24

rationalist spirit all these testimonies of Egypt's past – daily increased by a steady stream of new works yielded by the soil of Rome – was undertaken by Bernard de Montfaucon in his encyclopaedic *L'Antiquité expliquée*, published between 1719 and 1724.

Montfaucon illustrated his specimens of Egyptian art systematically arranged on densely filled plates and in his elegant text he was extremely critical of older Egyptological research. He refused to attempt an interpretation of hieroglyphs which cannot be undertaken 'without the risk of running wild'; he refused to admire Egyptian wisdom; and he regarded Egyptian religion as monstrous and Egyptian art as horrible. This was indeed a new spirit – it was the spirit of the eighteenth century. Archaeological erudition and discrimination went hand in hand with sober criticism and emotive disenchantment.

A little later in 1741 the much maligned Bishop of Gloucester, William Warburton, published his *The Divine Legation of Moses* – a work difficult to digest for a layman like myself – which, however, contains some enlightened thoughts about Egypt and hieroglyphic writing. Warburton derides Athanasius Kircher, who was still steeped in Neo-Platonic mysticism. He ridicules Kircher's 'Labouring through

345 Plate from Fischer von Erlach's *Entwurf einer historischen Architektur,* 1721, showing the Pyramids

half a dozen folios with writings of late Greek Platonists, and forged Books of Hermes [i.e. the hermetic writings] which contain a philosophy, not Egyptian, to explain and illustrate old monuments, not philosophical.' And Warburton suggests to leave him alone to pursue 'his shadow of a dream through all the fantastic regions of Pythagorean Platonism'.

The men of the Enlightenment brushed under the carpet the strange Renaissance aberrations in the interpretation of hieroglyphs. But the old conviction that Egypt was the source of occult and mystic revelations was difficult to kill; indeed, this conviction lived on as an undercurrent mainly in secret societies such as the Rosicrucians and Freemasons. In this connection Mozart's *Magic Flute* and the name of Cagliostro come to everybody's mind. Egyptological research was divorced from such survivals of esoteric beliefs.

While thus the spirit of Alexandrian Neo-Platonism and mysticism now held little attraction, Egyptian art as a style made its entry. At a first glance the course of events may appear paradoxical, but, in fact, it had its own logic. As long as Egypt was a riddle and a challenge captivating the minds and the emotions of people, no serious attempt was made (as I have tried to show) to grasp the peculiarities of

Egyptian art or to imitate more than isolated details. When the spell was broken and replaced by archaeological detachment, a door was opened to an understanding, appreciation and analysis of Egyptian art as a style in its own right.

Probably the first to approach the stylistic phenomenon of Egyptian art and architecture from a general conceptual point of view was Fischer von Erlach in his *Entwurf einer historischen Architektur,* first published in Vienna in 1721, a work in which he attempted to demonstrate by picture and word the unbroken development of the history of architecture from Asia and Egypt to modern times. For him Egyptian architecture excelled by its marvellous simplicity. His plate with the pyramids of 345 Gizeh certainly illustrates his point. Fischer had never been to Egypt; his illustrations of Egyptian architecture were derived from travellers' books. Certain other illustrations – such as Heliopolis and Thebes – show that Fischer's 346 ideas about Egypt were still somewhat foggy.

Fischer's work was intensely studied; Piranesi too was attracted by it. Early in his career, probably around 1743, he made rapid sketches after some of Fischer's plates and two such sheets showing pyramids, etc., are now in the 347 Morgan Library.

346 Plate from Fischer von Erlach's *Entwurf einer historischen Architektur,* 1721, showing tombs at Heliopolis

The ways in which Piranesi's attitude to Greek, Etruscan and Roman architecture developed have already been traced in a previous essay (pp. 235–246). Up to 1756 his work reveals no serious consideration of Egyptian art. But in the text of *Della Magnificenza ed Architettura de' Romani* (1761) he does mention Egypt, and it appears that he held determined views. Following Caylus,[6] he maintains that it was from Egypt that the Etruscans inherited their grandeur, truth and simplicity, qualities that he then admired. By 1765, when *Parere su l'Architettura* appeared, his aesthetic values had changed (see p. 239), and he now recommended the ornate style which he had condemned before, illustrating his new position with extraordinary designs of his own invention. All the rules are cast to the wind; the designs are overloaded with decorative motifs. Elements taken from Roman and Egyptian architecture and sculpture, from Etruscan and Greek vases and so forth appear side by side, to show how the whole heritage of antiquity can be combined in a personal contemporary style. Archaeological material has become a weapon in the hands of a revolutionary modernist, but the importance of Egypt as a source has not diminished.

Whether one likes these strange projects or not, to Piranesi they were extremely important, for they were visible testimonies of a process of intellectual liberation successfully accomplished. Looking back over twenty years of his life to the *Carceri*, one may feel that erudition and archaeology had a disastrous influence on a man who had been one of the greatest creative geniuses of the century. Instead of the sweeping unification of visions in the *Carceri*, we find here, it may be argued, an ill-judged conglomeration of heterogeneous motifs. But another more positive approach is possible. These designs are conceived, as a critic has said, in a typically eighteenth-century anthological spirit. If the *Carceri* are still tied to the Baroque, here one may discover the mentality of the encyclopaedists.

348
316–
318

266

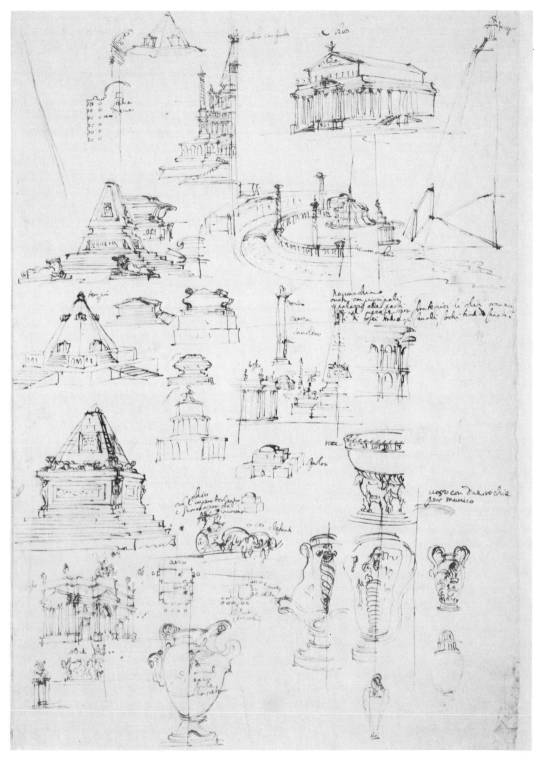

347 PIRANESI. Page of sketches from Fischer von Erlach's *Entwurf* (New York, Pierpont Morgan Library)

348 PIRANESI. *Parere su l'Architettura*, 1765, pl. VI

Piranesi's last excursion into the field of Egyptology was the *Diverse Maniere d'adornare i Camini* of 1769 (see pp. 245–246). He entitled his introduction to the *Camini*: 'Apologetic argument in defence of Egyptian and Etruscan architecture.' For him Egyptian and Etruscan art belonged closely together, but in the following remarks I shall concentrate on the Egyptian argument. He felt it necessary to defend himself against attacks he expected from critics. As we have seen, Fischer von Erlach, Caylus and others had created a tenor of opinion regarding the simplicity and massiveness of Egyptian art and architecture. The travellers' reports to which Piranesi refers had shown that Egyptian structures were colossal and bare. He felt that he had to meet two objections: first, that he perverted historical truth by representing the Egyptian style as ornate; secondly, that he was using and recommending manners which offended good taste, because according to general opinion both 'Egyptian and Etruscan architecture were bold and bare [*ardite e grette*] manners'.

The first objection he countered surely with his tongue in his cheek. He maintained that the present 'lack and poverty of ornaments' of Egyptian monuments were due to the ravages of time. The *Tabula Bembina*, 'the ornaments found in the Villa Hadriana', the richly ornamented Egyptian objects, the ornaments on Egyptian urns, and so forth – all go to show, he argues, that the walls of Egyptian palaces and temples were once enriched by ornament. This settled, he asks whether Egyptian artists wanted to show 'a mystery or delight with their ornaments'; and he answers that their ornaments were not mysterious 'but whims [*bizzarie*] of the Egyptian artists'. We have considered the anti-Renaissance, rationalist eighteenth-century approach to the Egyptian mysteries, and it is not astonishing to find Piranesi in the rationalist camp. But so far nobody had maintained that Egyptian artists were interested, as Piranesi himself was, in the representation of *bizzarie*. He concluded to his own satisfaction that his medley of hieroglyphs, mummies, scarabs, sphinxes, bulls, crocodiles and statues was no more than a recreation of the *bizzarie* of the ancient masters. In keeping with this programme the *Diverse Maniere* contains a large number of fireplaces in the Egyptian manner, which Piranesi quite correctly prides himself on having introduced for the first time. 336, 349, 350

His answer to the second objection (that his recommendations were offensive to good taste) leads him to even more revealing remarks. Let us assume, he argues, that the general view is correct that the Egyptian and Etruscan styles are 'bold, angry and harsh manners' [*maniere ardite, risentite, e aspre*]. What is wrong with that? Even 'the grotesque has its beauty and causes delight' as is proved by the modern infatuation with Chinese cabinets and Chinese rooms, a taste which according to him is 'awkward and far removed from any grace'. He concludes that 'mankind loves variety too much to enjoy all the time the same decoration: one is pleased by the alternating of the cheerful and the serious, one even enjoys the pathetic and the horror of battles has its beauty and out of fear rises delight' – most revealing ideas, because we see here Piranesi in command of the eighteenth-century language of the Sublime.

One should have thought that he had no need to go further, because one now expects him to

349, 350 PIRANESI. Two designs for Egyptian fireplaces from *Diverse Maniere d'adornare i Camini*, 1769

351 Table made to Piranesi's design (Minneapolis Institute of Arts)

352 One of the lions from the Acqua Felice, Rome (from an engraving in C. H. Tatham, *Etchings*, etc., 1799)

argue that he wanted to create horror and fear and therefore delight by a bizarre assembly of elements of the hard manner (*maniera aspra*) of the Egyptians. But historical situations are scarcely ever that simple. Piranesi was too much involved in partly contradictory thought processes old and new to accept such an easy solution. He had to prove as much to himself as to others that the 'hardness' (*durezza*) of the Egyptian manner was not the result of a lack of experience, but had been arrived at after mature consideration. It was a deliberate stylization developed by Egyptian artists in order to assimilate their statuary and decoration to the character of their architecture.

We have to remember that for classically trained minds non-naturalistic or anti-naturalistic styles had the stigma of primitivity, of a lack of know-how attached to them, and to prefer them to the Greco-Roman and western naturalistic tradition meant reverting to styles that were qualitatively inferior. We know what

353 PIRANESI. Wall decoration for the Caffè Inglese, Rome (from the *Diverse Maniere d'adornare i Camini,* 1769)

Piranesi means when he maintains that Egyptian works do not show 'a lack of art and knowledge'. Not unexpectedly he continues that the Egyptians knew 'the natural beauties' very well, but undertook to modify and correct them. Or else they would have been incapable 352 of creating such marvellous works as the lions of the Acqua Felice (what majesty, what severity, what wisdom! he exclaims) – lions which are infinitely superior to their non-Egyptian realistic counterparts.

These are remarkable observations, real eye-openers – nobody before Piranesi had ever seen Egyptian works in this way. Even though his reasoning may no longer be acceptable, his eye was impeccable and free from the bondage of *naturalezza* at any price. So far Piranesi's intellectual position seems defensible. At the end, however, all vestiges of reason seem to desert him. Since the Egyptians, he argues, had really digested nature, they were also capable of 'that delicate, that fleshy and palpable

manner which, it is maintained, only the Greeks knew'. He therefore calls upon artists to break away from the bondage of the Greek manner 'and where the Egyptians and the Etruscans show in their monuments grace, charm and elegance – let's make use of this richness'. This, surely, is an unexpected anticlimax, for charm and elegance – stylistic terms of the Rococo vocabulary – are the last things we can discover in Piranesi's Egyptian manner.

None of Piranesi's Egyptian *camini* and only two of the 'Roman' designs were executed, but are no longer extant. A table, now in the Minneapolis Institute of Art, also in the Roman 351 manner, executed for Cardinal Rezzonico, is the only piece of the *Camini* publication that survives. It gives at least an idea of the imaginative richness and density of this style. Even before the publication of the *Camini* Piranesi decorated two walls of the Caffè Inglese in 353 Rome in the Egyptian manner (the date 'about 1760' usually mentioned is certainly too early).

271

354 Porch of the Hôtel Beauharnais, Paris, 1803

This work, the earliest decoration of a room in the Egyptian style and the only one Piranesi executed in the manner of the Egyptian *camini*, did not survive long; but the two etchings in the publication have at least preserved a reliable record of the design, though it is tantalizing that we have no clear idea of the colours and the overall effect on the spectator.

It is not quite easy to assess to what extent Piranesi was responsible for the Egyptomania of the next decades. I think, however, one can say that, although artists like Mauro Tesi in Italy and Leqeu and Desprez in France began making Egyptian designs almost contemporaneously with, and independent of, Piranesi, it was the widely circulated *Camini* that prepared the ground for a general acceptance of Egyptian taste. When I say this I have in mind Piranesi's text rather than his designs.

Later works inspired by Egyptian art were hardly influenced by Piranesi's Egyptian style. In the 1780s Frenchmen like Boullée were once 356 again attracted by the bareness and hardness and the colossal of Egyptian architecture. Although Napoleon revived some of the mystique of Egypt and used hieroglyphic signs for imperial symbolism, his conquest of Egypt, the ensuing scientific survey of the country and people and Champollion's deciphering of the hieroglyphs robbed Egypt forever of the aura of strangeness. During the first decades of the nineteenth century I find in only one rare book, G. Landi's *Architectural Decorations . . . from the Egyptian, the Greek . . .* of 1810, a survival of Piranesi's spirit. As a rule, an archaeological facet of the Egyptian style found general approval. We find this style for instance in Thomas Hope's book *Household Furniture and* 355 *Interior Decoration executed from Designs by Thomas Hope,* published in 1807, or in Percier's and Fontaine's *Recueil de décorations intérieures* of 1812, or the façade of the Hôtel Beauharnais 354 in Paris of 1803 and of the Egyptian Hall in London of 1812.

All this is comparatively sober and tame. Against this foil, it becomes apparent how personal, quaint, exotic and eccentric Piranesi's 'stile egiziano' was. And these comparisons strengthen our awareness that this first creative effusion of eighteenth-century Egyptomania had its roots in a typically mid-eighteenth-century conception of sublimity.

355 Plate from Thomas Hope's *Household Furniture and Interior Decoration,* 1807

356 E.-L. BOULLÉE. Project for the entrance to a cemetery

273

NOTES

I Carlo Rainaldi and the Architecture of the High Baroque in Rome

1 *The Art Bulletin*, XVI, 1934, p. 123 ff. [to be included in a later volume of these essays.—Ed.]

2 For a monographic treatment see E. Hempel, *Carlo Rainaldi. Ein Beitrag zur Geschichte des roemischen Barock*. Diss. Munich, 1919. Also by the same author: 'Carlo Rainaldi', in *Biblioteca d'Arte Illustrata*, Series I, Fasc. II. Compare also the article by Mandl in Thieme-Becker, *Kuenstler-Lexikon*. XXVII, 1933, p. 578.

3 *Op. cit.*, p. 47 ff.

4 E. Coudenhove-Erthal, *Carlo Fontana*, Vienna, 1930, p. 36 ff.; and Mandl, *op. cit.*

5 Inscription above the inner door: ANNO JUBILEO MDCLXXV. See also Forcella, *Iscrizioni delle chiese . . . di Roma*, IX, p. 385.

6 Exterior inscription over the entrance: ANNO DNI MDCLXXVIII. Interior inscription over the entrance: MDCLXXIX. See Forcella, *op. cit.*, X, p. 621.

7 *Ammaestramento utile e curioso di pittura, scultura ed architettura nelle chiese di Roma*, Rome, 1686, p. 355.

8 In Giov. Giac. Rossi, *Il nuovo teatro . . . delle fabriche . . . di Roma . . . sotto Alessandro VII*, Rome, 1665, I, pl. 7.

In the analysis of the history of the construction one can disregard the drawing by Lieven Cruyl of 1664, which Egger was the first to publish in *Roemische Veduten*, I, 1911, pl. 5. This is merely a misinterpretation of the design on the foundation medal (see below and pl. 2). As late as 1692 Cruyl made an engraving after his drawing (copy in Rome, Corsini, Cart. 7000, Inv. 16796), which corrects the drawing in as much as the churches are represented in the same condition as on the foundation medal. But meanwhile the buildings had actually been completed in their altered form!

9 *Studio di pittura, scultura e architettura nelle chiese di Roma*.

10 Pp. 96–97.

11 P. 467.

12 *'Essendo stato Architetto della Cuppola e dell'Altar maggiore l'istesso Rainaldi, e di tutto il restante il Bernini e Fontana.'* For the documentary value of this *Guida* see L. Schudt, *Le Guide di Roma*, 1930, p. 54. In

Baldinucci's *Vita* of Rainaldi (*Vite . . . ed. F. Ranalli, Florence, 1847, V, p. 331) there is no special mention of a change of plan. A later engraving by Falda of S. Maria di Monte Santo in Giov. Giacomo de Rossi, *Insignium Romae Templorum prospectus*, Rome, 1684, pl. 47, bears the inscription: *'Graphia, et inventum Eq. D. Caroli Rainaldi Architecti Romani.'* The engraving does not indeed correspond with the actual building (which had already been long completed) and even represents the church with the octagonal dome which had originally been planned.

13 *'Dissegno per la nova cuppola della Chiesa di Monte Santo sotto li XX Marzo 1674.'* Below a dedication by Fontana from which it is evident that the plan dates from much earlier than 1674 and that meanwhile another plan had been executed: *'offero a V. S. Ill.ma una vittima, che è sua, con viva speranza d'esserle gradita, benchè non affetuata nell'opra.'* The meaning of this plan is made clear by the text and ground plan which can be seen respectively left and right above. *'Ragioni del Disegno. La figura della Chiesa, è Ovale Misto e non Ellipse seg.to A prodotto in virtù di pal. 100 di lon.a e larg.a pal. 80 varia solo alla rotondità pal. 10 per lato. Dunque facile sarebbe stato l'esecuzione circolare perche scemando la grossezza del tamburro sino a pal. 5 nelli lati BB* (i.e. longitudinal outer diameter of the dome 110 P.) *crescendo sino a pal. 12 nelli lati CC* (i.e., the transverse outer diameter of the dome 104 P.) *resta solo che pal. 3* (i.e., altogether 6 palms) *di variatione al circolo, alterando poi l'aggetti in proiettura in CC e diminuendo in BB. Certo che all'occhio più perfetto parsa sarebbe per la vicin.za del Circolo, e susequente megliore sarebbe stata la Cuppola in riguardo all'avanzo nella resega del Cornicione quale permetteva la Rotondità perfetta et ottangolare.'* Copy in Rome, Corsini 35 H 10, Inv. 37122. 39·8 × 26·9 cm.

14 Giovanni Incisa della Rocchetta published in *Il Messaggero* of 9 April 1926 a letter from Rainaldi to Mons. Gastaldi, unfortunately undated, concerning the completion of the foundation medal. The medal, the artist of which is G. F. Travani, has been occasionally reproduced in modern literature, last by F. Dworschak in *Jahrbuch d. preuss. Kunstslg.*, LV, 1934, p. 37, pl. III, 3. There exist two obviously simultaneous issues of the foundation medal, dated 1662; the one issue showing

on the reverse the inscription on a scroll above: *'Sapientia in plateis dat vocam suam'*, below: *'MDCLXII'*; the other showing the same inscription without a scroll, and below, instead of the date: *'Eq. Carolus Rainaldus Inventor'*.

15 Cartella 81, R 279. Left half-sheet, not reproduced here, with the *chiragrafo* of Alexander VII of 16 November 1661. On the left of our illustration: ground-plan of the whole square with the adjoining streets; on the right: ground-plan and elevation of one of the two churches which according to this project were to correspond exactly. Coloured pen-and-ink drawing. Size of the whole sheet: 525 mm × 750 mm (right-hand part which is here reproduced 525 mm × 420 mm). In the ground-plan of the site the existing structures are coloured brown and the proposed alterations violet. The *chiragrafo* deals with the purchase of the ground site. The churches are to be constructed *'nel modo e forma contenuta, et esposta nella sopra designata Pianta. . . .'*

16 In the Roman State Archives (Cartella 81, R 278) there is a large pen-and-ink scale drawing of the Piazza (815 mm × 420 mm) before the erection of the obelisk, i.e. before 1589, which depicts exact proposals for the re-organization of the site. The character of the drawing as well as that of the handwriting suggests that it was made at the end of the sixteenth century, and the idea itself indicates the period of re-organization under Sixtus V. It probably arose in connection with the relocation of the obelisk.

17 Codex Vaticanus lat. 13442, fol. 34r. 509 mm × 354 mm.

18 Bibl. Vat., cod. Chig. P VII 10, fol. 26r. Brown ink. 271 mm × 390 mm. The sheet is pasted into this volume of drawings.

19 Nearly all the published town plans, both old and new, eliminate the relatively small differences in size, but in the Maggi plan (pl. 8) they can be clearly seen.

20 The towers were erected only in the eighteenth century, but their existence is in harmony with Rainaldi's conception. They block the view of the domes from the Corso and give a clear indication from which point of view the churches should be seen.

21 Rainaldi's original solution (the foundation medal project) was the result of an objective consideration: the domes can only appear equally large if they are really

identical in size. Another deliberate optical illusion can be found in the façades. Owing to the exigencies of the site the façade of S. Maria di Monte Santo had to be 90 cm narrower than that of the other church. But the fact that the façade appears to terminate with the outer orders on each side and that by an unnoticeable extension of the wall beyond the outer orders the measurement between these orders was in both cases identical made it possible to conceal the actual disparity in size.

22 See Brauer-Wittkower, *Die Zeichnungen des Gianlorenzo Bernini*, 1931, pp. 102, 159. Also *Kritische Berichte*, 1931/2, p. 144.

23 Coudenhove-Erthal, *op. cit.*, pp. 26–27, confines himself to the remark: '*Fontana duerfte sich zuerst bei Rainaldi als Hilfskraft betaetigt haben.*'

24 Bibl. Vat., cod, Chig. P VII 13, fol. 26v/7. For the character of the different volumes of the Chigiana with drawings and plans see: Brauer-Wittkower, *Die Zeichnungen des G. L. Bernini*, 1931, pp. 11–12.

25 For other domes by Fontana see, for instance, the design for the decoration of the Colosseum, and the Jesuit Church in Loyola in Spain. See reproductions in Coudenhove-Erthal, *op. cit.*, pls. 6–8.

26 For the conception and significance of dual function, see *Art Bulletin, loc. cit.*, p. 208 ff.

27 In the Maderno ground-plan of St Peter's shown in the engraving by de Greuter in 1613, Bernini with hasty pencil strokes has added the outer isolated columns. The engraving is in cod. Chig. P. VII 9, fol. 30. Further material relating to this matter in Brauer-Wittkower, *op. cit.*, pp. 83–84, pls. 61, 164b.

28 Dagobert Frey, *Architettura Barocca*, Rome-Milan, Società Editrice d'Arte Illustrata, p. 47, even concluded that the portico was erected by Bernini himself when he took over the construction.

29 For the divergent functions of the pediment as conceived by Bernini and Rainaldi see below, note 38.

30 *Architektonische Handzeichnungen* . . ., Vienna 1910, pl. 28. After 1918 this sheet was transferred from the Hofbibliothek to the Albertina in Vienna.

31 *Rainaldi* . . ., p. 34, and also by the same, *Borromini*, Vienna, 1924, pl. 88, 2.

32 For Rainaldi's qualitative equalization of pilaster and column, see below, p. 21.

33 Hempel, *Borromini, op. cit.*, p. 141.

34 For the system of articulation in the façade of St Peter's see below, p. 20.

35 All details of the history of the construction are published by Hempel, *Borromini*, p. 138 ff.

36 Sheet in the Albertina. Published by

Hempel, *op. cit.*, pl. 90.

37 Design for the foundation medal in the Albertina. Published by Hempel, *op. cit.*, p. 138.

38 With Rainaldi the pediment, standing as it does in front of a flat wall surface, is merely a linear expression of emphasis and concentration, while with Bernini it forms the apex of the building and has always a sculptural character. As to this, compare Bernini's whole work from his S. Andrea al Quirinale and the churches in Castel Gandolfo and Ariccia up to the pediments of the colonnades of St Peter's. It is also most informative to compare Bernini's design for the apse of S. Maria Maggiore with the building as actually executed by Rainaldi. Rainaldi's apse stands against the plain decorative wall of the attic whereas in Bernini's project the entire structure is one dynamic entity of utmost sculptural value. For both projects see *Bernini Zeichnungen, loc cit.*, pp. 163–5. Hempel, *op. cit.*, p. 143 ff., already pointed out modifications of Borromini's plan in the region of the pediment; on p. 150 ff. he deals further with modifications of the design in the towers and lantern. The author of a drawing in cod. Chig. P VII 9, fol. 85—probably Giovanni Maria Baratta, who designed the towers—makes in his design of the region of the pediment, a clumsy attempt to mediate between Rainaldi and Borromini (pl. 17).

39 For the façade of S. Andrea della Valle see Baglione, *Le Vite de' Pittori*. . . . Naples, 1733, p. 197; Baldinucci, *Notizie* . . ., ed. 1847, V., p. 330; A. Boni, *La Chiesa di S. Andrea della Valle in Roma. Numero speciale della Illustrazione Cattolica*, 21 March 1907, p. 6 ff.; Hempel, *Rainaldi*, p. 54 ff.; Dagobert Frey, in *Jahrbuch für Kunstgeschichte*, III, 1924, p. 35; A. Muñoz, *Carlo Maderna (Bibl. d'Arte Illustrata, Serie I, Fasc. 12)*, p. 9 ff.; S. Ortolani, *S. Andrea della Valle (Chiese di Roma Illustrate, no. 4)*, 1923, p. 7 ff.; G. Giovannoni, *Saggi sulla Architettura del rinascimento*, Milan, 1931, p. 211 ff., 233; Caflisch, in Thieme-Becker, *s. v. Maderno*, XXIII, p. 531 and Caflisch, *Maderno*, 1934, p. 50 ff. Copy of the engraving in Rome, Corsiniana 47 H 7 Inv. 71588 (566 mm × 343 mm). The engraving later published in the work of Giacomo de Rossi, *Insignium Romae Templorum prospectus*, Rome, 1684, pl. 44.

40 For the analysis of S. Susanna see: *Art Bulletin*, 1934, p. 209.

41 Cod. Chig. P VII 9, fol. 91v/92r (58), 745 mm × 519 mm. Coloured pen and ink. Below on the right-hand margin the original signature: 'Rainaldi'. Pl. 18 does not include the signature. This drawing already published by Caflisch, *op. cit.*, fig. 27.

42 The inconsistency is still more accentuated here by the existence of the half-pilasters without entablature which must have been a legacy of the Maderno design.

43 Rainaldi in his design simply included the existing window by Maderno. The executed window has no apparent connection with the Maderno window although in fact this has not been altered. The window opens above the 'attic' and the balcony, now part of the attic, is placed in front of a blank wall so that it cannot be reached. Close observation however reveals the semicircular window of Maderno behind the present rectangular window frame. Here again one can see the exact point at which the subjective, psychological principle, which we noticed in the churches on the Piazza del Popolo, supersedes the 'objective' conception, characteristic of Rainaldi.

44 Bibl. Vat., cod. Chig. P VII 9, fol. 90 (57). Signature in Fontana's own writing: 'Carlo Fontana f.' The same technique of coloured pen and ink can be seen in a great number of Fontana's drawings. We reproduce only a detail of the much larger sheet on the left side of which is represented an extensive ground-plan of the site. Coudenhove-Erthal, *op. cit.*, p. 27 was acquainted with this sheet and held therefore the clue to the Rainaldi-Fontana problem.

45 The foundation medal was struck during the eighth year of Alexander's pontificate, i.e. between 7 April 1662 and 6 April 1663. Rainaldi's project (pl. 18) bears in the frieze the date 1662. The recommencement of the work may be dated that year; it was finally completed, according to the inscription of the façade, in 1665.

Small but significant divergences between the Fontana project, the medal design, and the completed structure must here be mentioned. In Fontana's project (pl. 21) the tabernacles in the outer compartments of the main storey are shown with 'ears' instead of with the actually existing triglyphs. There is, further, in Fontana's project—still in accordance with both Maderno and Rainaldi—a pillar in the centre of the balustrade of the balcony in the upper storey, while in the completed building there is no central motif in the balustrade. Finally—again in accordance with Maderno and Rainaldi—the large centre window is made to terminate in a semicircle, while it actually terminates in a straight lintel. The last two features are logical developments of a movement away from the original Maderno design. The details of the executed tabernacle frames, on the other hand, are definitely characteristic of Rainaldi's treatment of details. The fact that Rainaldi wished to assert his ideas against those of Fontana is also shown by the broken cornice above the outer pilaster of the medal design (pl. 22), implying hereby a return to the earlier Rainaldi project (pl. 18). Otherwise the medal design follows that of Fontana slavishly, except that it already represents the central window with straight lintel. It is evident therefore that in spite of the victory of Fontana, Rainaldi was not disposed to give way in all details. The engraving of Falda (G. G. Rossi, *Il Nuovo Teatro . . .*, 1665, *Libro* I) reproduces the plan of the medal, but shows at the same time a staircase before the façade in Rainaldi's style, which was not executed, but which was undoubtedly planned by Rainaldi himself.

46 We are speaking here of central structures up till about 1550. For the new possibilities of expression to be found in Baroque see below, p. 27 ff.

47 The essential differences between these types can be best appreciated in the elevation. The simple circular form (or forms developed from it) carries the dome directly, as in the Pantheon. In buildings of the Greek-cross type, there is between the lower and the upper structures the transitional zone of the pendentives.

48 The most exhaustive treatment, as far as I know, of the whole problem is that by Frankl, *Die Entwicklungsphasen der neueren Baukunst*, 1914, p. 148 ff. See also Dehio-Bezold, *Kirchliche Baukunst des Abendlandes* and Gurlitt, *Geschichte des Barockstils in Italien*, 1886, p. 58 ff.

49 An attempt was sometimes made to separate clergy from laity by placing a barrier round the altar under the dome. But such an arrangement was only adopted in conjunction with a nave (compare Florence: Cathedral, SS. Annunziata, S. Spirito).

50 It is no exaggeration to say that all the Renaissance centralized buildings received accentuated high altars at the time of the Counter-Reformation. In many cases long choirs had even been added to the building (such as S. Maria di Loreto and S. Anna de' Palafrenieri in Rome, S. Stefano in Milan).

51 For this building see Willich, *Giacomo Barozzi da Vignola*, 1906, p. 64 ff., with the elevation and view of the interior.

52 With the help of town plans, old engravings and guide books the history of the building can be completely reconstructed.

53 His life in Baglione, *Vite de' Pittori*, ed. 1733, p. 45. The building was completed by Carlo Maderno. Caflisch, *Maderna*, 1934, p. 9, on the basis of the documents, dates the laying of the foundation stone of the façade 11 April 1592, and names as architect Francesco Volterrano. Giovannoni, *Chiese della seconda metà del Cinquecento in Roma* (at first in *L'Arte*, 1912–13; reprinted in *Saggi . . .*, 1931, p. 226 ff.), considers Francesco Volterrano a typical reactionary artist of the Renaissance and does not even believe that he was responsible for the ground-plan of S. Giacomo, quite clearly against the evidence of the documents. Engravings of the church in G. G. de Rossi, *Insignium Romae Templorum prospectus*, 1684, pl. 59: longitudinal section; pl. 60: ground-plan (pl. 25).

54 In doing this the artist could refer to the Pantheon, where the vaulting of the entrance and choir intrudes into the high attic of the cylinder. Above, the actual cornice of the dome forms indeed one unbroken circle.

55 This complexity of structure is combined with a conception of detail which is very clear, definite and restrained. It is just this combination of a complicated, structural conception with a classical conception of detail which is a general characteristic of Roman art about 1590.

56 In the guide literature (see above, p. 12) the name of Mattia de Rossi does not appear. But in a collection of engravings of 1713 (Gio. Giacomo de Rossi, *Disegni di vari altari e cappelle nelle chiese di Roma*, pls. 30, 31) a longitudinal and transverse section of the choir is represented with the inscription below: 'Archit. Mattia de Rossi'. But it seems probable that de Rossi's participation was not confined to the choir and that Fontana's contribution, which is emphasized in the guide-books, was in reality very small.

In this connection I would recall the fact that Mattia de Rossi created an oval church, S. Galla in Via Bocca della Verità, which has since been destroyed. In this plan, however, Mattia followed in principle the plan of S. Maria de' Miracoli, i.e. he emphasized the transverse axis. This can be seen from the large plan of Rome by Nolli (ed. Card. F. Ehrle, 1932, no. 1040).

57 The collaboration of Fontana can be clearly recognized. It is the choir which is most markedly stamped with his style (for this see Coudenhove-Erthal, *op. cit.*, p. 40 ff.), but it is also unmistakable in the drum and dome. The style of the lower structure indicates that Rainaldi himself was responsible for the building as far as the drum.

58 Construction begun 1658. For Bernini's centralized buildings see Brauer-Wittkower, *op. cit.*, p. 110 ff.

59 The rest of the plastic decoration, adorning the base of the dome, depicts the world of St Andrew, the fisherman: we see representations of fishermen with oars and nets, of fish, shells and water plants.

60 For Bernini's psychological conception of architecture see above, p. 16, etc.

61 Construction began in 1635 and was only completed after 1650. An adequate work on Pietro da Cortona as an architect does not exist. The best treatment is by D. Frey, *Architettura barocca*, Rome and Milan, *s. a.*, p. 28 ff. See also: *Das Siebente Jahrzehnt. Festschrift zum 70. Geburtstag von Adolph Goldschmidt*, 1935, p. 137 ff.

62 The principle of a wall split into several layers was still further developed in Cortona's later works, notably in the entrance hall of S. Maria in Via Lata, where the wall has three distinct layers, one behind the other. It would be an extremely engrossing task to trace back this principle of a many-layered wall to its origin. Cortona developed it from the Mannerist principle of an intricate multiplicity of different wall planes (see *Art Bulletin*, 1934, p. 210 ff.).

63 The construction of S. Ivo was begun in 1642 and completed in 1660. See Hempel, *Borromini*, p. 114 ff.

64 It could easily be shown that in the case of S. Carlo alle Quattro Fontane the rhythmical succession of columns was also meant to express and emphasize the nature of the basic, dynamic structure. There were, however, still traces of Mannerist dual functions which were eliminated in his later buildings. Nor is there as yet, in accordance with the horizontal articulation typical of the first half of the century, any relation between the dynamic lower structure and the pure oval form of the dome.

65 See P. Francesco Ferraironi, *S. Maria in Campitelli*, Rome, 1934; *Le Chiese di Roma illustrate*, no. 33. One finds here supplementary material to Hempel, *op. cit.*, p. 35 ff.

66 L. Marracci, *Memorie di S. Maria in Portico di Roma*, 2nd ed., 1675, p. 117 ff. Paul V caused two medals of the church to be struck in 1619, one with his own portrait and one with a portrait of Cardinal Garzia Mellini, who laid the foundation stone. Marracci, *op. cit.*, p. 121 ff. speaks as follows of the structure of 1642: '[La Chiesa] fu ridotta in forma più ampia e vaga e tutta coperta di soffita dorata con quattro altari dentro cappelle adornate di marmi e di stucchi nel corpo della chiesa e due nei bracci della medesima, restando l'Altare maggiore con la tribuna à volta come era prima.'—Ferraironi, *op. cit.*, p. 10, wrongly described this building as consisting of three naves, an opinion which is disproved by Marracci's text and by the plans of the building which are here reproduced.

67 Drawing of the ground-plan: fol. 104 (555 mm × 382 mm). The inscription: '*Pianta della Chiesa di Sta. Maria in Campitelli*' does not appear in the illustration. Drawing of the longitudinal section: folios 107/8. For the arrangement of flaps on this sheet see further below, pp. 33, 34, and note 70.

68 The authority for this fact and for the other dates is still Marracci, *op. cit.*, 1st ed., 1667, p. 97 ff.

69 Bibl. Vat. Chig. G III 78, fol. 214v. See also Pastor, *Geschichte der Paepste*, XIV, 1, p. 520, note.

70 This drawing can be covered by a large flap on which the old choir of 1619 is depicted (pl. 41). Naturally this upper flap cannot be taken as an alternative solution but was only attached for purposes of comparison.

71 543 mm × 389 mm. Blue-grey wash.

72 The kneeling Pope depicted on the high altar would naturally have been Alexander

VII. There is no point in putting forward conjectures as to the identity of the other figures. But it seems to be fairly certain that they represent members of the great families (Capizucchi, Paluzzi, Costaguti, Muti) who owned and still own chapels in the church and who undoubtedly bore to some extent the cost of the rebuilding and upkeep of the church.

73 On fol. 109r (pl. 44) and on one of the flaps attached to fol. 107v/8.

74 Chig. P VII 10, fol. 116/7r: plan of the site of the surroundings with a ground-plan in dotted lines of the new church; fol. 119r: ground-plan of the new building; fol. 120r: elevation, signed 'Greg.o Tomassini' (pl. 45); fol. 121r: section, signed as above.

75 Marracci, *op. cit.*, p. 117.

76 Bonanni, *Numismata Pontificum*, Rome, 1706, II, p. 692. The erroneous date 1660, given by Marracci (pp. 119–20) was first disproved by Incisa della Rocchetta in the *Messaggero* of 18 February 1926. Nevertheless we find it again in the inadequate article by Mandl in Thieme-Becker, XXVII, p. 578.

77 Obverse: *'Alexander. VII. Pont. Max. Anno. MDCLXII'*. Reverse: *'Quae. vovi. reddam. pro. salute. Domino'*. The medal, a work by G. F. Travani, first published in modern literature by Stettiner, *Roma nei suoi monumenti*, 1911, fig. 580 (English edition, 1912, fig. 184). Ultimately published by F. Dworschak in *Jahrbuch d. preuss. Kunstslg.*, LV, 1934, p. 39.

78 The windows in the drum are alternately rounded and straight, as can be clearly seen on the original medal. In depicting the panels of the dome, the outer ones are shown as almost equal in width to those preceding them. If the panels had been in reality equal in width, they could not present such an appearance because of perspective foreshortening; in other words, the panels over the rectangular windows of the drum were planned to be narrower than those over the semicircular windows.

79 Bonanni, *op. cit.*, II, p. 692 and Marracci, *op. cit.*, pp. 121–22: *'Poco dopo essersi incominciato il Santuario, si pose mano alla facciata.'*

80 C. A. Erra makes a vague and confused reference to this project in *Storia dell'imagine e chiesa di S. Maria in Portico di Campitelli*, Rome, 1750, pp. 55–56. Churches showing a sequence of two domed buildings, a larger and a smaller one, are rather rare. Examples in Strack, *Central und Kuppelkirchen der Renaissance*, 1882 (e.g. pl. 4, S. Maria Coronata near Pavia).

81 The drawings preserved in the archive of S. Maria in Campitelli were referred to first by P. Fr. Ferraironi, *op. cit.*, p. 14. Albrecht Rosenthal, who made researches for me on the spot, found in all seven drawings with the following representations: 1, *'disegno dello Spaccato di dentro del Tempio (non eseguito)'* (pl. 48); 2, *'disegno della Facciata (non eseguita)'*, without dome (pl. 47); 3, *'Facciata eseguita'*; 4, longitudinal section (ill. by Ferraironi, p. 38); 5, ground-plan of the existing building; 6 & 7, *'Pianta del Piano Nobbile e superiore dell'Habitatione'*. They were kindly sent to me by Dr Kurt Cassirer when this article had already gone to press.

82 Obverse: *'Alexander. VII. Pont. Max. An. VIII'*. (the small letters 'G. M.' on the cutting of the arm stand for Gaspare Meolo, the artist). Reverse: *'Immaculatae Virgini. Vot.—Romae'*. According to the inscription therefore the medal was struck in the eighth year of Alexander's pontificate, i.e. between 7 April 1662 and 6 April 1663. So the alteration of plan must have been made during those months between the laying of the foundation stone 29 September 1662 and 6 April 1663.

83 The drawing in P VII 10, folios 105v/106r is signed in Rainaldi's own handwriting: 'Eq.s Carolus Rainaldus Inv.' (504 mm × 750 mm). The inscription in the frieze gives the supposed date of completion, not that on which the work was begun. It runs: *'S. P. Q. R. Vot. Sol. Alexan. VII. P. M. S. Mariae in Porticu A. Fundam. Pos. A. D. MDCLXVI'*. In the original the date 1666 is clearly legible, not 1665. On the medal the design is necessarily somewhat compressed through lack of space, but apart from this it corresponds exactly with the drawing. The only difference is that the pairs of flying cupids above the statues of the saints do not yet appear in the drawing.

The completed façade bears the same inscription as the drawing, but with the date 1665. This must represent the date of the completion of the lower storey of the façade. The whole façade was not completed till 1667 (see below). The actually existing upper storey differs from the design as shown in the drawing and on the medal by a further development on two points. The middle window is surmounted by a massive segmental pediment and the great triangular gable is now broken. Both elements represent an increased division and disintegration of the structural mass. More than three years had elapsed between the production of the medal and drawing and the completion of these parts of the building. The whole sculptural decoration, which alone gave to the façade the desired appearance of splendour, had finally been abandoned. The very insignificant coat-of-arms in the segmental gable of the upper storey was placed there only in 1747. The engraving by Falda (pl. 52) made during the construction of the church still followed the design on the medal as regards the crowning gable, but already differs from the medal design in the gable above the window of the upper storey.

84 Chig. P VII 10, fol. 102v/103r (530 mm × 724 mm). The drawing is by Rainaldi's own hand as the handwriting incontestably shows. Such a drawing of the site would only have been of value as long as the plans for the building had not entirely crystallized. The purpose was to make clear to the Pope the relation between the proposed structure and the requirements of the site, especially as regarded the apse, which according to this design projected slightly beyond the existing blocks of houses. The corrections in pencil at this point show that there had been discussions about this critical question, and that in this drawing Rainaldi is demonstrating a proposal whereby this part of the apse could also be enclosed by buildings (as were the entire sides of the church). In the actual construction this suggestion was not followed and the position of the building today corresponds fairly closely with the plan of the site.

85 Marracci, *op. cit.*, p. 122: Sanctuarium and façade completed *'circa la metà del presente anno 1667'*.

86 Marracci, *op. cit.*, p. 124 ff. For the later history of the completion of the building see: Marracci, 2nd ed., 1675, p. 140 ff. and Erra, *Storia dell'imagine e chiesa di S. Maria in Portico*, Rome, 1750, p. 53 ff. Also Ferraironi, *op. cit.*, p. 17. A *chirografo* of Innocent XI of 3 September 1679, directs that the fountain which till then had stood before the church (pl. 52) should be transferred to its present position at the east end of the piazza. For this there is a drawing in the Archivio di Stato, Cartella 81, R 304.

87 See especially Hempel, *Rainaldi*, p. 46.

88 The gable motif over the window in the outer division is repeated in the gable of the window of the upper storey. The 'Capitol motif' of the outer divisions is not repeated in the central division. The two columns of the main entrance are placed here not in recesses but in front of the wall, so that they seem to emphasize the dynamic concentration of the façade towards the centre. Yet the eye is bound to relate the outer and central columns, not only because of their equal height, but more especially because of the complete identity of the details.

The side bays are derived directly from Michelangelo's Capitol Palaces and not from the façade of St Peter's. In this connection we may recall that Rainaldi had special associations with the Capitol. It was his father Girolamo who was in charge of the rebuilding of the Palazzo Senatorio and who later began the construction of the palace on the left, the Capitoline Museum, which was completed by Carlo Rainaldi under Alexander VII. Carlo even planned to alter the aspect of the square to make it correspond with the taste of the Seicento. In a design by his own hand (cod. Chig. P VII 13, folios 5v/6r) the most important feature is the removal of the fountain before the Palazzo Senatorio far out into the square. This idea opens interesting vistas in regard to the problem of conflicting directions, for thereby a strongly accentuated longitudinal axis would have been introduced into Michelangelo's very definitely centralized square.

89 We shall confine ourselves to indicating the general principles without going too much into details. It can be seen that the wall piers behind the projecting orders are on a level, yet that at the same time the wall between and the entablature above project progressively from the outer to the inner division. The two recessed columns are a motif worthy of special treatment. We can only refer to it briefly. It is an extremely old motif; one can see it in the Pantheon, where the columns divide off the chapels lying outside the enclosing ring. In the Florentine Baptistry this Pantheon motif is converted into a typically flat Florentine design where the columns are directly contiguous to the wall. This Tuscan transformation remained alive in Florence from Giuliano da Sangallo and Cronaca (entrance hall, Sacristy of S. Spirito), to Michelangelo (Ricetto) and Ammannati (façade of S. Giovanni Evangelista in Florence) and even to Pietro da Cortona, through whom the motif was re-established in Rome. From Cortona it was adopted by Rainaldi, who at the same time took over other features of Cortona's architecture (first medal for S. Maria in Campitelli). Rainaldi, however, transformed the motif in accordance with Roman plasticity into a deep niche for statuary, so that the columns are, as it were, frames. The proposed statues were unfortunately never executed. The idea of placing sculpture between columns seems to have come from Longhi's façade of SS. Vincenzo ed Anastasio, where the statuary was equally never executed. The motif of the recessed columns is finally used by Fuga in the façade of S. Maria della Morte in Rome. This façade is very similar to Ammannati's S. Giovanni Evangelista, and is an interesting example of the revival or survival of tendencies of the Cinquecento in the Settecento.

90 It was Wölfflin, *Renaissance und Barock*, 1st ed., 1888, p. 84 ff., who first drew attention, and in a masterly way, to this development. See also Giovannoni's classical work: *Chiese della seconda metà del Cinquecento in Roma*, in *L'Arte*, 1912–13, reprinted in: *Saggi sull'Architettura del Rinascimento*, 1931, p. 179 ff. As we are here concerned with the general line of development only, we need not deal with the variations it presents, which could easily be demonstrated.

91 D. Frey in *Wiener Jahrbuch für Kunstgeschichte*, III, 1924, p. 29.

92 For the history of the construction see Hoffmann in *Wiener Jahrbuch für Kunstgeschichte*, 1934, p. 92. The construction was begun before 1619, but the façade was

only completed after 1630. Preliminary stages can be seen in Pellegrino Tibaldi's altars in Milan Cathedral of about 1585, where the same principle is already fully developed with different imaginative variations.

93 This project of 1623 was first published by A. Foratti in *Comune di Bologna*, 1932. Passeri, *Vite . . .*, ed. Hess, 1934, pp. 216–17, speaks of the church.

94 For instance S. Apollinare, S. Caterina della Ruota, SS. Trinità in Via Condotti. Rainaldi himself employed at a much earlier date a simplified form of the same type in small churches. In the Chiesa del Carmine in Ascoli Piceno, the façade, which was constructed in 1651 after a design by Rainaldi, represents two aedicules on different planes. In the same town he erected much later, in 1679, the small uncompleted façade of S. Angelo Custode, the completed form of which would have been necessarily such as Hempel describes it (*op. cit.*, p. 74). Here again he had planned two aedicules, the inner one of columns, the outer one of pilasters; as the façade, however, is very narrow there is no bay between the two orders.

95 Compare, for instance, S. Caterina in Casale Monferrato (eighteenth century) or the Cathedral in Syracuse. The façade of S. Maria ai Scalzi in Venice (architect Sardi, 1683–89) is a good example of the developed aedicule type with typical north Italian classicist features.

96 The drawings in the Uffizi for this church were published as designs for S. Giovanni de' Fiorentini in Rome by D. Frey, *Michelangelo-Studien*, 1920, p. 67 ff. The right attribution of these ground-plans we owe to Giovannoni, *Saggi . . . l.c.*, p. 111 ff.

97 L. H. Heydenreich, in *Mitteilungen des Kunsthistorischen Instituts in Florenz*, 1931, p. 282 ff., in his article on the Annunziata in Florence, was the first to discuss the two forms of structural grouping.

98 Traditional attribution of the building to Bramante. Ground-plan in Giovannoni, *Saggi . . .*, 1931, pp. 68–69, fig. 27.

99 The building was partly erected under Mascherino after the fire of 1591 up to 1600. Regarding Mascherino see Golzio in *Dedalo*, X, 1929–30, pp. 164–94. The history of S. Salvatore has been described by Astolfi in *Rassegna Marchigiana*, XI, 1933, p. 210 ff. P. Rotondi (in the same volume, p. 274 ff.) attributes too much importance to the influence of S. Salvatore upon S. Maria in Campitelli.

100 Titi, *Descrizione delle pitture, sculture . . .'* Rome, 1763, p. 103, gives the year 1614 as the date of the completion of the church interior.

101 See Vasari, ed. Milanesi, VI, p. 320–21.

102 The redecoration of the church may have been finished about 1656. See the inscriptions: Forcella, *Inscrizioni, . . . di Roma*, II, no. 152–53.

Of the greatest importance for Carlo Rainaldi was the Cathedral of S. Pietro in Bologna (pl. 57). A pair of coupled columns —very similar to those in S. Maria in Campitelli—are placed under the arch of the crossing and indicate a longitudinal orientation. On the corresponding place before the apse there is only one column, standing in an angle between two walls. About the history of the construction of S. Pietro see: Cantagalli, in *Comune di Bologna*, 1934, p. 48 ff.

103 Mandl in Thieme-Becker, XXVII, p. 578, rightly recognized that Rainaldi's domed space and choir were added to the older nave of G. B. Soria. The fact that there was an earlier and a later period of construction can be seen with singular clearness even from the exterior of the building (pl. 58). But I do not think Mandl is right in dating Rainaldi's contribution as late as the sixties. One finds in the outside wall of the transverse (closed from inside) a window in the 'Palladio-motif' exactly in the same style as was used by the father, Girolamo Rainaldi, in S. Teresa in Caprarola (completed 1620). This early motif alone, which Rainaldi never used in his later years, proves that Monte Compatri is one of his earliest buildings.

104 The half-columns have each a counterpart in the corners of the transept so that one has here a ground-plan which differs only from that of the church of the Madonna di Biagio in Montepulciano through the existence of the isolated columns.

105 Perhaps the earliest large building with the line of a pseudo-transept across the anterior of the church is Giov. Battista Bertani's S. Barbara in Modena (1562–65). Here the nave consists of a row of four rectangular spaces the first and third of which have cross vaultings and are dark, and the second and fourth are brightly illuminated through windows in curiously shaped turretlike domes. But only the first 'transept' consists of a real crossing with adjoining chapels, which emphasize its transverse effect. I am very much indebted to Dr Ernst Gombrich for directing my attention to this very important building.

106 Construction of the building: 1605–23. About Magenta's importance see Gurlitt, *Barockstil in Italien*, 1887, p. 142 ff. The article in Thieme-Becker, XXIII, p. 554, is inadequate.

107 The relation between S. Salvatore and S. Maria in Campitelli was already noticed by A. E. Brinckmann in the latest edition of the *Handbuch für Kunstwissenschaft (Baukunst des 17 und 18. Jahrhunderts in den romanischen Ländern)*.

108 The history of the transverse axis

across the nave has as far as I know never received proper attention. The question deserves a special and close examination. Only some points can here be noticed. In the one-nave type of church from the end of the sixteenth century onwards the accentuation of the transverse axis is not a rare feature. On Roman soil one could cite S. Brigida, S. Egidio in Trastevere, S. Francesco di Paola, etc. Rainaldi himself followed the same principle in the interior of the small church of S. Maria del Sudario (see below). The placing of a larger central chapel between two smaller ones can be seen for example in an interesting ground-plan, of 1593, for S. Maria della Scala in Rome (Uffizi, Dis. Arch. 6735). Girolamo Rainaldi's church of S. Teresa near Caprarola represents a unique solution of the problem. The accentuation of the transverse axis across the centre of the nave is effected by an interior structural arrangement derived from a Palladio motif. It is evident that the design of this church has been influenced by that of Pellegrino Tibaldi's SS. Martiri in Turin (laying of the foundation stone in 1577), where the same motif is twice repeated. Monumental double pilasters stand in the middle of the wall of the nave, thereby dividing the nave into two great quadrangles. The interior of Longhena's Chiesa degli Scalzi in Venice is a very interesting contemporary parallel to S. Maria in Campitelli. I do not believe that the conception of this church was uninfluenced by Rainaldi's work, although the construction of the Chiesa degli Scalzi is generally dated 1646–89. (Giulio Lorenzetti, *Venezia e il suo estuario*, 1926, p. 429, dates the beginning in the year 1660. Ground-plan in Gurlitt, · *Geschichte des Barockstils*, p. 312.)

There is a very close relation between Rainaldi's conception and Juvarra's first great design for St Philip Neri in Turin. See plan and section in A. E. Brinckmann, *Theatrum Novum Pedemontii*, 1931, pl. 221.

109 Bound together as a book: Bibl. Vat., cod. Barb. lat. 4411. On fol. 20 (14) signature and date: 'Carolus Rainaldus Archit.s fecit 1633.' See Pastor, *Geschichte der Paepste*, XIII, 2 p. 854 ff. and Oskar Pollak, *Die Kunsttaetigkeit unter Urban VIII*, 1927, I, Reg. 1507.

110 *Art Bulletin*, 1934, p. 208 ff.

111 In the course of this paper attention has several times been drawn to the importance of Girolamo Rainaldi as intermediary between the Mannerism of the sixteenth century and the art of Carlo Rainaldi. I would emphasize here again that Carlo Rainaldi's style is not imaginable without this link between the two centuries and between north and central Italy. As a characteristic example of Girolamo's style we may cite an altar in S. Maria della Scala in Rome from 1606. The function of the columns as frames of the central panel is counteracted by the isolat-

ing tendency of the small segmental pediment above each column. The details look like cabinet-makers' work. Although Carlo Rainaldi soon set out to modernize architectural details he never gave up his father's methods completely.

112 For the history of the towers see Brauer-Wittkower, *Die Zeichnungen des G. L. Bernini*, p. 39 ff. Judging from the style, we attributed the project here illustrated (pl. 67) to Girolamo Rainaldi (*op. cit.* p. 41, note 2), but on the basis of a contemporary report it has to be given to Carlo Rainaldi. A comparison with the project of Girolamo Rainaldi in cod. Vat. lat. 13442, fol. 10 (written on the back: 'Giron.o Rainaldi'), in which he preserves the first storey of Bernini's tower and replaces only the second storey by a structure of his own design, shows how far Carlo had moved from his father's Mannerist conception of detail, although the tradition inherited from his father was especially strong at this relatively early period.

113 For the technical reasons of this proposal see Brauer-Wittkower, *op. cit.*, p. 39 ff. See also especially pp. 67 and 97 for Rainaldi's further projects for the façade and the Piazza S. Pietro.

114 An exhaustive discussion of this drawing in Brauer-Wittkower, *op. cit.*, pp. 41 ff., pl. 156.

115 Vienna, Albertina.

116 The history of the construction first in Nogara, *SS. Ambrogio e Carlo al Corso (Chiese di Roma illustrate*, no. 3). See also Passeri, ed. Hess, 1934, p. 226. Martino Longhi was in charge of the building till about 1656–60 (died in Viggiù 15 December 1660). But the engraving showing Longhi's plan for the church was published before 1640, which can be proved by the fact that Francesco Biglia, to whom the engraving is dedicated, was '*primicerio dell'Arciconfraternità*' until 1640. All later architects in charge of that building worked on the basis of Longhi's engraving. On the sheet which is preserved in cod. Chig. P VII 10, fol. 21 (pl. 70) Alexander VII orders in March 1665 that the obstructing buildings at the back be pulled down and the street shortened, to make room for the rear part of the church. Between 1660 and 1665 Carlo Fontana superintended the construction. In 1672 the whole building was finished except for the façade. Possibly Rainaldi's design might be dated as late as that year. The façade was only erected in 1682–84 by Menicucci after plans by Cardinal Omodei.

117 In Longhi's project every column stands on a plane which is clearly differentiated from the plane of the next column. In the façade of SS. Vincenzo ed Anastasio the planes of the triad of columns are not separable, one plane, so to speak, overlaps the other; thus the three columns form one

entity of great plasticity.

A design by Longhi preserved in the Roman Archivio di Stato (Cartella 85, R 493; 807 mm × 382 mm—two examples differing very slightly one from another—pl. 72) is an earlier plan for S. Carlo than the engraved one. The design of the façade in this drawing derived from northern Italy in so far as it shows a distinct separation of planes. From here Longhi's development is clearly traceable past the engraved design up to the Roman features of SS. Vincenzo ed Anastasio.

118 For the façade of S. Marcello see Coudenhove-Erthal, *op. cit.*, p. 53 ff. In this connection I wish to draw attention to the fact that Carlo Fontana followed in his scheme Longhi's first project for S. Carlo al Corso (pl. 72) very closely. Sedlmayr in *Kritische Berichte*, 1931–32, p. 146 ff., tries to prove that Fontana derived his project from Longhi's façade of SS. Vincenzo ed Anastasio. This is obviously wrong.

119 In cod. Chig. P VII 9, fol. 94. It is probable that this drawing dates from about 1658, which was approximately when Rainaldi got the order for rebuilding the old church. But Rainaldi's plans were carried out only in the second half of the eighties. The church was finished in 1687. See Hempel, *Rainaldi*, p. 71.

II The Third Arm of Bernini's Piazza S. Pietro

1 T. A. Polazzo, *Da Castel S. Angelo alla Basilica di San Pietro*, Rome, 1948. Professor Polazzo's project is based on detailed studies and accompanied by a great wealth of illustrations and experimental designs. He rightly advocates going back to Bernini's solution, and believes he has made this the basis of his own; he proposes to enclose the wide space of Via della Conciliazione by placing there a carefully thought-out colonnade which would run from the point where Via Pio X joins Via della Conciliazione, to the old Piazza Rusticucci. The idea in itself is not new, as those familiar with earlier projects will know, but it is certainly an improvement on those of Busiri-Vici and of Armando Brasini.

2 On the 'bi-axiality' of the piazza, see V. Mariani, *Significato del portico berniniano di S. Pietro*, opening lecture in the course on 'The History of Medieval and Modern Art' at the University of Rome, 1935, especially p. 12 ff.

3 Brauer-Wittkower, *Die Zeichnungen des Gianlorenzo Bernini*, Berlin, 1931, p. 81, pl. 162 a.

4 Biblioteca Vaticana, cod. Chig. P VII 9, folios 17v–18.

5 Brauer-Wittkower, *op. cit.* p. 83.

6 Fraschetti, *Il Bernini*, Rome, 1900, p. 316.

7 Brauer-Wittkower, *op. cit.*, pp. 85–86.

8 *Ibid.*, pls. 62–64.

9 Biblioteca Vaticana, cod. Ottob. lat. 3154, between folios 347 and 348. See also the drawing by Lieven Cruyl of 1669, in the Ashmolean Museum, Oxford, published by Ashby in *Atti della Pont. Accad. Rom. di Archeologia*, Serie III, Memoria I, i, 1923, p. 221, pl. 9.

10 Brauer-Wittkower, *op. cit.*, pl. 62a.

11 Brauer-Wittkower, *op. cit.*, pl. 64.

12 Brauer-Wittkower, *op. cit.*, pl. 62b, 63a.

13 Biblioteca Vaticana, cod. Chig. P VII 9, fol. 15. Engraved by Bonanni, *Numismata summorum pontificum templi Vaticani*, Rome, 1700, pl. 70.

14 Dis. arch. 266.

15 The original drawing in the Biblioteca Vaticana was engraved by Bonanni, *op. cit.*, pl. 69.

16 Probably the idea was first conceived by Bernini in two rapid sketches, which are contained in a *Chigiano* codex (J VI 205, fol. 36) under an inscription which is unrelated to the sketches. The small sketch on the left represents the third arm on the perimeter of the oval, the larger sketch on the right shows the elliptical piazza between two straight-sided piazzas.

III A Counter-Project to Bernini's Piazza S. Pietro

1 Now in the Brandegee Collection, Faulkner Farm, Mass. The set consists of 15 sheets, some containing one, some two drawings, in three different inks: greyish blue, dark blue and brown. White paper with a star-shaped water-mark, such as was used in Rome in the mid-seventeenth century. Size of paper varies, on average *c*. 17 cm high, 36 cm wide. Remounted and bound in the nineteenth century. In their present arrangement the drawings are preceded by a nineteenth-century note on their provenance. From the Fabbrica di S. Pietro they passed into the possession of Luigi Vanvitelli, architect to the Fabbrica in the eighteenth century, who gave them to his assistant Andrea Vici. After 1899 they passed through the Corvisieri and Piancastelli collections.

As originals by Bernini first published by the owner A. Busiri-Vici, *La Piazza di San Pietro nei secoli III, XIV, XVII*. Rome, 1893. Later mentioned and in some cases treated in detail as Bernini drawings by Fraschetti, Posse, Escher, Riegl, Brinckmann, Cardinal Ehrle, Norton, *Encyclopedia Italiana* and others. Full bibliography in Brauer-Wittkower, *Die Zeichnungen des Gianlorenzo Bernini*, 1931, p. 98, where the true character of these drawings was briefly pointed out. In spite of this, the old attribution as Bernini was later revived, cf. G. Tardini, in *Illustrazione Vaticana*, VII, 1936, p. 935, ff.; Luigi Tombolini Barzotti, *La Basilica di S. Pietro in Vaticano nei simboli e negli elementi architettonici di Gianlorenzo Bernini*, 1937.

Busiri-Vici published only 17 out of the 25 drawings; two more were published by Norton, *Bernini and other Studies*, 1914.

2 The present arrangement does not coincide with the numbers written on the drawings in the brown ink which was used in them. A few sheets are without old numbers. In the following study they have been inserted where they logically belong.

3 The two circles appearing to the west on either side of the transept and repeating the dominant motif of the critic's scheme may be suggestions for sacristies, which had not been built at that time, and in their positions may recall the sun and the moon in pictures of the Crucifixion.

4 Cf. below, p. 79.

5 The principle of his structure appears in a schematic form.

6 The five small circles on which the arc of Heaven appears to rest may indicate the five planets and may be connected with the Crown of Eternity, about which below p. 80.

7 Without an old number.

8 Large palaces corresponding to those on each side of St Peter's are drawn in dotted lines behind the right-hand colonnades. This is an alternative proposal to the simpler drawn out arrangement.

9 For its history cf. Egger, 'Der Uhrturm Pauls V', *Mededeelingen van het Nederlandsch historisch Instituut te Rome*, IX, 1929, p. 71 ff.

10 Cf. Egger, *Carlo Madernas Projekt für den Vorplatz von San Pietro in Vaticano*, 1928, p. 14 ff. ('Röm. Forschungen der Bibl. Hertziana VI'), Brauer-Wittkower, *op. cit.*, p. 89.

11 To make the Scala Regia Bernini took the bold step of connecting his corridor (which replaced Ferrabosco's tower) with the old staircase, and thereby gave the palace its superb entrance in direct line with the Borgo Nuovo. It was an arrangement of great ingenuity which was probably planned after the critic's counter-project. Cf. p. 76.

12 They are detached from the palaces only at this particular spot.

13 This storey would at the same time hide the drum. Cf. below, p. 72.

14 Cf. below, p. 75.

15 For reasons which will be given below (p. 78) he insists on arcades, and as long as a single colonnade was planned it could still be attached to palaces.

16 The Corinthian capitals, never planned by Bernini, are probably due to the carelessness of the draughtsman.

17 It had been closed by Pius V (1566–72) and replaced by the road farther to the east running through Porta Angelica. Access to

the piazza from this road to an insignificant point of the north-eastern colonnades was very unsatisfactory. For the whole problem, cf. Brauer-Wittkower, *op. cit.*, p. 83.

18 Bibl. Vat., without inventory number. Probably made by Carlo Fontana, Bernini's assistant at that time. The engraving by Bonacina (cf. p. 75) of the Piazza S. Pietro has been cut out and pasted on to the lower part.

19 This is supported by similar observations which can be made throughout the series of drawings. Some instances may be quoted. In drawing 1 those portions vital for the exposition of the criticism—the face of St Peter and the broken parts of the arms—are drawn over by a clumsy hand. The *visuale* of drawing 3 is drawn with the same ink; both drawings in no. 5 seem to be by this hand, the figure of St Peter being slavishly copied from no. 2. The same hand is responsible for the small steps interrupting the large circle of steps in the view of the piazza facing the church (pl. 89) and for the repetition of the right-hand palaces on the other side. This hand seems to have done drawing 12 and overdrawn vital points in drawing 13.

20 The clumsily drawn portion with the Piazza Rusticucci is affixed to the sheet. Above the small church in this square opposite St Peter's are two inscriptions: '*Piazza de Rusticucci,*' and below: '*piaca putiguci*'.

21 Bears the no. 17, like the last drawing, although written by the same hand.

22 Ed. Padua, 1630, Pt. 3, p. 12.

23 The fountain by Maderno is here surmounted by the Chigi *monti*—another allusion to the critic's conception corresponding to drawing no. 3.

24 For the whole story of these discussions cf. Fraschetti, *Bernini*, 1900, p. 165 ff., Ehrle, 'Dalle carte e dai disegni di Virgilio Spada', *Atti della Pont. Acc. Romana di Archeologia*, serie III, memorie, Vol. II, p. 22 ff., Brauer-Wittkower, *op. cit.*, p. 38 ff.

The most important Roman architects criticized in long memoranda Padre Grassi's plans for S. Ignazio. Cf. Ehrle, *op. cit.*, p. 13 ff., D. Frey in *Wiener Jahrbuch f. Kunstgesch.* 1922–23.

25 Ch. Perrault, *Mémoires*, ed. Bonnefon, 1909, p. 52 ff.

26 Detailed account of the institution and organization of the Congregation in Ehrle, *op. cit.*, p. 19.

27 *Ibid.*, p. 34, note 156.

28 '. . . *per mero ornato, et fabrica non necessaria*'. Printed in full in Fraschetti, *op. cit.*, p. 314.

29 The two memoranda in Brauer-Wittkower, p. 71 ff., 97. It is worth noticing that one of Bernini's opponents managed

to submit to the Congregation his own plan under Bernini's name. Cf. Pastor, *Geschichte der Päpste*, XIV, i, p. 510. Avviso of 8 September 1556.

30 Published in Brauer-Wittkower, p. 70.

31 *Ibid.*, p. 101.

32 Discussion of this material *ibid.*, p. 96 ff.

33 *Ibid.*, p. 71 ff.

34 In Bernini's project the joining of the corridor and the tower must however have been different from the careless representation of the critic. It may have been similar to Carlo Rainaldi's project, ill. *ibid.*, pl. 189.

35 Fraschetti, *op. cit.*, p. 315.

36 After 7 April 1659. Cf. Brauer-Wittkower, p. 81. The engraving is shown in pl. 102, cf. above, note 18.

37 Cf. above, p. 71.

38 This idea had to be abandoned after 1661. The finished colonnades therefore show the protruding columns only on the inside.

39 Cf. above, p. 71.

40 Cf. above, pp. 67, 73.

41 Brauer-Wittkower, p. 93.

42 Even if Constanzo was asked to base his drawing of '*Religione Christiana*' upon Ripa, he could still claim to be the '*inventore*'.

43 Carlo Fontana, *Templum Vaticanum*, 1694, pl. 185.

44 *Ibid.*, p. 183: '*il Palazzo Pontificio . . . gl'impedì il dare la detta migliore forma; e per non distruggere quella parte del detto Palazzo, fù necessitato nel distribuirli à dare nel denotato difetto.*'

45 Cf. above, note 30. '*Antivedde* [the Pope] *subito gl'inconvenienti che s'incontravano in fare il Portico in forma quadrata, impercioche la sua altezza in quella forma haverebbe impedito al Popolo la veduta del Palazzo, et al Palazzo il prospetto della Piazza, accresciendosi l'Inconveniente mercè che solendo il Papa dalle fenestre dare la Benedittione a'i Pellegrini, e processioni che l'anno Santo vengono per riceverla in questo modo non poteva benedirli se non in grandissima lontananza . . .*'

46 '*Con esser uscito dalla forma quadra, ò piutosto parte rellogramma, si sono sfuggite molte cose cattive, e specialmente la perdita della vista di chi viene à Palazzo alle finestre di S. S.ta . . .*'

47 *Vita del Cavaliere Gio. Lorenzo Bernino*, 1682, p. 38.

48 The latter in Bibl. Vat., cod. Chig. P VII 9, fol. 36 (25) (published as an original by Bernini in Muñoz, 'Bernini architetto e decoratore' (*Bibl. d'Arte Ill.* I, 26–28, 1925,

pl. 58; and by D. Frey, *Architettura barocca*, 1925, fig. 112). The former (unpublished) in Vienna, Albertina (Rome, XXX, i, 717). H. 28·5 cm, w. 20·9 cm. Both drawings by the same hand.

49 Baldinucci, *Notizie de' Professori del Disegno*. Ed. 1847, V, p. 330. For the history of Rainaldi's projects cf. Brauer-Wittkower, p. 97 ff.
Bernini never planned a circular piazza, his oval form following directly on the rectangular one. The suggestion of a circular plan by Bernini goes back to a wrong interpretation of the drawing in Bibl. Vat. Chig. P VII 9, folios 32v–33 by Bonnani, *Numismata, op. cit.*, pl. 68, repeated always in literature. This drawing was actually a critical counter-proposal directed against Bernini. Cf. Brauer-Wittkower, p. 97.

50 Pastor, *Gesch. d. Päpste*, XIV, i, p. 509, note 6.

51 Based on Alberti's plans for the piazza, cf. Dehio, *Repertorium f. Kunstw.* III, 1880, p. 241 ff. Pius II (1458–64) inaugurated the construction of arcades which, however, came to an end with the three-storeyed Loggia della Benedizione. This fragment, existing until the days of Maderno's façade, never ceased to influence later projects.

52 The memoranda submitted at the meeting of the Congregazione on 17 March 1657 (in criticism of Bernini's project for a single arcade with *one* pilaster dividing *two* arches), argued that '*i pilastri nella forma designata in una piazza così vasta, possino apparire meschini, e che col dupplicarsi fossero per riuscire di maggiore magnificenza.*' (Brauer-Wittkower, pp. 71, 72). Cf. also Bernini's own treatise against the critics of his free-standing colonnade, mentioned above, p. 74.

53 I.e. the end bay on each side of the façade.

54 Cf. Bernini's own words in Chantelou's *Journal du voyage du Cav. Bernin en France*, ed. L. Lalanne, 1885, p. 42, and the words of his memorandum (Brauer-Wittkower, p. 70): '*il formare un Portico non solo apportava maggior bellezza e decoro al Tempio mà veniva à coprire molte imperfettioni di quello, essendo che la facciata che per se stessa è di forma quatta haverebbe spiccata, et in certo modo si sarebbe sollevata sopra se stessa.*'

55 Cf. his project, Brauer-Wittkower, pl. 189c.

56 Col. I, 24: 'Who now rejoice in my sufferings for you, and fill up that which is behind of the afflictions of Christ in my flesh for his body's sake, which is the church.'

57 Cf. J. Sauer, *Symbolik des Kirchengebäudes und seiner Ausstattung*, 1902, pp. 101, 111; Schlosser, *Quellenbuch zur Kunstgeschichte des abendl. Mittelalters*, 1896, p.

282. The main source for our critic seems to be Durandus (1275–1334), whose often reprinted *Rationale* starts with '*Dispositio Ecclesiae materialis modum humani corporis tenet*' (I, 14).

58 Müntz, *Les Arts à la Cour des Papes*, 1878, I, p. 341 ff.

59 Pastor, *Gesch. d. Päpste*, XII, p. 590.

60 Cf. e.g. the frontispiece to G. J. Rossi's *Nuovo Teatro delle Fabriche . . . di Roma moderna* and Bonacina's engraving after Courtois (Paris, Cab. d'Est. B. a. 20, p. 27).

61 Ill. in Stettiner, *Roma nei suoi monumenti*, 1911, p. 164; cf. E. Strong in *Town Planning Review*, 1917, p. 196.

62 Bibl. Vat., cod. Chig. R VIII. c. 1, fol. 10 contains the draft of a letter by Alexander VII to Holstenius with a sketch of the foundation medal at the top and the following words below: '*Così starà il medaglione per porre nel fondamento del Portico triplice trionfale et farà la piazza, e condurrà a coperto a S. Pietro. Nella Cartella sotto vi capiranno sei o sette parole cioè da 40 in 50 lettere. V. S. pensi, e me le mandi secondo il suo gusto, se può in più forme . . .*'

63 Cf. Sauer, *op. cit.*, p. 114 ff. The Pope is the Bishop of Rome.

64 Chantelou, ed. Lalanne, *op. cit.*, p. 42.

65 Brauer-Wittkower, pl. 62b.

66 *Ibid.*, p. 70: '. . . *essendo la Chiesa di S. Pietro quasi matrice di tutte le altre doveva haver' un Portico che per l'appunto dimostrasse di ricevere à braccia aperte maternamente i Cattolici per confermarli nella credenza, gl'Heretici per riunirli alla Chiesa, e gl'Infedeli per illuminarli alla vera fede.*'

67 Although the critic uses Leonardo's studies in human proportions, probably known to him from the editions of Vitruvius by Fra Giocondo (1511) or Cesariano (1521), his purpose is completely different; whilst in Leonardo the circle surrounding the figure is evidence of certain fundamental proportions in the human body, in the critic's drawing (no. 17) the figure illustrates the ideal character of his circular scheme.

68 Sauer, *op. cit.*, p. 110.

69 This and the following quotations from Durandus' *Rationale*, I, 1, 17.

70 Not visible in the reproduction.

71 Durandus, I, 9.

72 All that is known of Bartoli is preserved in a volume from the Fabbrica di S. Pietro, now in the Bibl. Vittorio Emanuele, Fondi Minori 3808. Extracts published by C. Scaccia-Scarafoni in *Accademia e Biblioteche d'Italia*, I, 1927–28, 3, p. 15 ff.

73 By Matthaeus Greuter, 1623.

74 Cf. Sauer, *op. cit.*

75 The towers and satellite domes are taken over from Sangallo's project, the big

pediment above the façade from Old St Peter's, and the arcades of the Piazza from those built under Pius II; cf. above, note 51.

76 The engraving of the mystical ship bears the legend: '*Delineavit Dm̄s Simon eius ex fratre Nepos J. V. D. per M. Greuterum are incidi curavit. 1623.*' It is probable that the engraving of the piazza was also ordered by him, after his uncle's death, in about 1620.

77 On parchment. Rome, Palazzo Venezia. Anderson 24647.

IV The Vicissitudes of a Dynastic Monument: Bernini's Equestrian Statue of Louis XIV

1 A. de Montaiglon, 'Le Louis XIV du Cav. Bernini', *Revue universelle des arts*, VIII, 1858, pp. 505–14; Stanislao Fraschetti, *Il Bernini*, Milan, 1900, pp. 358–64 (henceforth quoted: 'Fraschetti'); Marcel Reymond, 'La statue équestre de Louis XIV par le Bernin', *Revue de l'art ancien et moderne*, XXXIV, 1913, pp. 23–40; A. Bertini Calosso, 'Il monumento equestre del Bernini a Luigi XIV', *Bollettino d'Arte*, III, 1923–24, pp. 557–66. In addition, see the many documents published by L. Mirot (see note 2).

2 [The original publication of this essay in *De Artibus Opuscula*, XL, New York University Press, 1961, included a lengthy Appendix in which extracts from documents were printed in chronological sequence. The reader seeking justification for the statements in the essay is referred to this Appendix. The principal sources from which it was drawn were: Pierre Clément, *Lettres instructions et mémoires de Colbert*, Paris, 1868; A. de Montaiglon, *Correspondance des directeurs de l'Académie de France à Rome*, Paris, 1889 ff.; G. B. Depping, *Correspondance administrative sous le règne de Louis XIV*, Paris, 1850–55; J. Guiffrey, *Comptes des bâtiments du roi sous le règne de Louis XIV*, Paris, 1888–1901; Paris, Bibl. Nat., *Mélanges Colbert*; L. Mirot, 'Le Bernin en France', *Mémoires de la Société de l'Histoire de Paris et de l'Ile-de-France*, XXXI, 1904.]

3 The idea of such a square to be built on the left bank remained alive and turned up much later.

4 M. de Chantelou, *Journal du voyage du Cav. Bernin en France*, ed. L. Lalanne, Paris, 1885, pp. 96, 231 (henceforth quoted: 'Chantelou, ed. Lalanne'). The reference on 12 October was made during a talk Chantelou had with the Abbé Francesco Butti, a Roman by birth, who had acquired French citizenship in 1654 and enjoyed the full confidence of the court (see Mirot, p. 168).

5 See Anthony Blunt, *Art and Architecture in France 1500–1700*, London, 1953, p. 114. For the best view of the Pont Neuf with the equestrian monument (destroyed during the Revolution) and the next bridge downstream, see *Les Délices de Paris et de ses environs*, Paris, 1753, pl. 33.

6 The letters of patent mentioned in note 3 of the Appendix [of the original publication] have never been published.

7 *Op. cit.*, p. 278 ff. Reymond, *op. cit.*, p. 32, came to conclusions similar to my own.

8 The dates of the payment of the pension during the critical years may here be summarized: 1670 pension: paid after January 1671, probably in April; 1671 pension: paid before 10 May 1672; 1672 pension: paid before 6 June 1673; 1673 pension: after 27 October 1673. It is, however, by no means certain that the '*lettre de change*' mentioned in Colbert's letter of that date was really the pension for the current year. It is not quite clear whether the last pension paid out was for the year 1673 or 1675.

9 Unfortunately, there is a gap in the flow of information from 13 June 1670 to 31 January 1671.

10 Bernini's own letter of 30 December disproves the accuracy of the report that the block had been delivered to his studio on 27 July. In his letter of 31 January 1670 Colbert is concerned with this question of transportation. The statue was executed in the studio behind St Peter's; see Domenico Bernini, *Vita del cavalier Gio. Lorenzo Bernino*, Rome, 1713, p. 148 (henceforth quoted: 'Domenico Bernini'), and Fraschetti, p. 359.

11 Although rather free, the translation corresponds, I hope, exactly to what Bernini intended to express.

12 V. Martinelli, *Bernini*, Milan, 1953, p. 152, thought to discover the hands of pupils, but there is not the slightest reason to accept this view. For a full bibliography on the model, see Italo Faldi, *Galleria Borghese. Le sculture dal secolo XVI al XIX*, Rome, 1954, pp. 41 ff.

13 It should be pointed out that Bernini's 'rearing' horses are not 'curvetting', the high point of Italo-Spanish Baroque horsemanship where the horse rises slowly on its hind legs on which the whole weight of its body rests for a few seconds. The curvetting attitude is therefore the exact opposite of uncontrolled rearing: it is a studied performance which requires not only the highest discipline and intelligence on the part of the horse but also complete collaboration between horse and rider. Velasquez was, of course, the great master of this showpiece of correct horsemanship. Bernini's horses are too far down on the hind legs, a position which does not belong (so far as I can make out) to the seventeenth-century cycle of high-school horsemanship. Bernini sacrificed correctness to the impression of rapid movement which he needed.

14 See particularly R. W. Lee, 'Ut Pictura Poesis: the Humanistic Theory of Painting', *Art Bulletin*, XXII, 1940, p. 197 ff.

15 Chantelou (ed. Lalanne, p. 106) reports

a characteristic and somewhat dangerous play with words before the King of France when the talk turned to caricatures: '*et comme l'on a parlé de quelqu'un de femme, le Cavalier a dit que Non bisognava caricar le donne che da notte.*' Surely, Hans Rose's German translation (Munich, 1919, p. 122) of this passage ('*Eins von den Blättern nannten wir "Frauen-Karikatur". Der Cavaliere verbesserte aber: "Ich wollte nicht die Frau karikieren, sondern die Nacht"'*) would have given Bernini occasion for a deft application of wit.

16 On this and the following, see my remarks in *Art and Architecture in Italy 1600 to 1750*, Penguin Books, 1958, p. 108 ff. I have here to paraphrase some of my own sentences.

17 Domenico Bernini, p. 150 ff. Since Domenico was born on 3 August 1657, he was hardly younger than sixteen and possibly as old as nineteen or twenty at the time of the event he reports. There is a good deal of collateral evidence to prove that Domenico reproduced here the gist of a real conversation. The most telling piece of evidence is, of course, the work itself.

Domenico's *Vita* is rather rare, but for reasons of space I must forgo printing the long Italian passage. Domenico put in the margin of the page the following explanatory note: '*Intenzione del Cavaliere nello scolpire il Rè con faccia allegra, e gioviale.*'

18 According to Baldinucci (*Vita di Gian Lorenzo Bernini*, ed. S. S. Ludovici, Milan, 1948, p. 84; henceforth quoted: 'Baldinucci'), Bernini differentiated between '*qualche significato vero o pure alludente a cosa nobile o vera o finta*', i.e., between a historically correct and a poetical meaning; see Hans Kauffmann in *Jahresberichte der Max-Planck-Gesellschaft*, 1953–54, pp. 56 ff.

19 Doc. 60. Padre Oliva, the General of the Jesuit Order, was a close friend of Bernini's with whose work and mentality he was intimately familiar.

20 *Op. cit.*, p. 126.

21 The *consensus omnium* is that Girardon's alterations were negligible (see, e.g., Reymond, *op. cit.*, p. 36). According to the *Comptes des bâtiments* he reworked the head, and there is reason to believe that he really did so. I do not refer to the addition of the helmet, nor to the shortening of the locks which fell over the right shoulder, but to the face itself. The corroded surface and the broken nose make it difficult to arrive at reliable conclusions. Yet the face has no similarity with Louis's, which, according to eyewitnesses, it originally had. The Abate Benedetti reports on 14 September 1672: 'The head is already finished and it is very similar if the portraits sent here are similar.' The only document which might possibly solve the problem is not at hand. About thirty years ago I saw in the Berlin Print Room a weak copy after

Bernini's monument which had the following inscription: '*al 21 feb.o 1685 fui à vedere il ritratto del Rè di francia a cavallo tutto di marmo bianco fatto d[al] Bernino.*' I.e., this drawing was made before Girardon's alterations.

22 Wittkower, *Gian Lorenzo Bernini*, London, 1955, p. 234 and *Art and Architecture*, pl. 58B.

23 In this drawing Bernini was of course concerned only with the most important top strata of the rock. He here applied in reverse the principle of the curtain behind the *Constantine*. Instead of moving with the rider from left to right, the rocks sink down from right to left and help therefore to bring the horse's movement to rest: the King has arrived on top of the hill.

24 In Girardon's alteration the mass of flames under the horse's belly and the leaping flame in front are separated by a broad hiatus. This arrangement echoes the original formation of the flags.

25 The medals were first published by F. Dworschak (in *Jahrbuch der Preuss. Kunstsammlungen*, LV, 1934, p. 34 ff.), who dates them *c*. 1680.

26 The text says '*pellegrino*', i.e., '*peregrino*', which means '*singolare, vago, elegante*'. On Benedetti, see E. Hempel, in *Festschrift H. Wölfflin*, Munich, 1924, p. 277 ff.

27 It hardly needs emphasizing that for much of the following I am deeply indebted to Erwin Panofsky's *Herkules am Scheidewege*, Leipzig, 1930.

28 *Op. cit.*, p. 126. Baldinucci's last words are: '*ove ha sua stanza la vera gloria*'.

29 It is not possible in the present context to give an adequate idea of the richness and breadth of this tradition. For the euhemeristic tradition, see J. Seznec, *The Survival of the Pagan Gods*, New York, 1953, p. 25 ff. (Hercules as founder of the Burgundian dynasty and of the House of Navarre); for Hercules as exemplar of heroism, see Panofsky, *op. cit.*, p. 83 ff. See also J. R. Martin, in *Art Bulletin*, XXXVIII, 1956, p. 95 ff., and A. Pigler, *Barockthemen*, Budapest, 1956, II, p. 101 ff. For further material, see below in the text and the notes.

30 Lucian, *Heracles*, tr. A. M. Harmon (Loeb Library).

31 For the Hercules Gallicus, see E. Wind, in *Journal of the Warburg Institute*, II, 1938–39, p. 208 ff.; Pigler, *op. cit.*, II, p. 471.

32 Medals showing Louis XIV as Hercules are common; see *Médailles sur les principaux événements du Règne entier de Louis le Grand*, Paris, 1723, pls. 147, 230, 235, 247, 257, 268. A great deal of this symbolism is buried in occasional writings, pamphlets, etc., which are almost completely forgotten. In a pamphlet by the Abate Benedetti, published in 1682 (see below, note 61), the King is described as '*un novello Ercole Gallico, dalla cui bocca pende una Catena d'oro, per dinotare quella suovità, con la quale incatena i cuori degli Ascoltanti*'. The title of an ode, published anonymously in 1699, begins '*L'Apothéose du nouvel Hercule . . .*' (see note 79).

The anonymous author of an informative little work published in London with the title *The Grandeur and Glory of France, drawn in the Triumphant Portraitures of her present Victorious Monarch*, 1673, remarks satirically (p. 15) that Louis 'gave even in his Cradle infallible hopes of the wonders he would achieve when he should arrive at the Crown . . . Medalls were coyned, bearing his Effigies, His Head crowned with victorious Laurell, in his right hand holding Hercules Club, with his Infant Arm; with his left hand, he crusht to pieces a hideous Serpent, whilst at the same time he satt Mounted with one foot on the Neck of a Lion,' etc.

33 Many editions. The first Paris edition appeared in 1689; later editions 1693, 1700, etc. Menestrier (1631–1705) had a prodigious talent in every sense. He is credited with well over a hundred published works, many of them concerned with emblems and devices. From 1658 on he was in charge of the decorations for festivals and entries on official occasions. Information about him may be conveniently found in Mario Praz, *Studies in Seventeenth-Century Imagery*, London, 1939, I, p. 162 ff. and *passim*.

34 On the occasion of his visit to Avignon in 1600, Henry IV was celebrated as '*Hercule gaulois*' by means of 'a sevenfold labyrinth adorned with seven triumphal arches intended to commemorate the seven most glorious labours of Hercules' (Praz, *op. cit.*, p. 161). Another *entrée* of Henry IV, that at Rouen in 1596, interpreted the labours of Hercules as the houses of the Zodiac on an obelisk crowned by an image of the sun; see W. S. Heckscher, in *Art Bulletin*, XXIX, 1947, pp. 178, 180, notes 125, 139 and fig. 39. For the connection of Hercules with the Zodiac see also F. Saxl, *Lectures*, London, 1957, I, p. 59.

35 This motto was of course in line with the traditional role of the French kings as the rightful successors of Charlemagne, but in no way agreed with the political situation. Louis's relationship to the Vatican was extremely strained for long periods and it was only after 1693 that Paris and Rome found a *modus vivendi*.

36 On several occasions these figures are mentioned in Chantelou's diary (24 September, 12 October) and appear in Marot's engraving of the Louvre façade. See also Mattia de'Rossi's letter of 21 August 1665 (Mirot, p. 251).

37 *Le Imprese illustri*, Venice, 1566, p. 112 ff. For Charles V's *impresa*, see also Frances A. Yates, in *Journal of the Warburg and Courtauld Institutes*, X, 1947, p. 52.

38 Fifty years later the ball was returned to the German emperor. When Fischer von Erlach, in the façade of the Karlskirche in Vienna, revived the emblematical Hercules concept of Charles V for the Emperor Charles VI, he fell back on the Roman columns planned by Bernini for the monument of Louis XIV. Even before coming to Paris, Bernini had planned to transport the Column of Trajan to the Piazza Colonna where the Column of Marcus Aurelius stands (Chantelou, ed. Lalanne, p. 40). The idea lived on in projects for the Fontana Trevi and was kept alive by Carlo Fontana (Brauer-Wittkower, *Die Zeichnungen des Gianlorenzo Bernini*, Berlin, 1931, p. 148 ff.), in whose studio Fischer must have become acquainted with it. H. Sedlmayr ('Die Schauseite der Karlskirche in Wien', in *Kunstgeschichtliche Studien für Hans Kauffmann*, Berlin, 1956, p. 262 ff.) seems to have been unaware of these connections.

39 *Op. cit.*, p. 46 ff. and *passim*. Here also is the demonstration that Xenophon's well-known passage in the *Memorabilia* (II, i, 21 ff.) combined elements of the Choice-of-Hercules tradition from Hesiod and Prodicus.

40 T. E. Mommsen, 'Petrarch and the Story of the Choice of Hercules', *Journal of the Warburg and Courtauld Institutes*, XVI, 1953, p. 178 ff. In *De vita solitaria* Petrarch writes that Hercules 'took the path of Virtue, and marching indefatigably along its course, he was raised not only to the apex of human glory but even to a reputation of divinity.' Quite apart from the Hercules theme, both Petrarch and Boccaccio acknowledged the close connection between *Virtus* and *Gloria*; see Panofsky, *op. cit.*, p. 165.

41 Glory and Fame may here be regarded as synonyms although the iconologists differentiated, of course, between the two notions.

42 After Panofsky's fig. 87. The pointing Virtue with wings is not, as might be suspected, a hybrid Virtus-Fama personification. According to Cesare Ripa (*Iconologia*, ed. 1630, Pt III, p. 177), wings, laurel wreath, lance and sun emblem (here on the diadem and not on the chest as described by Ripa) are the correct attributes of Virtue.

43 The first edition of Erizzo's celebrated work appeared in 1559. I am using the edition of 1571, p. 274.

44 Panofsky, *op. cit.*, p. 117, note 3, quotes the passage from Fulgentius which was used almost verbatim by Erizzo.

45 *Op. cit.*, p. 233.

46 Panofsky, figs. 57, 65, 70, 71, 72, 74.

47 *Ibid.*, p. 124 ff. Panofsky showed that Annibale's painting became the 'canonical' formulation of the theme. For the Pegasus, see J. R. Martin, in *Art Bulletin*, XXXVIII, 1956, p. 95. It is here convincingly argued

that in Annibale's painting Pegasus is given a dual meaning: the horse stands for fame and for poetical inspiration, alluding to Cardinal Alessandro Farnese 'who bore an *impresa* showing Pegasus on Mount Parnassus, to signify his patronage of *letterati*.'

In a letter of 1563 Annibale Caro interpreted this *impresa* as '*d'un Pegaso, come si vede, che par che esca dal Sole; perchè si finge che nascesse dall'Aurora: e percuote con una zampa dinanzi il monte Parnaso, donde fa uscire un Fonte. Questo Cavallo alato significa l'Eloquenza, e la Poesia . . .*' (*Delle lettere familiari*, Padua, 1748, II, p. 346).

48 First ed., Venice, 1551. In the Cologne ed. of 1612, which I am using, the text (p. 949) runs: '*Nam Bellerophon & Pegasus idem sunt re ipsa, vis Solis scilicet, que variis nominibus appellatur.*' Identification of Pegasus and Bellerophon in Middle Ages: Mythographer V, 71, see Francis Hanning, *De Pegaso*, Breslau, 1901, p. 39, and article by J. M. Steadman in *Review of English Studies*, N.S. IX, 1958, pp. 407–10.

49 Erizzo, *op. cit.*, p. 511: '*il caval Pegaso con Perseo sopra, significa la virtù essaltata dalla fama. La chimera si può interpretare per il vitio, & cosi dare il significamento; che il vitio sia domato & superato dalla virtù, attribuendo questa virtù portata dalla fama, & che vola per la bocca de gli huomini, fatta chiara, alla persona di questo Principe . . .*' Ripa, *op. cit.*, Pt. III, p. 177 ff.

50 Erizzo, *op. cit.*, p. 418 ff. For the question of the authenticity of the Antinoüs medal, see E. Wind, *Bellini's Feast of the Gods*, Cambridge, Mass., 1948, p. 12.

51 *Op. cit.*, p. 233 ff.

52 Panofsky, *op. cit.*, pp. 38, 42 ff., 45 ff., 48 f. and *passim*.

53 Louvre Inv. 5966. The drawing was first discussed by R. Josephson (in *Revue de l'art ancien et moderne*, LIII, 1928, p. 24 ff.), who was, however, not interested in iconographical problems and does not even observe that the horse in the drawing is winged.

54 *Ibid.*, p. 25. Horse and rider are extremely close to some of the designs for the King, illustrated by Josephson. Instead of the commander's baton, Perseus brandishes the head of Medusa in the direction of a seated crowned figure, who is attempting to protect himself in an attitude borrowed from one of the rivers of Bernini's Four Rivers Fountain. He may be King Cepheus, Andromeda's father.

55 See F. M. Haberditzl, *Das Barockmuseum im Unteren Belvedere*, Vienna, p. 29 ff. and pls. 76–78. There are also illustrations of the base with the allegorical figures.

56 Similar to the Pegasus in Annibale Carracci's painting; see above, note 47.

57 Reference may be made to Mantegna's *Parnassus*, where Pegasus has his natural place as a symbol of poetical inspiration (see also Wind, *Bellini's Feast*, p. 12). A similar meaning may be assumed for the large Pegasus (painted as if it were a bronze) presiding over the grove of muses in a strange picture by Heemskerck in the Chrysler Collection (see *Paintings from the Collection of Walter P. Chrysler, Jr.*, Exhibition Portland Art Museum, 1956, no. 3). Pegasus is, of course, frequent on medals as an emblem of poetical flight; see G. F. Hill, *Corpus of Italian Medals*, London, 1930, nos. 406c, d, 940, 1203 (and also nos. 220, 559, 573, 574). In addition, Pietro Bembo's medal may be mentioned which shows on the obverse the fountain Hippocrene springing up under Pegasus' hoofs (formerly ascribed to Cellini; see G. Habich, *Die Medaillen der italienischen Renaissance*, Berlin, 1922, pp. 115, 121 ff.; pl. 83, i).

In the same context belongs a picture by Largillière with the portrait of a poet laureate and a rearing Pegasus on a high rock in the background (Galerie Heim, Paris, 1958). For Pegasus in a lost fresco by Niccolò dell'Abbate, in a relief by Pietro Lombardo, and in the *Hypnerotomachia*, see Sylvie Béguin, in *Journal of the Warburg and Courtauld Institutes*, XVIII, 1955, p. 119 ff.

Bertoldo's *Bellerophon taming Pegasus* (W. von Bode, *Bertoldo*, Freiburg, 1925, p. 88 ff.) may be mythological just as are a number of other bronzes (e.g., the charming German [?] bronze *Pegasus* of *c.* 1600 at Oberlin, the knowledge of which I owe to Wolfgang Stechow) or the life-size marble *Pegasus* in the garden of the Villa d'Este to which David Coffin drew my attention.

More relevant than all this is the rearing *equus alatus* with the victorious figure of 'Lucifer' (Morning star) over the triumphal arch erected by Rubens for Archduke Ferdinand at Antwerp. For the heavy-handed programme, see *Pompa introitus honori serenissimi principis Ferdinandi Austriaci . . .* Antwerp, 1635, p. 108 ff.

58 Georges Keller-Dorian, *Antoine Coysevox*, Paris, 1920, II, p. 33 ff. The groups, begun in 1701 and finished at the end of 1702, were made for the garden at Marly but transferred to their present position as early as 1719.

59 More precisely, the groups show the two main aspects of *Fama*, namely *Fama Buona* and *Fama Chiara*; see Ripa, *op. cit.*, p. 233. This has been overlooked so far as I can see.

60 In his *Histoire du Roy Louis le Grand*, p. 3 (see note 33).

61 *Le Glorie della Virtu Nella Persona di Luigi il Magno Re di Francia, e di Navarra Per La di lui incoronazione nel Tempio della GLORIA IDEA Esposta della Immitatione AL REAL DELFINO Con un breve cenno d'alcune della magnanime azioni di questo grand'EROE Dell'ossequiosa penna Dell'- Abate Benedetti Agente in Roma Di Sua Maesta Christianissima*, Lyons, 1682.

After the dedication the text begins with the words: '*Che al Tempio della Gloria Campidoglio delle Eroica Virtù Veggasi nel fiore degli anni asceso Luigi il Magno no sia che ne stupisca . . .*' The phrase 'Temple of Glory, Capitol of Heroic Virtue' or some such version may have originated with Bernini himself. This would explain the satirical dialogue between Bernini and the Capitol which seemed to have made the rounds during Bernini's lifetime.

62 Benedetti himself signed as inventor. Antonio Gherardi, an interesting artist, made the design; one cannot help noticing that he felt frustrated by the request to follow rigorously the pedestrian programme. Long before that date he had designed a Hercules at the Crossroads; see Panofsky, *op. cit.*, fig. 86.

63 The reviewer of Benedetti's little book in the *Journal des Sçavans*, 1683, p. 73, judged that the work was done '*avec une méthode aussi juste que véritable*'.

64 See Wittkower, *Bernini's Bust of Louis XIV*, London, 1951, pp. 18 ff.

65 The progress of the work can be followed in the documents [see Appendix to original publication.—Ed.]

66 According to Baldinucci (p. 126) the work was carried out in four years (i.e., 1670–73 inclusive), and this corresponds pretty well with the evidence of the documents. Domenico Bernini, who must be regarded as an eyewitness, claims that his father required eight years for it (p. 148) and outlived its completion by three years (p. 152 ff.). Since Bernini died on 28 November 1680, the period in question would be 1670 to 1677 inclusive. It may confidently be argued, however, that very little remained to be done after the end of 1673. On 14 September 1672 Elpidio Benedetti judged that the completion would take less than a year; Errard, too, believed that the work could be finished by July or August 1673, and this was a correct estimate. But it was then that Bernini fell ill, so that he hardly touched the statue during the following four years.

67 On this problem, see also E. H. Gombrich, 'Icones Symbolicae', *Journal of the Warburg and Courtauld Institutes*, XI, 1948, p. 163 ff.

68 See G. B. Depping, *Correspondance administrative sous le règne de Louis XIV*, Paris, 1850–55, IV, p. 624 ff.: '*Circulaire du Comte de Pontchartrain aux premiers présidents des parlements et aux intendants.*' Two sentences will convey an idea of the spirit of the circular: '*C'est un livre que tout homme public doit tousjours avoir ou dans les mains ou sur sa table pour fournir à une conversation utile et solide. C'est dans cette pensée que j'ay cru vous faire plaisir de vous destiner un exemplaire.*'

69 [See documents printed in Appendix to

to original publication.—Ed.]

70 P. Pecchiai, *La Scalinata di Piazza di Spagna*, Rome, 1941, p. 24.

71 E. Hempel, 'Die Spanische Treppe', in *Festschrift Heinrich Wölfflin*, Munich, 1924, p. 276 ff. Our pl. 134 from cod. Chig. P VII 10, fol. 31, first published by Hempel, is inscribed: '*dell'Abate Benedetti*'. Hempel correctly suggested that this drawing had the Abate's support but was not made by him. Pecchiai (p. 24) misinterpreted Hempel as having described Benedetti as the artist. It is not unlikely that the artist was François Dorbay, whom Benedetti employed to make a design.

72 This conclusion can be drawn from the Roman *avviso* of 27 July 1669 which mentions as a *fait accompli* that the statue was to be placed in front of Trinità de' Monti.

73 For this monument see mainly R. Josephson, 'Le monument du triomphe pour le Louvre', *Revue de l'art ancien et moderne*, LIII, 1928, p. 21 ff.

74 Cf. above, p. 87.

75 The earliest descriptions of the monuments, written in 1685 by Brice and Le Laire, have not been mentioned by modern scholars. Brice's text rather than Le Laire's shows dependence on Bernini's *concetto* by explaining that one sees '*ce grand Monarque arrivé au sommet de la gloire*'. Le Laire introduced a new element by pointing out the inaccessibility of the rock, and this, in fact, is a feature of Lebrun's project. Both authors maintain that Girardon was responsible for the design of the monument. But the series of drawings by Lebrun in the Louvre, first published by Josephson (note 73), as well as Tessin's description of his visit to Lebrun's studio in 1687 where he saw a large design of the monument (O. Sirén, *Nicodemus Tessin d.y:s Studieresor*, Stockholm, 1914, p. 102) leave no doubt as to the author.

It is not my intention here to try to disentangle the various projects drafted by Lebrun. I may mention only that the project described by Lafont de Saint-Yenne (*L'ombre du grand Colbert*, The Hague, 1749, p. 111, quoted by L. Hautecœur, *L'histoire des châteaux du Louvre et des Tuileries*, Paris, 1927, p. 159) as Bernini's, which envisioned a rock a hundred feet high decorated by rivers, maritime deities and Tritons, erected inside an enormous basin, crowned with the statue of Louis XIV, and placed in the square in front of the Louvre, can hardly be accepted as a correct attribution. It is much more likely that the author was here talking about one of Lebrun's projects.

A design in my possession (pl. 135) is clearly connected with Lebrun's project. Here a high base appears above the rock formation on which the personifications of the rivers are placed in analogy to Bernini's Four Rivers Fountain (see also *Exhibition of*

Architectural and Decorative Drawings, The Courtauld Institute, London, 1941, no. 39).

76 For payments for Girardon's models made in the '*Jeu de Paume du Louvre*', see J. Guiffrey, *Comptes des bâtiments du roi . . .*, Paris, 1888 ff., I, cols. 1229, 1287; II, cols. 137, 165, 169, 175, 182, 197, 201, 313, 352.

77 R. P. Wunder, in *Smith College Museum of Art. Bulletin*, no. 37, 1957, p. 10 ff

78 *La statue équestre de Louis le Grand, Placée dans le Temple de la Gloire, Dessein du Feu d'artifice élévé sur la Rivière de Seine, par les ordres de Messieurs les Prevost, des Marchands & Echevins de la Ville de Paris, le Jeudy 13. Aoust 1699*, Paris, 1699.

79 Published in Paris, 1699. The relevant verses are:

C'est icy qu'on immortalise
Le plus grand Roy de l'Univers

Le superbe Château qui brûle
Est l'Œte d'un second Hercule

The King's valet de chambre, De Bellocq, published an ode (*Ode Latine traduite en vers françois sur la Statue Equestre du Roy, Elevée dans la Place de Louis Le Grand*, Paris, 1700) in which he compared the rider with Perseus and the horse with Pegasus!

80 For the following see L. Réau, *Etienne-Maurice Falconet*, Paris, 1920–22.

V The Role of Classical Models in Bernini and Poussin

1 M. de Chantelou, *Journal du Voyage du Cav. Bernin en France*, ed. L. Lalanne, Paris, 1885.

2 G. P. Bellori, *Le vite de' pittori, scultori et architetti moderni*, Rome, 1672, p. 457.

3 The example shown here as pl. 144 was not found until 1824.

4 Pl. 145 after G. P. Bellori, *Admiranda romanarum antiquitatum ac veteris sculpturae vestigia*, Rome, 1693, pl. 55. The sarcophagus, in Poussin's day in the Villa Borghese, is now in the Louvre (Robert, *Die antiken Sarkophag-Reliefs*, Berlin, 1890, II, no. 195).

It should be recalled that Medea revenged herself for Jason's desertion by giving his new bride Creusa a poisoned garment. In the detail, pl. 145, we see Creusa dying in extreme pain, her father hurrying to her side with an expression of utter despair.

5 For transitional drawings, see Walter Friedlaender, *The Drawings of Nicolas Poussin*, London, 1939, I, p. 8 ff.

6 The youthful Bacchus and Faun (now in Florence) shown in pl. 151 is one of many examples that might be given for the general attitude of Poussin's group. But the attitude of the arm of Pharaoh's daughter

resting on her attendant's shoulder comes from a different source: it is close to that of the bearded Dionysus in the well-known relief of the British Museum (2190) which in Poussin's day was in the Villa Montalto in Rome. Our pl. 152 is after Bellori, *op. cit.*, pl. 43.

7 The detail in pl. 156, reproduced in reverse, after Bellori, *op. cit.*, pl. 52, shows Orestes' nurse with gestures that reflect her reaction to Orestes' murder of his mother Clytemnestra and her lover Aegisthus. The sarcophagus is still in the Palazzo Giustiniani, Rome (Robert, *op. cit.*, no. 156).

The detail of the Meleager sarcophagus shown in pl. 157 is reproduced after the sixteenth-century *Coburgensis* from Robert, *op. cit.*, 1904, III, ii, no. 278. The sarcophagus is in the Villa Albani.

8 For the entire series of Daniel drawings, see Brauer-Wittkower, *Die Zeichnungen des Gianlorenzo Bernini*, Berlin, 1931, pls. 42–47.

VI Pietro da Cortona's Project for Reconstructing the Temple of Palestrina

1 *Ichnographia Templi Fortunae Praenestae*. Monogram on the right: ⅅℂ.

2 *Orthographia Templi Fortunae Praenestae*. Monogram on the right: ⅅℂ.

3 *Sciographia Templi Fortunae Praenestae*. Left: *Illustrissimo et excellentissimo Principi / Maphaeo Barberino / Principi Praenestes ereti / etc. / Hoc obsequii monimentum / Dominicus Castellus D.D.C.* Right: *Petrus Berettin. Cort.s delin.* Beside this is a description of the building.

4 *Athanasii Kircheri Latium. Id est, Nova et parallela Latii tum veteris tum novi Descriptio*, Amsterdam, 1671. Plates between pp. 94 and 95.

5 In Domenico de Rossi, *Romanae Magnitudinis Monumenta . . .*, pls. 53, 54, 55.

6 *Josephus Roccus Vulpius Vetus Latium Profanum. Tomus Nonum in quo agitur de Praenestinis et Gabinis*, Rome, Bernabò 1743, pls. 4 (ground-plan), 5 (isometric projection), 6 (view).

7 Canina, *Gli edifizi antichi dei Contorni di Roma*, Rome, 1856, VI, pl. III.

8 There is a reference to these sheets (as Cortona originals) by H. Chalton Bradshaw, in *Papers of the British School at Rome*, Vol. IX, 1920, p. 245. The drawings (pen and wash) are in the volumes of the Albani estate Vol. 186, nos. 10382–10384. I am grateful to Dr O. F. Morthead, the librarian of the collection, for his kind co-operation and for various items of information.

9 The sheets, which should be in the Barberini collection, are now apparently lost.

10 While ground-plan and elevation A come from the same hand, that of a very weak but meticulous draughtsman, the

view B, although executed in the same pen and wash technique, exhibits a rather freer and more lively style. Both sheets for scheme A are set in a sepia frame; the view for scheme B has no such frame. The two scheme A sheets have an old numbering (as part of a continuing series) on the bottom right-hand corner—52 (ground-plan) and 53 (view); the scheme B view has no number.

11 (a) Ground-plan in the Albertina *Architekt. Handz. aus der Wiener Hofbibliothek*, no. 272. End of sixteenth century. Cf. Egger, *Krit. Verzeichnis d. Slg. arch. Handzg. d. Hofbibliothek*, Vienna, 1903, no. 272. Illustrated in Bradshaw, *op. cit.*, fig. 4.
(b) Rome, Cod. Vat. lat. 3439, fol. 50 (ground-plan), fol. 51 (view). Illustrated in Egger, *op. cit.*, pl. V and fig. 20. The view in Hülsen in *Hermann Egger Festschrift*, Graz, 1933 (pl. 5). Ascribed to Girolamo Rainaldi by Egger.
(c) Rome, cod. Ottob. lat. 3373, fol. 71, 72. Mentioned by Bradshaw, *op. cit.*, p. 244.

12 Cf. in the views, in each case, the cumulative graduation of the terraces, which not being subjected to any uniform concept, fade away indecisively at the sides.

13 Cf. for instance the brick wall with an order of columns in front closing off the courtyard of the lower temple area or the two-storey building above the uppermost terrace with the wide attic between the floors, etc.

14 Blondel's survey (*Mélanges d'Archéologie et d'Histoire*, Vol. II, 1882, p. 168, pl. IV, which is widely accepted as correct, agrees with the reconstruction scheme A with regard to the terracing, the layout of the niche system with order in front as a decoration of the two upper retaining walls and with regard to the double grotto of the main retaining wall.

15 Use of double pillars, simplification of the staircase ramp arrangement, etc.

16 Elements which are found with Domenico Fontana (the dome) and the group of architects of the turn of the century: band-framing of wall surfaces.

17 *Memorie Prenistine. Disposte in forma di Annali*, Rome, 1795, p. 233.

18 On Cassiano dal Pozzo see especially Carlo Dati, *Delle lodi del Com. C. d. P.*, Florence, 1664; Lumbroso in *Miscellanea di Storia Italiana*, Vol. XV, 1874, p. 129 ff.; Dumesnil, *Histoire des plus célèbres amateurs italiens*, Paris, 1853, p. 403 ff.; O. M. Premoli in *L'Arcadia*, Vol. II, 1917, p. 181 ff.

19 There has not so far been a critical treatment of Pozzo's collection, urgent though the task is. O. Kern's treatment of the theme promised by Robert in *Antike Sarkophag-Reliefs*, Vol. II, 1890, p. xi, never appeared.

20 This explains the secondary discrepancies between schemes A and B listed in note 10.

21 See above, note 3.

22 Cf. Petrini, *Mem. Pren.*, *op. cit.*, p. 252.

23 D. Castelli was unimportant as an architect, but had special connections with the Barberinis as an architectural official of the papal chamber (1623–57). He also made drawings of all the buildings of Urban VIII for an unpublished book of engravings. See Pollak in *Thieme-Becker*, Vol. VI, p. 149.

24 See Petrini, *op. cit.*, p. 242, where the hypothesis is advanced that Cortona's reconstruction scheme was developed on this occasion.

25 Suarez, *op. cit.*, p. 51: '*oculos, et animum convertamus ad Ichnographiam, et ad effigiem Templi, quas Eminentissimi Cardinalis Francisci Barberini munificentia typis expressas subjectimus . . .*'

26 The two halves are not identical. There is an alternative version; the right-hand corner shows recognizable connections with the engraving.

27 F. Burger in *Zeitschrift f. Geschichte der Architektur*, Vol. II, 1908–9, pp. 203–10.

28 Cortona's interest could have been rekindled by the publication of Suarez.

29 The only Quattrocento survey known to us is by the hand of Giuliano da Sangallo (cod. Vat. lat. 4424, fol. 43r). It shows a detail, the apsidal hall, reproduced in Delbrueck, *Hellenistische Bauten in Latium*, Strasbourg 1967, I, p. 52, where a summary of later schemes is also given.

30 The connections with Palestrina were first seen by Patzak in *Die Villa Imperiale in Pesaro*, 1908, p. 155. Probably without knowledge of this passage, Hülsen recently made a renewed reference to Bramante's ancient model in *Hermann Egger Festschrift*, Graz, 1933, p. 57 ff. See also D. Frey, *Michelangelo—Studien*, 1920, p. 36 ff.

31 Nearly all restorers agree that there were convex steps at Palestrina. The most recent tentative reconstruction by Bradshaw (*op. cit.*) supports this suggestion. The exedra staircase in the Vatican is known not to have been executed after Bramante's plan. With Bramante the motif is still used in the same way as in ancient architecture, but later it appears in quite new contexts. It plays a significant part in Michelangelo's designs for the Laurenziana, is then taken over by painters and serves in Mannerist fresco cycles to blur the frontier between real and painted space (e.g., Poccetti's in the Ospedale degl'Innocenti, Florence).

32 On the significance of the Villa d'Este see Patzak in *Zeitschrift f. bild, Kunst*, Vol. N.F. XVII, 1906, p. 51 ff.

33 The present form of the Nicchione is also attributed to Ligorio by Tolnay (then Tolnai) in *Jahrbuch d. Preuss. Kunstslg.*, Vol. LI, 1930, p. 29 ff.

34 See as early a commentator as J. Burckhardt, *Geschichte der Renaissance in Italien*, 1912, p. 240. Further, D. Frey, *Michelangelo-Studien*, *op. cit.*, p. 34. The engraving of the Villa by Specchi in Muñoz, *P. da Cortona (Bibl. d'Arte Illustrata)*, pl. 1.

35 The ancient Monopteros, which the 1614 scheme made into the chief motif of a dome with drum in the early sixteenth-century style, is now omitted altogether. From the Villa Sacchetti the way led directly to the free-standing belvedere.

36 On these schemes see Brauer-Wittkower, *Bernini-Zeichnungen*, p. 148.

37 Reproduced by Josephson in *Gazette des Beaux-Arts*, Vol. XVII, 1928, pp. 79, 81.

38 See Chantelou, *Journal du Voyage du Cav. Bernin en France*, ed. L. Lalanne, Paris, 1885, p. 257.

39 Already by the Neoclassical period the 'more correct' scheme by P. Ligorio was being rediscovered. It was first published by G. B. Cipriani, *Monumenti di Fabbriche Antiche estratti dai disegni dei più celebri autori*, Rome, 1797, Vol. I (under 'Tempio di Vesta', pls. 9, 10), after the sheets in cod. Vat. lat. 3439.

VII Santa Maria della Salute

1 The fullest collection of historical material concerning S. Maria della Salute appeared in Vittorio Piva, *Il tempio della Salute eretto per voto de la repubblica veneta*, Venice, 1930. Some of the conclusions of the present paper were first published in *Journal of the Society of Architectural Historians* XVI, 1957, pp. 3–10.

2 *La chiesa e il seminario di S. Maria della Salute*, Venice, 1842.

3 See note 1. Some documents appeared first in Flaminio Corner, *Ecclesiae venetae antiquis monumentis . . . VII–VIII*, Venice, 1749, pp. 74–76.

4 Venice, Archivio di Stato, Senato terra, filza 22 October 1630. Verbatim in Corner, *op. cit.*, p. 74 ff. and Piva, *op. cit.*, p. 29.

5 For the history of SS. Trinità and the Seminary, see Piva, pp. 13 ff., 73 ff.

6 See, e.g., Marco Antonio Sabellico, *Le Historie Vinitiane*, Venice, 1544, fol. 5v; H. Kretschmayr, *Geschichte von Venedig*, Gotha, 1905, I, p. 19 ff., with references to chronicles.

7 In Smeraldi's *inventario dei beni* compiled on 1 August 1648 after his death he is mentioned as '*Antonio quondam Francesco Smeraldi, detto Fracao*' (Arch. di Stato, Petizione 361, note 29).

8 In the beginning of the memorandum Longhena mentions that at an earlier date he had handed in measured drawings of his project, whereupon he had been asked to make '*un modello di rilievo sopra esse*

Piante. Io prontamente con ogni diligenza e studio il fabbricai . . .' He concludes the memorandum with the words: *'Il tutto mi obbligo prontamente mostrare nel mio modello e pianta presentati'.*

9 See Giovanni Casoni, *La peste di Venezia nel MDCXXX origine della erezione del Tempio a S. Maria della Salute,* Venice, 1830, p. 35.

10 Neither Moschini nor Piva published the result of the ballot. Longhena's project received 66 votes and Fracao's 39; see Arch. di Stato, Senato I, R.o 105, Terra 1631, fol. 222v.

11 Arabic numbers in brackets always refer to the documents mentioned in the previous section.

12 Among the other competitors were probably the Florentine Gherardo Silvani and the Venetians Matteo Ingoli, Bartolo Belli and the painter Padovanino. See G. Dalla Santa, *Il pittore Alessandro Varotari e un suo disegno per la chiesa della Salute di Venezia,* Nozze Lampertico-Feriani, Vicenza, 1904.

13 Reproduced in Casoni, *op. cit.,* frontispiece, and Piva, p. 34.

14 See Dalla Santa, *op. cit.,* p. 13 ff.

15 See Casoni, p. 37 ff. and Piva, p. 97.

16 Casoni, p. 40.

17 *'. . . mi sono posto, già mesi, a fare Pianta, Profili e Facciata in disegno . . .'.*

18 See note 8.

19 There is no full agreement as to the measurements of the execution. Discrepancies are partly due to the fact that different authors measured the same parts between different points.

Old measured drawings are in *Le Fabriche più cospicue di Venezia,* Venice, 1820, II, pls. 111–14; on these all later reproductions were based until recently. New edition of the same work: L. Cicognara, A. Diedo, G. A. Selva, *Le fabbriche e i monumenti cospicui di Venezia,* Venice, 1858, II, pp. 113–18, pls. 213–16, with additional notes by Francesco Zanotto. The text to the chapter on S. Maria della Salute is by A. Diedo (henceforth quoted as 'Diedo').

New measured drawings made under Bruno Zevi's guidance by Carlo Santamaria were published in *L'Architettura* I, 1955, pp. 53–57 (henceforth quoted as 'Santamaria'). I am greatly indebted to Professor Zevi for having put the original measured drawing at my disposal.

I checked up certain measurements inside the church. In addition I am under a great obligation to Signor Cattaruzza of the Ufficio Tecnico of the Fondazione Cini for having also verified the measurements of the elevation. He confirmed the correctness of Santamaria's work, but noted occasional errors in the figures inscribed in the

drawings, a fact that had puzzled me before.

Finally, it should be mentioned that Piva (*op. cit.*) gives the principal measurements in his text without revealing his source for them.

I should like to put on record my gratitude to the Fondazione Cini not only for the services of Signor Cattaruzza, but also for a number of new photographs which were specially taken for me and for the efficient and unfailing assistance given me by the staff of that admirable Institution.

20 Not only in my table but whenever mentioned in my text 'feet' are Venetian feet. One English foot equals 0·877 Venetian feet, i.e. the Venetian foot is *c.* 13 inches. 2·85 Venetian feet = 1 m.

21 Santamaria's 44 m. are 125·40 feet. According to Santamaria the greatest width (including the base outside) is 45·40 m., according to Piva 45·50 m.

As will be shown below the ideal measurements aimed at by Longhena are 124 feet (43·50 m.).

22 60 feet are 21 m. This is also the measurement given by J. Durm, *Die Baukunst der Renaissance,* Leipzig, 1914, fig. 863. Santamaria's measurements are not quite consistent.

23 According to Longhena himself (9) and the report of the commission (see Chronology, 14): 19 feet; according to one of the experts (13): *'18 in luce almeno'.* Diedo's and Santamaria's measurements agree. The latter's 6·50 m. = 18·5 feet.

24 According to Diedo: 10 feet from the balustrade to the pilasters of the wall and 11 feet to the wall itself. My own measurement is 3·65 m. = 10·5 feet. Santamaria's 3·80 m. = 10·8 feet.

25 Diedo's and Santamaria's figures are in agreement.

26 188 feet = 65·9 m.

27 43 feet = 15 m. It is to be noted that in Santamaria's plan the steps are wrongly placed. The first step is flush with the half-columns (as shown in Santamaria's section) and not with the pilasters under the arch.

28 80 feet = 28 m. Piva's measure is 27·75 m.

29 In Diedo's plan clearly 10 feet = 3·5 m. In Santamaria's section: 3 m. (section through the arch), but in the plan at the level of the base of the columns at least 3·40 m.

30 According to Diedo 20·5 feet to the pilasters of the back wall and 21 feet to the wall itself. Santamaria's *c.* 7 m. are almost precisely 20 feet. Piva's measurement: 6·60 m.; my own: 6·80 m.

31 Diedo and Santamaria almost agree. The latter's 13·5 m. = 38·5 feet. Confirmed by my own measurement.

32 Santamaria's 12·55 m. = 35·75 feet

seems to be correct.

33 5·25 m. = 15 feet.

34 The level of the high altar area—separated from the presbytery by the Communion rails—is raised one step above the level of the presbytery. This step appears in the correct position in Santamaria's plan, but is wrongly drawn in his section. Three further steps lead up to the high altar.

In the choir the level of the high altar area is maintained, so that the floor of the choir is one step above that of the presbytery.

35 Measured at the bottom of the double pilaster shafts, according to Santamaria 1·85 m. = 5·27 feet.

36 See note 21.

37 See note 8.

38 Moschini, p. 9: *'. . . mentre colla sola distanza che si trova presentemente di piedi dodici incirca esso corridore non si stima a sufficienza fianchegiata . . .'.*

39 A comparison of the figures under *g* and *k* makes it evident that between the stage of the model and that of the execution Longhena added 6 feet to the presbytery and took 6 feet off the length of the choir.

40 The detailed measurements of the model taken along the central axis were: 12 (wall and entrance, corresponding to the chapels), 15 (ambulatory), 5 (pillar), 60 (Rotonda), 5 (pillar), 15 (ambulatory), 37 (presbytery), 10 (high altar area), 26 (choir). The sum is 185 feet to which should be added about 2 feet for the wall of the choir. This brings us within one foot (or 35 cm) of the overall measurement of 188 feet given by Longhena—but only if he planned the ambulatory 15 and not 12 feet wide.

41 See below, p. 143.

42 A common procedure in medieval rotundas with ambulatory. Among late examples Carlo Fontana's Jesuit church at Loyola, Spain, is particularly interesting because Fontana knew the Salute but did not accept the system employed in that church.

43 *'18 in luce almeno';* see note 23.

44 *'Mi oppongo alla Rotonda, bisogna alterarla. Si è esteso nei difetti espressi dai Comini della sproporzione dei volti tra gl'intercolumnii e i corridori; onde si converrebbe alterare tutto il corpo della Chiesa da chi volesse allargare i corridori, come si perderia il terreno per il Monastero, e si perderia il confine alla fondamenta, et sic juravit.'*

45 *'difetto patente, insuperabile, conosciuto da tutti e affermato, dopo che dalla perizia di alcuni è stato raccordato, che conoscemmo di dover portare puntualmente alla notizia delle EE. VV. come punto essenzialissimo.'*

46 J. Durm (*op. cit.,* fig. 863), too, who seems to have taken measurements in the

building, incorporated into his section this and other mistakes made by Diedo.

47 This was first noticed by Dohme in *Jahrbuch der Preussischen Kunstsammlungen*, III, 1882, p. 127.

One must not exclude the possibility that the Venetian double-arched window, familiar from such palaces as Corner-Spinelli, Vendramin-Calergi and the Scuola di S. Rocco may have influenced Longhena's choice. But before Longhena no such windows are to be found in Venice in the drum of a dome.

48 This type of plan was the north Italian contribution to the old problem of axial direction in centralized churches (see the essay on Carlo Rainaldi in this volume, especially p. 23, and *Architectural Principles in the Age of Humanism*, London, 1965, pp. 11, 99 ff.). By placing the high altar into an architecturally isolated presbytery, axial ambiguity was reduced, for the centralized character of the congregational room was preserved without abandoning emphasis on the high altar.

49 See Lorenzo Santi, *Ricordo di Fra Francesco Colonna e ragionamento sull'estetica architettonica*, Venice, 1837, who was the first to claim Longhena's dependence on the *Hypnerotomachia*. See also P. Selvatico, *Sulla architettura e sulla scultura in Venezia*, Venice, 1847, p. 415.

50 The kind of influence which the *Hypnerotomachia* may have had on architectural thought was admirably demonstrated by E. Gombrich in *Journal of the Warburg and Courtauld Institutes*, XIV, 1951, p. 119 ff.

51 '*Avendo essa Chiesa mistero nella sua dedicazione, essendo dedicata alla B.V., mi parve per quella poca virtù che Dio benedetto mi ha prestato, di farla in forma rotonda, essendo in forma di corona, per essere dedicata a essa Vergine . . .*'.

52 S. Beissel, *Geschichte der Verehrung Marias im 16. und 17. Jahrhundert*, Freiburg, 1910, p. 478 ff.

53 Figures of angels are placed on the balustrade over the entrance, at both sides of the Virgin, as well as on top of the chapel fronts.

54 L'Abbè Auber, *Histoire e théorie du symbolism religieux*, Paris, 1871, II, p. 225.

55 The figures are so much corroded and mutilated that it is virtually impossible to name them. But their number leaves hardly any doubt that the Apostles are represented.

56 Inscriptions make it possible to identify the figures of the Prophets. Apart from the four main prophets—Isaiah, Jeremiah, Ezechiel and Daniel—three minor Prophets, Simeon, Hosea, Baruch and, in addition, David are represented. The reasons for this choice are not obvious and would require further investigation.

The rest of the decoration is not of absorbing iconographic interest. The main features may be mentioned briefly. *Façade:* left niches: St Mark, St Matthew; right niches: St Luke, St John. On the scrolls left and right of the Virgin: Moses and David.

Subsidiary fronts: left of centre: in the niches: Courage, St Michael, Justice; above the pediment: Eve. Right of centre: in the niches: Prudence, St George, Temperance; above the pediment: Judith. Thus these two subsidiary fronts have a uniform programme: two antitypes of the Virgin, the two Archangels and the four Cardinal Virtues.

Presbytery: in the spandrels of the arch above the high altar: St John and St Mark; opposite: St Matthew and St Luke. In the niches left and right of the high altar: SS. Peter and Paul.

Chapels of the ambulatory: on the altars, with one exception (second left, Liberi's St Anthony of Padua), pictures illustrating the life of the Virgin: Birth of the Virgin, Presentation in the Temple, and Assumption by Luca Giordano, Annunciation by Liberi; Descent of the Holy Spirit by Titian.

57 The close alliance between the crown and centralized buildings in contemporary thought finds welcome support in Domenichino's *Madonna of the Rosary* (Pinacoteca, Bologna: 1617–25), where the angel holding the crown appears next to one with a small round temple, both resting on clouds close to the Virgin. For the identification of the rosary with the crown of stars, see Beissel, *op. cit.*, p. 44.

58 R. Krautheimer, 'Santa Maria Rotunda', in *Arte del primo millenio. Atti del Convegno di Pavia*, 1950, pp. 21–27, discussed this problem at length and has shown that the roundness of churches dedicated to the Virgin was originally the result of their being derived from the martyrium erected over the tomb of the Virgin.

59 See R. Wittkower, *Architectural Principles, op. cit.*, p. 1 ff.

60 See, among others, the sequences of differently shaped domed spaces in Roman thermae.

61 With the exception of the Venetian window-type altars of the centre chapels; see pl. 191.

62 First observed by Diedo who called the presbytery a '*felicissima imitazione di quanto praticò il Palladio nella Chiesa del Redentore*'.

63 In addition, their diameter is *c.* 90 cm as against the Rotonda columns' *c.* 95 cm.

64 The colourful marble shafts—the only architectural members of precious material in the church—stem from the Roman theatre at Pola. Longhena obviously adjusted their height for his purpose.

65 See note 34.

66 Originally the three arches visible in

pl. 205 opened in windows; they were blocked when the organ was built in. Professor Nicola Ivanoff informs me '*che nel' 700 vi è stato inserito l'organo bloccando le finestre, in modo che non è più, come era in origine, la parte più luminosa della chiesa*'.

67 Longhena does not mention the size of the pillars. It seems almost certain that they were executed as planned in the model stage. Measured at the base of the pilaster shafts their size appears to be slightly over 5 feet; see note 35. The diameter of the columns may possibly have been Longhena's module, but it seems to be slightly too large, namely 2·6 feet (95 cm) instead of 2·5 feet.

68 It is possible that the ambulatory of 12 feet survived from an earlier plan to which the series 10, 12, 18 might well have belonged. In this plan the main measures of the ambulatory would have been related as 12:18. The present ratio is 15:18·5 (see note 23). The latter figure (opening of the arches into the octagon) is the only major measurement that does not fit into the series of the execution, but the distance from column shaft to column shaft in the octagon is 20 feet.

69 The 43 feet of the length of the presbytery (g) are the measure taken from the steps on, as we have noted. The measure from the far end of the pilasters at the entry into the presbytery to the columns of the high altar —i.e. the presbytery proper—is exactly 40 feet.

70 It appears now that the intended overall measure must have been 124 feet (120 plus 4 feet for the walls); see above, note 21.

71 The width of the choir falls short of the ideal measurement by 40 to 50 cm (see *l* and note 31). The reason cannot be determined without further investigation. However, the difference between the actual and the ideal measurement does not seem large enough to voice doubt as to Longhena's intentions.

72 Diedo's, Piva's and Santamaria's measurements differ considerably. Diedo committed the error, always repeated until it was corrected by Santamaria, of drawing the inner vault of the dome semi-spherically. In Santamaria's section the sum of the single measurements is at variance with the corresponding overall notation (mainly owing to the wrong inscription 8·92 m. for the height of the drum). The entire interior height to the ring of the lantern is given by Santamaria as 41·70 m. (118·8 feet) and by Piva as 42·20 m. (120 feet). Diedo mentions in his text: '*tutta l'altezza dal pavimento alla sommità equivale a due larghezze dell'ottagono*' (i.e. twice 60 feet). The measurement taken for me by Signor Cattaruzza is 42·57 m. (121·3 feet).

73 To be exact, according to Santamaria: 13·80 m., 13·90 m. and 13·70 m. = 41·40 m. (instead of the inscribed overall measure

41·70 m.) or 39·3, 39·6, 39 feet.

74 The height from the pavement to the top of the figures in the octagon is 21·65 m. according to Santamaria (21 m. = 60 feet); the height of the dome and inner lantern is also 60 feet; the height of the drum, measured from the top of the balustrade, is exactly 30 feet.

75 Santamaria's inscribed measurement '29 m.' (82·65 feet), shown in our pl. 192, refers to the height from the pavement to the top of the interior balustrade under the dome. The top of the outside entablature lies about 2 feet lower, i.e., the whole height is 80 feet.

76 According to Signor Cattaruzza's measurements it is 16·13 m. to the top of the entablature above the giant pilasters. Since the entablature is 2·20 m. high, the entire height without the entablature is 16·13–2·20 m = 13·97 m. (14 m. = 40 feet).
The computing of Santamaria's figures for drum and dome results in 13·90 m. The radius of the dome is 20 feet (that of the large dome is 30 feet); its centre lies 1·50 m. above the entablature of the drum, and the full circle drawn from this centre touches, of course, the lower edge of the balustrade of the drum.
The radius of the semi-vaults of the apses seems to be 15 feet and the height of the giant pilasters 30 feet.

77 R. Wittkower, *Architectural Principles, op. cit.*, p. 101 ff.

78 See note 66.

79 Longhena also thought that the ambulatory plan had practical advantages for the smooth functioning of the service and religious ceremonies. He wrote (Chronology, 9): '*tra la nave grande di essa Chiesa ed esse cappelle vi sarà sito per poterci andare intorno colle processioni nel tempo delle feste principali senza impedimento del popolo che si troverà nel mezzo della Chiesa, e delle Messe che vi saranno agli altari*'. Such later authors as Selvatico and Zanotto thoroughly disagreed. In any case, it seems unlikely that these were primary considerations in determining the choice of the ambulatory plan.

80 Moschini, p. 13: '*ed essendo nel mezzo della Cupola grande, cioè nel mezzo di essa Chiesa si godranno benissimo tutte le cappelle e gli altari*'.

81 Wittkower, *op. cit.*, p. 97 ff.

82 The breaking up of the uniform floor space by steps is to be found, of course, in Palladio's churches. But the tradition went further back; see, e.g., Codussi's S. Michele all'Isola. Moreover, examples in the rest of north Italy are not rare, e.g. S. Fedele in Milan.

83 With the exception of the step of the Communion rail.

84 *L'architettura di Baldassare Longhena*, Padua, 1954, p. 18.

85 C. Hussey, *The Picturesque*, London, 1924; N. Pevsner, 'The Genesis of the Picturesque', *Architectural Review*, Vol. 96, 1944. [Reprinted in *Studies in Art, Architecture and Design*, 1968.—Ed.]

86 It is perhaps not out of place to compare Longhena's approach to space with that of seventeenth-century perspective theory and practice. The spectator can, of course, take up any position inside the church; he is free to move about, but the views appearing in his field of vision may be distorted—just as Padre Pozzo's illusionism collapses when seen from a wrong standpoint.

87 Further to Brunelleschi's 'perspective' conception of architecture, Wittkower, 'Brunelleschi and "Proportion in Perspective"', *Journal of the Warburg and Courtauld Institutes*, XVI, 1953, p. 275 ff.; G. C. Argan, *Brunelleschi*, Mondadori, 1955; C. Brandi, *Arcadio—Eliante*, Milan, 1956, p. 155 ff.

88 In the illustrations the capitals look darker, but this is due to the effect of shadows.

89 [When this essay was written (1958) the pilasters had also been painted grey. The colour scheme has now been changed again and both columns and pilasters are white; bases, capitals and architraves are yellowish natural stone.—Ed.]

90 See Antonio Visentini, *Osservazioni che servono di continuazione al trattato di Teofilo Gallacini sopra gli errori degli architetti*, Venice, 1771, pp. 68, 69; see also Diedo's text. Selvatico, *op. cit.*, p. 414, defended Longhena against the purists.

91 In S. Giorgio Maggiore Palladio also worked with two colours, the grey stone colour and a yellowish hue which he used for arches and windows and for the arches of the crossing and the architectural parts of the drum.

92 See the criticism by Diedo, Selvatico and Francesco Zanotto in the 1858 edition of *Le fabbriche e i monumenti cospicui di Venezia*, II, p. 113 ff.

93 The ribs are set off against white bands which form the lateral frames of the coffers. These white bands reverse the grey of the window surrounds in the drum and return to the white of the pilasters in the body of the church. [After this essay was published, Elena Bassi ('Una domanda a Rudolf Wittkower', in *Critica d'Arte*, no. 62, 1964) suggested, on the basis of a later document, that Longhena intended to decorate the interior of the main dome with stuccoes and paintings. Rudolf Wittkower was not convinced, and in an unpublished draft for a reply wrote: 'The structural decoration of the dome makes it quite evident that it can never have been planned for painted decoration. The conception belongs as clearly to the anti-painterly dome constructions as the domes by Cortona, Borromini and Bernini. None were designed for

taking paintings. The approach changed after about 1660, when dome surfaces were planned to be smooth·and painting was envisaged from the start. Bassi's document dates from 1679. By then it had apparently been decided to go along with the times and fit in paintings, whether appropriate or not, but the incongruous project was evidently abandoned.'—Ed.]

94 The use of colour at the exterior would deserve a special discussion. I only want to mention that the tripartite façade, the scrolls and the entablature and balustrade over the drum form a 'pictorial' unit by virtue of the use of white stone and are set off against the grey plaster of the drum itself and of the chapel walls of the rotonda farther back.

95 It is worth while studying the use of colour in later Venetian churches such as the Gesuati, the Gesuiti and S. Geremia. Nowhere will similar complexities be found.

96 Labacco, *Libro di architettura*, 1558, fols. 24, 25. See G. Fiocco in Thieme-Becker, *s. v.* Longhena.

97 See W. Lotz in *Römisches Jahrbuch für Kunstgeschichte*, VII, p. 22 ff.

98 The weight of the dome rests on the free-standing pillars; the scrolls rest on the arches of the ambulatory.

99 But for the form of the towers he returned to the square design traditional in Venice.

100 The comparison of pls. 215 and 216 makes it evident that the assumption of a direct influence of the Santo at Padua on Longhena (Semenzato, p. 20) is unjustified.

101 See also p. 145 above.

102 Illustrated in Piva, *op. cit.*, p. 53.

103 Carlo Fontana's Jesuit church at Loyola (above, note 42) is unthinkable without the Salute. Gibbs's Radcliffe Camera at Oxford is a late descendent of the Salute, via Fontana's work at Loyola. The church of St Mary at Gostyn, Poland, built by Pompeo Ferrari c. 1725 is almost a straight copy of the Salute (ill. in Zbigniew Dmochowski, *The Architecture of Poland*, London, 1956, pp. 262, 263).
Vanvitelli's Caserta with the octagonal vestibules with ambulatories spells a last great triumph for Longhena's principles.

VIII Francesco Borromini: His Character and Life

1 The original testament is in the Archivio di Stato, Rome, and a more easily readable copy is in the Archivio Capitolino among the papers of the notary Olimpius Ricci. Ugo Donati, 'Il testamento di Francesco Borromini', in *Urbe*, VII, no. 7, July 1942, pp. 18–22, was the first to quote from this document; it was published *in extenso* by Paolo Portoghesi, *Borromini nella cultura europea*, Rome, 1964, pp. 381–84. The

verbal account of Borromini's interrogation about his suicide on the part of an official representing the Governatore of Rome was published twice by Bertolotti, first in *Archivio*, ed. F. Gori, IV, 1880, pp. 220–21, and again in *Artisti lombardi a Roma*, Milan, 1881, II, pp. 37–40. A new transcription was published by Sergio Samek Ludovici, in his ed. of Baldinucci's *Vita di Bernini*, Milan, 1948, pp. 273–75, from the Archivio Communale di Roma, Processi, Parte I, 1667, folios 30–35. For the suicide, see also Appendix IV. The entire text of the inventory (not without some blunders in the transcription) is in Portoghesi, *op. cit.*, pp. 385–400.

2 *Die Architektur Borrominis*, Vienna, 1930 and 1939 (2nd ed.), p. 119 ff.

3 *Ibid.*, p. 124.

4 *Ibid.*, p. 121.

5 Such as delusions, incoherent associations and psychosensory or psychomotory disturbances.

6 Carlo Giulio Argan, *Borromini*, Verona, 1952, especially p. 14 ff.

7 *Vite* (written between about 1655 and 1677), ed. Jacob Hess, Leipzig and Vienna, 1934, p. 365: 'Francesco was good looking; but he was always a conspicuous figure, because he insisted on dressing the same way all the time, and preferred not to follow everyday customs as regards clothes. He always wore a Spanish-type *randiglia*, and rosettes on his shoes, and likewise leggings round his legs; he made no unnecessary effort, yet he was always decorous in his dress.'

8 *Vite* . . ., Rome, 1730, I, p. 305. It is true that Pascoli's *Life* of Borromini is largely dependent on Baldinucci (see Eugenio Battisti, 'Lione Pascoli scrittore d'arte', *Acc. Naz. dei Lincei Rendiconti Classe di Scienze morali* . . ., Serie VIII, Vol. VIII, Fasc. 3–4, 1953, p. 134), but it also contains some important independent passages. (The last sentences of the *Life* indicate that Pascoli knew Bernardo and his family; see note 27.) The whole passage to which I refer in the text, reads as follows: 'He was of a healthy, robust nature, not bad looking, even though somewhat gloomy and difficult; tall, well-built and brawny, black-haired, swarthy-faced, chaste and clean-living; and to the very end he conserved the inborn nobility of his generous manner and refined spirit. He always wore black, almost Spanish-type clothes, but with a wig and side-whiskers.' The only known portrait engraving of Borromini (published in *Opus architectonicum*, Rome, 1720 and 1725), datable shortly after 26 July 1652, when Innocent X personally draped him with the mantle and cross of the Cavaliere (see below, note 26), shows him without whiskers; he may, however, wear a wig.

9 *Notizie dei Professori del Disegno*, Flor-

ence, 1681–1728. Baldinucci's *Vita* of Borromini was probably written after 1688 (see Appendix I). I am quoting from the edition: Florence, 1847, V, p. 139: 'Fu Francesco Borromini uomo di grande e bell'aspetto, di grosse e robuste membra, di forte animo, e d'altri e nobili concetti. Fu sobrio nel cibarsi, e visse castamente.'

The MS *Life* of Borromini in the Magliabechiana in Florence (see Appendix I), usually wrongly regarded as a draft by Baldinucci but, in actual fact, his principal source, contains the following passage (fol. 171v): 'He was a tall, well-built man of good appearance and he dressed in ancient Roman fashion in finely woven stuff, and in his mode of life he was most frugal . . .' If, as I have reason to believe, this *Life* contains reliable information, it would seem that at some time, possibly quite late in life, Borromini changed his clothing habits.

10 Baldinucci, p. 139: '*Stimò molto l'arte sua, per amor della quale non perdonò a fatica . . .*'; p. 140: 'A few days before his death he burnt all the drawings he had intended to be used for engravings, which he had not been able to carry out: he did this for fear that they might fall into the hands of his adversaries, who might have either had them engraved as their own work, or else altered them. He was not in the least ruled by a desire for possessions . . . he did not want to take money so that, he said, he could work in his own way.'—Passeri, p. 366: '. . . he never allowed himself to be dominated by business interests . . . he had no wish to accumulate money for his heirs.'—Magliabechiano, *Life* (Appendix I): '. . . he was a disinterested man—he never at any time valued money and he never asked for anything from his employers so that he would be more free to work in his own way . . .' See also note 82.

11 *Ibid.*, p. 137 ff.: '*Era egli stato solito di patir molto d'umore malinconico, o, come dicevano alcuni dei suoi medesimi, d'ipocondria, a cagione della quale infermità, congiunta alla continua speculazione nelle cose dell'arte sua, in processo di tempo egli si trovò si profondato e fisso in un continuo pensare, che fuggiva al possibile la conversazione degli uomini standosene solo in casa, in null'altro occupato, che nel continuo giro dei torbidi pensieri, che alla sua mente somministrava del continuo quel nero umore.*'

12 See also Passeri's remark, quoted above (note 7), that he always attracted attention because of his dress.

13 Passeri does not mention the profession of Giovanni Domenico Castelli, Borromini's father. According to Baldinucci (p. 132; see Appendix I, 7) he worked as an architect in the service of the Visconti. But since no architectural work by him is known, since he appears to have spent his life in Bissone on Lake Lugano, Borromini's birth-place—the area that gave Italy so many stone-

masons—and since Borromini was apprenticed with a stonemason in Milan, the conclusion seems justified that Giovanni Domenico was a *capomastro* rather than an architect.

14 Baldinucci (p. 132) and Passeri (p. 360) disagree about Borromini's arrival in Rome. According to the former he was in Milan between his ninth and sixteenth year (i.e., 1608–15), while the latter dates his Milanese stay between 1614 and 1624. The truth lies probably half-way. The first Roman document in which his name appears dates from 1619.

15 Domenico Bernini, *Vita del Cav. Gio. Lorenzo Bernini*, Rome, 1713, p. 32, reports a strange story. When an important personality complained to Bernini that Borromini, who had been a good designer, had exchanged the ancient Roman and good modern manner for the Gothic manner, Bernini said smiling: 'In my opinion it is less harmful to be a bad Catholic than to be a good Heretic.' In his answer Bernini shifted from the architectural to the religious field; he likened Borromini to a good heretic, to him less acceptable than a bad Catholic. This may have been a purely metaphorical manner of speech. On the other hand, knowing Bernini's love of puns, *double entendres* and overlaid meanings, we can be almost certain that for him, the religious conformist, Borromini's Gothic heresy was paralleled by religious heresy. See also Argan, *op. cit.*, p. 18 ff.

16 The house, traditionally regarded as Borromini's, is situated in Via Giulia facing the Vicolo Orbitelli. It was first described in *Arti e Lettere. Scritti raccolti da Francesco Gasparoni*, Rome, I, 1863, p. 23 (see also Luigi Mazio, *Studi storici letterari e filosofici*, Rome, 1872, pp. 355–57). It was completely 'overhauled' in 1937, but the original entrance remains; see Portoghesi, *op. cit.*, p. 373, note 1. Thelen (see postscript) locates Borromini's house to the north-west, rather than to the south, of S. Giovanni de' Fiorentini.

17 Apart from some fifty plaster casts, among them one of a life-size lion, he owned about an equal number of original sculptures and *bozzetti*, more than 130 paintings, many drawings and manuscripts, medals, coins and fragments of Roman inscriptions; there were also pieces of polished marble, small pieces of jewellery made of pearls, corals and amber; there were crystals and sea-shells; see the sensitive discussion in Portoghesi, *op. cit.*, pp. 374–78; and Guglielmo de Angelis D'Ossat, 'Francesco Borromini e la mole vallicelliana', in *L'Oratorio di S. Filippo Neri. Rassegna di cultura e arte oratoriana*, XXIV, no. 3, p. 45 ff. The inventory also mentions wax models of most of Borromini's buildings, and this attests to the correctness of Baldinucci's information who writes (p. 139): 'in order that his models should turn out completely correct,

he made them of wax, and sometimes of clay, with his own hands.'

18 In various sections of the inventory the books are lumped together in ten lots ranging from 4 to 293 items; 933 items in all.

19 Once only has a lot been characterized: *'libri 123 in foglio d'Architettura e scritti'.* This figure shows that Borromini must have owned almost every architectural treatise that had appeared up to his time not only in Italy but also in France, Spain and Germany.

20 Of course, in the seventeenth century these disciplines would have included works on astrology, number symbolism and mysticism, hermetism, hieroglyphics, emblematics, etc.; and I would venture a guess that all these fields were represented in Borromini's library.

21 See L. Montalto, in *Palladio*, N.S. VIII, 1958, p. 165; *'si lasciava vedere ora nelle librerie di Piazza Navona, scartellando, senza porre il piede nella fabbrica.'*

22 *Opus Architectonicum*, Rome, 1725, Preface.

23 'For the inconvenience he was causing her by wanting to be buried in her father's tomb.' This passage appears only in the original of the testament and not in the copy of the Archivio Capitolino.

24 'He wishes that his Body, having become a corpse, should be taken privately to the Church of San Giovanni de' Fiorentini in Rome, without being exhibited . . . and that for his Burial a Hundred candles should be given: but if his Body should be exhibited, the candles are to be given to another Church . . .' The stipulation not to have his body exhibited is mentioned by Pascoli, p. 304, but not by the other biographers.

25 *'Item lascia a M.ro fran.co Massari sc. Cinquecento m.ta in recognit.e delle grandi scommodi hauti, e fatighe fatte per lui . . .'* Massari had worked under Borromini at the façade of S. Carlo alle Quattro Fontane and supervised the work in S. Giovanni de' Fiorentini. Baldinucci, p. 139, mentions that it was Massari who 'out of pure concern for his [Borromini's] health had denied him a light'. The correctness of this fact is attested to by Borromini himself in the report referred to in note 1.

26 Not to be confused with the papal architect Domenico Castelli (d. 1658), who was *inter alia* responsible for the rebuilding of S. Girolamo della Carità (1652–58) and as early as the 1630s had worked with or rather under Borromini in S. Carlo alle Quattro Fontane (see Appendix II, under pp. 263–316).
One of the main beneficiaries was the Cardinal Ulderico Carpegna (d. 1679), an old friend and patron, who, on 14 October 1646, had consecrated the church of S. Carlino (O. Pollak, *Die Kunsttätigkeit under*

Urban VIII, Vienna, 1928, I, pp. 49, 115 ff.); at about the same time Borromini rebuilt the family palace (E. Hempel, *Francesco Borromini*, Vienna, 1924, p. 127 ff.), now the seat of the Accademia di San Luca. As a sign of gratitude 'for endless benefits received' Borromini bequeathed to him, apart from 2,000 scudi, 'his two gold Necklaces, one of which is plaited, and has an ornate cross, which he wore around his neck in holy memory of His Holiness Innocente X, who had presented him with the robe of Knight of Christ, with the two small gold Crosses . . .'; furthermore, the silver, the marble inscriptions, six pictures and the terracotta Christ at the Column 'varnished to imitate bronze, made by the hand of a skilful man'. Finally, the will stipulates that the Cardinal advise Bernardo Borromini in investing about 8,000 scudi in government debentures (*'monti Camerali e non vacabili'*).—Once again, Baldinucci (p. 139) shows himself very well informed.

27 Moreover, he requested Bernardo to study architecture: '. . . makes him his sole heir and he verbally nominated his nephew Sig.r Bernardo Castel Boromino, son of the late Domenico, on condition, however, that he must take as his wife a daughter of the above-mentioned Sig.a Giovanna Maderno, daughter of the above-mentioned dearly remembered Sig.r Carlo Maderno, and must live in Rome in order to study architecture . . .' Giovanna Maderno was born in 1621 to Maderno's third wife, Elisabetta Malucci. Only Pascoli (p. 305) mentions that the name of Giovanna's daughter was Maddalena; he also informs us that Giovanna was married to the *Capitano* Giovanfrancesco Pupi. If Donati (in *Urbe*, VII, 1942, no. 7, p. 21) had read Pascoli he would not have given play to his imagination and suggested that Maddalena might have been Borromini's natural daughter. Pascoli further reports that Bernardo was twenty at the time of Borromini's death, that the marriage was contracted (as requested in the testament) and that Bernardo settled down to a leisurely life enjoying the money left to him by his uncle.

28 *Storia de Milano*, Vol. X: 'L'età della riforma cattolica' (1559–1630), Milan, 1957, p. 14: 'Neither Philip II nor his immediate successors Philip III (1598–1621) and Philip IV (1621–65) . . . ever ceased to consider Milan not only as a pearl of the crown, but as a possession necessary both for the maintenance of the other Italian dominions and the Spanish pre-eminence in Italy . . .'; also pp. 19, 71 and passim. In Rome, Borromini must have proudly referred to his Milanese upbringing; otherwise it is hard to understand why he is called 'Milanese' in the well-informed *Ritratto di Roma* of 1645, p. 515. Baglione (1642) calls him 'Lombardo' (see note 78). At the official interrogation on his deathbed (see note 1) he is recorded as son of the

Milanese Domenico (*'Eques Franciscus Boromini q. Dominici mediolonensis'*).

29 F. Gregorovius, *Urban VIII im Widerspruch zu Spanien und dem Kaiser*, Stuttgart, 1879. Gregorovius prints a report by Fulvio Testi, the Roman agent of the Duke of Modena, dated 12 January 1633, in which Testi writes (p. 157): 'The Pope is of a nature more French than any citizen of Paris.' See also the relevant passages in Pastor, *Geschichte der Päpste*, XIII, 1, 1928.

30 In his Roman diary, Giacinto Gigli reports a number of incidents, also between the Spaniards and the French; see Gigli, *Diario romano (1608–1670)*, ed. Giuseppe Ricciotti, Rome, 1958: 8 April 1636 (p. 162); Fight between Spaniards and French in Piazza Navona; the disorder lasted several days.—25 June 1646 (p. 286): The Spaniards kill seven Frenchmen in a brawl inside the monastery of S. Giacomo degli Spagnuoli.—14 April 1650 (p. 354 ff.): Riot during a procession; 'the Spaniards said that the riot had been against them' . . . July 1650 (p. 367): The people of Rome are up in arms against the increase in food prices which they attribute to the fact that the Pope (i.e., Innocent X), 'who was fond of the Spaniards', had sent them victuals as a support in their struggle against the French. This affair led to a public revolt against the Spaniards. See also Pastor (*Geschichte der Päpste*, XIV, i, p. 47) about the bloody skirmish between Spaniards and French on 29 April 1646.

31 E.g., the Procurator General of the monastery of S. Carlo alle Quattro Fontane, Fra Giovanni di S. Bonaventura, and, above all, the Spanish Ambassador Extraordinary, Marchese di Castel Rodrigo (also Rodriguez), to whom Borromini dedicated the *Opus Architectonicum*; see Appendix III. Virgilio Spada apparently had a Spanish background; as a youth he had enrolled in the Spanish army in Lombardy; see Card. Franz Ehrle, 'Dalle carte e dai disegni di Virgilio Spada', in *Atti della Pontifica Accademia Romana di Archeologia*, Serie III, Memorie II, Rome, 1928, p. 3. With the rebuilding of the Palazzo di Spagna Borromini entered the service of the Spanish Crown. According to Pascoli (I, p. 301) King Philip IV rewarded him with a handsome sum of money and the decoration of the Order of St James. The information is correct, for Borromini had in his estate two gold chains (see note 26), one of which belonged to the Cross of the order of Cavaliere, while the second must have belonged to the Spanish Order.

32 René Taylor, 'Architecture and Magic', in *Essays in the History of Architecture Presented to Rudolf Wittkower*, London, 1967, p. 87.

33 For general information about melancholy and astrology, see Rudolf and Margot Wittkower, *Born under Saturn*, London, 1963, chap, V. For further study, R. Klibansky, E. Panofsky and F. Saxl, *Saturn*

and Melancholy, London, 1964, particularly Part II.—Black had, of course always been associated with Saturn and hence with melancholy. These matters were even available in treatises on art; see, e.g., Paolo Lomazzo, *Trattato dell'arte della pittura*, Milan, 1584 (ed. Rome, 1844, II, p. 427 ff.): 'Black signifies melancholy, sadness, grief, gravity and steadfastness, and its deity is Saturn.'

34 The literature on this problem is vast. A good introduction: Richard Mott Gummere, *Seneca the Philosopher and his modern Message*, London, 1922.

35 Lipsius' stoic publications began with his *De constantia*, 1583; later he published a critical edition of Seneca's works: *L. Annaei Senecae Philosophi Opera*, Antwerp, 1605. Further to the problem of neo-Stoicism, Léontine Zanta, *La renaissance du stoicisme au XVIe siècle*, Paris, 1914 and Jason L. Saunders, *Justus Lipsius*, New York, 1955.

36 For this and other problems of Borromini's stoicism, see Appendix IV.

37 Passeri, p. 366: '*si compiacque di vivere sempre a se stesso con libertà, e con quiete d'animo*'. For the other passages to which reference is made in the text, see notes 8–11.

38 See note 15.

39 Passeri, p. 360: 'during the lunch and dinner breaks, withdrawn and alone, he carefully drew many parts of the famous Temple of St Peter, for, he said, he was enamoured of the ingenious architecture of Michel'Angelo Buonaruoti, and he made a special study of it'.—Baldinucci, p. 133, embellishes the story: 'that is, during this time allotted for the afternoon break when the others went to eat or to play quoits, he would enter that great Basilica, and begin to draw . . .'

40 Passeri and Baldinucci, *loc. cit.* Passeri (p. 360) states that the family relation between Borromini and Maderno was through the female line ('*per cagione di donna*') and the author of the Magliabechiano *Vita* makes the same assertion. While this is essentially correct, the exact family bonds between the two have only recently been clarified. See H. Hibbard, *Carlo Maderno*, London, 1971, p. 100 ff.

41 One is, of course, inclined to date these studies very early, in any case before 1622, but H. Thelen, in *70 disegni di Francesco Borromini dalle collezioni dell'Albertina di Vienna*, Catalogue, Rome, 1958–59, nos. 2–4, for reasons not revealed by him, dates them much later, between *c.* 1624 and 1628.. In Thelen's *Catalogue*, 1967, nos. 74–76 (see Postscript) the three drawings are dated about 1627–28.

42 N. Caflisch, *Carlo Maderno*, Munich, 1934, p. 141, note 102.

43 This fact is differently reported by the biographers. Passeri (p. 360) is least emphatic; he only says that Maderno used Borromini for translating his sketches into measured drawings. Baldinucci (p. 133), and, following him, Pascoli, attribute to Borromini a more important share: 'Maderno, who was already weighed down with age, wanted Borromini, so that he had to abandon the craft of cutting stones altogether, and dedicate himself entirely to the art of architecture . . .'; p. 134: '*e molto anche si adoperò intorno a'disegni e modelli per lo palazzo Barberini*'.

44 Baldinucci toned down the much more outspoken account of the author of the MS *Vita* (Appendix I) who maintains that all Maderno's work in St Peter's and the Palazzo Barberini was executed by Borromini: 'Maderno, who was by now very old, left Borromino completely in charge of the said palazzo and the other works at St Peter's—delighted to have as a relative a young man such as this, who could take his place in his old age, carrying out drawings and work for him.' (The entire passage in Hempel, *op. cit.*, p. 21 ff.)

45 *Vite* . . ., Rome, 1649. The sentence referring to Borromini is missing in the first edition of 1642 and seems to have been added by the editor of the second edition; cf. A. Blunt, in *Journal of the Warburg and Courtauld Institutes*, XXI, 1958, p. 263 and note 22.

46 O. Pollak, *Kunsttätigkeit*, I, p. 251 ff.; Blunt, *op. cit.*, p. 259 ff., makes it likely that Maderno's first project dates from 1625, but the contracts with the craftsmen were not drawn up until January 1629, though work on the present building began in December 1628.

47 Pollak, *Kunsttätigkeit*, II, no. 1121 ff.

48 U. Donati, in *Urbe*, VII, 1942, no. 7, p. 21: 'Why Francesco Castelli at a certain point in his life decided to call himself Boromino, is a problem which still remains unsolved and which is perhaps not worth trying to solve . . .' A. Muñoz, in *Scritti in onore di Bartolomeo Nogara*, Vatican City, 1937, p. 318: 'it was not until 1628, perhaps to distinguish himself from the many other Castellis from the same district, that he began to give himself the name, which I believe was his mother's, of Borromini'. Similarly, Portoghesi, *op. cit.*, p. 33 suggests that he changed his name because he wanted to distinguish himself from others with the same surname.

49 Corrado Ricci in his Preface (p. vii) to the Italian edition of Hempel's book also introduced Carlo Borromeo in this context: '"borromei" or "borromini" were used to describe those Swiss belonging to the Golden League of the Seven Cantons of Catholic Switzerland, the league being called "borromea" because it was founded under the auspices of Carlo Borromeo. Francesco Castello, born at Bissone, on Lake Lugano, was therefore a "borromino" . . .'.

50 As suggested by authors quoted in note 48.

51 M. Del Piazzo has discovered documentary proof that Radi was married to Bernini's sister; he was therefore brother-in-law to Bernini and not to Borromini.

52 Pollak, *Kunsttätigkeit*, I, nos. 132–56.

53 The following list extracted from Pollak's two volumes gives an idea of their collaboration: *1626–31*: Quirinal Palace (I, nos. 1068–71, 1185, 1186); *1626–32*: Vatican Palace (I, nos. 1259–66, 13252–56); *1626–28*: Pantheon (I, nos. 597, 598, 603–6); *1627–29*: St Peter's (II, nos. 1120 ff., 1628 ff., 2360–61, 2393–95); *1629–32*: Palazzo Barberini (I, nos. 859, 887–92); *1631*: St Peter's (II, nos. 446, 450).

54 Passeri, p. 361.—Baldinucci (p. 134), viewing the situation as Bernini's partisan, says 'it was not difficult [for Borromini] to approach Bernini himself, and not only learn from him some useful lessons in art, but also to be used a great deal in tasks connected with the position held by Bernini', and he claims to have no knowledge of the reasons for the break between the two.

In the *Vita del Cav. G. L. Bernino*, 1682, p. 81, Baldinucci is even more outspoken: 'The Cavaliere [i.e. Bernini] employed Borromini many years in the House of our Creator [i.e. St Peter's] to learn the art of architecture, and he became a very practised Master, except for the fact that in trying to innovate too much in the decoration of Buildings, following his own whims, sometimes breaking the rules [of architecture], he came too near the Gothic manner.' See also Baldinucci's damnatory comments, note 76.

55 For this *Vita*, see Appendix I. The most important passages run as follows: Bernini 'knowing that Boromino had done the fabric of St Peter's for Maderno and that, also for Maderno, he had supervised and executed the Palazzo Barberini—begged him not to leave him on that occasion—promising him that he would acknowledge his hard labours with a fitting recompense . . . and Bernini attended to his sculpture, while as far as architecture was concerned, he left all the work to Boromino; and Bernino made himself out to be the architect of St Peter's and the Pope's architect—while in fact Bernino at that time was a complete beginner in that art . . . Bernino drew the stipends and wages, and he never gave anything at all to Boromino for all those years of toil—only kind words and great promises, and Boromino, seeing himself deceived and derided, left Bernino, abandoned him—with these words: "I do not mind him having the money but I do mind that he should enjoy the honour for my hard work" . . .' The last sentence fits very well into the impression we have won of Borromini's character; the gist of the accusation was probably often repeated in the company of

intimates.—The entire passage was published by Hempel, *op. cit.*, pp. 11–12.

56 The documents supply evidence that Borromini had to abandon much of his mason's work after 1629. Thus, from March 1628 onwards he is paid, together with Radi, for work on the tribuna niches of St Peter's, but in November 1628 he drops out of the accounts (Pollak, II, nos. 2358–61, 2370); for work on the tomb of Urban VIII he received payments until December 1629 (Pollak, II, nos. 2393–5), while Radi carried on alone; he disappears from the accounts of the niche of St Andrew under the dome after April 1629 (Pollak, II, nos. 1628 ff.), etc. But he continued to work through most of 1630 in the Cappella di S. Sebastiano, the niche of Veronica and elsewhere.

57 Pollak, I, no. 867: final payment for drawings and models. Borromini, however, continued to serve the palace in his capacity as stonemason until the autumn of 1632 (*ibid.*, no. 892).

58 *Ibid.*, II, nos. 1274 ff., 1287.

59 Niccola Ratti, *Notizie della chiesa interna dell'Archiginnasio Romano*, Rome, 1833, p. 19 ff. Pollak, *Kunsttätigkeit*, I, p. 160, no. 506.

60 The contracts with the master bricklayer (*capo mastro muratore*) and the master mason (*capo mastro scarpellino*) date from 6 July 1634, i.e., before this date not only the drawings but also all the specifications had to be ready and approved.—All the documents for S. Carlo alle Quattro Fontane in Pollak, I, pp. 36–116.

61 Hempel, *op. cit.*, p. 66.

62 *Ibid.*, p. 62; see also Portoghesi's Preface to his facsimile edition (1964) and his contribution to *Essays in the History of Architecture presented to Rudolf Wittkower*, London, 1967, pp. 128–33; Giovanni Incisa della Rocchetta, *L'oratorio borrominiano nella descrizione del P. Virgilio Spada* ('Quaderni dell'Oratorio', 13, XXX, 1967). For the part played by Spada in the construction of the Oratory, see *Opus architectonicum*, 1725, p. 9: '. . . many drawings done, each one censored [i.e., criticized] by Father Virgilio Spada . . .', and Passeri, p. 361 ff.: 'The Fathers . . . put Borromini in charge [of the building], and the promoter [of this appointment] was Father Virgilio Spada who was delighted with Boromini's precision and diligence . . .'

63 For Virgilio Spada's life, see especially Ehrle (note 31) and Carlo Gasbarri d.O., *L'Oratorio romano dal cinquecento al novecento*, Rome, 1963, pp. 169–71.

64 *Opus architectonicum*, Preface: 'Prego . . . a riflettere che ho avuto a servire una Congregazione d'animi così rimessi, che nell'ornare mi hanno tenuto le mani, e conseguentemente mi è convenuto in più luoghi obedire più al voler loro, che all'arte . . . e se in alcuna cosa eccedei qualche poco

la regola prescrittami, per un pezzo udij dei brontoli.'

65 Hempel, *op. cit.*, p. 86; Adolfo Pernièr, 'Documenti inediti sopra un'opera del Borromini. La fabbrica dei Filippini a Monte Giordano', in *Archivi d'Italia*, Series II, ii, 1935, p. 206.

66 Hempel, p. 94 ff. It is true, Borromini's restoration remained fragmentary; the vault planned by him over the nave was never carried out, see H. Thelen, in *Kunstchronik*, VII, 1954, p. 264 ff. In addition, the remarks of Giovanni di S. Bonaventura in his MS history of S. Carlino (see Appendix II): Borromini 'was obliged by our Signore to preserve the old form of the church, nor was he allowed to vault it, for the old ceiling was to remain' (Pollak, *Kunsttätigkeit*, I, p. 42).

67 Papal *chirografo* of 15 April 1646; see Hempel, p. 97.

68 Cesare Rasponi, *De Basilica et Patriarchio Lateranensi*, Rome, 1656, p. 81: 'And so [Innocent X] placed Francesco Borromini, the famous architect of our times, in charge of the work that was to be done, and he added as general adviser and arbiter Virgilio Spada, member of the Congregation of the Oratory, his Groom of the Bedchamber [*interior Cubicularius*] and Papal Almoner [*elemosinarum Praefectum*], and a man of the most consummate judgment.'

69 For the history of S. Agnese, see Hempel, p. 138 ff.; R. Wittkower, *Art and Architecture in Italy 1600 to 1750*, Pelican History of Art, 1965, p. 140 ff., with further literature; and, above all, Lina Montalto, 'Il drammatico licenziamento di Francesco Borromini dalla fabbrica di Sant'Agnese in Agone', in *Palladio*, N.S. VIII, 1958, pp. 139–88. Based on a wealth of new documents, she has skilfully disentangled the events of the critical years 1653–57. The following facts and quotations are abstracted from the documents published by her.

70 From the summer of 1655 onwards Don Camillo was alone responsible for the continuation of building activity; see Montalto, p. 141 ff., 148 and note 24.

71 *Ibid.*, p. 162, doc. X: '22 January 1657. Since Santini, Procurator of the fabric of S. Agnese has reported that for over a month Cav. Borromini has not been to see the fabric and to give orders . . . and that . . . he spends his time on all his important jobs and that on many occasions the multitude of works he has on hand have caused him to give differing and contradictory orders . . .'. From the document giving the reasons for Borromini's dismissal (p. 164, doc. XIII): 'Very few wished to have any more dealings with him, fearing that he would throw indecisive orders at them . . . He neglected his work, and others were blamed for it.' It was also pointed out that when faults in the foundations were mentioned to him 'he gave no other

satisfactory excuse but that he was persecuted'—a characteristic reference to his persecution mania.

72 From Imperiali's statement (p. 163, doc. XI): '. . . nelle mani di quell'Architetto si credea impossibile (di finire la fabbrica) . . . è stata una meraviglia, che S.a Ecc.a [i.e., Don Camillo] habbia potuto haverci pazienza tanti mesi, essendo intrattabile la natura di tal huomo'. For the correct date of this document, see Montalti, p. 160, note 30. Cardinal Lorenzo Imperiali (d. 1673) had not only as papal '*tesoriere*' but also as '*comprotettore della fabbrica*' an authoritative voice in the deliberations.

73 'Si è licenziato il Borromini per non esser possibile durar seco per la sua natura difficile, inflessibile' (p. 164, doc. XIII).

74 In support of this assessment I quote at random (in addition to the quotations in notes 71–73) the following passages from the documents. One of the reasons for his dismissal: 'because after two months there was still no sign of the drawings for the fabric' (p. 164, doc. XIII). Moreover, Borromini 'has made enemies of all the workmen; he has never sent them money, and in desperation they have all sued' (p. 165, doc. XIV). 'The orders which the Cavaliere gave to the masons and masterbuilders led one to suppose that either he had not established what the building was to be like, or that he had neglected to adjust the drawing, because every day, and almost from one moment to the next, he changed the orders themselves in such an uncertain and irresolute manner that after several very experienced workers had given in their notice, the rest were on the point of leaving, fed up with such an unstable manner of directing Architecture' . . . (*ibid.*). And finally: when one wanted to consult him, he had gone home and if one went there 'one was told he was not there, though in fact he was' (*ibid.*).

75 In any case, until about a year before his dismissal Borromini's expertise cannot be questioned, even though on the face of it everything seemed to point to the contrary. When his difficulties increased, he compiled, apparently in self-defence, a meticulously detailed survey of all the work ('*Misura e stima*') executed under him in S. Agnese. This most impressive document, signed and dated 13 January 1656, covers no less than eighty-three manuscript pages and twenty printed pages in Montalti's paper (pp. 169–88). He handed this document over to Pope Alexander VII and, it seems, deposited a copy with Virgilio Spada (p. 163, doc. X), but obstinately refused to let Don Camillo see it or anyone else connected with the building.

76 The tragedy of the towers has often been recorded; cf. Wittkower, *op. cit.*, p. 126, note 71, with further literature. In addition, see S. Fraschetti, *Il Bernini*, Milan, 1900, p. 165, and Hempel, p. 91 ff.

At the most critical moment the towers were discussed in five sessions of the *Congregazione generale della Rev. Fabbrica* (27 March 1645–23 February 1646); see Ehrle (note 31), p. 22 ff. For the negative reception of Borromini's criticism, referred to in my text, see Baldinucci, pp. 134–5: 'indeed, this craftsman [i.e. Borromini] received little praise for treating the master [Bernini] in this certainly none too seemly manner'. In addition, see the long expositions in Baldinucci's *Vita del Cav. G. L. Bernini*, 1682, pp. 24–29, and in Domenico Bernini's Life of his father (*Vita del Cav. Gio. Lorenzo Bernini*, Rome, 1713, pp. 76–80) which in parts correspond literally (Baldinucci claiming that his text was based on documents in the Archive of the Fabbrica). Both report that the true reason for Borromini's excessive criticism was his desire to succeed Bernini as architect to St Peter's. Baldinucci: 'In the opinion of many, all this warring was waged not so much for lack of affection for the person of Bernino . . . as for the desire . . . that the Pope should on this account take a dislike to our Craftsman, that he should allow Borromino, who had been Bernino's Pupil, but to say the truth, not a very grateful one, to succeed him in the position of Architect of the great Fabric, because . . . only in the presence of the Pope did he inveigh against him [i.e. Bernini] with all his heart, and with all his energy . . .' In Domenico Bernini's words, Borromini had learned the rules of architecture from Bernini, but had 'degenerated into an altogether different manner, and at the same time he made himself very disagreeable to the Master . . . because of the propitious circumstances mentioned, he had the idea of using all his powers to occupy Bernini's position as First Architect to the Great Fabric of St Peter's,' but did not succeed.

77 Bertolotti, *Art. lomb.* (*op. cit.*, note 1), p. 32 ff.

78 Among Bellori's marginal notes in the copy of Baglione's 1642 edition in the library of the Accademia dei Lincei, Rome (used for the facsimile edition of Baglione's *Vite*, ed. Valerio Mariani, Rome, 1935, p. 180). Baglione's favourable mention of S. Carlino (*'bella chiesetta, la quale è leggiadra, e capricciosa architettura di Francesco Borromini Lombardo'*) received Bellori's comment: '*brutta e deforma. Gotico ignorantissimo e corruttore dell'Architettura, infamia del nostro secolo'.* For the 'Gothic' quality of Borromini's architecture, see also notes 15, 54.

79 The MS is in the archive of the monastery of S. Carlo alle Quattro Fontane, Vol. 77. For further details, see Appendix II.

80 Pollak, *Kunsttätigkeit*, I, p. 40: 'But where the said Sig.r Francesco showed himself to be the nephew of that most skilful Architect Carlo Maderna . . . was in

the fabric of the Church of this Convent . . .'

81 *Ibid.*, p. 48: Borromini's rivals say in order to 'obscure or diminish the glory which is due to his fabrics . . .: that his fabrics are beautiful, but that they are very costly; the first . . . everyone says so, even his Rivals, and it is true; but the second is false: as can clearly be seen in the fabric of this church' . . .—p. 40: That S. Carlino is the most extraordinary church 'in the whole world . . . is proved by the people of various nations who on arriving in Rome continually ask to have the design: often we are asked . . . by Germans, Flemings, Frenchmen, Italians, Spaniards and even Indians . . . and the said Sig.r Francesco . . . is continually pestered both by foreigners and Italians to have this design'. Fra Giovanni returns twice to the same story (not published by Pollak), once where he says (p. 45 of MS) that all those foreigners who come to see the church 'do nothing but gaze above them and move round the whole church because all its features are arranged in such a way that the one calls attention the next, and the observer is struck by one thing in such a way that he then considers another'—a fine observation which catches the essence of Borromini's innovation; and a second time (p. 45, not in Pollak), where a French *Padre* asks for the design and Fra Giovanni answers him: 'I wished to have the design to send it to Spain . . . and even though Sig.r Francesco Borromino, the architect of this church, is my Benefactor, and for more than six years I have been begging him, it has been impossible to obtain this favour . . .'.

82 *Ibid.*, p. 40: Borromini 'has always been most generous and in his fabrics and works he has acted in a completely disinterested way; we can vouch for many instances, but in particular we can affirm that in the case of our fabric he never wished to receive a *giulio*'. It will be recalled that this is a point also made by the biographers (see note 10); their reliability is confirmed by the present text.

83 *Ibid.*, p. 41: '*qualsivoglia persona de buon sapere che vol fabricare, non si sodisfà di altro che di d° Sr Francesco'.* As a proof of this assertion there follow the passages on the Oratory of St Philip Neri and S. Giovanni in Laterano.

84 *Ibid.*, p. 48: '*lui medesimo governa al murator la cuciara; driza al stuchator il cuciarino, al falegname la sega, et il scarpello al scarpellino; al matonator la martellina et al ferraro la lima: Di modo che il Valor delle sue fabriche è grande; ma non la spesa come censura li suoi emuli'.*

85 Hempel, p. 61.

86 Further to the problem opened up by this date, see Appendix III, a–c.

87 These terms appear in chapters 6, 7, 11 and 26 of *Opus architectonicum*.

88 *Opus Architectonicum*, Preface to the Reader: '*nell' inventare cose nuove, non si puo ricevere il frutto della fatica se non tardi'.*

89 The reader will notice that this statement, as well as the opinions expressed in the next paragraph, are utterly at variance with Sedlmayr's results, to which I referred at the beginning of this paper.

IX Guarini the Man

1 *Le vite de' piu celebri architetti*, Rome, 1768. Translated from the fourth edition, which has the title *Memorie degli architetti antichi e moderni*, Bassano, 1785, II, p. 199.

2 *Dizionario degli architetti, scultori, pittori . . .*, Milan, 1831, II, pp. 223–24.

3 'Il Padre Guarino Guarini', in *Atti e memorie della R. Deputazione di Storia Patria per le provincie modenesi e parmensi*, V, 1888, pp. 483–534.

4 Vol. VI, i, p. 68 ff.

5 Terzaghi, in *Atti del X Congresso di Storia dell'Architettura*, Rome, 1959, p. 396 ff., believes that possibly Guarini went to Lisbon between 1656 and 1659 to carry out his project for the church of S. Maria della Divina Providenza.

6 On Sainte-Anne-la-Royale see David R. Coffin, in *Journal of the Society of Architectural Historians*, XV, ii, 1956, pp. 3–11.

7 Sieur de Chantelou, *Journal du voyage du Cavalier Bernin en France*, ed. L. Lalanne, Paris, 1885, p. 33.

8 All the material concerning Wren's stay in Paris was published by Margaret Whinney, in *Gazette des Beaux Arts*, LI, 1958, pp. 229–42. It is interesting that Wren gives a list of architects in Paris, mentioning Bernini, Mansart, Le Vau, Le Pautre and even the minor Jean Gobert, but not Guarini. In a memorandum of 1 May 1666 Wren speaks of the buildings he had seen in Paris, 'while they were in rising, conducted by the best artists, French and Italian . . .'. It is probable that he was referring to Sainte-Anne-la-Royale. See the interesting analysis by Portoghesi in *Critica d'Arte*, 1957, note 20, p. 114 ff.

9 For Guarini's literary career see E. Olivero, 'Gli scritti del Padre Guarino Guarini', in *Il Duomo di Torino*, II, 1928, no. 6, pp. 5–9.

10 See Andreina Griseri, *Le metamorfosi del Barocco*, Turin, 1967, p. 211, note 2.

11 See the masterly edition of *Architettura civile*, Milan, 1968, provided by Nino Carboneri, with an ample introduction, complete bibliography and copious notes. See also Daria De Bernardi Ferrero, *I 'Disegni d'architettura civile et ecclesiastica' di Guarino Guarini e l'arte del Maestro*, Turin, 1966, which contains many penetrating remarks and is important for its discussion of the controversy between Guarini and Caramuel. The same author

has published the only modern work on Caramuel, in *Palladio*, 1965, pp. 91–110.

12 E. Olivero, 'Il Padre Guarino Guarini teologo del Principe di Carignano', in *Il Duomo di Torino*, II, 1928, note 4, pp. 22–24.

13 *Architettura civile, Trattato I*, Capo III, Oss. 3.

14 *Tratt. I*, Capo III, Oss. 11.

15 *Tratt. II*, Capo VII, Oss. 9.

16 *Tratt. I*, Capo III, Oss. 6.

17 *Ibid.*

18 *Tratt. I*, Capo III, Oss. 9.

19 *Tratt. III*, Capo III.

20 *Tratt. III*, Capo III, Oss. 1.

21 Guarini himself always stresses the supreme importance of reason, free from all passions. See also Carboneri's note 1 to p. 17 of his edition of the *Treatise*.

22 *Tratt. II*, Capo VII, Oss. 5.

23 *Tratt. II*, Capo VIII, Oss. 1.

24 *Tratt. III*, Capo XXV, Oss. 1.

25 *Tratt. III*, Capo XIII, Oss. 1.

26 *Tratt. IV*, Introduction. There is a splendid article by Werner Müller on the mathematics of *Trattato IV*: 'The Authenticity of Guarini's Stereotomy in his *Architettura civile*', in *Journal of the Society of Architectural Historians*, XXVII, 1968, pp. 203–8.

27 P. 165.

28 *Tratt. I*, Capo III, Oss. 7.

29 *Tratt. I*, Capo III, Introduction.

30 *Tratt. I*, Capo II, Oss. 3.

31 Henry Millon, *Baroque and Rococo Architecture*, New York, 1961, p. 20.

32 Paolo Portoghesi, *Guarino Guarini*, Milan, 1956.

33 Sandonnini, *op. cit.*, p. 505.

34 In the dedication of *Euclides*.

X A Sketchbook of Filippo Juvarra at Chatsworth

1 I wish to thank His Grace the Duke of Devonshire and his librarian and curator, my friend Francis Thompson, for permission to publish in the *Bollettino Società Piemontese d'Archeologia e di Belli Arti* this new contribution to the knowledge of Juvarra's works.

2 Albertina, Vienna. Rovere-Viale-Brinckmann, *Filippo Juvarra*, Milan, published for the City of Turin, 1937, Vol. I, p. 116, pl. 6.

3 *Ibid.*, p. 158 and pls. 7, 9.

4 Turin, Museo Civico, Vol. I, pp. 21–23, 26, 28–30, 63, 64, 67, 68. Rovere-Viale-Brinckmann, *op. cit.*, pls. 18–23. The dimensions of these drawings correspond with those at Chatsworth (approx. 22·5 cm

× 33·5 cm); however, the dimensions of four of them (pp. 63, 64, 67, 68) are slightly different (22·3 cm × 34·7 cm).

5 Rovere-Viale-Brinckmann, pp. 117, 162 and pls. 24–30. One drawing dated 1730 proves that the series, at least in part, had been executed before 1732.

6 See also Rovere-Viale-Brinckmann, *op. cit.*, pl. 27.

7 *Cf.* for example the lighthouse of Alexandria, in the engraving by Martin de Vos, in his series *The Seven Wonders of the World*.

8 Well known from the many editions of Palladio's *Quattro Libri*.

9 Vol. VI, no. 49.

10 Reproduced in Rovere-Viale-Brinckmann, pl. 28.

11 Also in the Dresden sketchbook. Rovere-Viale-Brinckmann, *op. cit.*, pl. 27.

12 For example in the editions of the *Descrizione di Roma antica*. On fol. 26 there is a large monument with a gryphon. Juvarra used it also in the Dresden volume, no. 37; and, less prominently, in no. 15 of the Chatsworth album. It seems to derive from classical monuments such as the frieze of the Trajan Forum with facing gryphons and candelabra.

13 The same group was used in other drawings: Turin, Museo Civico, Vol. I, p. 58 and Dresden, no. 5.

14 The she-wolf is also in Dresden, no. 29. A similar architectural arrangement is in Dresden, no. 21.

15 The Dioscuri seen from behind appear in Dresden, no. 21.

16 Rovere-Viale-Brinckmann, p. 117 and pl. 23.

17 *Archit. civ.*, especially p. 133.

18 A. E. Brinckmann, *Theatrum Novum Pedemontii*, Düsseldorf, 1931.

19 Burlington was the great-grand-nephew of the famous scientist Robert Boyle who died in 1691.

20 Chatsworth, MS 75A.

21 Rovere-Viale-Brinckmann, *op. cit.*, p. 55.

22 *Ibid.*, p. 56.

23 On the subject of Juvarra's stay in Rome see the note published in the *Bollettino Societa Piemontese d'Archeologia e di Belli Arti*, III, 1949, p. 153.

24 He signed sketches for an altar 'Rome, 24 Feb. 1715', and later a detail of the dome of the Pantheon '27 March 1715'. See Rovere-Viale-Brinckmann, *op. cit.*, p. 59 and pl. 104.

25 See on Kent: M. Jourdain, *William Kent*, London, 1948 and R. Wittkower, in *The Archaeological Journal*, Vol. 102, 1947,

pp. 151–64. [Reprinted in R. Wittkower, *Palladio and English Palladianism*, 1974.—Ed.]

26 Leoni was born in Venice. As a young man he went to the Palatinate court and in about 1713 went to England where he remained until his death in 1746.

27 For fuller information on Campbell and the whole Burlington circle, see the article referred to in note 25.

28 Rovere-Viale-Brinckmann, *op. cit.*, p. 70.

29 These drawings, mostly unpublished, are now at the RIBA in London.

30 *Fabbriche Antiche disegnate da Andrea Palladio Vicentino e date in Luce da Riccardo Conte di Burlington*, London, 1730.

31 Cicognara, *Catalogo ragionato dei libri d'arte e d'antichità*, Pisa, 1821, Vol. I, no. 597. Cicognara confirms my theory that 'this first edition was presented by the publisher to the men of letters of his day'.

32 *Vita di Benvenuto Cellini . . . dedicata all'eccellenza di Mylord Riccardo Boyle, Conte di Burlington*, Cologne, Pietro Martello, 1728.

33 Chatsworth, 80D.

34 *L'architettura di Leonbattista Alberti*, Florence, 1550. Chatsworth, 81C.

35 Letter at Chatsworth.

36 Rovere-Viale-Brinckmann, *op. cit.*, p. 30.

37 Turin, National Library, Vol. VI, nos. 4, 49.

38 See *Wren Society*, Vol. XIX, p. 138 ff.

39 No. 49.

40 It cannot be ruled out however that both Hawksmoor and Juvarra might have found the prototype in the *Hypnerotomachia Poliphili* by Francesco Colonna (Venice, 1499).

41 See for example the drawings of non-European architecture in Fischer von Erlach, *Entwurf einer historischen Architektur*, 1725, which would certainly have been known to Juvarra.

42 All the documents concerning this mausoleum were published by G. Webb, in *Walpole Society*, Vol. XIX, p. 111 ff.

XI Vittone's Domes

1 Paolo Portughesi, *Bernardo Vittone*, Rome, 1966.

2 I refer here to the very extensive inventory compiled by several lawyers now in the Turin Archivio di Stato (Sez. II, libro II, Vol. I, p. 463 ff.), first excerpted by Eugenio Olivero, *Le opere di Bernardo Antonio Vittone*, Turin, 1920, p. 30, and now fully published by Paolo Portoghesi, *op. cit.*, p. 237 ff.; see particularly nos. 434, 761–66.

See also 'Descrizione, o sia Nota delle scritture spettanti all'Eredità del fu Sig. Architetto Bernardo Vittone' in the Archivio Comunale at Carignano, published by G. Rodolfo, 'Notizie inedite dell'architetto Bernardo Vittone', in Atti della Società Piemontese di Archeologia e Belle Arti, XV, 1933, p. 450.

3 R. Pommer, Eighteenth-Century Architecture in Piedmont, New York–London, 1967.

4 N. Carboneri and V. Viale, Mostra del Barocco Piemontese, Catalogo, Turin, 1963.

5 W. Oechslin, 'Un Tempio di Mosè . . .', in Boll. d'Arte, 3, 1967.

XII Vittone's Drawings in the Musée des Arts Décoratifs

1 These volumes were discovered and first mentioned to me by Sir Anthony Blunt.

2 Height of the volumes 50·5 cm, width 36·5 cm.

3 As a rule each drawing has its own number, but the two drawings mounted on the first page of the second volume have only one number (no. 133); on the other hand, there is no no. 234.

4 The librarian originally stated on the 'fly-leaf' of the first volume that the two volumes contain 233 drawings; but this number was crossed out and changed to 237 (corresponding to the pagination but not to the actual number of drawings).

5 The librarian noted that three sheets were transferred and, in fact, the present numbers 3433, 3434 and 3435 of the 'mixed' volume bear Cattaneo's signature. But it seems that, together with the three signed Cattaneo drawings, two other closely related drawings were removed from the Vittone volumes, viz. nos. 3431 and 3436. It is reasonable to conclude that these five drawings were originally located in the Vittone volumes under the missing nos. 4, 11, 55, 63, 234.

6 On nos. 8, 10, 19, 46, 66, 67, 115, 130, 166, 188, 194, 221, 236 the reading is uncertain owing to cutting; on nos. 13 and 215 only traces are preserved.

7 On nos. 94, 96, 162, 176 the reading is again uncertain; on nos. 12, 13, 203 there are only traces. The 111 sheets with ink numbers correspond to 121 modern numbers and the 118 sheets with red numbers to 128 modern numbers because in some cases two unconnected drawings on one large sheet were given two modern numbers, but only one old number.

8 These numbers never coincide, e.g., red 3, 4, 5 correspond to old ink 21, 22, 12 and old ink 19, 20 to red 12, 145, etc.

9 No. 3431 is old ink 199 and red 156 (crossed out and changed into 157). No. 3434 (signed 'Cataneo 1794') is red 195.

No. 3435 (signed 'Andrea Cattaneo fec. 1795') is red 194.

10 Once on copies after Carlo Fontana, corresponding to the modern nos. 200, 219, 223, 220, 9; and once on Vittone drawings corresponding to the modern nos. 51, 196, 29, 232, 1/2.

11 'Spidery' numbers on nos. 116 (old 186), 143 (old 193, crossed out in pencil and replaced by pencil no. 178; this number repeated in red, partly cut), 193 (old 185). Two old ink numbers appear on 51 (old 8, in the normal position, centred on the long side of the sheet, and spidery 115 in the lower right-hand corner); 53 (old 9 in the normal position and 10 in the top left corner); 155 (old 174 in the normal position and spidery 98 in the left bottom corner). With the possible exception of no. 193, all the drawings mentioned in this note are original designs by Vittone. The 'spidery' ink numbers, especially those not in the 'right' position, may be serial numbers used before 1770 in Vittone's collection.

12 E.g., no. 50—old ink 187, red 40; no. 51—old ink 8, red 48; no. 52—190 and 47; no. 53—9 and 49; no. 54—140 (crossed out and replaced by 141) and 53.

13 Cf. the following large sheets: nos. 61, 62—old ink 7, red 39; nos. 70, 71—86 and 36; nos. 72, 73—87 and 34; nos. 74, 75—58 and 38; nos. 86, 87—89 and 123; nos. 96, 97—34 and 131 (?).

14 No. 236 (old ink 171?, red 184). In a letter Dr Petzet mentioned to me that he has handed over his discovery to E. Hubala for publication in a forthcoming paper on Zuccalli.

15 'Ein unbekanntes Projekt Chiaveris für die Dresdener Hofkirche', Alte und Moderne Kunst, III, 4, 1958, p. 16, no. 197 (old ink 144, red 205) and no. 218 (old ink 145, red 206). In this case, as in others, the re-arrangement of 1903 broke up the connection between the two drawings which was preserved in the old sequence.

16 The plan corresponds to an engraving dated 1739 by Chiaveri's collaborator, Lorenzo Zucchi (E. Hempel, Gaetano Chiaveri, Dresden, 1955, fig. 14), but the section differs in some details from the engraved one (Hempel, fig. 20). The copyist had access to a section otherwise unrecorded. I have no doubt that the two drawings are by the copyist of the Fontana drawings.

17 No. 146 (old ink 148, red 204); no. 148 (red 203).

18 Nos. 177 and 182 (old ink 153). I am grateful to Dr Hager for communicating his important discoveries to me. He intends to publish the original projects, together with the other concorso material in the Accademia di S. Luca.

19 S. Carlo al Corso—no. 205 (red 192); S. Lorenzo—no. 187 (red 183).

20 Nos, 8, 9, 13, 14, 15, 19, 21, 22, 30, 33, 37, 41, 48, 67, 68, 83, 84, 85, 88, 89, 93, 101, 107, 108, 109, 111, 112, 114, 117, 131, 133, 139, 140, 141, 147, 150, 153, 154, 156, 157, 158, 161, 163, 164, 166–172, 174, 175, 176, 179, 181, 183, 188, 189, 191, 200, 202, 210, 211, 212, 214, 216, 219–224, 226, 227, 228.

In his paper 'Carlo Fontanas Entwurf für das Liechtensteinpalais', in Alte und Neue Kunst, II, 1957, no. 5, p. 16 ff. M. Petzet published no. 214, but left unmentioned the fact that nos. 133, 139, 150, 154, 156, 157, 158, 169 also represent the same Fontana project. Nor did he know the long series of Fontana's originals at Windsor, nos. 9552–9565, from which the 9 Paris drawings are copied.

21 Bibl. Estense, MS λ B.1.16; see Paris volumes nos. 131, 179, 188, 189, 200, 202, and also no. 153 (see above, note 20). I am much indebted to Dr Hager for this information.

22 Nos. 7, 10, 32, 34, 35, 42, 82, 86, 87, 90, 91, 92, 98, 102, 103, 105, 106, 110, 159, 180, 213, 215, 217.

23 No. 20 (altar, very Fontanesque, but with trabucchi, i.e. Piedmontese scale). However, the cut of this sheet indicates that it originally formed a larger sheet with no. 41, which shows an altar copied after Fontana 9498. (The plan above this altar, copied from Fontana 9739, belongs to no. 20 rather than 41.) In addition, nos. 24–28, 46, 96, 97, 134, 135, 151, 152, 178, 186, 192, 193, 201, 225.

24 This statement is a simplification. In reality some sheets combine Fontana and Vittone material; see p. 232.

25 Nos. 1–2 (one sheet), 3, 49, 50, 53, 54, 56, 57, 59, 81, 206.

26 Nos. 3, 5, 6, 9, 13, 16, 17, 23, 29, 32, 36, 38, 44, 50, 51, 52, 68, 90–93, 98–100, 106, 107, 110, 114, 120, 129, 138, 143, 145, 160, 165, 168 verso, 174, 181, 198, 199, 206, 206 verso, 207, 208.

27 Nos. 78, 122, 125, 132 and perhaps also 5, 7, 184.

28 Nos. 39, 40, 42, 43, 45, 60, 65, 66, 116, 155, 209, 229, 230.

29 Nos. 12, 47, 104.

30 Nos. 69–80 (for 78 see above, note 27), 94, 95, 123, 124, 126–128, 130, 162. Towers: 31, 184, 185; 184 close to Instruzioni elementari, pl. LXXV.

31 Nos. 18, 61, 62, 64, 113, 136, 137, 142, 144, 190, 196, 231, 232.

32 Counting no. 78 (see notes 27 and 30) only once.

33 Of the 13 sheets not accounted for, I regard the portals and doors on nos. 58, 118, 119, 121 as marginal Vittone drawings, while the remaining nine drawings are by different hands.

34 Nos. 7, 9, 13, 32, 42, 68, 90–93, 98, 106, 107, 110, 114, 168 verso, 174, 181. See above, notes 20, 22, 26, 27, 28.

35 Cf. above, p. 214, and notes 10, 11.

36 Cf. p. 228, and notes 54, 55.

37 The history of the Fontana volumes will be discussed in the forthcoming Windsor Catalogue by A. Braham and H. Hager. Robert Adam negotiated the deal; see John Fleming, *Robert Adam*, Harvard University Press, 1962, p. 297.

38 Cf. above, note 34.

39 The centre group with Faith and the skeleton, and the ground-plan—Fontana 9393; the two candle-holders—Fontana 9394; the armature top left—Fontana 9389 and 9403. There are altogether seven sheets with copies after Fontana's S. Antonio dei Portoghesi decoration. Apart from nos. 93 and 114, nos. 108 (F. 9396), 109 (F. 9369), 111 (F. 9370 or 9371), 112 (F. 9376 or 9377 and 9369), 181 (F. 9405).

40 See also the tomb design, *Istruzioni diverse*, pl. CVII top left, which is derived from Fontana 9905 (ill. in A. Braham, 'The Tomb of Christiana', *Analecta Reginensia*, I, Stockholm, 1966, fig. 11), but there is no copy after Fontana in the Paris volumes.

41 Cf. Henry A. Millon, 'Alcune osservazioni sulle opere giovanili di Bernardo Antonio Vittone', *Bollettino Piemontese della Società di Archeologia e Belle Arti*, XII–XIII, 1958–59 (offprint, p. 3).

42 Of course, none of the copies bears his signature.

43 Millon, *op. cit.*, and Paolo Portoghesi, *op. cit.*, p. 83 ff.

44 Cf. Nino Carboneri, in the catalogue of the *Mostra del Barocco Piemontese*, Turin, 1963, 'Architettura', no. 136, and Portoghesi, *loc. cit.*

45 For ill., cf. Portoghesi, figs. 1–6.

46 *Istruzioni elementari*, pl. LXXIII. The design also contains Borrominesque elements.

47 No. 230 (old ink 163, red 177). Unfortunately, I have not been successful in finding out whether this project was executed.

48 Cf. L. Rovere, V. Viale, A. E. Brinckmann, *Filippo Juvarra*, Milan, 1937, p. 95 ff.

49 Cardinal Annibale Albani had been Juvarra's patron for many years; cf. Brinckmann, *op. cit.*, p. 95 and *passim*.

50 For instance, one would not hesitate to attribute the altar drawings 21, 22, 41 to the same hand as no. 3435 (which is signed by Cattaneo), if they were not copies after Fontana's Windsor drawings 9494, 9495, 9498. Cattaneo was probably born in the mid-1760s (see below, p. 234), i.e., after the Fontana volumes had left Italy. One might also feel inclined to attribute to Cattaneo a

number of drawings in Fontana's manner such as nos. 24–28 and even the church design 198 and 199; but the latter design is in all likelihood an early project by Vittone for S. Maria Maddalena at Alba.

51 19 October 1705. Windsor Vol. 177, nos. 9807–59.

52 The peculiar oven at the top centre of the sheet represents the '*machina*' shown on F. 9855 which absorbed the fumes produced by the eight cannons of the catafalque.

53 In this case Vittone simply turned the pages of the volume copying page after page.

54 Windsor, Vols. 176 and 170.

55 E.g., no. 30 combines F. 9500 (Vol. 174) and 9717 (Vol. 176); no. 141, F. 9341 (Vol. 170) and 9735 (Vol. 176); no. 153, F. 9514, 9516 (Vol. 174) and Soane 33; no. 176, F. 9309 (Vol. 168), 9556 (Vol. 174) and Soane 23.

56 Cf., e.g., pls. XCIII (catafalques; for half of the plate see our pl. 299) and pl. CV (tombs). On occasions the engraved designs are so closely connected that they are not easily separated, e.g., on pl. XXVIII different designs with wrought iron railings are firmly joined; other examples are on pls. X and XI.

57 See above, note 16.

58 Cf. above, note 19. The underlying pencil drawing, not entirely drawn over in pen and ink, has auxiliary lines radiating from the centre, a typical Vittone device. I have not been able to trace the drawing he copied. It may be in the Bianconi Collection, Castello Sforzesco, Milan. For similar drawings of S. Lorenzo, cf. A. Calderini, Chierici, Cecchelli, *La basilica di S. Lorenzo*, 1951, pl. LXVI. On the verso of Vittone's drawing there are not easily decipherable pencil sketches of characteristically Vittonesque church plans.

59 Cf. e.g., Caprarola: *Istruzioni elementari*, pls. LXIV, LXVII, LXVIII, LXXIX; *Istruzioni diverse*, pl. XIX. Scala Regia: *Istruzioni elementari*, pl. LXXVIII; *Istruzioni diverse*, pl. XX; Four Rivers Fountain, Piazza Navona: *Istruzioni diverse*, pl. XXXV; and so forth.

60 *Istruzioni diverse*, pl. XXXII: '*casa di campagna*'. Fontana's originals of 1689: Windsor, nos. 9706–9712. A sheet by Vittone, no. 174, shows at the top the elevation after F. 9708; in the centre a plan after F. 9710 and below it a second plan after F. 9712. The same plan appears once again on Vittone's sheet no. 69. It is interesting that Portoghesi, *op. cit.*, p. 171, believed this project to be an original design by Vittone.

61 A large proportion of the 26 designs on pls. CIII–CVII are derived from Fontana. Vittone used at least 19 of his copies for these plates. It is not astonishing that Vittone was much attracted by Fontana's

decorative and 'pictorial' designs, i.e. by designs with a distinctly Baroque flavour (see pls. 297–99). Characteristically, he copied on large sheets (corresponding to the size of the originals) Fontana's series of projects for the Fontana Trevi made in 1706 for Pope Clement XI (Windsor, Vol. 169, nos. 9312–36). In the Paris drawings nos. 219–224 and 226–8, he made use of 15 originals.

62 Cf. Millon, *op. cit.*, note 17. Portoghesi, *op. cit.*, p. 219, dates the altar '*c.* 1730' without giving specific reasons. The drawing no. 38 (pl. 304) differs somewhat from the execution (see Portoghesi, fig. 64). The concept of the altar reveals the influence of the popular *Sacri Monti* sculpture on Vittone.

63 For the date, cf. Millon, *op. cit.* The engraving in *Istruzioni diverse*, pl. LXXI shows a different altar design, but the connection of the drawings with S. Chiara is confirmed by a drawing in the Museo Civico at Turin published by Carboneri, *op. cit.*, pl. 136 and Portoghesi, *op. cit.*, fig. 16.

64 In all the plans there appears a projecting wall next to the façade (belonging to an existing building). The engraving, *Istruzioni diverse*, pl. LXXII, shows this situation in reverse.

65 Portoghesi, *op. cit.*, p. 223 ff., no. 21, dates the building '*c.* 1750'. If my analysis is correct, this date would be much too late. It would seem tempting to connect the plan no. 209 with the same church, but this is not possible because the building is freestanding on all sides. This interesting project, which clearly reveals its derivation from Guarini's Cappella SS. Sindone, may be dated in the late 1730s.

66 Cf. *Istruzioni diverse*, pl. LXXIV.

67 They were designed in 1750 and executed in the following two years; cf. Portoghesi, *op. cit.*, p. 225, no. 28.

68 Ill. in Portoghesi, fig. 283 (with wrong date 1767). Engraved in *Istruzioni diverse*, pl. XC. Although the execution dates from 1761, the design must have been made some time before that year; cf. below, note 77. It may also be mentioned that the door design no. 129 corresponds to *Istruzioni diverse*, pl. XXIII (below, centre), and the side doors of the façade of S. Francesco.

69 Ill. in Portoghesi, fig. 278.

70 The whole sheet originally had the red number 120 (now on 44) and the old ink no. 90. The digits '9' and '0' were separated when the sheet was cut.

71 Communicated to me by Dr Hellmut Hager.

72 The two tabernacles on 44 have their counterparts on pls. XCV and XCVI of *Istruzioni diverse*, but are not directly connected with any of the illustrated designs.

73 Not a single sheet in the Paris volumes shows a layout similar to the plates of the publications.

74 Bibl. Reale, Varia 203. A bound volume of 135 pp., 44·5 cm × 28 cm. All the drawings are laid down on paper. Size of the drawings: 36·1 cm × 22·3 cm. The volume was exhibited at the *Mostra del Barocco Piemontese*; cf. Carboneri, *op. cit.*, p. 64, no. 176. A study of the volume announced by Carboneri had not appeared at the time of writing.

75 The title-page consists of an engraved cartouche with the following hand-written title: '*L'architetto civile volume originale delle opere del Signor Bernardo Vitone insigne allievo dell'Accademia di Roma MDCCLX*'. (The 'LX' of 1760 is super-imposed upon another figure that has been erased.) Bottom left: '*Babel sculpteur*'; centre: '*A Paris, chez Jacques Chéreau, rue St. Jacques au grand St. Remy*'. Vittone's idea of publishing in Paris was abandoned and both books came out in Lugano.

76 *Istruzioni diverse*, pls. XXIII, XXV, LIX, IC are not in the Turin volume.

77 Vittone's façade of S. Francesco at Turin and his altars inside the church are among the Turin drawings. The date *ante quem* for these projects is therefore 1760 (see above, note 68).

78 C. Brayda, L. Coli, D. Sesia, *Ingegneri e architetti del Sei e Settecento in Piemonte*, Turin, 1963, p. 28.

79 Luigi Mallè, *Le arti figurative in Piemonte*, Turin, 1961, p. 328.

80 *Ibid.*, p. 419.

81 The watermarks, for instance, require a thorough study. This task is now made difficult because a great number of the drawings have been laid down.

XIII Piranesi's Architectural Creed

1 *The Investigator. A Dialogue on Taste* (2nd ed., 1762). Cf. J. L. Caw in *The Walpole Society*, XXV, 1936–37, p. 67 ff. The problems of Piranesi's theories on art have never been properly dealt with, although much valuable material can be found in various books on Piranesi, chiefly in A. Giesecke, *G.-B. Piranesi*, 1912, p. 20 ff. ('Meister der Graphik', Vol. 6) and in H. Focillon, *G.-B. Piranesi*, Paris, 1918.

2 Allan Ramsay was a champion not only of Greek but also of Gothic art.

3 Chap. 62: '*I Greci coll'applicarsi agli ornamenti, alle subdivisioni delle parti, e agl'intagli, hanno atteso forse troppo ad una vana leggiadria, ma poco per altro alla gravità.*' They used '*poco a poco la libertà di farvi tutto quel che volevano*'.

4 Chap. 62: '*. . . gli architetti incominciarono a ricever per legge il capriccio de' Greci.*' Chap. 58: The Romans use the Greeks '*stando il capriccio in luogo della ragione*'. And: The Romans '*corressero molti e molti*

difetti, infra i moltissimi, che ritrovarono nell'architettura de' Greci'.

5 E.g., chap. 67 about dolphins in capitals: '*Qual cosa mai posson questi sostenere colla coda, o che luogo hanno eglino ne' capitelli, essendo la loro abitazione nel mare. Tali cose, ed altri di simil genere, che hanno poco relazione al vero, si posson vedere nelle tavole 14, 15, 16, 17, 19.*'

6 By means of an illusionistic device a page from Le Roy is, so to speak, fixed on Piranesi's plate and is clearly marked by the heading: '*Les plus beaux Monuments de la Grèce*', and the quotation from Le Roy's text.

7 First French ed. 1758. Quotation from English ed., Edinburgh, 1761, II, p. 201.

8 The view of a decline from Greece to Rome appears for instance in M. Guys, *Voyage littéraire de la Grèce*, Paris, 1771, II, p. 3 ff. in J. F. Blondel, *Cours d'Architecture*, Paris, 1771, p. 44 ff., or in Stuart's preface to the *Antiquities of Athens*.

9 *Recueil d'Antiquités*, Paris 1752–67, I, pp. ix, 119 ff., etc.

10 *De Etruria Regali*, Florence, 1723–26.— A comprehensive chapter on the history of Etruscology in Justi, *Winckelmann und sein Jahrhundert*, 3rd ed., 1923, II, p. 283 ff.

11 Cf. H. Focillon, *op. cit.*, p. 73 ff.

12 *Origini Italiche o siano Memorie Istoriche-Etrusche*, 1767–72. Cf. mainly Vol. II, liber 7.

13 *Vite*, ed. Milanesi, 'Proemio', I, p. 220 ff.

14 *A Treatise on the Decorative Art of Civil Architecture*, London, 1791, p. 26. Cf. Miss Lawrence's article in *Journal of the Warburg Institute*, Vol. 2, no. 2, p. 136.

15 *Nouveau Traité de toute l'Architecture ou l'Art de bastir*, 1st ed., Paris, 1706.

16 *Essai sur l'Architecture*, Paris, 1753.

17 Although Lodoli never published a line his personal influence seems to have been more vital than that of any other theorist of architecture of the eighteenth century. It is known (cf. J. v. Schlosser, *Die Kunstliteratur*, 1924, p. 567) that Laugier is in many respects dependent on Lodoli, but as a Frenchman he turns against the Romans and declares the Greeks to be perfect. The views of Francesco Milizia, the most important classicist theorist of the end of the century, are based on Lodoli's ideas. The latter's system was summarized by Andrea Memmo, *Elementi d'Architettura Lodoliana ossia l'Arte del Fabbricare con solidità scientifica e con eleganza non capricciosa. Libri due*, Zara, 1834.

18 Cf. Mariette's correspondence with Bottari, published in Bottari's *Raccolta di Lettere*, Milan, 1822, Vol. V, nos. 157, 162, 167. Mariette asserts that the letter in the

Gazette littéraire was published without his knowledge.

19 *Collection of Etruscan, Greek, and Roman Antiquities from the Cabinet of the Hon.ble M. W. Hamilton*, 1766, I, pp. 52 ff., 72 ff., 94, 104, 108 ff.

20 Apart from the aesthetic judgment, the idea of the simplicity of the Etruscan style and the ornateness of the Greek coincides with Piranesi's view of 1761.

21 Piranesi dedicated his *Campus Martius Antiquae Urbis* to R. Adam (1762) and engraved four plates for his *Works in Architecture* (1778).

22 In their *Works in Architecture*, 1774, Vol. I, 2, p. 4. In Vol. II, 1, 1779, Robert and James Adam acknowledge the Etrusco-Roman continuity without Greek influence. Ashby, (*Burlington Magazine*, XXXIII, 1918, p. 187) refers to the fact that the Etruscan origin of the Tuscan order was in the nineteenth century still defended by Rivoira, *Origin of Lombard Architecture*.

23 The left hand is represented. This might point to the 'sinister' intention of Mariette's letter.

24 Three of the plates accompanying Piranesi's text show ornaments which he had discovered in Etruscan underground chambers. The title of the first of them is: '*Essais de différentes Frises ou peintures qui se trouvent dans les souterrains des anciens Etrusques près de Corneto*.' And below it bears the satirical remark: '*Problème historique à l'avantage des Tailleurs. Qui des Etrusques ou des Grecs a été l'inventeur de ces espèces de gallons qui ont été découvertes par Piranesi en Toscane dans les cavernes de Corneto et de Chiusi*.'

25 For the ancient origin and history of the two notions *pulchritudo innata* and *ornamentum*, which are the basis of Winckelmann's conception, cf. Panofsky, *Idea*, 1924, p. 92 and *Hercules am Scheidewege*, 1930, p. 174. The distinction was codified in Kant's *Kritik der Urteilskraft*, where the superiority of '*reine Schönheit*' over '*anhängende Schönheit*' is made the subject of an *a priori* argument (§ 16).

26 Walpole, naturally, sympathized with this tendency. In the advertisement to the fourth volume of the *Anecdotes of Painting in England* (printed 1771) he advises English architects, who have become too dainty for his taste, to 'study the sublime dreams of Piranesi, who seems to have conceived visions of Rome beyond what it boasted even in the meridian of its splendour. Savage as Salvator Rosa, fierce as Michael Angelo and exuberant as Rubens he has imagined scenes that would startle geometry, and exhaust the Indies to realize. He piles palaces on bridges, and temples on palaces, and scales Heaven with mountains of edifices. Yet what taste in his boldness! What grandeur in his wildness!

What labour and thought both in his rashness and details!'

27 Mariette was also misled by the standard type of book produced by the Neoclassical 'discoverers'. It consists of a series of engravings accompanied by a scholarly text with a didactic purpose. Le Roy as well as Stuart and Revett, Robert Adam, Clérisseau and many others manifest the same double intention: to spread knowledge and to serve the advancement of the arts. For all these architects and authors the survey of the ancient buildings which they illustrate falls into line with their aesthetic creed.

28 'A celebrated Italian Artist whose taste and luxuriance of fancy were unusually great, and the effect of whose compositions on paper has seldom been equalled, knew little of construction or calculation, yet less of the contrivance of habitable structures, or the modes of carrying real works into execution, though styling himself an architect. And when some pensioners of the French academy at Rome, in the Author's hearing, charged him with ignorance of plans, he composed a very complicated one, since published in his work; which sufficiently proves, that the charge was not altogether groundless.' In Piranesi's oeuvre no such plan seems to exist. If it were not an anachronism—Chambers left Italy in 1755—we should assume that he refers to designs similar to those reproduced here.

29 In the first edition the plates bear no numbers. They seem to be differently arranged (cf. copy in the Royal Institute of British Architects) from the numbered edition which we follow here.

30 'Aequum est vos cognoscere atque ignoscere quae veteres factitarunt si faciunt novi.' Conclusions as to Piranesi's knowledge of Latin seem to be allowed from the fact that he engraved 'vas' instead of 'vos'.

31 Sallust, in Bell. Iugurt. 'Novitatem meam contemnunt, ego illorum ignaviam.'

32 Op. cit., I, p. 132 ff.

33 Op. cit., I, 1, p. 6. For the idea that even the ancients broke the rules, cf. Piranesi's dedication to Robert Adam in Campus Martius, 1762: the observer 'non ritroverà

inventate più cose dai moderni, che dagli antichi contra le più rigide leggi dell'architettura.'

34 Antiquités de la France, Paris, 1778, p. xii.

35 Cf. Hans Thüme, 'Beiträge zur Geschichte des Geniebegriffs in England', Studien zur Engl. Philologie 71, Halle, 1927; B. Rosenthal, 'Der Geniebegriff des Aufklärungszeitalters', Germanische Studien, 138, Berlin, 1933, p. 15 ff.

36 Gedanken über die Nachahmung der griechischen Werke in der Malerei und Bildhauerkunst, 1755.

37 D'Hancarville (op. cit., preface), for instance, says: 'In every art good models give birth to ideas, by exciting the imagination.' Similarly for Reynolds originality develops from imitation (Discourse II, ed. 1905, p. 22 ff.). Cf. E. Wind, 'Humanitätsidee und heroisiertes Porträt', Vorträge der Bibl. Warburg, 1930–31, p. 181.

38 Schiller, Ueber naive und sentimentalische Dichtung, 1795–96.

39 About these principles cf. the author's article on the Biblioteca Laurenziana in Art Bulletin, 1934, and on Carlo Rainaldi, pp. 9–52 of the present volume.

40 All Piranesi's biographers accept, sometimes with a certain suspicion, Bianconi's (Piranesi's first biographer) statement that Piranesi had no theoretical views of his own, but was used as a mouthpiece by a group of erudites. The reader will by now, I hope, be convinced that this is not the case.

41 It was precisely in 1764–65 that Piranesi received his one relatively important commission as a practical architect, namely the restoration of the church of S. Maria del Priorato on the Aventine (see pp. 247–58).

42 For Piranesi's Egyptian style, see pp. 259–73.

43 The volume was published by his son, Francesco. Piranesi died two months after the papal imprimatur, in November, 1778 (cf. A. M. Hind, G.-B. Piranesi. A critical Study, 1922, pp. 3, 19). He is thus responsible for the texts under the engravings

which clearly reveal that Piranesi had not only discovered the beauty of the Doric but also the essentially Greek character of this grand style.

XIV Piranesi as Architect

1 Werner Körte, 'Giovanni Battista Piranesi als praktischer Architekt', Zeitschrift für Kunstgeschichte, II, 1933, p. 16 ff. The basic study on Piranesi as architect.

2 Felice Stampfle, 'An Unknown Group of Drawings by Giovanni Battista Piranesi', Art Bulletin, XXX, 1948, p. 122 ff. Catalogue of the drawings in the Morgan Library.

3 Giulio Pediconi, 'Un particolare piranesiano', Quaderni dell'Istituto di storia dell'architettura, 1956, no. 15, p. 15 f. Measured drawings of the high altar of S. Maria del Priorato.

4 Giuseppe Fiocco, 'La facciata di San Nicola in Carcere', Palladio, IV, 1954, p. 131 ff. It is not quite clear whether the author wants to attribute the whole or part of the façade to Piranesi.

5 'S. Maria della Salute: Scenographic Architecture and the Venetian Baroque', see above, pp. 125–52.

XV Piranesi and Eighteenth-Century Egyptomania

1 L. Volkmann, Bilderschriften der Renaissance: Hieroglyphik und Emblematik in ihren Beziehungen und Fortwirkungen, Leipzig, 1923, and Bilderschriften der Renaissance, Nieuwkoop, 1962.

2 G. Boas, The Hieroglyphics of Horapollo, New York, 1950.

3 Erik Iversen, The Myth of Egypt and its Hieroglyphics in European Tradition, Copenhagen, 1961.

4 S. Morenz, 'Der Gott auf der Blume', in Artibus Asiae, Ascona, 1954. [Also a later book by the same author, Die Begegnung Europas mit Egypten, Berlin, 1968.—Ed.]

5 J. Baltrušaitis, Le Moyen-âge fantastique, Paris, 1955, and La Quête d'Isis: Introduction à l'Egyptomanie, Paris, 1967.

6 Comte de Caylus, Recueil d'Antiquités Egyptiennes, Etrusques, Grecques, Romaines, et Gauloises; 7 vols, 1752–67.

PHOTOGRAPHIC ACKNOWLEDGMENTS

The editor and publishers wish to thank the following owners, institutions and photographers for permission to reproduce photographs: Her Gracious Majesty Queen Elizabeth II (Royal Library, Windsor. Crown Copyright reserved): 174, 175, 176, 298, 300; The Devonshire Collections, Chatsworth (reproduced by Permission of the Trustees of the Chatsworth Settlement): 244–274; Biblioteca Apostolica Vaticana: 180; Musée des Arts Décoratifs, Paris: 297, 301, 302, 303, 304, 306, 307, 308, 309, 310, 311; Bibliothèque Nationale, Paris: 356; Fogg Art Museum, Harvard: 166; Pierpont Morgan Library, New York: 323, 325, 326, 333, 334, 347; Minneapolis Institute of Art: 351; Avery Library, Columbia University, New York: 322; The Brandegee Collection, Faulkner, Mass.: 85–101; Soprintendenza ai Monumenti, Venice: 215; Fondazione Giorgio Cini, Venice: 191, 196, 203, 204, 208, 217; Gabinetto Fotografico Nazionale, Rome: 321, 324, 328, 329, 330, 335; The British Museum, London: 75; National Monuments Record, London: 278; Royal Institute of British Architects, London: 177, 178, 179, 227, 344, 345; The Mansell Collection: 224, 225, 231, 338; G. E. Kidder Smith: 182, 211, 214, 240, 242; Giraudon: 140, 142, 150, 153, 355; Bulloz: 154; Osvaldo Böhm: 193, 194, 205, 206, 209; Archivio Artistico Borlui: 198, 200, 202; F. A. Mella: 284.

INDEX

Names in the Notes are indexed only if they are more than expansions of text references; they are referred to by chapter and note number.
Numbers in *italics* refer to illustrations.